Why is this
Lying Bastard
lying to me?

ROB BURLEY

Why is this Lying Bastard lying to me?

Searching for
THE TRUTH
on Political TV

MUDLARK

Mudlark
HarperCollins*Publishers*
1 London Bridge Street
London SE1 9GF

www.harpercollins.co.uk

HarperCollins*Publishers*
Macken House, 39/40 Mayor Street Upper
Dublin 1, D01 C9W8, Ireland

First published by Mudlark 2023
This edition published 2024

1 3 5 7 9 10 8 6 4 2

Rob Burley asserts the moral right to be
identified as the author of this work

Excerpts on pages 61–64 © *The Independent*

A catalogue record of this book is
available from the British Library

ISBN 978-0-00-854251-1

Printed and bound in the UK using 100%
renewable electricity at CPI Group (UK) Ltd

This book is produced from independently certified FSC™ paper
to ensure responsible forest management.

For more information visit: www.harpercollins.co.uk/green

To Holly, Noah & Louis
and with love to Pat & Sid

The plain fact is that Westminster's time-honoured procedures for calling our leaders to account are in some respects vastly inferior to those of television ... When it comes to uncovering truth there is no substitute for sustained questioning in public by a single individual armed with a clear purpose ... We should be proud that we in Britain have made the political interview a more effective instrument of liberty than any of the other people of the democratic world.

Brian Walden, 1990

Why the fu*k wd we put a gaffe machine clueless about policy & government up to be grilled for ages? This is not a hard decision.

Dominic Cummings, former chief adviser
to Boris Johnson, 2021

CONTENTS

INTRODUCTION
Bottler

It started – to misquote pop/soul hit-makers Hot Chocolate – with a fridge.

It's just after 6 a.m. but still dark on a freezing December morning in Yorkshire on the day before the UK general election of 2019, the pre-dawn gloom illuminated by the lights of a film crew sent by ITV's morning news programme *Good Morning Britain* (*GMB*). Jonathan Swain – known as 'Swainy' to his colleagues – is one of the show's senior correspondents, and he's been sent to the Modern Milkman dairy in Pudsey near Leeds by his editor Neil Thompson to track down the prime minister, Boris Johnson.

Swainy is there to 'doorstep' Johnson, a TV news term for showing up unannounced, usually at someone's front door or place of work, and – from the doorstep – asking for an interview or simply shouting questions. Thompson has resorted to such drastic measures after months of the prime minister and his ministers boycotting the programme.

Johnson's people have never said that *GMB* is on the banned list, but nobody is ever available and it's hard to see this policy as anything but cowardice. The show is presented by brash inquisitor Piers Morgan and razor-sharp journalist Susanna Reid, neither of whom are attractive options for scrutiny-shy

Johnson. During the election campaign Johnson's team repeatedly promises the *GMB* team – including Morgan personally – that he will do an interview on the show, but it's the day before the election and time has run out. All those promises have turned out to be lies.

So Swainy has to wait in the cold, and when Johnson arrives at 6.35 a.m., Piers Morgan goes live to Pudsey. There's a minor media scrum, but not much is happening. Johnson is inside the dairy, being briefed by staff. The plan is for the prime minister to load one of the milk vans with a few crates of semi-skimmed while the assembled press take pictures. Swainy explains all this to viewers while Morgan urges him to shout a question at Johnson, but the GMB reporter has other ideas. He wants to get up close and personal.

At 6.37 a.m. Johnson, who has finally grasped the logistics of the photo opportunity, saunters towards the cameras in the direction of the milk van where Swainy is hiding. As his prey approaches, the *GMB* man politely calls out his question: 'Good morning, Prime Minister. Will you come on *Good Morning Britain*, Prime Minister?'

Before Johnson can answer, one of his media minders – Vote Leave veteran Rob Oxley – blocks Swainy's way and, with a look of utter contempt, spits, 'Oh, for fuck's sake' on national television.

There are gasps and hoots of glee back in the studio. Morgan and Reid are less worried about an impressionable child viewer hearing the F-bomb on breakfast television than they are amused at the tetchiness of Johnson's henchman.

'The look on his face, that minder!' exclaims Reid.

Swainy asks Oxley to stop pushing him around.

'Wow!' says Morgan.

Then the *GMB* camera swings to the left to find the prime minister loading the milk van.

'Will you deliver on your promise to speak to Piers and Susanna?' asks Swainy, striding towards Johnson, who is about to head back to get another crate. 'We're ready to go. We're live on ITV right now, Prime Minister. We have an earpiece in my pocket. You are more than welcome to come on.'

Johnson pretends not to hear him.

GMB editor Neil Thompson, watching from London, is worried about his senior correspondent, concerned that Johnson's minders – or 'suited gorillas', as he describes them[1] – will resume what looks to him like physical and verbal intimidation. But Swainy knows what he's doing, and so do his film crew, who turn their camera on Oxley. The meaty adviser looks shiftily at the camera, perhaps aware that he might become the story. Swainy, clearly starting to enjoy himself, asks him to 'tone your language down'. Oxley, his bravado extinguished, disappears into the darkness. Swainy 1, Suited Gorilla 0.

Johnson, now unprotected – never a smart move for him – reappears, this time carrying a crate of orange juice. Swainy is quickly upon him. He asks, again, whether the prime minister will keep his promise. Johnson, cornered, lies.

'Of course I will!' he says.

Swainy is well aware that this is bullshit, so he thinks he should probably ask for some specifics. 'This morning?' he wonders. 'Now?' But Johnson says nothing. There's a sense of panic in the air. Swainy has Johnson trapped. Every time he heads to the milk van he gets asked another question. So he retreats a safe distance, standing still, doing nothing, waiting. He needs somewhere, anywhere, else to go. Oxley, pretending to play it cool while studying his phone, materialises next to him. Neither knows what to do.

Swainy knows. Vacating his spot next to the milk van, the intrepid reporter heads towards Johnson for another go. 'You're live on *Good Morning Britain*,' he says. 'Will you talk to Piers and Susanna?'

Johnson looks at Swainy helplessly. 'I'll be with you in a second,' he lies, 'I'll be with you in a second,' before instinctively turning to run away.

The problem is that there's nowhere to run. The only place he can head to, the only place that might allow him to escape Swainy and his questions, is the building directly behind him.

'Come on!' he says to his team, faking jollity and marching purposefully towards a white door. As he approaches, a member of the dairy staff obediently slides it open, and Johnson, Oxley and team make their escape like absolute legends. Not cowards, legends.

Boris Johnson, the prime minister of Great Britain and Northern Ireland, is so scared of mild-mannered Jonathan 'Swainy' Swain, so terrified of Piers Morgan and Susanna Reid, that he's hiding in an industrial-sized, walk-in fridge.

The fridge farce is just the most ridiculous and vivid example of Boris Johnson's contempt for democratic norms. I watched all this unfold from home, still feeling bruised from my own encounter with Johnson's scaredy-cat political operation. As the editor of BBC's live political programmes, I was in charge of the general election party leaders' interviews fronted by Britain's toughest political interviewer, Andrew Neil. These 'long-form' interviews have been part of our general elections for as long as anyone can remember. Lasting half an hour and airing in prime time, they're the toughest test of the campaign. Until 2019, however reluctant politicians might have been to participate, they showed up because they saw them as an important moment in the campaign. No wonder, then, that Boris Johnson and his team decided to wait until the Labour leader Jeremy Corbyn had done his interview – spoiler alert: it didn't go well – before gradually and disgracefully backing out of their own.

Clearly, something had gone badly wrong. My memory of political interviews down the years was of titanic clashes between heavyweight interviewers and political giants, encounters relished by both sides: Sir Robin Day vs Neil Kinnock, John Humphrys vs Tony Blair, Andrew Marr vs Gordon Brown and, most titanic of them all, Brian Walden versus Margaret Thatcher.

The final and most consequential interview between Walden and Thatcher, in October 1989, took place two days after Thatcher had been plunged into her greatest political crisis, when her chancellor Nigel Lawson unexpectedly resigned. This enormous blow to her authority immediately ignited plotting against her by Conservative MPs. Despite this, Thatcher honoured a long-standing commitment to sit down on national television with the country's most feared political interviewer at the most precarious moment in her premiership. She could have made up a reason to cancel, but that's not how she operated. Even when she was in political trouble, she saw television interviews as opportunities to teach the public about her ideas. So she fronted up. Thatcher was not a coward.

The contrast between Thatcher's conduct and Johnson's antics that morning in Pudsey is startling. In thirty years, we'd gone from a prime minister in crisis willing to face the nation's most feared inquisitor for a forty-six-minute interview to a man so scared of a quick chat on breakfast TV that he was prepared to climb into the deep freeze until the coast was clear.

And as for me, I'd been along for the journey from hot seat to chilled section. At first I was a viewer, wowed by Walden and Thatcher, decoding the language of politics and loving the political theatre. And then, over more than twenty-five years, my vantage point moved progressively closer to the action; from lowly researcher to editor of ITV's political programme in my early thirties, then on to the BBC and *Newsnight* and editing *The Andrew Marr Show* before running the BBC's political programmes department. After that, I put in a stint at LBC before landing at Sky. I made political interviews my speciality and worked with the modern greats: Andrew Marr, Jeremy Paxman, Emily Maitlis, Andrew Neil, Laura Kuenssberg, and now Beth Rigby at Sky News.

Over those years I prepared, practised and helped prosecute political interviews with eight prime ministers, numerous chancellors and more cabinet ministers than you could shake a stick at. Oh, and Russell Brand too, if you must mention it.

Maybe, I thought, getting up from the sofa and turning the TV off, I should write some of this down.

However absurd Johnson's game of hide and seek, and however depressing what came next – the disgrace of the Johnson administration, the new low of the Truss interregnum – I don't approach this story wearing rose-tinted spectacles. This is a book about lying and equivocation in political interviews, but in 2019 Boris Johnson decided that the techniques of deception that politicians had used for decades were not enough to protect him against Andrew Neil or Morgan and Reid. This was also Liz Truss's approach when running to become Britain's most short-lived prime minister in 2022. But these are the extremes. Most politicians in these pages show up rather than make up excuses not to come. But that doesn't mean they all tell the truth when they get there.

Academics at the University of York, led by Professor Peter Bull, have spent decades conducting 'microanalysis' of techniques of political equivocation. They have identified thirty-five different ways that politicians don't answer the question. I won't list them all – you can find them online – but there are eleven principal categories. Thirty years later these techniques remain familiar: ignoring the question; acknowledging the question without answering it; questioning the question; attacking the question; attacking the interviewer; declining to answer; making a political point instead of answering the question; repeating the answer to a previous question; saying that they've already answered the question; and 'apologising' (this one is refreshing when it happens but is rare).[2]

Peter Bull's meticulous work has given us a sense of the direction of travel when it comes to political deceit. One measure is what he calls the 'reply rate'. This means the proportion of questions that receive explicit answers from politicians – in other words, straight answers to straight questions. Bull's study of interviews with party leaders between 1987 and 1992 found, on average, that 46 per cent of questions were given straight answers. This fell to 38 per cent between 2015 and 2017 and, when applied specifically to a series of interviews with Theresa May, dropped to just 27 per cent. The academics even had to come up with a brand new, thirty-sixth category – 'the non-specific answer to a specific question' – to take account of May's creative methods of obfuscation.[3] She may only have lasted three years in Downing Street, but you can't say she didn't make her mark.

If Tory politicians have forced academics to come up with new categories of bullshitting, then New Labour elevated it to an art form. Peter Mandelson, Labour's director of communications between 1985 and 1990, had worked with Brian Walden on ITV's *Weekend World* and knew the risks and opportunities of television interviews for politicians. Under Mandelson's influence, New Labour perfected the art of being 'on message'. For political interviews, this was bad news.

In practice, it formalised the long-standing technique of going into an interview with a clear idea of the answers you wanted to give, irrespective of the questions you were asked. This required interviewees to attempt to camouflage the transition from a question about X to an answer about Y. Academics called this 'bridging' – the arching across from the subject being asked about to the subject that was covered in the answer. The result was boring interviews that left viewers none the wiser. This was useful for New Labour in opposition – it allowed them to wang on at length without saying anything that could be used against them – but enjoyed diminishing returns after that.

In 2014, reflecting on his part in creating the soul-destroying New Labour interview, Lord Mandelson issued a mea culpa. Sort of.

Given the state of Labour in my early days, a little bit of discipline hardly went amiss. But when I coached Tony Blair, Mr Brown and others of their day, I said: 'Deliver your core message first, but always have something more to say when they come back for a second and third question.' You have to make an argument for what you believe in, not go round on a loop repeating the first thing you said. I think too many politicians have forgotten – or have never heard – the second part of this advice.[4]

Gordon Brown and the generation of New Labour politicians who sought to succeed him could not escape Mandelson's loop. 'Message discipline' ingrained a way of communicating that might have helped Labour get elected in 1997 but was ultimately alienating to voters who just wanted politicians to answer the question.

This is not a textbook. I don't intend to count up or classify the lies told, the deceptions deployed or the obfuscations observed. I will talk a little about the techniques of evasion, but not systematically. Instead, this is the inside story of a life spent setting up, planning and executing political interviews with some of the biggest names in British politics. It's also a view behind the scenes with star presenters and tells some of their stories too. This is a history of the last thirty years in British politics viewed through the prism of political interviewing, from the decline of Mrs Thatcher to the crash and burn of Liz Truss, via the Iraq War, austerity, Brexit and Partygate.

This, too, is a history of political television and a love letter to its highest form: the long-form, forensic political interview. I want to celebrate and chart its development, from its infancy in 1958, when Robin Day dared to ask Harold Macmillan a proper question, to today, when the form is at risk of dying out in an age where clicks and clips trump depth and analysis. The BBC should be doing something about it, but they seem to have lost their way. I agree with Andrew Neil when he says, 'I've never understood a public service broadcaster not wanting to make the long-form interview a key part of its political coverage.'[5] So, I'm proud to be part of the team at Sky News, where – working with the political editor Beth Rigby – we are trying to keep the long-form flame alive.

In many ways, in terms of her integrity and commitment to facing scrutiny, Margaret Thatcher is the anti-Johnson, but I'm not here to canonise her. She once said that as a politician, 'you don't tell deliberate lies, but sometimes you have to be evasive.' And she was. In 1993 the York academics Peter Bull and Kate Mayer wrote a paper titled 'How Not to Answer Questions in Political Interviews' studying set-piece TV interviews given by Thatcher and Labour leader Neil Kinnock in the 1987 election. Their analysis revealed that, more often than not, viewers urging politicians on television to 'answer the question' are right to feel frustrated. Thatcher gave what Bull and Mayer call 'non-replies' 56 per cent of the time. Proof positive that Thatcher was sometimes dishonest? Well, yes, but then she wasn't alone. Kinnock scored 59 per cent.[6]

A significant portion of this book is devoted to an interview featuring Margaret Thatcher because it's the high watermark of political interviewing in Britain: that day in 1989 when she sat down with Brian Walden for a forty-minute-plus televised conversation in the middle of her most serious political crisis. The interview marked the beginning of the end of the Thatcher era and was the single-most important reason why I started my journey into political television. More importantly, as I learned more about the relationship between Walden and Thatcher, a new story emerged about their friendship, their controversial political partnership and a personal choice that had to be made by television's star interviewer. The rest of the political interviews that feature in the book exist in the context created by this encounter, and the shape of the book reflects that.

I want this book to be fun too. I'd like to apologise in advance to anyone, politician or presenter, who might be offended. This is political and TV history with jokes and gossip thrown in. It's serious stuff, but I've sweetened the pill for my own sake as much as yours. There's also some swearing. Sorry.

This is a personal journey, and my peculiarities play their part in the story. Chief among these is a sort of social anxiety or inadequacy that emerges whenever I find myself mixing in the social circles that swirl around politicians. In this company, I'm mostly uncomfortable and unable to drum up the requisite small talk and faux fascination for the intrigue of Westminster politics. I'm not suggesting this reflects well on me – it may have held me back in ways I'll never really appreciate – but it has been useful. I'm sure it's created a healthy distance between myself and those we interview that has helped me adopt an approach that's rooted in the kinds of things that ordinary people might ask or think.

Detachment from politicians and their circles is desirable when you're holding them to account, not merely because you don't know your victims personally but also because you don't want your judgement to be clouded by appreciating their predicament *too* well. It's worthwhile understanding the difficulties and imperfect options that politicians must choose but ultimately you are there to ask questions on behalf of the viewer rather than to feel the politician's pain. In any case, few are willing to talk openly about these realities, at least not when they're in office. When they leave power you often can't shut them up on the subject, but before that, the political interview tends to be a performance predicated on a story the politician wants to tell the public about themselves and their grasp on events. The interviewer's job is to test whether that story can survive contact with scrutiny.

Sometimes politicians really are lying bastards. But *why* is this lying bastard lying to me? In their defence, maybe it's because sometimes – to paraphrase Jack Nicholson in *A Few Good Men* – we can't handle the truth. Every slip of the tongue is a 'gaffe', every apology a humiliation, every tentative conversation about policy options a pretext for a political row. These responses offer some mitigation, but only some. Every few years there are calls for a 'reset' of the rules of engagement in the political interview to create a safer environment for the politician and, in theory, encourage an outbreak of candour. The results are usually disappointing because, as my former colleague, producer Jason Keen, put it, the 'reset' tends to involve unilateral disarmament on the part of the political interviewer. So the journalists lay down their arms, and the politicians shoot them anyway.

But it's important to be fair. With this in mind, I developed an approach to political interviewing over the years that comes down to the question: what is the truth? This is a way of framing an interview in a way that is reality-based. So the truth might be, for example, that a particular policy will be effective at the margins but won't address the most pressing or significant problem. Armed with this truth, you can devise questions that stress test the story the politician is trying to tell and, if you're right, might reveal the reality to the viewer. This works because it enables you to produce nuanced and fair-minded interviews, as well as the more dramatic and theatrical sort – 'Will you resign, Prime Minister?' – that should only be deployed when the moment really demands it.

All this matters because we're in a political crisis. Survey after survey, study after study tell us that the British people don't trust politicians. A 2022 report by the Office for National Statistics conducted *before* the downfall of Boris Johnson and the car-crash premiership of Liz Truss found that only 35 per cent of the public said they trusted the government. Lies and incompetence, disgrace and chaos are unlikely to have pushed that number up.

Both Johnson and Truss avoided serious, long-form, forensic political interviews in their election campaigns. This was not accidental. They did so because they were frightened that their inadequacies might be revealed and that this would endanger their chances to hold on to, or gain, political power. They were right. Nothing is as effective as the political interview at testing the suitability of a candidate for the highest office. It's far more revealing than the pantomime of Prime Minister's Questions or the arcane tedium of a parliamentary debate watched by virtually nobody. And it's far harder to wing it or fake than a general election debate where you are able to draw on your muscle memory of an Oxbridge debating society to emerge unscathed.

Yet the question of whether politicians should submit themselves to this forensic and testing job interview or performance assessment doesn't get the attention it deserves. It's regarded as something that only matters to the journalists who work on them or the interviewers who want to conduct them. In reality, everyone who wants to avoid the elevation of the untrustworthy and unqualified to the highest offices in the land should demand they take place week in, week out, and especially at elections. Such interviews are the best means our political culture has devised to reveal character, competence and credibility. We must demand them.

Political interviews exist to hold those in power accountable. They're not for the politicians' benefit but for the public's. The politicians get to run the country. We get the chance to watch and listen when Andrew Neil or Emily Maitlis, Andrew Marr or Beth Rigby ask them the tough questions about how that's going. We then enjoy the opportunity to vote them out if they fall short.

This book is about the search for truth when a powerful person sits down with a first-class interviewer to answer the important questions.

The cameras are rolling. We are recording.

Time to decide. Truth or lies?

1

MARGARET & MARGO

For me, Margaret Thatcher's fateful TV interview with Brian Walden was a long time coming.

In 1975, when I was six years old, two things happened that, over time, melded in my youthful mind. The first, in February, was the election of Margaret Thatcher as Tory leader and leader of the opposition. The second, in April, was the arrival of Margo Leadbetter of Surbiton on the tiny black-and-white television that I already loved more than anything in the world.

I wouldn't have made the connection immediately because I wasn't yet paying attention to politics, but I'm sure I watched Margo, played to perfection by Penelope Keith, in the hit BBC sitcom *The Good Life* from the start. The show centred on Tom and Barbara Good, a couple who gave up the rat race to go self-sufficient and struggled to survive on the fruits of their suburban garden, with predictably hilarious results. As the show grew in popularity, so the Goods' uptight, dominating Conservative next-door neighbour Margo emerged as the real star. Margo elevated *The Good Life* to the status of a comedy classic, concerned with class as much as carrots. At the same time, uptight, dominating Conservative Margaret Thatcher was never off the TV news. It wasn't long before I understood that unlike Margo, whom we thought was funny, we didn't like Mrs Thatcher in our house.

We were a Labour family, and my parents liked Harold Wilson, the prime minister. I didn't really understand why, but he was a Yorkshireman like my dad, so it wasn't difficult to share the sentiment. I can still remember the shock of Wilson resigning when I was seven. His successor James Callaghan smiled a lot and seemed nice too. So that was it – we liked Labour, we didn't like the Tories.

We might have been a solid Labour family, but we weren't quite a typical one: we were from the north – Dad from Leeds, Mum from Liverpool – yet by 1972, when I was three years old, we were living in a derelict thatched cottage in the middle of nowhere, Sussex. Dad was a teacher, Mum a nurse, but by 1975 – that year of Thatcher and *The Good Life* – we were three years into our own experiment in self-sufficiency. Like Margo's neighbours Tom and Barbara in the sitcom, my dad had quit his day job to cultivate the back garden, keep pigs and grow vegetables, a move that was both ahead of its time and very 1970s.

Tom and Barbara were more middle class than us, and the sitcom's setting in Surbiton was, well, more suburban, but the essential tensions and challenges were the same, just not as funny. Dad had stopped earning, which meant Mum had to provide the actual money to support the family from her job as a district nurse. The enterprise was doomed from the start. The goats and chickens provided milk and eggs, and Rosie the pig – don't give your pig a name, you'll never eat it – produced copious amounts of shit to fertilise the vegetable garden, but we never grew enough.

As the experiment wore on, the tensions between my parents – financial and otherwise – boiled over into arguments and recriminations. It was less Richard Briers and Felicity Kendal, more *Who's Afraid of Virginia Woolf?*

The tiny black-and-white television was my refuge from all this and from the isolation of our weird rural life. I watched everything, from *Nationwide* on weeknights to *Seaside Special* on summer's long Saturday evenings. Those last years of the 1970s in Britain played out with comedy and tragedy in equal measure: the Holy Trinity of *Fawlty Towers*, *The Fall and Rise of Reginald Perrin* and *The Good Life*, making comedy from class, suburbia and provincialism, counterpointed by the industrial strife at Grunwick and British Leyland every night on the news. Finally, deciding the matter, the Winter of Discontent arrived, and the unions and the Labour government brought each other down.

There throughout were Margo and Margaret: Margo from the Home Counties, Margaret from provincial Lincolnshire. They both despaired at what Margo called the 'present rabble', which meant the trade unions and the Labour Party. Both were determined to wrest control from the wet Tory men who surrounded them, be it Margo's limp husband Jerry or Thatcher's defeated rival Ted Heath. What's more, they shared something quite identifiably political: a rejection of collectivism, a celebration of self-reliance and the private sphere. As Margo declared – anticipating Thatcher's declaration that there was 'no such thing as society' – 'I am not a citizen, I am a resident.' My mum, paradoxically using their sort of language, declared them both 'ghastly'.

'Ghastly' was a word reserved for women, but in comedy and politics there were other words too: battle-axe, hen-pecker, harridan, shrew. From Thatcher to Margo via Sybil Fawlty and the hippopotamus that stood in for Reggie Perrin's mother-in-law, they complained, nagged, fussed and even bellowed. I remember watching a news report featuring Mrs Thatcher herding her shadow cabinet of boy-men, corralling them like school kids, arranging them like matron, patronising them like Joyce Grenfell. She was simultaneously a walking stereotype direct from sitcom land and a revolutionary demanding something women were denied: power, including power over men.

This contradiction was most clearly on display in her early days as leader of the opposition. Thatcher adopted a persona that was unthreatening to men just as she prepared to smash the glass ceiling. She smuggled herself into power in the guise of a woman whose candidacy for Tory leader was seen by men like Michael Heseltine – who later joined her cabinet – as 'incredible'.[1] This was a woman who maintained her domestic role – ironing her husband Denis's shirts between late-night votes in the House of Commons – while pursuing the most senior job in the country. Jonathan Aitken, the former MP who was Thatcher's daughter Carol's boyfriend in the 1970s, told the BBC in 2019:

> Margaret was a force in the home and kitchen just as she was in the House of Commons. She bossed everybody around. She was rather a good cook, I seem to remember, Coronation chicken being one of her specialities.[2]

Aitken's recollections of Margaret were pure Margo – a force in the home, bossing people around in the kitchen – and Margo's televised traits were pure Margaret too.

I was a child who loved television, pop music and Liverpool FC, but I began to be drawn to politics too, primarily because it was available on the telly. As I started to pay more attention to Thatcher, the similarities between the two women made an impression on me. I wasn't alone. It's interesting to discover that some in the Tory Party saw an opportunity to draw upon the 'Margo factor' to help persuade voters that a woman could run the country.

Richard Kelly, who went on to be the head of politics at Manchester Grammar School for many years, was a Tory activist in Leeds in 1979, and he encountered scepticism on the doorstep about the possibility of a female prime minister. Canvassers were looking for ways to convince voters that, far from being a reason to reject Thatcher for the top job, her sex was why they should back her. The most effective way to do that, Kelly recalled party officials telling him, was to suggest to voters that 'what this country needs is a Margo to shake things up'.

'I think, to the activists that I met,' Kelly remembers, 'the parallels between Margo and Maggie were obvious.' Margo, like Thatcher, was

> not necessarily a loved figure, but someone who was seen as fascinating and kind of unstoppable and admirable. Thatcher, like Margo Leadbetter, was a formidable woman and, my God, don't we need a formidable woman right now with all the stuff going on with the unions and all the rest of it?[3]

This wasn't an isolated case. Kelly later discovered that Marcus Fox, one of the Conservative Party's most prominent northern MPs, had deployed the 'Margo factor' a few miles away in his Shipley constituency, persuading socially conservative voters who 'weren't quite sure about a woman prime minister' that their admiration for Margo Leadbetter should translate into a vote for Thatcher.

Kelly also recalls how the similarities between the two women's marriages and husbands helped make the case:

> Parallels were drawn between Jerry and Denis because Denis and Jerry were both world-weary guys who were ultimately content to step back and let their formidable wives do the business. They could make sense of how you could have a situation where a bloke stands back and lets his very bossy wife sort things out.[4]

Bossy wives and long-suffering husbands: the stuff of sitcom sexism alchemised by Margaret Thatcher into a reason to give a woman the chance to lead.

The orthodox view is that it was only when Margaret's more Margo-ish characteristics – her voice, her taste in floral prints, her presence in overwhelmingly domestic settings – were jettisoned by her image advisers that the electorate signed up. But perhaps that's wrong. Maybe those first impressions went deep, and many responded by deciding that Britain did indeed need a Margo.

The show's viewing figures support the theory: *The Good Life*'s final run in 1977 regularly reached 15 million people, the Christmas special a mind-blowing 21 million. Margot's cultural power was undeniable, and Margaret had unconsciously harnessed it. Sitting at home glued to the box, I could feel the power of television, and I wasn't alone.

My kids have grown up with hundreds of channels, streaming services and everything on demand, and yet, unsurprisingly, TV means less to them than it did to me. In the early 1980s we had three channels. By 1982 we'd gone colour and there was a fourth, developments that felt intoxicatingly futuristic. Meanwhile, my family's experiment in self-sufficiency rumbled on long after the Goods had gone, until sometime after I'd gone to secondary school, when my dad finally threw in the trowel and got a proper job again.

Meanwhile, my interest in politics was deepening. Not in a William Hague-ish way, I'd like to think (I didn't read *Hansard* and found parliamentary politics quite boring), but I was a little precocious. None of my friends at Manhood High School – stop sniggering at the back – shared my interest in the news, but then they had other things to do. They'd visit each other's houses, go to the cinema in nearby Chichester or take part in seaside life on Selsey Bill, where most of them lived. My house was three miles away, which might as well have been the moon, given how insular our home life was. This wasn't a deliberate policy by my parents; they just weren't interested. So I retreated further into books, music and, most of all, television.

And my amusingly named school was also edgier than West Sussex sounds. There was something about comprehensive school culture in the late 1970s and early 1980s that held menace, and that was just the teachers. My brother bailed out early for a job in a butcher's shop and left home at seventeen. My sister got herself suspended for throwing eggs at a teacher. I'd like to think they were from our 'Good Life' chickens, but I never checked. I just wanted to get in and out of school as fast as possible then disappear into my room, where the old black-and-white set was now all mine.

The political stories that pumped out of the BBC news-room, *Channel 4 News* and *ITN News at 545* – with its very cool early synth theme music – in the 1980s were compelling. The early years of the Thatcher government were gripping, terrible and exciting. Unemployment, riots and amazing music were the staples of early 'Youth TV', like *Something Else* on BBC2, which demonised Thatcher and all her works. So much for BBC impartiality! Developing my own authentic position on the issues, I decided I agreed with my mum and dad: I hated Thatcher and despised the Tories, and it seemed obvious that the country felt the same; she'd be out on her ear at the next election. Then came the Falklands War, and things got weird.

The way that military triumph in the South Atlantic trans-formed Thatcher's domestic political fortunes is well documented, and it changed the political conversation in our house too. My dad and I did most of our politics 'up the garden', where he'd weed, dig or cultivate while I asked questions about politics. But it was in the kitchen during that spring of 1982 where Dad told me the news.

'Argentina has invaded the Falkland Islands,' he said, 'and they're British.'

'Is that bad?' I asked him. I'd never heard of the Falklands and was unsure whose side I was supposed to be on.

'Of course it's bad,' he answered. 'It means war. The bastards.'

We talked more a few days later. Absorbing the arguments that swirled around the news from the left, I was more ambivalent than Dad. Bastards they may be, I thought, but weren't these islands theirs, really? Weren't they much closer to Argentina than Britain? What right did we have to claim them, and why did we care so much about a bunch of rocks and some penguins?

Dad kept returning to the essential truth: the Falkland Islanders were British citizens, and a brutal military dictator had invaded their home. Of course we had to protect them, Dad said. Of course Mrs Thatcher was right. This was the first time I'd encountered a situation where it was unclear where to stand and where a simplistic rejection of all things Margaret seemed inadequate. There were obviously more complex political justifications involving words like 'imperialism' and 'colonialism' for not supporting the decision to retake the islands, but they seemed theoretical and unconvincing. Even Labour, half-heartedly, backed the war in the end.

By the time the British Task Force arrived in the South Atlantic to liberate the islands, I was caught up in the drama of events and was enthusiastically rooting for our boys. I was still gutted when this paved the way for Thatcher's victory in the 1983 election, but I'd started to grasp that things were more complicated than goodies and baddies. I also realised then that political parties had to consider how issues might be viewed by the ordinary, non-party political people who decide elections.

All this fed my appetite for political argument. I was ready for the hard stuff: the political interview.

The best thing that can happen on television when you're a kid is the unexpected. Those are the moments you remember. Sport was constantly exploding with them: Tommy Smith's bullet header in his final match for Liverpool in the 1977 European Cup Final; Coe and Ovett at the Olympics in 1980; Botham and Willis executing, to mix my war film metaphors, the great escape to victory at Headingley in 1981. These were the times when things went unexpectedly right, but the real gold came when TV went wrong.

There was the time an elephant shat all over the *Blue Peter* studio floor, creating a real danger that John Noakes or Valerie Singleton might slip over on shit, live on TV. There was the Saturday morning *Swap Shop* phone-in when someone used a massive swear word to and *about* jazz popsters Matt Bianco, and there was the shocking moment when Jools Holland said 'fucker' on the music show *The Tube*. Jools's career on Channel 4 never recovered, which may have indirectly led to his subsequent domination of BBC2 pop music programming and, therefore, his relentless boogie-woogie piano grandstanding. It was a 'fucker' with a lot to answer for.

For me, the best moment of them all came in politics and involved one of the greats of political television: Sir Robin Day.

It was October 1982 and the Tories were at their party conference in Brighton, basking in the afterglow of victory in the Falklands four months earlier. That success had been made possible by the heroism and professionalism of the armed forces, including the Royal Navy. Despite that, the government had decided to make cuts to the number of ships and personnel. This provoked a furious response from the navy's top brass, including the First Sea Lord. At the conference the Tory grassroots were equally upset and numerous critical motions were tabled, but the government had a cunning plan: they'd ignore the angry members, not bother debating the critical motions and hope it would all go away. But it didn't quite work out like that.

Sir Robin, the BBC's star political interviewer, had been granted an interview with John Nott, the usually mildmannered and unflappable defence secretary. Sir Robin did not intend to gloss over the controversy, and focused directly on the arguments between Nott and the Royal Navy establishment over the proposed cuts.

From the start, the defence secretary seemed incensed by Day's audacity, accusing him of sowing division between politicians and the services. Nott had recently announced that he would be leaving parliament at the next election and, appropriately enough for a defence secretary, there was a sense that he was, if not demob happy, then demob grumpy. He was tired of the stress; he was tired of the questions; he was tired of Sir Robin Day. At this point, with Nott's irritation rising, Day pressed the issue:

'Why should the public,' began Day, expressionless, 'on this issue, as regards the future of the Royal Navy, believe you ...'

So far, so normal.

'a transient ...'

That's an interesting word; where's he going with this?

'here-today ...'

Robin is smiling.

'and ...'

Robin's eyebrows dart upwards as he leans towards Nott, eyes filled with mischief. This is the moment the word 'impish' was invented for.

'if I may say so ...'

Oh, that's the killer.

'gone-tomorrow politician, rather than a senior officer of many years' experience?'

At this, Nott, seventeen years in parliament, four in the cabinet, has no more fucks to give. This is the end of his political road, and he is offended. Hasn't he earned the right to a modicum of respect?

He glances around to reorient himself towards the studio exit and pushes himself up from his chair.

'I'm sorry, I'm fed up with this interview, really,' he says wearily, his hand clattering against the microphone that's clipped to his tie as he struggles to remove it, then mutters, 'It's ridiculous.'

'Thank you, Mr Nott,' says Sir Robin.[5]

Nott glances at his tormenter one more time before throwing the microphone across the desk in the general direction of TV's grand inquisitor, striding off the set and disappearing through the studio door.

For the thirteen-year-old me, this is a moment of pure delight. I love the drama; I love Sir Robin's face and the glint in his eye as he hits upon 'here today, gone tomorrow'. I love how beautifully he slides 'and if I may say so' into the middle of the question. Most of all, I love the glimpse it offers of a side of politicians and the dominant Tory government that we never usually see. It's a little chink in armour that seemed impregnable.

I like to imagine the thoughts in Nott's head as he fumes out of the Brighton Centre onto the seafront, 'Thank you, Mr Nott' ringing in his ears. *I'm in the cabinet, I'm the defence secretary, who is Sir Robin fucking Day to call me transient and, if he may say so, here today, gone tomorrow? What's Day ever done?*

The answer: everything.

It's genuinely no exaggeration to say that Robin Day, almost single-handedly, invented the political interview on British television. The age of deference that started lifting in the late fifties and became obsolete somewhere between Lady Chatterley and the Beatles' first LP didn't end by itself; it required courage. Day had it. With the support and ambition of ITN, which launched itself and Day's career in 1955, he changed Britain.

On 23 February 1958 Robin Day conducted an interview with the prime minister Harold Macmillan that started it all. Until then, interactions between politicians and TV journalists had either taken place at controlled press conferences or been hurried encounters at airports where obsequious posh men asked politicians softball questions.

This time was different. Day had negotiated thirteen minutes with the prime minister, which was unusually long. He'd also resolved to ask about the big political question of the day: the future of Selwyn Lloyd, the foreign secretary. There were rumours in Westminster and all over the newspapers that Macmillan was planning to sack Lloyd, who'd been in post during the Suez Crisis under the previous prime minister, Anthony Eden. The problem for Day was the convention, well entrenched in the BBC in particular, that television should shy away from impertinent questions to politicians in general and the prime minister in particular.

When the time came, Day went for it. 'What do you say, Prime Minister,' he offered a little gingerly, 'to the criticism which has been made, especially in Conservative newspapers, about Mr Selwyn Lloyd, the Foreign Secretary?'

Macmillan played a straight bat and betrayed no particular annoyance, so Day, smiling, persisted.

Day: Is it correct, as reported in one paper, that he would like, in fact, to give up the job of foreign secretary?

Macmillan: Not at all, except in the sense that everybody would like to give up these appalling burdens which we try and carry.

Day: Would you like to give up yours?

Macmillan: In a sense, yes, because they are very heavy burdens. But of course … we've gone into this game, and we try to do our best.[6]

This is innocuous by today's standards, but was daring at the time. I particularly enjoy Day's off-the-cuff follow-up: 'Would you like to give up yours?' No politician today would dream of offering Macmillan's surprising and honest response. Good luck to the modern politician who complains about the burdens of government and suggests they quite fancy giving the 'game' up. Here was the brief period where modern political interviewing was emerging, and professional political communications were not yet there to get in the way.

Mild stuff, but it sparked a furore that seems incomprehensible now. The press attacked Day for, variously, prolonging Lloyd's career by asking about his future, promoting entertainment over information and threatening parliament's status as the venue for political debate in favour of television.

After a failed attempt to enter the House of Commons for the Liberal Party in the 1959 election, Day joined the BBC. As more and more homes acquired television sets he quickly became a household name and face. There's wonderful footage of the comedian Frankie Howerd doing his ooh-ing and aah-ing routine on the hit satirical TV show *That Was the Week That Was* in 1963. His mention of Day and his tough questions draws immediate recognition from the studio audience as Howerd riffs on the interviewer's persona.

'He's a strange man, isn't he?' he says, pausing and camping it up beautifully, looking at the camera and elaborating with emphasis, '*funny* man'. The audience roars. Day *is* a funny man with his trademark polka-dot bow tie. Howerd smiles and lets the laughter grow, then subside. 'And uh,' he starts and stops again, 'and, hasn't he got cruel glasses? Have you noticed?'[7]

They *have* noticed, and the place erupts. Day is a star, and he often dazzled more brightly than the mostly grey politicians he interviewed. The dawn of Day and the dawn of the sixties roughly coincide, and, combined, they made the former stance of the political class towards television untenable.

By the early sixties politicians were waking up to the opportunities and the risks of the TV interview: the chief opportunity was access to the electorate, the biggest risk was exposure under its stark lights. Television demands an intimate, conversational style quite different to the rhetorical skills that politicians employ in parliament. Could they make the adjustment?

Harold Wilson went for it. He became Labour leader in 1963, and presented himself as a leader for a new and exciting decade harnessing the 'white-heat' of technology in a 'new Britain'. Television went with the grain of this modernising offer, so he used the new medium to help articulate his vision. It also helped him to project and reinvent himself as an affable man of the people rather than a slightly stuffy Oxford don. This interest in being on television was shared by the exceedingly stiff Edward Heath, who became Tory leader the year after Wilson won power in 1964. All of this was good news for TV producers and interviewers, but these young leaders and their advisers were not naive; as quickly as they embraced television, they sought to try to control it. So began the wary dance between politicians and the broadcasters.

Was this where it started? Was this where the lying bastards began lying to us? Well, yes and no. There are gradations of lying. Few – there are some – will come out with bare-faced lies. Brazen falsehoods are too easily found out, too crude and too dangerous as long as the norms of political behaviour are maintained. Instead, politicians, faced with interviewers holding them to account on behalf of the public, quickly began using now-familiar techniques: evasion (the action of escaping or avoiding something), dissembling (concealing or disguising one's true feelings), distraction (introducing ideas or arguments designed to throw interviewers off the line of questioning) or obfuscation (the act of making things obscure, unclear or unintelligible).

From the start, men like Wilson and Heath tried to manage the political interview. Faced with questions they'd rather not answer, covering topics they didn't want to discuss, politicians needed to find a way to answer without answering, to be less than candid while giving the impression of candour. They couldn't refuse to answer questions outright – although that happened occasionally – and would rather avoid overt defensiveness. Edward Heath was blunt about his strategy. 'The thing to do before a big programme,' he said, 'is to be clear in your mind about what you want to say because the interviewer will always try to deal with something else.'[8] This was pure cynicism and contempt for the process, but it was highly effective and anticipated New Labour's approach to 'message discipline' by thirty years. It remains the go-to approach to many political interviews today.

But it was not just about what was said in the interview; the rules agreed in advance were also constantly fought over. From early on, politicians sought to pre-agree the topics, dictate the location, determine the recording time, influence what the set looked like and decide who conducted the interview.

Harold Wilson played this game to perfection during the general election of 1970. He'd accepted a request for an interview from the BBC, as long as it was filmed at 10 Downing Street. Wilson – or probably his press secretary Joe Haines – knew that under BBC rules at the time, such an interview, recorded outside of the studio, would be conducted by a BBC interviewer who wasn't in the political team. That meant he could avoid Robin Day.

Accordingly, a political interview in the soothing environment of the prime minister's garden provided an easy ride for Wilson. Worse still, later on the same day the BBC unleashed Day on both Heath and Liberal leader Jeremy Thorpe under the harsh lights of a TV studio. It's a kind of poetic justice that Wilson lost that election. It has echoes in Boris Johnson's behaviour in the 2019 general election, but we'll come to that.

Later, by the time I was watching these shows in the 1980s, the two dominant leaders of that era – Margaret Thatcher and Labour leader Neil Kinnock – were frustrating Sir Robin (he was knighted in 1981) with their own evasion game, as he recalled in his memoirs:

For different reasons, but with similar results, Margaret Thatcher and Neil Kinnock developed a technique which devalued the interview as an instrument of democratic scrutiny. They were both determined to make a television interview a platform of their own. The interviewer's questions, or attempts at questions, were treated as tiresome interruptions to the statistical hammering of Thatcher or the repetitious rhetoric of Kinnock.[9]

What I loved most about Day was his high-minded approach to the political interview. He saw his role as asking questions on behalf of the electorate and regarded this as a very serious, very difficult, almost heroic job:

> In live interviews the interviewer has a responsibility heavier than may be imagined. He has to work in a combination of circumstances which few other journalists experience. He can't write up an interview afterwards in his office or a hotel room. He has to perform in the presence of a world-famous statesman, a powerful cabinet minister or an accomplished parliamentarian. The moment may be one of political tension or high drama; the situation may be of the upmost gravity or fraught with intense emotion. Lives may be at stake.[10]

My very favourite Day interview turned the tables on the 'Grand Inquisitor' – a title he revelled in – when newspaper columnist and public intellectual Bernard Levin had him on his BBC show in 1980. Levin asked the best question I've seen asked of a political interviewer. He mused whether it was fair for interviewers to interrogate politicians as they did, given how challenging their jobs were. Who was Day to tell them off for not performing well enough?

Day's answer, forty years on, remains relevant and brilliant:

> I do feel that responsibility very acutely, and whenever I go before a politician or a politician comes into the studio, I have that feeling in my stomach, in my guts. But

I have not to let it unnerve me, because I have to remember not only that he or she has enormous responsibilities and burdens, but I have also to remember that history shows that politicians make mistakes ... And I like to remember some words of Montaigne, which translated say, 'Sit he on never so high a throne, a man still sits on his own bottom.'[11]

In other words: politician, get over yourself and answer the question.

With that, then, what became of John Nott? When asked in 2000 about his encounter with Day, he was philosophical, accepting that 'you are only remembered for one thing, and all I'm remembered for is walking out on Robin Day'. If he isn't an entirely here-today-and-gone-tomorrow figure, it's only thanks to Sir Robin.

More recently, in his little-read and unreliably titled second memoir, *Memorable Encounters*, Nott pours barely concealed contempt on Day in an unpleasant little chapter. He remains affronted by his behaviour that day in Brighton, angry with the BBC in general and more than a little bitter about his association with the 'Grand Inquisitor', of whose panache and wit he still seems jealous writing thirty-six years after the event. However upsetting he found Day's elegant put-down, he was being asked important questions about public policy on behalf of the viewers. Day was right to ask; Nott was ridiculous for walking.

As the eighties wore on, my dislike of Thatcher and the Tory government became my genuine position, not just what my parents told me to think. The rest of the 1980s was full of political disappointments for people like me. The Westland affair was an argument about helicopter manufacturing that was important but also quite dull. When it led to the departure of cabinet minister Michael Heseltine, my hopes rose. I was doing my A levels by then, and my English teacher Molly – all first-name terms, split ends and pacifism – declared that this was it for Thatcher. 'She'll have to go now!' Molly proclaimed in the middle of a lesson that was supposed to be about Chaucer. She didn't.

And then there was 1987, the famously 'successful' Labour campaign that resulted in a reduced but healthy Tory majority of 102 seats. The power of an effective political TV interview struck home during this election. In possession of a dud unilateralist defence policy, Labour leader Neil Kinnock was tempted by David Frost into war-gaming a scenario involving a Soviet invasion of a non-nuclear Britain.

> **Frost:** If you haven't got nuclear weapons, the choice in that situation would be to subject your forces to an unfair battle.
>
> **Kinnock:** Yes, what you're suggesting is that the alternatives are between the gesture, the threat or the use of nuclear weapons, and surrender. In these circumstances, the choice is posed, and this is a classical choice between exterminating everything you stand for and the flower of your youth, or using all the resources you have to make any occupation totally untenable.[12]

It's a typically baroque piece of Kinnock-speak. My generation of Labour supporters loved the man, but he could be infuriating – one minute the peerless orator, the next utterly baffling and impenetrable. Whatever *he* meant by his answer, Tory Central Office and the Labour-hostile press interpreted his words to Frost as a hint that Britain, unable to deter a Soviet invasion because we had no nuclear weapons, would resort to a *Dad's Army* last line of defence, waging guerrilla warfare against Soviet guns and tanks. The Labour leader protested that he had been talking about NATO, but the damage was done and he never really recovered. Despite my dismay about its effect on the Labour campaign, it seemed appropriate that Kinnock should pay the price for not having a better answer to Frost's question.

When the election defeat came it felt brutal and terminal. It seemed like Margaret Thatcher might go on forever. She'd been in power since I was ten, and I resented her total domination of my childhood. How could this woman, this Margo, have managed that?

A little over two years later, with Lisa Stansfield's search for her baby sending her inexorably towards the top of the singles chart and Madchester on my mind a good deal more than Westminster, I was up by one o'clock on the last Sunday in October in my grotty student house in Nottingham. I was twenty years old.

2

BRIAN & MARGARET, PART ONE

Saturday 28 October 1989,
London Television Centre

Margaret Thatcher arrives at the London Television Centre on the South Bank of the Thames shortly before 10 a.m. She is accompanied by her police protection officers and her press secretary Bernard Ingham, who, by law, we must refer to as 'gruff'. Mrs Thatcher doesn't keep Brian Walden waiting for long. She greets her friend as she steps onto the studio floor and takes in the grand, gladiatorial set of ITV's *The Walden Interview*.

The studio is beige and brown, apart from a grey circle containing two smaller white circles. In the middle of both of these white circles are a black and silver chair, a microphone and a small table for water. Mrs Thatcher takes her seat; she is sitting at screen-right and looks directly at Walden. The interview will be pre-recorded this week for transmission at lunchtime on Sunday, which is unusual. It's also unusual for her to agree to come into a TV studio these days. The pair's interviews normally take place in the softer, more intimate environment of 10 Downing Street, her home turf, but not today. Today is going to be different.

Margaret Thatcher is sixty-four years old, she has been prime minister for more than ten years and Brian Walden is her favourite interviewer. Seven years her junior, Walden is a former Labour MP turned TV star who has been on a political journey towards Thatcherism. Given his job, he hasn't been entirely explicit about this, but his opinion pieces in *The Sunday Times* and sometimes unguarded praise for Thatcher have given the game away. He was already lost in admiration in 1979. 'This country needs someone like Margaret Thatcher,' he said. 'In years to come, great novels and poems will be written about her.'[1]

Thatcher is flattered by the sympathy and support of Labour renegades like Walden; they are among her favourite people. No wonder, then, that Walden and Thatcher became, according to Thatcher's official biographer Charles Moore, 'close friends'.[2] Their television encounters are coloured with unmistakable mutual admiration, but they are also revealing and significant. It was to Walden that Thatcher said we only remember the Good Samaritan because he had money; Walden was the first to suggest – on television – that she embodied 'Victorian values'. He gets her; they get each other. That's why these conversations stimulate her. Rather than wilt under pressure, she tends to blossom when speaking to him. That's what she needs today.

As recently as the previous year, Walden had been sent by Andrew Neil, the then editor of *The Sunday Times*, to interview the prime minister. 'I knew that she loved Brian,'[3] recalls Neil today. The feeling was mutual, as Walden's piece for the paper made clear.

> The Margaret Thatcher I know is not the one I read about. I find her frank, good-humoured, entirely without snobbery and willing to tolerate a fair measure of leg-pulling, vulgarity and impertinence. I have never met this other Thatcher, the arch-fiend, who has no human feelings and cannot be contradicted.[4]

There is tenderness in the way Walden writes about Thatcher. He's sensitive to the real woman behind the image and stands firm against the stereotype. He reveals to readers that 'the personal attacks do wound her'. The Iron Lady feigns indifference, he says, and uses that indifference as a shield.

This Saturday she is in full battle dress, her hair creating a golden helmet framing her face, pearl earrings matching her white blouse, a purple suit with a pattern of swirls that creates an impression of armour, a diamond Art Deco-style brooch high on her left side, her shoulders emphasised by the cut of her jacket. She is more Ma'am than Margo: imperial, regal, in charge.

Walden is a less physically striking figure. He wears a blue pin-stripe suit, a pale blue shirt and a tie of various shades of purple. What everyone remembers about Walden is his voice: it's slightly squeaky, with a West Bromwich accent, and he can't pronounce his rs.

Walden prepares himself and is counted in; it's time to record his 'pre-title' introduction to the programme as Thatcher watches on.

They're friends together, ready to go.

She's confident: this is Brian.

This time he's the nervous one.

After today they'll never speak again.

8.30 a.m., Thursday 26 October 1989, 10 Downing Street

Margaret Thatcher has just had her hair shampooed and set, followed by half an hour under the hairdryer. This process creates the famous Thatcher helmet of hair that helps project her aura of invulnerability.

But she's not as confident as she looks.

She believes that she's right, there's no doubt about that. She's more certain than ever despite a turbulent economy and rows over Europe, as well as the poll tax (or as she calls it, the community charge), which is igniting dissent across the country. Nor is she fazed by Conservative MPs who are increasingly critical of her policies and personality. They say she's losing her grip, losing touch with reality after so long at the top.

But she's sure of her politics, policies and principles, and she's never been afraid to stick to her guns, however unpopular she may be. She's been prime minister for ten years, knows what she's doing and doesn't want to stop.

But she's always aware of the threat to her position, which becomes a threat to her project. Politics is ego, ambition, conviction and mission, a dangerous mix. She never forgets this, but cannot let on. And she believes that her sex is relevant; there are no second chances for women in politics. If she stumbles, she believes nobody will be there to catch her.

In the previous year's *Sunday Times* interview, her friend Brian Walden asked her about fear, wondering why she was risking so much for the deeply unpopular poll tax. 'I feared for her,' he confessed. Did she fear for herself?

'No,' she told him.

'Are you ever afraid of anything?' Walden asked.

'No.'[5]

But she is really, she's always on guard, and Walden sensed it when he wrote this about her:

> I claim to understand Margaret Thatcher, but I wonder if I do. I wonder if anybody does. How much does this passionate, repressed woman keep to herself? Is the certain sound of the trumpet a necessary outer protection for a deep loneliness within?[6]

We don't know whether she feels lonely that morning under the hairdryer – she's probably catching up with her never-ending work. But she may sense the threat. It's in the air more than ever. It's the state of things and the time of year that puts her on edge: under Conservative Party rules, autumn is the season of the leadership challenge and she's worried that someone is waiting with a knife. Maybe she's turning that over in her mind or trying to push it away when she hears the footsteps of Andrew Turnbull, her principal private secretary, who has arrived with a message. The chancellor, Nigel Lawson, is waiting outside her study on the first floor and would like to see her. She is due to see him that day anyway, but not until quarter to ten. They have a meeting about the Atomic Weapons Establishment at Aldermaston, but this might be a different sort of explosive: some sort of political grenade much more personally directed.

Her relationship with her chancellor is broken. He's been there for six years, and they've been an effective and impressive team, but they've fallen out over the economy and Europe. Lawson still commands her respect, but not her trust. Trust has been fraying since 1987, when Lawson started secretly pursuing an exchange rate policy of ensuring that the pound shadowed the value of the Deutschmark. It was the kind of thing you might mention to the prime minister, but Lawson hadn't, and when the papers started talking about it and she realised, she was furious. It was humiliating and ominous.

But the serious damage had been done earlier that summer when Lawson joined forces with Sir Geoffrey Howe, the foreign secretary, to try to force a change in European policy. Lawson retained her respect and kept his job, but Howe paid the price with a brutal demotion. It was unpleasant, but the danger had passed. Hadn't it?

At ten minutes to nine, she walks downstairs and finds the chancellor waiting there outside her study: Nigel Lawson and the beginning of the end.

At the end of the day on which Lawson resigned from Thatcher's government, there's a glimpse of Margo. With the atmosphere of poisonous recrimination, betrayal, bad faith and bad blood now all played out in the offices on Downing Street and the grandeur of the House of Commons, Thatcher returned to the flat above No. 10, where she lived with her husband Denis.

> He [Denis] came in, and we sat down and he asked what had happened and I told him. In a matter of minutes, both my children were on the telephone ... Do you know that made me more cheerful than anything else. 'Mum, are you all right? Do you want me to come round?' Just marvellous to talk to them ... Then I talked and Denis was in for supper. So I must have got some supper. Someone's got to do it.[7]

Someone's got to do it.

Oh, hello, Margo.

You'd think somebody else might have thrown something together after the day she'd had.

This painful moment of reckoning with the chancellor had been coming for months. At its heart was a principled difference over policy and a related, more personal disagreement about character. It was this aspect that ultimately tipped Lawson over the edge or gave him the way out he was looking for, depending on your point of view.

As ever, Europe was at the heart of it. With the UK economy in trouble in the summer of 1989 – inflation stood at just over 5 per cent, interest rates just below 14 per cent – Lawson wanted Thatcher to commit to British membership of the European Exchange Rate Mechanism (ERM). The ERM, a precursor to a fully fledged European single currency, was anathema to Thatcher, but Lawson, also a Eurosceptic, thought it offered the best chance of economic stability in the here and now, and that had to come first.

All this came to a head at the end of June. Lawson and Geoffrey Howe told Thatcher they would resign on the eve of the European Council meeting in Madrid unless she used the occasion to commit herself to joining the ERM and, crucially, to set a timetable for British membership. These threats were a betrayal – forever known as the 'Madrid ambush' – and they backfired on Lawson and Howe, at least in the short term.

Thatcher did tell her fellow European leaders that Britain would join the ERM, but only once a stringent set of difficult-to-achieve conditions were met. She did not say when, only how. The prime minister was forever furious with both men. Thatcher's biographer, Charles Moore, told me that the long-term significance of these events should not be underestimated. They left her 'driven crazy with rage, and making her feel embattled and duped'.[8]

On her return to London, Thatcher found Lawson and Howe very much still in her Cabinet. 'No resignations, I see?' she goaded them.[9] The following month, still angry, she made a decision that set a time bomb ticking under her premiership: she demoted Howe from foreign secretary to the non-job of deputy prime minister (he would detonate spectacularly later). She left Lawson where he was, but things would never be the same between them after Madrid.

And then, Sir Alan Walters came home. Walters was an economics professor who'd profoundly influenced Thatcher's economic policy when he advised her in the early 1980s. He'd spent the rest of the decade in the United States until, in 1989, Thatcher asked him to come back. His return as an adviser would trigger the unravelling of Thatcher's premiership.

Born into poverty in the 1920s, Walters was highly intelligent but failed his eleven-plus. He achieved the status of celebrated academic and economic adviser to the prime minister the hard way. Thatcher must have admired what today we'd call his 'journey', and his Euroscepticism too. He stood out in a crowd of Tory men like Howe, Lawson and the coming man, John Major, who were caught in the slipstream of the drive towards European monetary union in the late 1980s.

Walters' return in June of 1989 was always going to get thoroughly up Lawson's nose. Getting up people's noses was a Walters speciality. He had a habit of saying and writing unwisely brutal things about the chancellor and his policies. His indiscretions were never dealt with because, Charles Moore says, 'Mrs Thatcher was inclined to indulge Walters.'[10] Walters told it like it was, and if that made for good copy, what harm could it do? Thatcher was fond of him:

> (He) is a very sweet man but very naive politically. If a
> journalist rings him up and asks him a question, he
> innocently answers it, saying what he thinks.[11]

In politics, that will never do.

In the summer of 1989 Margaret Thatcher, usually so alive to threat, did not see the risks in bringing Walters back. To her, Walters was the adviser, Lawson the decider, and she didn't think her chancellor would care too much about a few noises off. She was dead wrong about that. Lawson took Walters' comments as a true expression of the prime minister's feelings. This was unfair on Thatcher, who couldn't always have known what Walters planned to say, but her insouciance about his big mouth and her personal loyalty to him set the stage for the explosive events of October.

In politics, autumn offers the chance for a fresh start. So it was in 1989: the Madrid ambush had faded somewhat, and at the Conservative Party Conference in Blackpool Thatcher was back in her pomp, surveying the 'ruins of socialism' as the Soviet Bloc crumbled. But this turned out to be papering over the cracks. On 18 October the *Financial Times* carried an article Walters had written eighteen months earlier for an American magazine. The piece had suddenly become very newsworthy, as Walters suggested that the ERM – the system Lawson and Howe had tried to bounce Thatcher into joining in Madrid –

was 'half baked', and was openly sceptical about Britain joining. Lawson later said this article was the last straw: as long as Walters was around, shouting his mouth off, the split between the chancellor and prime minister was impossible to disguise. Resignation was on his mind.

But Lawson didn't go immediately. Mrs Thatcher was on the other side of the world at a Commonwealth Conference in Malaysia at the time, so he waited, stewing. From this distance, there's something a little performative about the chancellor's slow-motion resignation. It was as if taking offence at Walters' rehashed comments offered a way out. He had an increasingly difficult job, working for an increasingly difficult boss who didn't trust him anymore. It's tempting to think that being outraged about Walters' article presented an opportunity that was too good to miss. Lawson, unsurprisingly, rejects that interpretation, but he does say that Walters' comments were the pretext for his resignation, not the sole reason for it. As Charles Moore put it to me, one way or another, the Lawson/Thatcher project had 'run out of road'.[12]

By the time Thatcher was back from Kuala Lumpur and sufficiently rested, Lawson had decided and was ready to drop his bombshell. Both he and Thatcher published memos and memoirs recalling what happened next. Here's Mrs Thatcher's account, as given in a memo now in her official archive:

> The reason for his visit – which he had considered very carefully – was that unless I agreed to sack Alan Walters, he would hand in his resignation as Chancellor.
>
> This seemed to me an absurd, indeed reprehensible proposition, and Alan was a trusted consultant & Nigel a Chancellor.
>
> Nigel explained that Alan took a different view from him, his views sometimes came out in the press & this made his task intolerable. I duly countered that Alan was

an adviser and that Nigel and I made the decisions – so what was the problem?

Moreover, no Chancellor allowed himself to be offput by an adviser, and in my view, no one could possibly resign on the basis of such a flimsy and unworthy proposal.

I said, go away & think again. I will see you after questions – I have a very busy day ahead – briefing for questions, Cabinet, Statement, Questions, Statement.[13]

Lawson, in his very long memoir, agrees on the essentials:

I came straight to the point … Given [Walters'] position as the Prime Minister's personal economic adviser, this made my job as Chancellor impossible … I had therefore come to the firm conclusion that Walters would have to go.[14]

Thatcher told him that if she sacked Walters at Lawson's insistence, her authority would be destroyed. Lawson said this was 'absurd' – which it wasn't – before reiterating that 'if she were not to get rid of Walters, I did not see how I could possibly remain as Chancellor'. The reasons for the resignation, and the means to avert it, were crystal clear.

After that, Lawson did go away, but he didn't consider the matter any further. As long as Thatcher kept Walters, there was nothing to reflect on. At two that afternoon they met again. According to Lawson, Thatcher 'begged' him to stay, lavishing praise on him and talking up future opportunities, before asking him to wait until after Prime Minister's Questions before doing anything. At this point his emotional antennae finally twitched, and he realised how shocked and upset she was. He agreed to put off the final decision until later that day, but there was no change of heart. Meeting her once more, Lawson, in an 'atmosphere of suppressed emotion', confirmed his resignation. Shortly afterwards, Walters had no choice but to resign too.

Thatcher was left seriously damaged, the resignation creating a sense of crisis unprecedented in her premiership. There was a feeling that something was ending or starting to end, although it was not yet inevitable. If she could control the political narrative again, perhaps she could move past this. Over the years, her interviews with Brian Walden had helped her generate a cogent political narrative, sparking her passions and igniting the fire behind her eyes. Perhaps, the old friends could work their magic together once again.

Brian Walden, like Margaret Thatcher, was from the Midlands (West in his case, East in hers), and, like her, he attended grammar school before heading to Oxford and then to parliament. Walden arrived with the Wilson government in 1964 as MP for Birmingham All Saints at thirty-two, five years after Thatcher's arrival as Tory MP for Finchley in October 1959, just before her thirty-fourth birthday.

While Thatcher's background was hardly privileged, Walden had much further to travel than she did. His mother, whom he revered, died young, and his father was often unemployed. As an intelligent boy interested in politics, joining the Labour Party was automatic – 'with my background,' he said, 'you take it in with your mother's milk'[15] – but Walden was essentially a meritocrat, not a socialist. The significance of his own story was not to escape him.

While at university Walden met Labour leader Hugh Gaitskell, who became his political hero. Gaitskell's sudden death in 1963 left him shattered. 'I don't believe I ever really adjusted,'[16] he said years later, but he pressed on with his plan to become an MP. 'Everybody seemed to want to help me,' he recalled, 'my vanity was flattered, and my head was turned.'[17] Once he reached Westminster he made an immediate impact as an orator. Given his reputation, it's likely Thatcher and Walden's paths crossed in the 1960s when Walden was, briefly, the future. In 1967 he was even tipped as a potential prime minister in one of those magazine pieces that always tips the wrong people. And so it was in Walden's case: nothing really happened for him. Looking back, he said, '[I was] disenchanted before I even took my seat.'[18]

> I shouldn't have been [an MP]. The fact that I was, was entirely my own fault. Nobody else was to blame. I made the mistake, perhaps an understandable one at the time, but a mistake nonetheless. The party I joined ... was the Old Labour Party. But I was never a Socialist. You can see how that might be a problem.[19]

By the 1970s it certainly was. Walden was dismayed by the growing influence of the left in the Labour Party and the trade unions in the country. When Thatcher won the Conservative leadership against the odds in 1975, Walden quickly became first Thatcher-curious, then smitten. Walden was a prototype Labour convert to Thatcherism, a meritocrat who quickly understood her significance. According to Charles Moore, this was not lost on her:

> I think Brian flattered her because he was one of the people who, from very early on, took her ideas seriously and wanted to sort of coax them out of her and never looked at her with condescension. She noticed very much whether men were condescending or encouraging.[20]

There was also a special place in her affections for a convert to the cause and, as their friendship developed, Moore says it became 'almost flirtatious':

> Mrs Thatcher's relationships with men were, to some extent, affected by whether she found them attractive or not. I don't mean that she behaved improperly, she never did the slightest bit, but she had a strong idea of men

who were charming, men who were handsome, men who were well-dressed and men who weren't. She liked people who could write well or were intellectual or were scientific experts. There were certain sorts of categories she liked: [like the] military, and then there were types she didn't like, like sociology lecturers or whatever. And she hated people with beards.[21]

Brian, the beardless intellectual and brilliant writer, appealed to Margaret.

Walden was rescued from his unhappy political career two years after Thatcher became Tory leader. In 1977 the call came from London Weekend Television: they wanted him to host the weighty Sunday lunchtime political interview programme *Weekend World*. This was a gamble on both sides, but it started to pay off from day one – 18 September 1977, when Walden made his debut. His first guest was Margaret Thatcher, leader of the opposition.

While reviews focused on the new presenter's nerves, his 'shocking-blue terylene suit' (well, it was 1977, and for those of us watching in black and white the colour was immaterial) and his strange voice, from the beginning Walden and Thatcher enjoyed a rapport. He really wanted to hear what she had to say, and she really wanted to tell him.

As Walden became more at ease in the role and increasingly skilled at the craft of interviewing, he concluded that television offered an opportunity for real scrutiny that Parliament couldn't match:

> The plain fact is that Westminster's time-honoured procedures for calling our leaders to account are in some respects vastly inferior to those of television … When it comes to uncovering the truth, there is no substitute for sustained questioning in public by a single individual armed with a clear purpose.[22]

He might have added, 'especially when that individual is Brian Walden', because over the years Walden became the master of the long-form, sustained and forensic political interview, establishing himself as a household name and arguably the greatest of all political interviewers through the late seventies and eighties. Robin Day was more flamboyant and watchable, but less strategic and precise. More than thirty years after Walden's heyday, only Andrew Neil can contest Walden's crown as a forensic interviewer.

Walden's process is legendary. David Cox, editor of *Weekend World* when Walden joined in 1977 and his executive producer, knows how the Walden plan was constructed better than anyone:

> The work would culminate in the preparation of a document setting out not only the questions to be asked but all the possible responses we could imagine, together with the follow-ups appropriate for each. At each point where the interviewee had a choice, two completely different lines of questioning would have to be provided, so the whole thing would have the underlying shape of a family tree.[23]

Once this exhaustive document was ready, there would be numerous meetings with Walden and the production team before a final plan was produced for the presenter to study, as Cox recalled:

> In the hours that remained, he would pore over this, pacing about the room until he had consigned its contents to some deep level of consciousness. There they would fuse with his instinctive attitudes and equip him to engage his interviewee without the benefit of notes in apparently spontaneous discourse.[24]

Nothing was left to chance, and that included how best Walden should approach his interviewee. He was sometimes abrasive, but only when he had to be. He preferred to find a way to open his guests up and engage in a real conversation. His most famous encounters were with Mrs Thatcher, and these were different from the others. With her he was essentially sympathetic, and at their most successful the result felt like a genuine exchange of ideas that provoked unguarded revelations.

From the very outset, however, there was an alternative narrative when it came to these interviews: that Walden was a fanboy, burnishing her achievements and amplifying her power. Rather than holding her to account, the high esteem in which he held her meant that he granted her special treatment as the dominant politician of her age, someone who'd truly earned her own 'ism'. He was, or so the critique went, too close to the powerful, too remote from the people. That was why Walden was Thatcher's favourite interviewer and why she granted him an audience more readily than she did to the Dimblebys or Days of this world.

This characterisation is too simplistic and is rejected outright not only by Cox but also by John Wakefield, who worked on *Weekend World* and was editor of the 1989 Walden/Thatcher encounter. While both men accept that Walden had a particular approach to Thatcher interviews that was more sophisticated than simply launching into a broadside attack, they maintain that his approach produced revealing interviews that weren't always helpful to the then prime minister.

The fact remains, however, that the relationship between Thatcher and Walden was unusually close for a politician and a star TV interrogator, and this closeness delivered Thatcher to Walden's programme. It would be wrong to suggest the interviews were soft, but they were sympathetic. It's a credit to them both that this atmosphere produced interviews that revealed more than Thatcher sometimes intended, but it would be a stretch to suggest she was ever in trouble or under the cosh.

Between 1977's first *Weekend World* encounter and 1983, the prime minister and her favourite television journalist grew closer, personally and ideologically. Walden was in particular lockstep with Margaret on the biggest, most divisive issue of the time: the trade unions. Charles Moore told me that 'despite his theoretical impartiality as a television interviewer, Walden was passionately concerned that union power should be broken'. Given the centrality of that debate in the 1980s, this is an important revelation. No wonder, as Moore put it to me, Margaret considered Brian 'one of us'.[25]

But how could Walden be 'one of us' and ITV's star political interviewer at the same time? In the 1983 general election campaign, his answer to that question tarnished his legacy.

Sunday 5 June 1983, Wembley Conference Centre

A man with wild eyes, an oversized rosette and a pair of enormous, monstrous foam hands is building the crowd to a frenzy. After a sedate start featuring naff snooker star Steve 'Interesting' Davis, old-school comic Jimmy Tarbuck and ingratiating film director Michael Winner, the election rally at the Wembley Conference Centre in north London is going wild. This is the Young Conservatives, as you've never seen them before.

The man on stage could not be more incongruous in a Tory get-together in the 1980s: he is camp, bearded and even has the remnants of a Liverpool accent. It's four days before the 1983 general election, and DJ and TV comedian Kenny Everett has them rolling in the aisles. 'Let's bomb Russia!' he proclaims. The crowd is silent for a moment to process this, have a little think, and then decide to laugh in joyful, naughty release. Everett responds by waving his enormous comedy hands around like a twisted evangelical.

'Let's …' – he pauses, as if pondering what beastly Tory thing to do next – '… kick Michael Foot's stick away!' (Michael Foot, the leader of the Labour Party, is a frail-looking man about to celebrate his seventieth birthday, and sometimes uses a stick.)

The young Tories go bananas, only to find that they have extra bananas to go when Everett is joined on stage by Margaret Thatcher herself. The prime minister is basking in the adulation. Maggie – as they call her here – looks at Kenny, Kenny half bows his head towards Maggie. Jimmy Tarbuck claps, Steve Davis appears mildly animated.

The event will spur an ersatz controversy about the jokes told and the choice of comedian, but as Thatcher leaves Wembley she's feeling pumped up, convinced that the rally proves the unique, modern appeal of Thatcherism. Wild crowds and celebrity endorsements are usually the preserve of the left, but Maggie refreshes the parts other Tories cannot reach.

Elsewhere that afternoon, Sir Ronald Millar is waiting for the prime minister in a studio space in Maddox Street in the West End of London, where she is to film the final TV election broadcast of the 1983 campaign. Millar is a veteran playwright and actor who began working as a Tory speechwriter for Edward Heath in the 1960s. He wrote Thatcher's 'The lady's not for turning' line and has been drafting her election broadcasts throughout the campaign.

Millar is a keen observer of Thatcher's mood and appearance, and he's alarmed by what he sees at the rally. He doesn't like Everett's jokes, which he thinks are in poor taste, but is more troubled by the 'showbiz hysteria' affecting Thatcher. Most of all, he's worried about her 'exploding bouffant', which is 'over the top in more ways than one'. He thinks the hair is ominous. 'Women's hair, like their clothes,' he writes in his memoir, 'can be soft and soothing or striking and provocative, the outer image signalling the inner mood.'[26]

When Thatcher arrives she's with her friend and confidant Ian Gow MP, and, seeing her in the flesh, Millar is even more worried. The broadcast they are here to record is the final sell, scheduled to air two days before polling day. Millar has prepared something low-key and reflective, what he calls a 'mood piece', to seal the deal with the electorate, but Margaret is not in the mood for a mood piece, not after that rally.

'No! No!! No!!!' she explodes. Thatcher wants the broadcast to list facts: her achievements, the same things she's been banging on about all campaign long. Millar wants to change the tone in the final week and offer something else.

'I don't know what you're after,' Thatcher tells him, and Millar, ever the thespian, suggests a little warmth, perhaps 'a little night music'. Thatcher detonates again. She doesn't want night music, she wants politics.

Wearily, Millar tells her he was speaking figuratively, but the damage is done. 'We're heading for the finishing-post. We want people cheering and shouting "Maggie, Maggie, Maggie!"' she insists, her mind drifting back to the rally. 'My word, you should have heard them at Wembley.'

'I did,' says Millar. 'I thought it was vulgar.'

At this, the prime minister is done with Millar and turns to Gow: 'Ronnie's gone wobbly,' she says, 'you better find a rewrite man.'[27]

This is a big deal. The broadcast must be nailed down to ensure it's ready for transmission on Tuesday evening. Gow racks his brain for someone with the talent, flair and ideological fervour to step in and find the words for his leader's final appeal to the country. Surely, there's a copywriter from the party's advertising agency Saatchi & Saatchi or someone from Party HQ who can turn their hand to writing? But Gow has a better idea: his mind turns to a man Mrs Thatcher spent an hour with earlier in the day, broadcasting live from Downing Street between noon and one o'clock, someone she trusts and who understands her intimately. He turns to a man whose journalistic ethics should make him run a mile from the idea: Brian Walden.

Midnight, Monday 6 June 1983, Maddox Street, central London

It's taken Ian Gow several hours to track Brian Walden down. After finishing the interview with the prime minister at Downing Street, Walden had gone drinking with the *Weekend World* team to celebrate the end of their general election campaign.

Following the drinking session, the famous TV interrogator returned home and collapsed into a deep sleep. It took some time for Gow's phone calls to rouse him, but when they finally did, and the proposal was made, he said yes. He didn't say what he should have said: 'No, I'm sorry, Ian, but I can't do that. You know I'm an admirer of the prime minister, and I think you know where I am on the issues, but this crosses a line. I can't credibly hold the government to account in the years ahead if I've played a role in getting it elected. Given my job, this is an inappropriate proposal. Good night.'

Instead, Walden decided his loyalty lay with Thatcher, not journalism. Ronald Millar had been dismissed by Thatcher earlier in the evening, but was still in the building when Walden showed up.

> When he [Walden] finally arrived, he looked wobblier than anyone, staring around at this strange building, almost devoid of furniture, in which he found himself as though he had no idea where he was or what he was doing there. Strong black coffee was poured down him, and eventually, a sort of mishmash central section of the broadcast was devised by the two of us.[28]

After that, things went smoothly and eventually everyone got to go home. For Walden and Thatcher, it had been a long, strange day.

Three days later Thatcher won a landslide election victory and a second term with a majority of 144.

Brian Walden's involvement with Margaret Thatcher's campaign for re-election in 1983 is troubling. The idea that such a prominent journalist, whose job involved holding politicians to account, was willing to work on a Conservative election campaign broadcast is mind-boggling. It's particularly shocking to learn that Walden's appeal to the electorate to vote Conservative came just hours after he had been inside Downing Street conducting a live interview with the prime minister.

Perhaps Walden felt that his personal and ideological allegiances were in plain sight anyway, or maybe he didn't consider it likely anyone would ever find out.

That we have done so is thanks to Sir Ronald Millar's colourful but obscure 1993 memoir *A View from the Wings*. His entertaining account has occasionally been referred to in the thirty years since but has never been corroborated. Until now.

Charles Moore, who spoke to Brian Walden for his official biography of Margaret Thatcher, told me that Walden did do some work for her when she was prime minister that was 'probably improper'. While Moore can't know for certain whether that included helping her with the 1983 election broadcast, he did tell me that Walden openly claimed to have contributed to it. In other words, via Moore, Walden confirms Millar's account of his unwise involvement in Thatcher's campaign a few days before her landslide victory.

We'll never know how Walden justified it to himself. It would really depend on who, and what, he thought he was: a politician and player, or a journalist and spectator. Maybe having been both he would always straddle the two roles. In any case, his political side, now devoted personally and politically to Thatcher's cause, had won the day. He wanted to help her because he believed in her and liked her. It was understandable, but wrong.

Andrew Neil, who didn't know about Walden's political moonlighting until I told him about it, agrees: 'I think Brian crossed the line. Are we journalists or speechwriters?'[29] And Andrew Marr, one of the great political journalists and popular historians of our time, offers this verdict on Walden's behaviour:

> I revere Brian Walden as a journalist and interviewer, and we have to remember that he was himself a politician with very strong political views before he became a TV interviewer. He was a passionate right-wing Labour politician who felt that the country had gone in completely the wrong direction and who I'm sure genuinely felt that Margaret Thatcher was saving Britain. All that aside, this is a completely disgraceful episode. Interviewers should never, ever, ever be helping politicians behind the scenes like that. Never. You're on the side of the viewer, or you're on the side of the politician; you can't be both.[30]

Sunday 29 October 1989, 51 Bute Avenue, Nottingham

Thatcher has just lost her chancellor and she's about to sit down with the toughest interviewer on TV. Nobody has laid a finger on her in a TV interview for years. Even Walden, who's interviewed her many times, rarely lands a blow. She'll almost certainly be fine, emerging unscathed, enhanced – but you never know. I'll watch the first ten minutes, see how she gets on.

What happens next is the beginning of the end of Margaret Thatcher's political good life.

3

BRIAN & MARGARET, PART TWO

As the 1980s wore on, the fortunes of *Weekend World* began to wane. Thatcher appeared on the programme twice more after the 1983 election, but Walden left in 1986, two years before ITV axed the show.

After that, Walden's devotion to Thatcher only seemed to grow. His television career appeared to be over, but he had cachet as a Thatcher confidant. In the late eighties, Andrew Neil, editor of *The Sunday Times*, hired Walden as a columnist. His access to Thatcher – something Neil himself was denied – could only have helped him land the job.

During this period Walden sometimes met Thatcher late at night for a drink at Downing Street, and the conversation was candid but not always confidential. Walden told John Wakefield – one-time *Weekend World* producer and later Brian's editor – that he'd called Thatcher, to her face, an 'extraordinary animal that should be in a zoo'[1] on one of these nights. Meanwhile, Andrew Neil would make a point of meeting Walden at the Savoy Hotel after he'd seen Thatcher. 'And,' Neil recalls, 'Brian would tell me everything she'd said that was off the record.'[2]

In 1988 Neil asked Walden to try to get an interview with the prime minister. In his pitch to Bernard Ingham, Walden was clear he 'wanted to be helpful'. Very helpful, as Ingham revealed in a memo to a colleague about Walden's bid:

> He [Walden] says he wants to kill stone dead, the idea propagated by her enemies, that she is authoritarian, humourless, without human feelings and has no concern, e.g. for dying babies.[3]

A glowing and highly sympathetic piece followed. In it, Walden asked Thatcher whether she planned to stay on and run for re-election in 1991 and even 1995. She ruled neither possibility out, thrilling Walden. 'This was promising stuff,' he wrote, 'and I wanted more. I said, quite truthfully, that I did not want to see her go.'[4]

Then, quite suddenly, things changed for the two of them. ITV wanted a new political interview show. They wanted Walden back in the chair, this time with his name in the title. Thatcher's confidant and media cheerleader would once more be her interrogator too.

Monday 8 August 1989, London Weekend Television

John Wakefield is the editor of Walden's new programme, *The Walden Interview*. The show, which airs on Sundays at just after one o'clock, marks a return to Britain's TV screens of the master of the long-form, forensic political interview.

Wakefield has just got off the phone with Michael Bates, a press officer in 10 Downing Street who works for Bernard Ingham. Wakefield is pleased to have made the most important booking of the current series and, as it turns out, of his professional life. Ingham has agreed to a pre-recorded interview on Saturday 28 October at 10 a.m. to be broadcast, unedited, on the following day. What's more, the prime minister will come into the ITV studios. The interview is almost three months in the future but as was the way with Wakefield and Ingham's team, business is done well in advance.

Although Wakefield doesn't know it, he's just become the luckiest man in political television.

Friday 27 October 1989

There was a brief moment where the most consequential television interview of Thatcher's political life and the crowning achievement of Walden's interviewing career may never have happened, cancelled at the eleventh hour for want of a bouquet of flowers.

The call from Downing Street came on Friday morning, the day after Lawson's resignation. All was ready for the interview to be recorded the following morning in the *Walden* studio on London's South Bank, the set having been specially designed for adversarial sparring. But Downing Street had called, and they wanted flowers; something, Wakefield suspected, they hoped would soften the prime minister's appearance and lighten up the programme's carefully constructed atmosphere.

He said no.

For a few hours that Friday afternoon there was a stand-off. Wakefield would rather forgo the interview than bring an incongruous bouquet onto the *Walden* set. Up to this point he couldn't believe his luck: he'd fixed the interview three months previously and, by pure chance, it had coincided with the moment of maximum danger for the prime minister. But his luck might just be running out.

By then, Walden had arrived in the office in London from his Guernsey home. Walden, Cox, Wakefield and their team of journalists had been preparing for the interview for days in the usual way, but Lawson's resignation had changed everything. Brian and the team pored over the newspapers, absorbing the commentary and speculation. The significance of the moment for Thatcher was sinking in. This was her most serious crisis, but could the interview of the decade be slipping through their fingers?

Then, finally, the call came from Downing Street. They were still asking about flowers, but now said they needn't be on set. They just needed to be in the prime minister's line of sight. Mrs Thatcher liked to look at them. To Wakefield the request seemed all the more bizarre; he was non-committal but heard no more about it. Perhaps Downing Street had realised that cancelling an interview because of a lack of flowers would have made a damaging story in its own right.

The final obstacle overcome, the three men and the team of researchers started to turn their minds to the interview itself. The team, and Brian, had to rise to the occasion. Everyone would be watching this.

Saturday 28 October 1989

Thatcher has been up for several hours before she makes the short journey south of the river from Downing Street to the studios on the South Bank. She's had breakfast with Denis, done some work – of course – and the usual shampoo and set in Downing Street. Today is the sort of day she needs to look the part.

As her make-up is applied, she's not worried about the interview. No one has interviewed her on television as often as her friend Brian, and she trusts him. She knows where he stands and what he's done for her. She can rely on him to focus on the really important issues – Europe, the economy – and not spend too long on gossip and Westminster tittle-tattle. She knows there'll be questions about the resignation. Of course he'll have to ask about it, but it needn't go on forever. Then, all that will blow over, and she can talk about the issues they both agree really matter. As Bernard Ingham remarks in his briefing note for the interview: 'You are unlikely to have a more sympathetic interviewer than Brian Walden.'[5]

She has already read the newspapers – she has some time for that at the weekend – and knows that her defiant comments to the *Daily Express* have been widely reported. She's made clear that she has no intention of resigning and will stay on and win the next general election. And who's to say she can't? She's been underestimated before and has always emerged victorious. This morning's interview is a chance to remind viewers that she's still the prime minister they elected a little over two years ago, and she's still right about the things that matter to the British people. Brian understands that better than anyone.

As for Walden, strangely perhaps, his morning is a little more troubled than the prime minister's. He awakes, as usual, in the Savoy, the hundred-year-old luxury hotel on the Strand in central London where he stays on programme weekends.

He arrives at the office on the seventeenth floor of the London Television Centre at around half past seven, as he always does on the morning of an interview. He likes to set aside time for final conversations and a review of the newspapers with Wakefield and the executive producer David Cox over coffee and chain-smoked cigarettes.

Nobody can remember whether Walden had already seen that morning's *Independent* by the time he arrived at work or whether the profile of him, which dominates the editorial opinion pages, was drawn to his attention by Wakefield or Cox. Either way, everyone remembers how it set the stage for the encounter to come.

Above a black-and-white cartoon of Walden with an exaggerated quiff are the words:

PROFILE: Brian Walden, Thatcher's favoured interviewer

The choice of word is deliberate: Walden is 'favoured', given special access and trusted. He's more than simply her favourite. Beneath the cartoon comes the big question:

Is she safe in his hands?

Independent readers are almost certainly thinking the answer is 'probably', and they haven't started reading yet. From there, the piece – a 'profile', but one without a byline – is brutal. 'Tomorrow lunchtime,' it begins, referring to the day of transmission, 'the eyes of the world will be on Brian Walden.'

> Some months ago, Margaret Thatcher agreed to appear on her favourite television interviewer's programme to discuss her plans for the new parliamentary term. When it was arranged, it looked like being a passably interesting media event; after this week's political blood-letting, it could prove the sharpest television confrontation since David Frost met Richard Nixon. Walden's critics, however, would claim that in her time of crisis, the Prime Minister could not be in safer hands.[6]

If anyone at London Weekend Television has failed to appreciate the gravity of the moment before they read that paragraph, they're put straight afterwards. The piece, possibly written by veteran political commentator Tony Howard, slowly turns the screw on their star interviewer. Walden, the profile notes, has been granted a 'media audience' by Thatcher more times than any other British journalist. Why? Well, his style – 'polite, deferential, even gentle' – appeals to her, as well it might. Walden, whom the paper helpfully points out is 'now living in tax exile in Guernsey', does not wear the 'bovver boot' of the 'journalistic rough trade' the prime minister despises.

From there, the focus turns to Walden's back story, getting really stuck in when recalling his 'reputation as a flamboyant embellisher of the truth' at Oxford and his tendency as an MP to accept lucrative consultancies from organisations like the National Bookmakers Association: 'Dennis Skinner coined his parliamentary nickname: the bookie's runner.' The most damaging assertion comes next: noting he'd become a newspaper columnist at *The Sunday Times* after the demise of *Weekend World* in the late eighties, the profile is blunt:

> Here he could expound on his conversion to Toryism and
> enjoyed revealing to readers his place in the centre of
> things. 'I have been anticipating the current situation for
> many years,' and 'It was I who coined the phrase
> "Victorian Values."'[7]

The *Independent* characterises Walden as a soft interviewer who goes easy on Thatcher; he's vain, venal and untrustworthy; worst of all, this supposedly impartial journalist is basically a Tory.

From there, it gets nasty:

> Walden's mother died when he was in his teens but he
> continued to be devoted to her. Perhaps because he
> idolised the old-fashioned, working-class matriarch, a
> figure he could not immediately replace in his own life,
> he has had three wives and an apparently hectic
> emotional life.[8]

After a quick detour, noting that Brian's second wife Jane once wrote a piece about their relationship for a pornographic magazine entitled 'Is Your MP Good In Bed?', the paper returns to the main event: the weekend's interview with Thatcher:

> If he lets her off the hook, which may well be his natural
> instinct with his 'Let us not forget, Prime Minister, you
> are a figure of historic importance,' Walden will have

blown his great chance. Two imperative questions attach themselves to tomorrow's programme. Will Walden's producers insist he go for the jugular? And, more important, is he capable of doing it?[9]

So although this is a high-stakes political interview billed as make or break for Thatcher, it's Walden – not the prime minister – who is in the crosshairs. The piece brims with frustration that now, just as the moment of reckoning has arrived for Thatcher, it falls to one of her most enthusiastic cheerleaders to deliver it.

For Walden the risk – and opportunity – is enormous. It's all on the line that morning in October 1989, and he knows it. He's known it before the *Independent* weighs in, and he knows it more clearly than ever now. He also knows that there can only be one winner on a day like this: himself or Thatcher, but not both.

It's up to him to choose.

David Cox had been recruited by John Birt to *Weekend World* when it was launched in 1972, although he didn't actually join until the following year. In a team that at various times included Peter Mandelson, Trevor Phillips and David Aaronovitch, Cox was editor by the time Walden arrived at the South Bank in 1977. When the programme morphed into *The Walden Interview* Cox returned as executive producer, and he remained pretty much a constant at Walden's side throughout the interviewer's television career.

That October week in 1989 was unlike any other that Walden, Cox and editor John Wakefield had worked on. The usual period of intense planning, preparation and debate, followed by the production of 'the document' or interview plan, went out of the window when Lawson resigned on Thursday night. The economy and Europe were the big issues, but they would have to take a back seat now. Cox was a purist when it came to political interviews and wanted to send Walden into the studio with a plan that focused on Thatcher's future plans for government rather than dwell too much on the events of the previous few days.

Brian and Wakefield had other ideas: at this stage, the content of the conversations between the prime minister and chancellor remained a mystery. Something had gone terribly wrong at the top of government, and part of Walden's job was to deliver what Wakefield called a 'forensic police interview', establishing who said what, when and why. Only then could viewers, MPs and journalists assess Thatcher's handling of the crisis and determine whether she could have averted it.

Cox could tell that Walden grasped the significance of what he recalls as a 'very hot', 'very electric moment'. The *Independent* wasn't alone in seeing Walden as a Thatcherite who went easy on Thatcher. The question, says Cox, was whether Walden 'would have the bottle to attack her properly or would he suck up to her given their political and personal closeness'.[10]

Wakefield, Walden's editor, acknowledges the pressure on Walden to perform but dismisses the idea that Walden and Thatcher were friends in the sense you or I would understand the word. 'She didn't really do friends,' Wakefield told me, 'and nor did Brian.'

> Friendship implies a type of mutual feeling, a certain sort of loyalty that involves caring. None of that pertained between Brian and Thatcher. Brian was not a friend of Thatcher but rather a supporter of hers.[11]

Accordingly, any choice Walden might have made about how to approach an interview with Thatcher did not, says Wakefield, contain any component of personal loyalty or concern. What's more, despite the evidence that Walden betrayed his journalistic ethics by helping Thatcher to win re-election in 1983, Wakefield is firm in his belief that Walden's support for Thatcherism never influenced his conduct of interviews with her. He never had to resolve conflicting loyalties because he didn't have any, Wakefield says. He was 'always intent on being single-minded in doing his job as an interviewer'.[12]

David Cox, who essentially created Brian Walden the TV persona, takes a different view. This was personal for Walden: 'He did like her, and she was his friend, and he knew that he had to choose.'

> The idea was very much around that he liked Thatcher very much, and she liked him. They were great mates, and there were a lot of suspicions that he was favouring her in some sort of way when he interviewed her. It [the interview] happened to have fallen to him, so it was interesting that this interview, at this key moment, was going to be done by somebody who was thought to be in her pocket.[13]

Walden knew all this and felt it acutely. On that Saturday, when he was reading the *Independent*, he was very aware that the interview was a critically important moment for him and that he absolutely had to show that he wasn't going to be soft on her.[14]

Cox is certain that Walden had made his choice, even before that Saturday morning. The coverage 'just rammed it home'. He knew which way he would jump and, says Cox, so did the team.

> It was just obvious to all of us. It didn't really need to be said. Brian looked it in the eye and thought: it's her or him. And it's going to be her. He knew that he could go soft on her, but that would be very bad news for him, and he decided he would rather it was bad news for her.[15]

Before they begin the interview, as they glance across the studio, waiting for the recording to start, what's in their minds? Are they clear about where Brian and Margaret end and where Walden and Thatcher begin? Has Thatcher considered that where those lines are drawn has been changing in real time?

You can forgive her for a little complacency, given her history with Walden, but there's also a sense, here in Thatcher's late period, that she has become disconnected from reality in general. After Lawson, there's blood in the water, and while she's acutely aware of the political threat, she doesn't recognise that erstwhile friends can quickly morph into sharks.

In those days, far away from power, Westminster, Downing Street and the media world, I remember that we talked about Thatcher being 'mad'. Not just students like me, but mums and dads and people you'd chat to in the street. They might have liked her once, but she seemed more and more peculiar by the late eighties, transformed by power and years of dominance into an unyielding and remote figure who was simply unable to entertain alternative views or relate to ordinary people. Thatcher in furs in Moscow was imperial and sort of majestic, miles away from Margo in floral prints in Surbiton, but this regal Thatcher was also slightly ridiculous.

All this crystalised one day in March 1989 – six months before sitting down in the *Walden Interview* studio – when, again in fur, the prime minister bowled out of the front door of No. 10 towards a waiting camera to confirm the arrival of her first grandchild. She starts walking slowly, normally, but picks up pace, her shoes clip-clopping across the street like a jumpy horse, racing over to the film crew. She's going so fast that she slightly overshoots, her face coming to rest too near the camera, looming into the lens. Then, with the cameraman mid-rapid reframe, she announces, 'We have become a grandmother.'

This use of the royal 'we' sounded genuinely weird and delusional at the time. It seemed to indicate that Thatcher's self-image had been so warped by ten years in office that she'd begun to see herself as some sort of quasi-monarch. Charles Moore has a more prosaic explanation for her strange choice of words: she'd expected to make the announcement alongside her husband Denis and had planned to say, 'We have become grandparents,' but Denis couldn't make it. According to Moore, these words had been in her mind when she bounded into the street. But, as Bernard Ingham noted, people didn't believe Mrs Thatcher made mistakes. Her strange words must have been meant. As a result, the feeling that here was a woman starting to come off her rocker stuck. This, combined with her persistence with the disastrous poll tax and her growing conviction that she was right about everything, amplified the suspicion that there might be something wrong with her, that she might be losing it. This view was gathering pace in 1989, but it wasn't new, as Charles Moore told me:

> There was always a school of thought that Mrs Thatcher was mad. I don't mean literally mad, but that's what people said, because of her very intense way of saying things and also, through a certain sort of misogyny, in which a very earnest, emphatic woman is considered to be bonkers. People would say, 'She's a mad witch.'[16]

These sentiments were repeated more widely in senior party and cabinet circles after the 1987 general election campaign, when, as Moore describes it, she behaved particularly erratically:

> Everybody who was close to her during the 1987 campaign found her an incredible nuisance and very, very unbalanced. I don't mean suffering from mental illness, but very, very nervous and angry and difficult, much more than before.[17]

So all this was in the bloodstream by the time the poll tax, the Madrid ambush and the Lawson resignation came around in 1989. Unfairly or otherwise, arrogance and madness had become associated with Thatcher, and these sentiments were about to surface in the mainstream.

Even Walden was having his doubts. Not long before his death, in 2019, he spoke to Moore about his relationship with Thatcher. Walden told him that his view of her began to change towards the end of the 1980s. He felt she was losing her grip, becoming a '[modern-day] Napoleon thinking she can do whatever she likes'.

So perhaps that's what's going on in the studio on the South Bank. Maybe she is in her own world, divorced from reality, unaware of the depth of the political crisis and what that will mean for the next forty-six minutes. She expects a certain propriety from Walden. He's a serious interviewer and this will be a serious interview looking to the future. She won't need to spend too long on Lawson. She knows what she plans to say about him and will stick to saying it, whatever Walden asks.

But she's forgotten something about Walden. It's one of the reasons this ambitious, dirt-poor, working-class boy turned away from socialism and towards Thatcherism when she arrived on the scene: he's highly competitive. He's not here simply to take part. He's here to win.

The interview

Walden: Nigel Lawson's shock resignation from the Chancellorship has plunged the Prime Minister into the most serious political crisis of her career. It has also confronted her with a full-scale economic crisis. Can she resolve her political and economic problems? The Prime Minister is with us here today.[18]

The camera cuts to Thatcher, who blinks rapidly and steels herself. The two stare impassively at each other as the title music begins, all jolly piccolos that morph into staccato violins as the piece resolves. Walden looks up at Thatcher, smiles briefly and begins. There are no more jolly piccolos.

Walden opens, as he often does, with a half statement, half question, his distinctive West Midlands accent and difficulty pronouncing the letter 'r' combining to create its usual, strange effect. Then he asks, a little strangely, whether Thatcher is 'to blame' for Lawson's resignation.

Thatcher is untroubled – 'blame' is a matter of opinion and not specific enough to bother her for now – so she sidesteps. Her first, heavily prepared answer contains all the main elements she'll fall back on during the course of this interview: she lauds the successes of her six-year partnership with Lawson, suggests that his position as chancellor was 'unassailable' and, touching on the Walters problem, says that she was always clear with Lawson that 'advisers are there to advise, ministers are there to decide'.

Thatcher delivers these lines confidently. She is smiling and unruffled. The plan is clear: repeat, repeat, repeat. Walden returns to the question of blame, putting Lawson's suggestion to her that they were seen to disagree on economic policy because of her troublesome adviser. These weren't bitter disagreements, she answers, batting him away, just healthy discussions.

The first two and a half minutes have been Thatcher's, but it won't get any better than this for her.

Walden asks about Sir Alan Walters and what Lawson said to her about him. Here are the first signs of trouble.

Walden: It's pretty obvious from the [resignation] letter what it is he objects to … Professor Alan Walters … now he must have made it very clear to you, what did you say to that?

Thatcher: Nigel's position, as I said to him, is
unassailable. He was a very strong Chancellor ...

Walden: It isn't now, is it? He's gone.[19]

Come on, Brian, this is Margaret.

I remember watching that moment and thinking for the
first time that day – and maybe for the first time ever – that
Mrs Thatcher seemed a bit silly. Not strong or scary, but
silly. You can't say someone is unassailable – adjective: unable
to be attacked, questioned or defeated – when you've just
chosen your adviser over him and allowed him to walk out the
door.

At this point Thatcher makes her first really serious mistake:
she attempts to give the impression that she doesn't know why
Lawson resigned, as if the reason he left her government was
somehow obscure and unclear to her. This was hard enough to
believe on its own, but even less convincing as, her voice softening regretfully, she painted an intimate portrait of her
discussions with Lawson about his resignation.

Somehow, Nigel had made up his mind that he was
going. I spent a long time just talking, just the two of us
together, trying to dissuade him, but his mind was made
up. I was sad.[20]

In police interview terms, this is where Officer Walden starts to
smell a rat. How could she be unaware of the reasons the chancellor departed when she'd spent such a long time alone with
Lawson discussing them?

So Walden turns more precisely to the reason: Sir Alan
Walters embarrassing the chancellor by going around having
opinions. Thatcher can't help herself. She defends Walters and
then says she cannot believe that this can be the real reason for
the resignation: 'It is just not possible that this small particular

thing [Walters' troublemaking] could result in this particular resignation.' So what is the reason? She cannot say.

From there, she tries to shut down the line of questioning and direct Walden to where she wants to go, insisting, 'Now we must turn to the future.'

Not so fast, Margaret.

Walden is relentless. He returns to Walters, citing his indiscreet lunches in the City with journalists, telling anyone who would listen about his disagreements with the chancellor. Thatcher takes the bait: many people 'go out and have lunches in the City', she says, not just Sir Alan. Then she senses she's being walked towards danger and stops herself. 'I am not going to get involved with this tittle-tattle.'

For an answer or two, the prime minister regains control, rejecting gossip and rumour, and turning to the subjects she came here to talk about, things like the economy and Britain's standing in the world. Lawson is history, Brian. The future is what matters.

'It is,' answers Walden, 'but it is also, of course, your political position, Prime Minister, and I have to question you on that, and you know that I do.' He says those five words – 'you know that I do' – in his very particular way. He says them to signal empathy for his guest. It's a sort of apology for having to go through all this stuff, and a way of saying that both of us – me, Brian, you, Margaret – know how this works and how it has to go.

Thatcher forces a smile and playful nonchalance. 'Yes, do', she says, 'go question, go ahead.' A crucial stage has been reached: the prime minister's attempt to exert her authority over Walden has failed. He simply refuses to move on.

Now Walden turns up the heat. The big question, he tells her, his voice becoming louder for emphasis, is why. Why did Lawson resign if he was unassailable and everything was going so well?

'People are going to want to know why,' he reasons.

'I think that's a question you must put to him and not me,' she answers.

Walden, twinkling, tells her that he will. Mr Lawson will be on the programme next week.

Thatcher winces.

Walden switches back to police interview mode. He asks how many times she spoke to Lawson on the day he resigned, establishing they had discussed the issue several times. Then he turns the screw, using repetition to drive his point home powerfully:

Walden: He was unassailable, you say, you were in agreement, you say, everything was going well, you say, and he said to you, 'Margaret, you have got to get rid of Alan Walters.' Why didn't you and keep your Chancellor?[21]

Come on, Brian, let's move on.

At this, eleven minutes in, Thatcher is rattled, and she finally complains: 'You have asked me, Brian, the same question about five times, and I have given you the same answer. If you continue to ask that same question, I shall continue to give you the same answer.' She wants to turn to the future, but he will not let her, and then comes the key exchange:

Walden: A last question: do you deny that Nigel would have stayed if you had sacked Professor Alan Walters?

Thatcher (shaking her head): I don't know. I don't know.

Walden (raising his voice): You never even thought to ask him that?

Thatcher: That is not … I don't know.

She is visibility exasperated, shading into anger:

Thatcher: No, you're going on asking the same question. I have nothing further to …

Walden: That's a terrible admission, Prime Minister.

Thatcher: I have nothing further … I don't know … of course, I don't know.[22]

Of course, I know.

Thatcher wants to be somewhere else. Nobody has seen her like this on television before. 'I'm not going on with this,' she flounders, sounding forlorn, appealing to her friend to stop. She's on the ropes, and for a moment Walden seems to hesitate, as if he's ready to accept that he's done enough damage. But then he asks again, 'Did he [Lawson] ask you to sack Walters?'

She smiles weakly, trying to recover her composure.

'I'm not going to disclose the conversations which the two of us had.'

She returns to her talking points about Lawson being unassailable and how advisers only advise. It's desperate.

Briefly, Walden eases off a little. He moves on to the economic differences between prime minister and chancellor, and here she can regroup. The conversation remains heated, but Thatcher is on the offensive, at last, pushing back at Walden about his obsession with tittle-tattle. She's almost her old self again, urging Walden to face the future and move on.

But Walden is not done. Just when it seems the argument over Lawson and Walters has run out of steam, he changes tack and goes in for the kill. He starts by suggesting that Thatcher cannot work with independent figures and that she likes to surround herself with yes-men. She has heard this before, and she disputes it. It wasn't long ago that Walden himself had rejected this caricature in *The Sunday Times*.

'You know,' she answers, 'from many, many years arguing with me, that I enjoy a good argument.'

Walden can't help himself here: 'I know,' he agrees under his breath.

'So what you are saying again is nonsense,' says Thatcher, 'and you know it from having talked with me over the years!'

She connects with Walden here but can't shake him off. This appeal to their history – on television and in life – won't work today. Walden has more to say.

> **Walden:** Let me put this to you, Prime Minister, it is a point that has always interested me, and I think it is now politically relevant. It may be the case that in private, you will have a lusty argument and you will listen to other people's opinions and that you are only too happy to accept a suggestion if it is correct, but you never come over in public like that. Ever.[23]

He slams down 'ever' in front of Thatcher with a thwack. You can sense his real exasperation as her secret ally, with her increasingly high-handed manner. Maybe that's why he goes further:

> **Walden** (his voice gradually rising to a climax): You come over as being someone who one of your backbenchers said is slightly 'off her trolley', authoritarian, domineering, refusing to listen to anybody else – why? Why can't you publicly project what you have just told me is your private character?

> **Thatcher** (half-whispering but with controlled power): Brian, if anyone's coming over as domineering in this interview, it's you.[24]

Walden chuckles, and the laugh is genuine, his body bobbing up and down with real delight. This is Thatcher's wittiest and most effective moment because it's heartfelt and honest.

'It's you,' she repeats for emphasis.

Off my trolley. Really, Brian?

That second 'it's you' is melancholy and disappointed, and Walden's 'off her trolley' jibe has clearly stung. Despite her brilliant comeback, she's hurt. This is Brian; she is Margaret. He knows the domineering Thatcher caricature is untrue, yet he is brandishing it, as near as dammit calling her insane. She's used to the double-standard women must put up with – male politicians are strong, powerful and single-minded; she is authoritarian, domineering and mad – but she expects better from Walden.

She accuses him with some sadness of 'hammering things out instead of just talking about them in a conversational way'. It feels personal, as does her observation that 'you are very domineering at the moment'. She wants to talk to her friend Brian, but she finds Walden in his place, and he's giving the *Independent* and everyone else what they want instead: confrontation.

After her pointed comments fail to hit home, she makes a stab at contrition over the breakdown of relations with Lawson – 'Neither of us is faultless' – but it feels a little hollow. As the advert break nears, Thatcher tells Walden off once more for obsessing over gossip. He punches back, warning that far from tittle-tattle, 'when you get down to the House of Commons next week, you will hear very little else'.

He's not wrong.

It's been a bruising and extraordinary thirty-three minutes of political and personal theatre. To Thatcher's relief, most of the second part of the programme focuses on the economic problems facing the government and the argument over whether or not Britain should join the ERM. This is safer ground, and she is formidable. But Walden is still not done.

As the interview closes, he drags the conversation back to his earlier theme, pointing out that to the public she appears unyielding and that this interview will only confirm that impression.

'Nonsense, Brian,' she says, dripping with attitude, 'I'm staying my own sweet, reasonable self.'

As Walden runs out of time and closes the show, she interrupts with a promise: 'Strong leadership will continue.'

She has exactly thirteen months left to run.

Back in my Nottingham student house I was staggered. For the very first time, there seemed to be a real possibility that the political figure who had dominated throughout my teens and into my twenties might actually be vulnerable. The idea that Thatcher didn't know why Nigel Lawson had resigned and how she could have stopped it was absurd. That someone like Brian Walden called her 'off her trolley' was thrilling. Such an encounter was only possible on television. The procedure and pomp of parliament just didn't allow such drama. Imagine, I thought – before almost certainly heading to the pub for cheap pints of Festival bitter and the Sunday papers – having a job on a programme like that!

Those that did work on *The Walden Interview* that day had mixed feelings. John Wakefield's memory of it is uncomplicated: 'I think we were pretty pleased,' he told me.[25] David Cox's feelings were characteristically more complex. He recalls thinking that 'it was technically an absolutely terrible interview'.[26] Cox had some sympathy with Thatcher's view that the questions should have focused more on what she planned to do next, not the mechanics of the Lawson resignation.

If that was the battle plan before the interview started, Walden threw it away once the battle was under way. Walden made his choice, as Cox makes clear:

It was a sort of pantomime event, really. It wasn't in any way like the interviews we normally did. It was pantomime instead of a forensic examination. As it turned out, that was fine because the pantomime was what was really needed. That was what the *Independent* wanted to see. They wanted to see the world take on Thatcher. It was quite clear that Brian, who was thought to be a mate of hers, was confronting her with the suggestion that she was wrong; she was a bit bonkers; she was losing it. And that was what it turned out to be about.[27]

Having said that, Cox confirms that the decision to suggest that Thatcher was 'off her trolley' was in the interview plan.

There was a wider view that she was going bonkers. That was a genuine part of what her downfall was about. She'd lost touch with reality, which was an important part of the case against her. So we thought we had to engage with the idea that she was actually going nuts.[28]

Elsewhere in London, Nigel Lawson was watching his former boss lock horns with Walden. Lawson knew she wasn't telling the truth about their conversations. He'd made it 'perfectly clear' that Walters was the issue and that if the adviser had been fired, he'd have stayed. His worry now was how to avoid having to call her a liar on the same programme when he appeared the following Sunday.

But the truth is she *was* lying. Later she revealed her true feelings: she thought that Lawson had resigned because the economy was in trouble, and he didn't want to have to fix it. That this was her actual view explains her odd position in the interview. During the encounter, she hints that Lawson had other reasons than just Walters for leaving but doesn't state them.

In assessing Thatcher's interviews, I think her most admirable characteristic was her willingness to straightforwardly tell interviewers, colleagues and anyone else who'd listen what she really thought. When she did that, she found herself on safe ground, rooted in genuine conviction and the truth as she saw it.

The day before the Lawson resignation, Bernard Ingham had written Thatcher a note to help prepare her for the interview. In it he reminded her that 'your guiding principle, learned from your earliest years, is to thine own self be true' and suggested she stick by it. Perhaps the shocking events of the following day shook her, but this was not her approach. Instead, she was essentially defensive, a record stuck on pre-prepared grooves, disingenuously feigning ignorance of the heart of the matter.

Allow me, then, to offer you a remix, a mash-up, if you will, of two interviews.

The question comes from Brian Walden that day in October 1989. The answer is from a section of the *Downing Street Years* documentary series based on Thatcher's memoirs broadcast in 1993.

Walden: Why did Nigel Lawson resign? You say he knew that he was unassailable, he knew that you loved him and that everything he did was marvellous, but he resigned. Now people are going to want to know why?[29]

Thatcher: I think Nigel was looking for an excuse to resign because of the inflation he had created, and I think he was pestering me to get the information out because he feared that I might otherwise ring up Alan [Walters], and Alan would say, 'Well, of course, I will go,' and then his excuse would have been no longer valid, and he would have had to have stayed on and deal with the inflation himself.[30]

However blunt that would have been, it's hard to believe the truth would have been more damaging than the lie.

After the interview, Thatcher and Bernard Ingham headed to the eighteenth floor of the London Television Centre, where drinks were served in a huge hospitality area with stunning views of the capital. John Wakefield was already there, waiting to greet the prime minister. He remembers her protesting that the interview had spent so much time on what – several times – she called 'tittle-tattle' rather than 'the great issues of state'. However much this irritated her, Wakefield believes she knew it was a feeble objection. The Lawson resignation was bound to dominate the discussion and Wakefield had the sense that she knew that to be the case, really.[31]

When Walden arrived, Thatcher changed the subject and concealed her annoyance. The old friends spent an hour up there with the team of producers, enjoying a drink and discussing German reunification or Spanish fishing quotas, depending on whom you ask. Her temper seemed to have cooled.

It was only in the hours afterwards when the reviews started coming in that Thatcher began to stew. Her mantra that Lawson was unassailable was widely seen as ridiculous, and her suggestion that she didn't know why he'd gone was utterly preposterous. Woodrow Wyatt, another Labour renegade who'd become devoted to Thatcher, was also a friend of Walden. In his famous journal Wyatt refers to conversations he'd had with Walden in the days before the interview that had implied the interviewer would go easy on the prime minister. We can't be sure those conversations ever actually took place, but we do know that Wyatt was angry about how the interview turned out:

He [Walden] was obnoxious. I was furious ... the questioning was outrageously impertinent to a Prime Minister. Brian then accused her of being dictatorial and autocratic and said she appeared to people to be going off her trolley. I was amazed at Brian, who had pretended he was going to be helpful, carrying on in this extraordinary way to damage her as much as he possibly could.[32]

There can be no doubt that this sentiment found its way back to Mrs Thatcher, who must have shared Wyatt's sense of betrayal and hurt about the interview and the suggestion that she was in some way mentally unstable.

The front pages of the following day's newspapers were dominated by the Walden/Thatcher interview, with several titles printing long sections of the transcript. Subsequently, the *Daily Telegraph* diary speculated that Walden had been 'stripped of his title as Mrs Thatcher's Favourite Interviewer' and reported on one 'insider' who claimed it had cost him a knighthood.

In the House of Commons, the shadow chancellor and future Labour leader John Smith marked the importance of the moment:

> That interview was an event of enormous political significance, a revelation of the Prime Minister's style and approach to the problems of government, as an example of which it could not be bettered. It will be as indispensable to historians as it is to those of us who view these matters in a more contemporary frame.[33]

As for the man and woman involved, the interview was the end. Walden and Thatcher never spoke again.

As she always feared, within weeks, damaged by the Lawson affair and the Walden interview, the knife went in; she survived that first leadership challenge, but a line had been crossed. A year later, her time was up.

Thank you, Brian.

4

I THINK PADDY ASHDOWN HATES ME

It's April 1997 and we're in the middle of a general election campaign.

I'm standing at the back of the control room at the London Weekend Television studios on the South Bank, watching the *Jonathan Dimbleby* programme go out live. I'm a junior researcher, and I'm exhausted. I've spent a week preparing for this moment: our first leader's interview programme. Labour leader Tony Blair is due soon, and the Conservative prime minister John Major will appear on the last Sunday before polling day. Today it's the turn of Paddy Ashdown, leader of the Liberal Democrats. They're the third party, but it's still a big deal, and this is the biggest show I've worked on yet.

I've spent the week immersed in Lib Dem policy documents, principally the party's manifesto for the general election. I know it backwards, better than anyone should really have to.

Its centrepiece, and the main theme of Ashdown's campaign, is education. He's promising that a Lib Dem government – no sniggering – would put an extra penny on income tax and spend the proceeds on education. But there's a problem: central government might be able to raise taxes to provide extra money, but they can't tell local government, where the money ends up, what to spend it on. Ashdown likes to say this money is 'ring-fenced' for education, but it isn't as far as I can make out from his manifesto.

Most of the time, Ashdown and his party escape close scrutiny. Most interviewers can't be bothered with the Lib Dems, but Jonathan Dimbleby is different. We've spent hours over the course of the past few days wargaming. This involves Jonathan and the team role-playing the interview. Jonathan stars as himself while assorted team members, including me, pretend to be Ashdown. Perfecting a Paddy impression requires the ability to project a degree of sanctimony, and his holier-than-thou persona becomes a running joke through the course of the week.

Jonathan opens the show with a joke about Ashdown's telephone answering-machine message – look it up, kids – which asks callers to leave their message 'after the high moral tone'. Ashdown's back story – he's a former Royal Marine – has enhanced the Liberal Democrat leader's image, and he milks it relentlessly. He enjoys standing between the main two parties and condemning them both, the guardian of truth pitching his bivouac permanently on the moral high ground.

This image of probity surrounding Ashdown and his party must be maintained, or the whole enterprise risks crumbling. The Lib Dems have a reputation as electoral street fighters, well known for pumping out dodgy election literature that usually exaggerates their chances of winning a particular seat. They're also known to modify their policies depending on the audience they're trying to attract. So the opportunity to prick this particular bubble is delicious. What better than proving to viewers that Ashdown's guaranteed cash for schools isn't guaranteed at all?

So, here is Jonathan, entirely dependent on my briefing and understanding of the manifesto, taking on Ashdown, live on TV. 'JD', as I'm thrilled to be allowed to call him, wants to know how Ashdown can square his promise that all the extra money will go to schools with his party's belief that local authorities get to choose how to spend their money. You can't promise the money, says Jonathan, if you can't deliver it.

Ashdown smirks.

'Wrong, wrong, wrong,' he says confidently. 'I mean, forgive me; you've obviously been rather badly advised by your researcher.'

I wince.

'It was all absolutely in the detail of the manifesto.'

I swallow nervously.

'I'm sorry your researcher didn't inform you about that, Jonathan.'

Jonathan, whom I've briefed on this precise point, pursues it, but it seems to me he looks a little worried. I wonder if he'll let me call him 'JD' after this.

But Jonathan hasn't given up yet. He points out that Charles Kennedy, then the Lib Dem education spokesman, has made it clear: local councils will decide how the money will be spent. The Lib Dems believe power should be devolved to the local level. There's nothing in their manifesto to suggest any dilution of that principle regarding this money.

Ashdown is unmoved. His answer is a long-winded version of 'whatever'. As he answers, I see movement from the corner of my eye. My producer, Andy Harrison, a very lovely but currently rather worried man, swings his chair around to face me.

'Rob,' he asks me as a sickly wave of *oh shit* washes over me, 'are we right?'

'I, um,' I stammer, my mind racing to the closely typed pages of the Lib Dem manifesto, 'I think so,' I say weakly.

Before Andy can answer, Ashdown is coming back at Jonathan, pressing the point again.

Ashdown: I can understand why you're trying to explain why you didn't know about this. But the truth of it is that this has been made absolutely clear ... you were misinformed. I'm sorry about that.[1]

My face reddens and I look at Andy. 'I'll go and get the manifesto,' I say, running for the control room door. I sprint along endless corridors in the LWT building to the lift, which I take all the way up from the second to the seventeenth floor. I scan the office for the document but can't see it. The TV is on, and Ashdown is burbling on about education and the penny and, for all I know, how useless I am. Then I see it on Jonathan's desk: a yellow document called *Make the Difference*, with black-and-white images of ordinary people, and, in the centre, Ashdown's face with his trademark crinkly smile. I grab it and run full pelt back down to the studio.

But by the time I get there it's all moved on. The audience is asking questions, and Ashdown is chilled once again. I sit down and try to read the manifesto. Maybe if I can check it to make sure he's wrong it'll be OK, and there'll be time for JD, or should I say, Jonathan, to restore our honour. But the words swim in front of me as I read them: education, tax, £2 billion, words, words, words.

When the show is over I don't want to be there for the post-mortem/drinking session. I hang back downstairs, not ready to show my face. It's made worse by the fact that a journalist from the *Independent* has been shadowing us all weekend and now has a story about how rubbish the researchers are. I usually love the alcoholic post-show wind-down on the eighteenth floor, with its panoramic views of London and warm white wine, but I'm dreading it today. When I finally pluck up the courage to join the party, Ashdown is there, deep in conflab with the man from the *Independent*, who is earnestly making notes.

I enter the room and walk towards Jonathan, who's holding court surrounded by producer Andy, the rest of the production team and Ashdown's advisers. He seems happy, but I say nothing, standing on the periphery, waiting for someone to talk to me. Then Ashdown appears at my side. The reporter has gone.

'Paddy,' says Jonathan loudly enough so everyone can hear, 'this is my researcher. His name is Rob.'

I turn to Ashdown, who smiles his crinkly smile at me. I steel myself.

'Oh, sorry about that,' he says, half-laughing, lighting a cigarette. He's immediately much more likeable in person than he comes across on television. 'You were quite right, of course. There's nothing in the manifesto that absolutely guarantees the money, but I had to say something to get out of the hole.'

And everyone laughs. I feel relief wash all over me, followed by something close to disgust.

The next morning I rush to the newsagent to read the piece in the newspaper. Maybe the reporter has seen through Ashdown's protestations and made us look like heroes.

The headline is promising: 'Backroom army plots to outflank Paddy'.

The story runs through the on-screen spat over the penny on tax and my mad 'scurry' to retrieve the manifesto but gives Ashdown the last word:

'You see, I wrote our manifesto,' says Mr Ashdown afterwards. 'I spent seventy hours writing it, and I know where the skeletons are hidden.'

In the final analysis, even Jonathan Dimbleby and his team haven't spent as long studying Mr Ashdown as Mr Ashdown has.[2]

Moments before confessing to his fabrication in the green room, Ashdown had embellished his bullshit to the reporter, who duly wrote it up. I had to hand it to him.

Cheers, Paddy, I thought, *you cheeky lying bastard*.

Jonathan Dimbleby replaced Brian Walden's Sunday interview programme in 1994, and I joined the team in 1997, just a few months before Ashdown slated my research live on television. Somehow I'd made my way from that grimy student house in Nottingham in 1989, watching in wonder as Thatcher wobbled, to the offices on the South Bank of the Thames where Walden, Cox and Wakefield had plotted that historic interview.

Don't worry, I'm not going to chart every twist and turn that got me there because that would be too boring, but there were a couple of important moments. The first was the day I didn't get a job with Ron Davies MP. Ron is most famous for his 'moment of madness' on Clapham Common, a well-known gay cruising spot, where the poor guy got mugged in embarrassing circumstances. My encounter with him a few years before was much less racy and took place in the Norman Shaw building on the parliamentary estate where MPs had their offices.

It was 1992, and I was living in London, looking for a job. Since graduating, I hadn't had a sniff of work. I knew no one in politics or the media and had no connections whatsoever. As for the Labour Party, I'd steered clear of student politics so had no experience of how the party worked or what people inside it thought. In fact, despite coming from a Labour family as I did, I wasn't really a joiner. But I was interested in politics. So, through the spring and summer of 1992 – when humiliation for Labour at the general election was followed by humiliation for England in Euro 92 – I wrote to every Labour MP, a few Lib Dems (there *were* only a few) and even a couple of wet Tories. Nothing came back.

Then Ron Davies advertised for a researcher to join his team. This was a big deal. Ron was in the shadow cabinet, and breaking into the higher echelons as a Labour staffer was an exciting prospect. So, more in hope than expectation, I applied. I couldn't believe it when I got the call inviting me to an interview. I was sick to my stomach with nerves and excitement.

When the day came I did well. Ron was friendly, I was well prepared and we seemed to get on. Was it possible that I was going to walk into a job with a shadow cabinet minister on the strength of a patchy CV and a decent interview? Did a career in politics beckon? Could I help Labour win their first election since 1974? The answers, in order, were no, no and no. I'd come close, but Ron gave the job to a smooth character called Andy, and I missed out.

I'm grateful for that rejection, not because Ron's career ended in embarrassment a few years later, but because I know that a career as an aide to a Labour shadow cabinet minister or even an actual government minister wouldn't have worked out. I was too immature then. I was also uncomfortable among the Oxbridge set who dominated Labour's adviser class. Most of all, I was not tribal enough. I was more interested in asking questions than pretending to be certain of the answers – blame it on those conversations up the garden with my dad. In theory, joining Labour's roster of advisers on the cusp of the Blair years could have taken me to the stratosphere, but the theory would have been wrong.

Instead, the good impression I'd made on Ron got me a meeting with Paul Flynn, the MP for Newport West, who was looking for a researcher. Paul was a small, hairy man with warm eyes who was the ultimate backbencher. We got on straight away, and because he was kind and knew his own mind, he offered me the job there and then.

Paul was motivated by two things: helping people and making mischief for the Conservative government. He was a master of parliamentary procedure – something I never really grasped – tabling a blizzard of parliamentary questions, early day motions and ten-minute rule bills. This way, he could raise important issues and cause maximum trouble. He had a razor-sharp mind and was adept at identifying the most important details in complex pieces of policy. He was also politically brave.

For instance, we had a conversation one morning in his office about illegal drugs. I explained that I was from a generation for which recreational drug use was unremarkable, particularly in the wake of the 'Second Summer of Love' in 1988. In that context, I wondered, is it sensible to allow criminals to profit from illegal drugs and expose people who smoke cannabis or take ecstasy to the risk of prosecution or the dangers of taking impure or dangerous substances? Quite a bold thing to bring up with the boss. Luckily for me, Paul was receptive and became one of the most prominent drug law reform advocates, campaigning on the issue long after I'd moved on. Today, such views are commonplace, if not completely accepted, but in the early 1990s this was courageous stuff.

This environment of open discussion and interest in policy detail was valuable preparation for my future career. Paul took my ideas seriously but taught me to seek out the evidence to back them up. The devil may be in the detail, but so are the angels. You can find the truth and arm yourself for future battles if you have the patience to dig as deep as possible into the data. Paul – who served on numerous select committees and spoke in the House of Commons on diverse issues – lived for the detail because it made him better at his job and more politically effective. I learned a lot from him.

Unlike Paul, however, I never loved parliament. Some are drawn to the pageantry and procedure, the green benches, the red velvet and the rhetorical flourishes. I wasn't. It felt like a place for pointless wanging on, populated by boring middle-aged men who loved the sound of their own voices. I just wasn't that interested in this bunch of wangers even though I knew how important the big stuff that happened there was. Even then, to echo Brian Walden, I thought television was much better at holding those in power to account than parliament. Interviewers could go deeper than the leader of the opposition at Prime Minister's Questions. Dodging Ron and working for Paul – much as I will always love the man – convinced me that parliament was not where I belonged.

So I quit.

My mum was not happy, and she may have had a point. After that, it was the usual story: travelling in South America, teaching English as a foreign language and going on the dole to try to make it in a Britpop band. Trust me; you don't want to know.

Eventually, I was twenty-seven and back in London, a brilliant career postponed or possibly gone forever. Most rock stars – and I'd just proved I wasn't one of those – had done their life's work by my age, and here I was, working in an off-licence. I was still interested in television and politics but had no idea how to force my way in. Then, in the spring of 1996 I got wind of a new TV station offering a chance to get into television while paying very, very low wages. It sounded ideal!

The channel was called Granada Talk TV, a satellite station owned by the same media company that owned London Weekend Television, producers of *Walden*. I found out the name of the people running the new venture, sent in my CV on the off chance and was called in for an interview. I remember turning up feeling very self-conscious. I was too skint to get a haircut and didn't own a serviceable suit. Luckily Neil Thompson, head of programmes (and later boss of Piers Morgan-era *Good Morning Britain*), was a fan of Paul Flynn and was ready to give me a chance. However unkempt I looked, I was in.

When I arrived a few weeks later, I was allocated a job working on the new channel's daily news and current affairs show. It was called *Britain Talks Back* and was presented by an ex-*Mirror* editor called Roy Greenslade.

Ever since the Walden interview with Margaret Thatcher in 1989, I'd dreamed of getting the chance to come up with tough interview questions and see them put to politicians. The opportunity to do so seemed distant, impossible even, but here I was. After working countless gruelling fifteen-hour days in the run-up to the channel's launch in October, I was sent to the Tory Party conference in Bournemouth to persuade ministers and MPs to appear on the new channel. We were using the latest technology: the 'video phone'. This clunky device sent heavily pixelated and jumpy images of our guests in the conference hotel to our presenter in the studio back in London.

We do it on our phones today, but in October 1996 it was the cutting edge.

It's hard to remember all the guests we processed through the Talk TV videophone that week, but I mainly recall an angry Anne Widdecombe protesting about our unfair questions. I realised that I could do this and loved the process of interview preparation from the beginning. Then Roy – with whom I got on very well – persuaded the *Guardian* to publish a diary of his first few weeks at the channel. For the second week of October he included the following entry:

> It's Tory Conference week, and researcher Rob Birley
> [sic] manages to persuade some high-profile MPs to sit in
> front of the video phone. He also suggests a line of
> questioning for John Redwood that has him ducking for
> cover; Bill Cash, forewarned by Redwood, deals with it
> better.[3]

Roy may have spelt my name wrong, but I loved it and so did my mum. 'Ducking for cover' was what I was after. Roy's generosity immediately bore fruit; the article was noticed over at London Weekend Television by the team that ran *Jonathan Dimbleby*. They asked to see me and offered me a job. By January 1997, six months after I'd started in television, I'd jumped from tiny Granada Talk TV, channel number 59, to ITV1 – channel number 3 – and on to the Sunday lunchtime political slot on which I'd always dreamed of working.

I wasn't the only person who got my start in television from Neil Thompson at Talk TV. Numerous other producers, editors, commissioners and camera crew started there. Sadly, it only lasted until the end of August 1997, when the death of Princess Diana brought the channel off the air for what turned out to be a permanent blackout. In its short life, it provided early exposure for future household names, including Graham Norton and Natasha Kaplinsky.

I vividly remember one morning in the pre-launch summer when my colleague Jamie Glassman brought in a VHS tape to show the management. It was a showreel his mate had given him, and it was hilarious. The guy on the tape was quickly snapped up and given the channel's children's programme to present. He was a lovely guy, and the show was the best thing on the channel.

I was sad to leave Talk TV behind, and I still have my leaving card all these years later. At the top right there's a scrawled note from that children's show presenter reading: 'Dear Rob, good luck baby, have fun and things, see you soon, Sacha.' His name was Sacha Baron-Cohen. My career was about to take off, baby. I often wonder what became of him.

It's early 1993, and Tony Blair is nervous.

He's sitting opposite Brian Walden, still Britain's most formidable interviewer. He's the shadow home secretary and is road-testing a line that will become a New Labour classic: 'Tough on crime, tough on the causes of crime'. Walden is trying to find the substance in Blair's soundbite, asking him for an assurance that it means he wants tougher action against criminals.

Blair pauses for a moment before he starts to (indirectly) answer the question. He says he wants to deal with both sides of the problem because, well, he wants to be tough on crime and tough on the causes of crime. From there, Blair launches into an unwieldy list, somehow keeping count of how many points he's made: first, second, third, fourth, fifth and 'finally, sixthly'. He is not yet forty years old, and his voice is squeakier and less assured than we later become accustomed to. At the end of his mammoth answer, Blair slips a little boyishly on the words 'criminal activity', almost as if his voice is only just breaking. It's nothing major, but he's not quite the finished article.

Then, in the space of a few minutes, he starts to warm up. Walden keeps asking for clarification, returning to the same question, and finally the young politician gets into his stride. Blair fends off the challenging questions, and now he's free-wheeling, using the interview to challenge his party to rethink their approach to crime and punishment. New Labour is emerging a year before it's officially born.

All of this suggests that it was business as usual for *Walden* in the early nineties: forty minutes of proper policy discussion and a new face offering fresh challenges to the great interviewer. In reality, the show is in trouble. One reason was Mrs Thatcher's departure in November 1990. Until then, even after she came unstuck in her interview with him, she instructed cabinet ministers to go onto *Walden* and make the government's case.

After she'd gone, ministers began reassessing. John Wakefield recalls Michael Howard, environment secretary in the Major government and no slouch at arguing his case, emerging from a long-form roughing-up by Walden and observing to an adviser, 'I'm not sure what's in it for us, doing these interviews.' The answer from too many was 'nothing'. It was becoming harder and harder to persuade senior government figures to come on. Bidding for guests, once a relative breeze, became a slog. The lifeblood of *Walden* – the long-form political interview – was drying up.

A few miles away in west London at BBC Television Centre, things are very different for Barney Jones. The editor of a new Sunday morning politics, news and entertainment programme called *Breakfast with Frost* is off to a flying start on BBC1. After opening with the prime minister in the first week and the leader of the opposition in the second, Jones and his presenter Sir David Frost need to keep the momentum going. They've been knocking ideas around all afternoon but haven't hit upon the right one. Frost's chauffeur is waiting, and the great man's about to leave. And then it came to him.

'I tell you what would really do it,' said Frost. 'Let's see if we can get George!'

Jones isn't precisely sure who he means at first. Then he twigs. 'You mean the president?' he asks.

He does mean the president.

Frost makes his way to Jones's tiny office, sits down and, referring to his notebook, starts making calls and leaving messages with his network in Washington, DC. Within a few minutes, Jones's landline rings. Frost picks up.

'Mr President!' exclaims Sir David, now connected to the world's most powerful man. 'How *are* you?'

Barney can hear the faint voice of George Herbert Walker Bush, the 41st President of the United States, coming through the receiver. Frost looks over at him, smiling.

'And how *is* Barbara?' Frost asks, weighing up the necessary amount of small talk and listening patiently. It's been a rough few months for Bush, who will leave the White House in a few days and hand over to Bill Clinton.

'Now look,' said Frost, finally cutting to the chase, 'I know you've got a lot on your mind, Mr President, but do you think we could do a recording on Friday or Saturday, and we'd play it on our Sunday show?'

Jones waits. Frost smiles. 'Oh, you can? That's fabulous, George. Thank you, Mr President!'

Barney Jones has just seen the power of Frost's charm and peerless contacts book in real time. Looking back, Jones realises this was the moment everything changed. 'I was operating in a different league now,' he told me.[4]

If Frost was the master at landing the absurdly ambitious international bid, Barney Jones was no slouch when it came to contacts in Westminster or the creative side of television production. *Breakfast with Frost* emerged fully realised and was an immediate hit. It was the perfect vehicle for the man Frost had become by the early nineties.

Frost was in his early fifties by then. He was no longer the anti-establishment exponent of 'trial by television' that he had pioneered in the sixties, nor was he the glamorously urbane version of the seventies, later played to perfection by Michael Sheen in *Frost/Nixon*. He married Lady Carina Fitzalan-Howard, daughter of the 17th Duke of Norfolk, in the early eighties, and by 1993 Frost *was* the establishment. Jones recalls that the presenter's attitude to the rich and powerful was pure admiration and fascination. 'He liked them,' he says. 'He was intrigued. What's it like to have all this power?' Jones decided the new show would lean into all that.

For a start, this would not be a political interview show *Walden*-style.

> I thought we've got to do something really different. If we try and ape the Sunday lunchtime programmes, if we have a hard table and people saying, 'I'm going to take you apart for forty-five minutes,' a) Frost isn't very good at taking people apart and b) it's just not what people want to watch.[5]

Instead, Jones wanted a softer, more relaxing space with real carpets, plush leather armchairs, actual curtains hanging in the background and views to die for:

> I wanted to create a room that looked like Frost's study if it was in Jeffrey Archer's house, overlooking the Commons, with a bit of a sense of being near the centre of power. And the room itself is a centre of power. This is where Frost and his mates – who are all world leaders or whatever – would come.[6]

Jones had to find ways to entice reluctant politicians who'd rather spend Sunday morning at home onto the programme. 'I really went out of my way to make it as pleasant an experience as possible for a politician who doesn't want to be working at the weekend,' he remembers. And it worked. The programme's popular mix of domestic and international figures, alongside guests from the world of entertainment, attracted two to three million viewers. Politicians liked *that*, and they enjoyed rubbing shoulders with the stars too. It was, says Jones, 'fun for both sides'.

Talking to Jones about the genesis of *Breakfast with Frost*, it's hard not to feel that something had gone wrong. The BBC's pre-eminent political interview programme seemed too often to celebrate and accommodate the powerful, not challenge them. The studio was imagined as a 'centre of power', a place where Frost could be close to power and feed off it. It was too cosy, providing a safe space for the powerful to address the people, rather than holding them to account on the people's behalf.

There is, of course, a defence. It goes like this: Frost could attract names nobody else could get and bring interviews to a bigger audience than a Walden interrogation could ever manage. Jones was within his rights to make the experience as enjoyable as possible for these interviewees. None of this meant that the interview was 'soft'. On the contrary, Frost would lull his interviewees into a false sense of security, bewitching them through exploratory and friendly questioning into revealing more than they planned to. Frost himself put it like this:

> If you can enter into a real conversation with someone, then you get more of the real person. It's really to do with absorbing somebody in a conversation, not so much catching people out but just surprising them in some way with something that's a more thoughtful question than they realise at the time. Then you get something more real, more special, more newsworthy.[7]

Examples of this are hard to come by, but the contention did win some support. Jones recalls former Labour leader, the late John Smith, telling Frost that he was more anxious about appearing on *Breakfast with Frost* than going into battle with a more predictable attack-dog interviewer. Frost was proud of the accolade, and other politicians such as Tony Blair and John Major expressed similar sentiments about the programme.

Unsurprisingly, this was not the view from the South Bank and ITV. *Walden*'s executive producer David Cox is characteristically blunt:

> We were of the view that the idea was to deliberately ask soft questions and make it very nice in the hope that they would then suck up politicians who wanted an easy ride and deny us access. We viewed the Frost show as an enemy who was cheating.[8]

The key to a successful political-interview is not the first question you ask – coming up with a list of 'difficult' questions isn't hard in itself – but mastering the supplementary ones that can disrupt the politician's pre-prepared lines. In Cox's view, Frost's guests knew he simply didn't have them. And as for the legendary Frost technique of softening guests up before tempting them into saying something unguarded:

> There was the great pretence that Frost and his lot had, which was that if you were nice and friendly to them, you'll lull them into a false sense of security, and they'll start blurting out all sorts of revelations. The politicians played along with this because it suited them. They liked going on being asked easy questions.[9]

Sour grapes or jealousy? Maybe a bit of both. But he has a point.

Eddie Morgan, a producer on the *Walden* team at the time, agrees with his former boss. In his view, Frost 'poisoned the well' for political programmes in the UK:

> The case for Frost was that it looks easy but he's bowling all these devilish googlies. I basically think it's bollocks. It was softer interviewing, and the longest they did was

eight to twelve minutes. No wonder they got everyone. If I were a politician, I'd far rather face one over from a slow bowler than an entire session from the world's best fast bowler. I mean, wouldn't you?[10]

Frost's arrival was disastrous for *Walden*. The show was saved, for a little while, by Labour. Tony Blair and Gordon Brown were regulars while making their names in John Smith's shadow cabinet. They were happy to use *Walden*'s fast green wicket as a testing ground for nascent New Labour. The opposition will usually come out to bat because facing a few bouncers is better than no innings at all. The sitting government, not Walden himself, was the problem. But in the end it wasn't sustainable. As Eddie Morgan puts it:

> The premise of *Walden* was that it was the biggest and the best: we will get who we want, when we want. This wasn't just any old programme. The Thatcher programme in 1989 was so great. It was the *Sgt. Pepper* of political interviewing. If you've been that great, you can't just be one of the pack.[11]

So then, against the backdrop of Granada's takeover of London Weekend Television and the cost-cutting that followed (at £15,000 per show, Walden did not come cheap), *Walden* was quietly axed. Although LWT told the press that Walden had decided to retire and that the suits in the boardroom were sorry to see him go, the truth was very different. John Wakefield recalls that Walden had 'no wish to stop doing the programme', but by December 1994 it was all over. By then, Tony Blair had become Labour leader, and he would loom large over my own time at ITV's new political show.

* * *

I felt properly intimidated on my first day at *Jonathan Dimbleby* in January 1997. The office I walked into, high on the seventeenth floor of London Weekend Television's famous 'tower' on the South Bank, retained the culture of *Walden* and some of the personnel. This was the spiritual home of the long-form political interview and the place where people like Peter Mandelson and John Birt had worked on *Weekend World*. I was one of a small team of researchers alongside a slightly bigger team of producers crammed into a small room next to the editor's office.

The first thing I noticed was the silence: it was like a highly competitive library, where everything you said was heard by everybody else and, my paranoid self imagined, judged too. Among the wider team of LWT journalists and TV producers we were known as the 'pointy-heads'. We were weird people who knew about select committees, national insurance rates and the Exchange Rate Mechanism. To me, the other researchers seemed wildly clever, relatively friendly but scary, and out of my intellectual league.

The editor, former *Walden* producer Eddie Morgan, was the most intensely clever of them all. He'd left *Walden* aged twenty-five to make an acclaimed documentary series about Labour's years under the leadership of Neil Kinnock. Then, with *Walden* on death row, he was asked to devise a new Sunday lunchtime political show for ITV, which he would run.

Morgan's idea was a programme that brought together the forensic interview with an audience of a hundred voters at lunchtime on Sundays. It drew inspiration from the traditional American town hall debate (think Bill Clinton versus George H. W. Bush in the 1992 election). To present it, Eddie landed Jonathan Dimbleby, most recently presenter of the BBC's *On the Record*, who would give the programme its name and who relished the chance to take on his old BBC show. 'We were going to have a more accessible programme than *On the Record*,' he remembers, 'and we would get the political "big beasts" along with our studio audience. I bought into that completely.'[12]

After a difficult first few weeks I started to figure out how things worked, found my rhythm, made some friends and made my mark. Over the following years I worked my way through the ranks at *Jonathan Dimbleby*, from researcher to producer. But you probably don't know, more than a little vaguely, what these job titles even mean. Fair enough. Let's run through them.

Researcher

In TV, researchers are on the lowest rung proper of the editorial ladder, but their work is vital – and nowhere more so than on political programmes. Their job is to provide the information the producer needs to brief the presenter and plan the interview. In 1997 Google did not exist and our office had just one internet-connected computer. Nobody took your calls or faxed you information after five-thirty in the evening, so you'd better have everything you need for Sunday by the close of play on a Friday night.

The less effective researcher leaves it at that, simply providing what's been asked for by the producer or the presenter, writing it up in a brief and going home. The best researchers are more proactive, seeking out information that will make a difference on screen. Good research is like panning for gold, sorting through a mass of data to find the most valuable nuggets.

The most commonly discovered piece of political gold is the killer quote: a statement made by the interviewee, their current boss or another authoritative figure that contradicts their current position. For example, a minister may come onto the programme to express support for same-sex marriage only to be presented with a killer quote from his past saying homosexuality is the work of the devil.

Killer facts are even more golden. These expose the claims made by the interviewee, showing that they are not supported by the evidence. They may involve statistics that reveal, for example, that a much-heralded policy to reduce crime or bring down youth unemployment has had the opposite effect. When they land, killer facts can create moments of genuine drama.

Sometimes these moments are derided, especially by American politicians, as mere 'gotcha' interviews that reduce political encounters to entertainment and unfair ambushes. Actually, it's about accountability. 'Gotcha' moments only really work if they're significant and serious. The effrontery displayed by some politicians at being called out on their actual record is depressing. Unsurprisingly, most shameless of all is Boris Johnson, whose team would switch to outrage mode if asked, for example, about his previous comments on race or women. Quotes are always 'out of context' and facts are always 'more nuanced', say the spinners. They usually aren't.

The hunt for the most inconvenient truths is one of the thrills of journalism and makes impartiality possible. Being equally fair and tough on all sides becomes imperative when looking for gold. You realise this the first time you cause problems for the side you secretly support (most political journalists have political preferences), and it feels good. If you don't get a thrill taking on your own 'side' you're probably in the wrong job. I loved it, but not everyone can do it. I worked for a while in the late 1990s with the future Labour MP Stella Creasy, who was a researcher on the programme. She was highly intelligent and very politically switched on, but she didn't want to make trouble for her own side. It didn't take her long to move on to the career she was born for: politics. Gloria De Piero also had a spell on *Jonathan Dimbleby*. She wasn't like most of my colleagues in political TV, coming from a working-class background in Bradford and with an attitude I could relate to. She was also a laugh, which helped. De Piero was tribal Labour but didn't have Creasy's problem when it came to challenging her own side. Later, like Creasy, she became a Labour MP herself before eventually returning to a successful career in journalism.

Researchers are also expected to get their heads around policy. It sounds boring, but it's critical stuff, and any interview about policy is skewed in favour of the minister. They'll live and breathe their department, and have multiple civil servants and political advisers making sure they're across every conceivable question that could come up. Up against them is the researcher, trying to master a new brief, speaking to experts and trying to understand how the policy works and what's wrong with it. The stakes are high – and it's an unfair fight. If the researcher gets it wrong, their presenter is humiliated on national television, but when it goes right it's golden.

Producer

I always wanted to be a TV producer. It sounded cool. It sounded like a grown-up thing to be. The term can mean different things, depending on the work the producer does. A producer on a documentary does very different work from a producer on a live news programme. For political interview programmes it centres on finding the right framing for the programme or big guest slot, and then devising and managing the interview or programme plan.

In addition, if I can adjust my gold-related metaphors slightly, the political programme producer is in the business of alchemy. They should focus on how to transform an unpromising proposition – a person talking to another person in a room for a long time – into a piece of meaningful drama. While there are easy ways to create drama and spectacle such as building a huge set, recruiting a massive studio audience or asking provocative questions just for the reaction they get from the guest or audience, the more rewarding route is to concentrate on the content. This will involve seeking out the essential truth in the argument or personality of the guest and, using logic and careful production, exposing these to the viewer.

Once the producer has decided what the interview or programme is about, they need to translate it into something the presenter can deliver on air through a set of questions backed up by evidence. A good producer must bring order to the battle plan but build in sufficient flexibility to respond to unexpected developments as they occur on the ground. As we've seen, Brian Walden built an entire architecture that told him where to go in the interview plan depending on the answer to a question. For most presenters, this is unwieldy and unhelpful. For Walden – who may have had some sort of photographic memory – it was the best way to embed the plan in his mind.

Other presenters, like Andrew Neil, take the list of questions in with them and refer to it regularly, while always being ready to ditch any questions that are irrelevant or distracting if necessary. Jonathan Dimbleby's method was to translate the producer's plan into a shorter set of prompts that would trigger questions and comebacks in his head. Others, like Andrew Marr, work hard on the plan but don't want to look at a piece of paper during the interview, as this will break eye contact with the interviewee. The most frustrating are those interviewers who are given a producer's plan but prefer to ignore it. This is usually a sign of extreme self-confidence or arrogance, and doesn't often produce the best interview.

Editor
Basically, they're the boss.

The editor will take an overview of the entire series, think about the subjects a programme should aim to hit, liaise with the political parties about booking the guests, and provide editorial leadership and guidance for producers. Editors should be creative and, with any luck, visionary. They should be passionate about programme making and analysis, not just providing updates on incremental change or acting as stenographers for the political class. They should not get too near to politicians or their staff.

Editors are the main point of contact with the presenters, reporters or other correspondents on a programme. They are not there to do the presenter's bidding and shouldn't grow too close because they need to stand up to them when necessary. They should be brave and inspirational – the best care more about their programme and staff than their career progression.

Being an editor is the best job in television.

It's funny how things come full circle. After I was promoted to producer on *Jonathan Dimbleby* in the late 1990s, Paddy Ashdown returned to the show. Unlike that painful day when I was a junior researcher, I don't remember much about the details. I do, however, recall that during a fiercely argued section of the interview, Ashdown suggested that Jonathan was mistaken, adding, 'I don't know who your producer is, Jonathan, but you've got this wrong …' It was as if this ex-Royal Marine was out to get me, having taken note of my new job title before trashing me on national television. Again. This time, though, like everybody else, I just laughed.

I don't really blame Ashdown. His party was not used to serious scrutiny and he was bound to come a cropper when the details were examined, which must be embarrassing. I'm sorry that he passed away a few years ago at a relatively young age. His heart was in the right place, and we miss him. I also reflect on my producer on that first interview, Andy Harrison, who is also no longer with us. He was a kind and talented man.

In the end, I dissent from Ashdown's approach that political argument is somehow all a game that a talented politician can wing if necessary. Many of those who work in politics covering politicians or working for them go along with the idea that we should expect and accept deception from those who rule us. Of course, the argument goes, we understand that sometimes politicians have to be less than truthful. It's all part of the game.

Perhaps naively, perhaps idealistically, I've always resisted that approach. We are there on behalf of the public. They don't get to play the game or even see the rules. The game goes on around them.

That's not good enough at the best of times.

It's worse than not good enough in those times when political truth and lies become a matter of life and death.

5

WORDS DON'T MEAN WHAT THEY MEAN

I supported the Iraq war, and I was wrong.

There were no weapons of mass destruction, but that wasn't the only reason I backed it. I thought it was right to remove Saddam Hussein and end his brutal dictatorship. That was wrong. Regime change made life worse for the Iraqi people, not better.

I also thought, just two years after 9/11, that promoting democracy in the Middle East might make the world a safer place. As it turned out, imposing democracy was impossible and counter-productive, and the invasion has made the world more dangerous, not least by sowing the seeds of ISIS.

I heard all the warnings in the run-up to war through 2002 and 2003. I put them all on air and gave them justified prominence on ITV's *Jonathan Dimbleby* show. As in every newsroom, there was a range of powerfully held views on both sides in the programme team. People who make it to that level usually have opinions on issues like Iraq. The important thing was to leave those views at the entrance to the ITV Tower.

I'm proud of how we interrogated the build-up and the aftermath of the Iraq war, but I'm personally embarrassed. All those I disagreed with in pub arguments and over tense dinner tables were right, and I was wrong. The whole enterprise was an unmitigated disaster that cost hundreds of thousands of human lives, and I'm ashamed that I believed the case for war. It's hard to admit getting something so big so wrong, but now, twenty years later, I can acknowledge the truth.

It's a relief, actually. I feel better. I can't imagine how it must feel to have been part of that decision and to carry that around every day.

So that's me. Anyone else want to step up and share?

Anyone?

Tony?

The arrival of New Labour and the agonies of John Major's Tory government were good for business. Both political parties had a reason to come onto *Jonathan Dimbleby*: Labour to seal the deal ahead of the 1997 election, the Tories to avert their slow-motion political car crash that played out in the mid-nineties. In April 1995, when the programme first aired, Labour's lead in the polls hit a staggering 30 per cent. What choice did the Tory government have but to put up more ministers onto more programmes to answer more difficult questions and absorb more audience anger? As *Dimbleby* editor Eddie Morgan recalls, it was 'rich terrain'.[1]

One big problem for the Tories was Europe, just as it had been under Thatcher and would be under Cameron. The argument then centred on the euro, scheduled to launch in 1999, and whether Britain would join. John Major – the chancellor who took the UK into the ERM and the prime minister who crashed us out of it – didn't want to sign up in January 1999, but he didn't want to say so in public because he thought it would weaken his negotiating position in Brussels. Tory Eurosceptics, meanwhile, wanted him to rule it out forever. A truce, agreed by a cabinet with divergent views on the subject, was in place by early 1997, with the general election looming on the horizon. The policy was to keep all options open but promise voters that any future plan to join the euro would need to be endorsed in a referendum. Sorted.

Then one Sunday, along came Stephen Dorrell.

Dorrell was a grey politician and a safe pair of hands. He was secretary of state for health, but in March 1997 he was on the programme for a general political interview, ready to talk about whatever we wanted to throw at him. What we wanted to throw at him was Europe.

Here was the problem: Dorrell knew that the UK wouldn't join the euro in the first wave in 1999, Dimbleby knew that the UK wouldn't join the euro in the first wave in 1999, Eurosceptic MPs knew that the UK wouldn't join the euro in the first wave in 1999 and anyone who read a newspaper knew it too. But nobody was allowed to say it.

Then Stephen Dorrell did.

Asked the inevitable question, Dorrell started well enough:

Dorrell: The government's position, I would have thought, on the single currency is now as clear as you could ask for it to be.

Well, it is, but we've all got to pretend it isn't. Anyway, go on …

Dorrell: And that is: first of all, no single currency without a referendum …

Yep, yep, usual formula …

Dorrell: And, secondly, we shan't be joining a single currency on January 1, 1999.

Come again? Jonathan, could you clarify?

Dimbleby: You said there, and I'm sure you meant to say it, we will not join on January 1, 1999.

Meant to say it? Surely that's a fuck-up.

> **Dorrell** (emboldened and, if you pardon the pun, in for a penny in for a pound): I said we shall not be joining on January 1, 1999, because we shan't be putting the legislation through on the time scale that makes that possible.

Wow.

> **Dimbleby:** I may be wrong, but I think that is the first time a cabinet minister has said we will not be doing it because it will not be possible.[2]

This exchange and the reaction to it sum up the absurdity of much of our political discourse, an absurdity that encourages and rewards caution and dishonesty over candour. Dorrell wasn't lying. He was telling the truth, and that was seen as a gaffe. He was saying something we all knew to be true but no minister was allowed to say, while everyone else was saying something different. This was particularly apparent because Michael Heseltine, the deputy prime minister, was holding the line on BBC1 at the same time as Dorrell was abandoning it on ITV. Deputy Labour leader John Prescott crowed: 'This smacks of disarray at the heart of government.'[3]

By telling the truth on television, Dorrell had made himself and his colleagues look stupid. Here was another reason not to do interviews, although the problem wasn't the interviewer or the questions but the line the government had decided to take, which everyone knew to be deceitful. It always risked somebody blurting out the truth. And so it came to pass.

In the green room after the show, Dorrell's mobile rang – you'd notice that sort of thing then because we didn't all have them. I watched as he took the call. He listened for a long time but said very little. Given his usual grey pallor, it was hard to tell if he'd gone pale, but the secretary of state for health had been on the receiving end of a bollocking for telling the truth and did not look well.

A few hours later he was forced to 'clarify' his comments. 'I entirely agree with the Government's position,' his climb-down statement read, 'and no words I used on the *Dimbleby* programme were intended to question it.'[4] Despite this Sunday roast of humble pie with all the trimmings, Dorrell was still all over the newspaper front pages the following morning.

At the same time as the Tories floundered, New Labour was in its pomp. Much is made, rightly, about the downside of Labour's new-found professionalism – on-message politicians giving boring interviews – but in the years before the 1997 election, many were also able to communicate more effectively and openly than the staid, formal Conservatives. Sometimes New Labour politicians dared to say they didn't have all the answers or that the Conservatives hadn't got everything wrong. This candour – or faux candour depending on your point of view – was disarming.

Guests like Clare Short and Mo Mowlam lit up the studio, and Blair, even going back to a 1994 appearance on *Walden* shortly after becoming leader, saw the TV studio as a place to think aloud and sketch out values. Labour's thirteen years of government might cloud the youth and freshness of the New Labour team and its approach, but it was real back then. Like all political programmes at the time, *Jonathan Dimbleby* was given new energy by the sense that the government was crumbling in real time and a changing of the guard was imminent.

When the change came, however, the going got tough.

Landslides are bad for political programmes. These thrive when issues are contested and when politicians have an incentive to take the risk of appearing on them. They benefit from back-bench voices whose opinions can influence those in power and an opposition within striking distance of government. Landslides create precisely the opposite conditions.

Labour won with a majority of 179 in May 1997. The Conservative opposition was a rump of 165, with more than its fair share of weirdos and oddballs. Labour's own backbench malcontents – like one Jeremy Corbyn of Islington North – were like so many gnats on an elephant's hide. Furthermore, there was a brief consensus that Blair's synthesis of neo-liberalism and social democracy had settled the contested issues. The truth was that neither the right nor the left had gone away but Blair's dazzle and a recovering economy had created conditions unfavourable for their resurgence.

Surveying the post-1997 scene, Eddie Morgan recalls feeling pessimistic about the long-form political interview:

> New Labour's got a massive mandate. It's got a massive majority, Blair's pretty competent, Brown is commanding on the economy. Where does that leave the Socratic interview? The answer is high and dry.[5]

Most weeks, he was right, but it didn't take too long for the political interview to start making a comeback.

In the early nineties Labour had taken full advantage of the sexual and financial scandals that engulfed the Tory government, inflicting serious damage on John Major's administration. Blair had profited politically and had promised to 'restore faith in public life', but in November 1997 he had a full-blown 'sleaze' scandal of his own.

In January 1997 Labour had accepted a £1 million donation from Formula One motor racing boss Bernie Ecclestone. The tycoon was worried about a European directive that would ban tobacco sponsorship in sport and he wanted an exception to be made for Formula One so that it could carry on accepting cash from tobacco companies. In October, when Blair was in Downing Street, Ecclestone met the new prime minister to make his case in person. Blair – whose party had received the donation from Ecclestone just nine months earlier – bought the argument that a ban would cost jobs and might mean Britain losing its Grand Prix. On 4 November Blair ordered his public health minister Tessa Jowell to exempt Formula One from the tobacco advertising ban.

Once the news was made public, journalists started asking tricky questions. They wanted to know whether any financial links between Labour and Formula One might be relevant to the government's screeching U-turn. These questions prompted Blair and his team to pursue what can only be described as a cover-up about the donation, its size and, er, the fact that there were already discussions about more money coming Labour's way from Ecclestone.

As part of this effort to avoid embarrassment and the appearance of dodgy dealings, Blair asked Labour's general secretary to seek advice about a second donation from Sir Patrick Neil, the chairman of the Commission of Standards in Public Life. The idea was that referring the matter to Sir Patrick would make it look like Labour had proactively raised the donation and sought advice about it. Great idea! The only problem was that they did so after journalists had started asking questions.

Over the course of ten days, the details came out in punishing dribs and drabs, creating the impression that a donor had not only influenced Blair into adopting a policy position but also that Blair had covered it up. As the crisis deepened, Blair reportedly feared for his premiership, with the allegations risking his image being tarnished irreparably just six months after becoming prime minister. Drastic action was needed to draw a line under the story and move on. The answer, according to Blair's press secretary Alastair Campbell, was a TV interview.

The easy and most convenient option was an outing on Sir David Frost's sofa, which was Blair's preference. Looking back,

Frost's editor Barney Jones is unsure his man would have been up to the job. 'I couldn't rely on Frost really putting the knife in,' he told me. 'It was not Frost's way.'[6]

Campbell didn't think Frost would cut it this time, either. He felt his boss needed to take a 'kicking' if he was to deal with the issue effectively. So on Saturday 15 November Campbell called David Jordan, editor of *On the Record*, the BBC's most weighty political programme, presented by one of the BBC's toughest interviewers, John Humphrys. Campbell wondered if Jordan would like an interview with the prime minister live from his country residence Chequers the following lunchtime. Jordan said he would.

The *On the Record* team had twenty-four hours to prepare. On Sunday morning Humphrys and Jordan spent the car journey from London to Buckinghamshire role-playing the interview. Humphrys was best known for his many years presenting the *Today* programme on Radio 4, but Jordan produced a different variety of interview with him on television. 'John's best interviews were done on *On the Record*,' Jordan told me. 'At his best, he was very, very good, but he required a lot of handling. You needed to make sure he didn't get into his *Today* programme interruptive mode.'[7]

The interview had been trailed in the press as an apology for the Ecclestone affair, but it didn't quite work out like that. Blair told Humphrys that while he regretted how the issue had been 'handled', he rejected criticism of the decision to exempt Formula One or any suggestion that he had done so because of the £1 million cheque from Ecclestone. David Jordan regarded the affair as 'disgraceful corruption', yet had no way of proving it.

Audaciously, Blair presented himself as the wounded party, saying he was 'hurt and upset' that people might think he would 'ever do something wrong or improper', adding, 'I couldn't understand that anyone would impugn my motives.' As for the idea that Labour had only contacted the Standards

WORDS DON'T MEAN WHAT THEY MEAN

Commissioner after journalists started asking questions, this was an outrage:

> Before any journalist had been in touch about anything to do with donations and Mr Ecclestone, we had informed his people that we couldn't accept further donations. The question then arose, the question that was uppermost in my mind, what about the original donation? We decided to seek the advice of Sir Patrick Neil.[8]

As Andrew Rawnsley points out in his book about New Labour, *Servants of the People*, Blair was being 'creative with the veracity' here.[9] The letter to Sir Patrick had not asked about the original donation but sought advice on whether it would be OK to take *more* money from Ecclestone. As for Blair's claim that the Labour Party had sought Sir Patrick Neil's advice 'before any press enquiry had been made whatever', this was, in the words of John Rentoul, a journalist with a reputation for being scrupulously fair to Tony Blair, 'simply untrue'.[10]

So Blair, within moments of expressing his sense of hurt, upset and resentment at any suggestion that he could behave with anything but absolute propriety, gave an account to viewers that he must have known to be false.

The Ecclestone crisis had put the long-form political interview back where it belonged: at the centre of events. Humphrys' persistence left Blair with nowhere else to go as he endured his 'kicking' but to resort to what Jordan described to me as 'an emotional trump card':

> I hope that people know me well enough and realise the type of person I am to realise that I would never do anything that harmed the country or anything improper. I never have. I think most people who have dealt with me think I'm a pretty straight sort of guy, and I am.[11]

The interview did the trick for Tony Blair because he intuitively understood what the electorate had invested in him. Jordan, who was there, describes it brilliantly:

> The public didn't want to believe that Tony Blair was bent or had done something corrupt because they'd only just put him into office with a huge majority. They didn't want to think that this knight in shining armour was just the same as the rest of them, so they didn't.[12]

You can only fall back on the goodwill of the electorate like that once. But it doesn't mean you can't try a second time. Blair's focus on his feelings of hurt that anyone could question his integrity would resurface before and after his biggest call: the decision to go to war with Iraq.

My first few years working on *Jonathan Dimbleby* were some of the most exciting of my professional life. They were my first taste of the thrill and fear of live television. Every week we got the opportunity to pit our wits against the most powerful people in the country, and sometimes we came out on top. But the routine of weekend work was exhausting. At the end of the nineties, I followed my partner when she got a new job in the north-west and spent a couple of years making films for ITV's current affairs programme *Tonight with Trevor McDonald* at Granada Television in Manchester.

One was about the American singer Eva Cassidy, who had found posthumous success in Britain after the BBC's Terry Wogan played her version of 'Over the Rainbow' on his radio show. Eva's family were so happy with my film – which they believed helped take her album to the top of the UK album charts – that they agreed to let me write her authorised biography. The success of the book led to more writing work, including a collaboration with former Spice Girl Geri Halliwell.

Politics is showbusiness for ugly people, but for a brief period I had access to the world of real celebrity in places like Los Angeles and the poshest bits of west London. This technicolour world was a long way from the black-and-white television that started me off in the 1970s, but in the 2000s the celebs I met didn't seem to be having much fun behind the velvet rope. One afternoon I found myself lying on a sun bed in the Sunset Marquis hotel in Los Angeles, yearning for another round with Stephen Dorrell or, better still, a shot at Tony Blair. Then midway through 2002 my chance arrived: there was a job going as deputy editor of *Jonathan Dimbleby*, and I was soon on my way back to LWT.

Almost immediately there was one topic that dominated: Iraq. In the months that followed, the programme chronicled the road to war. Blair's ministers argued for it, and critics from across politics and beyond came on to warn of its likely bloody aftermath. The audience was passionate on both sides. The production team was also divided over the issue.

I travelled with Jonathan to Iraq, where he interviewed Iraq's deputy prime minister Tariq Aziz twice, including in the very final days before the war. Jonathan recalls the 'panic, deep anxiety and fear' in Aziz's eyes and came away convinced that Iraq did not possess WMD.[13] He was right, of course, but he couldn't voice this view publicly at the time. We were at the United Nations in New York as Britain's efforts to secure a second resolution authorising military action ran out of road. On that day the UK's ambassador to the UN, Sir Jeremy Greenstock, waited with us as we set up to interview Jack Straw, the foreign secretary. Greenstock looked shattered and, after the interview, confided gloomily to Jonathan that the UK was about to break international law.[14]

We covered the aftermath of the war as well: the looting, the chaos, the realisation that politicians had built the case for war on weapons of mass destruction that did not exist. Alongside that, we chronicled the anger that followed. Our studio audience felt cheated, hoodwinked and lied to. We examined the Hutton report into the use of intelligence by the government in the production of the notorious 'September dossier' and the circumstances of the death of Dr David Kelly, and then the Butler report into the intelligence failures that led to a false case being made about the WMD.

In 2004 I was promoted to editor – that's right, the best job in television – and the following year, when an election was expected, the focus shifted to the political reckoning for all this. Many voters not only disagreed with Tony Blair's decision to go to war but thought he had lied about it. As the expected election neared, Blair pursued what became known as his 'masochism strategy': turning up in TV studios in front of prosecutorial interviewers and hostile audiences to defend what felt increasingly indefensible. Just as Blair had used *On the Record* to give him the cleansing 'kicking' that would help people move on from the Ecclestone scandal, he hoped his resilience, apparent sincerity and bravery would be rewarded with a third term.

As it turned out, we were to have two bites at the Blair cherry that spring and early summer. These programmes were a challenge because they combined audience questions with sections of forensic interview. The audience's questions were emotionally powerful but less precise than the interview sections. Blair was highly skilled at getting through these encounters unscathed and was actually under less pressure when the audience weighed in because their questions offered more escape routes to a man of his lawyerly talents. So we had to ensure that the short sections of one-on-one interview counted.

Increasingly, I thought it was important to approach these interviews with a clear proposition in mind. I hadn't developed this idea as I later tried to do, but the idea of identifying the truth of a politician's predicament and going from there was already part of my thinking. Of course, the truth is contested, but this approach enabled us to come up with what you might call a theory of the case, which was the basis for every interview.

For Blair in early 2005, our case was this: the prime minister had been driven by a conviction that whatever the United States wanted to do about Iraq, he was with them and would go along. This meant, one way or another, a war that would change the regime in Iraq. The disarmament aspect of this – the weapons of mass destruction – was important in its own right, and was the best way to attract public and diplomatic support, but it was not the reason for war.

Disarmament might theoretically give Saddam Hussein the chance to stay in power and avoid war, but the Americans and British did not exhaust this route. Saddam staying in power was unthinkable. They had a definition of compliance and a timetable they would not deviate from. The UN route was always likely to fail. When it did, Blair delivered on his promise to support regime change, which was always the explicit policy of the US government and, in reality, the UK government too.

This case was not that Blair had knowingly lied about the WMD that weren't there, nor that those weapons weren't an important factor in his decision. Instead, we'd maintain that he had made clear his support for regime change to the US administration in private and that he had been less than transparent with the British people that this was the case.

Blair vs Dimbleby 1 – 13 March 2005

In March 2005 Blair came face-to-face with an audience of women voters who had grown disillusioned with Labour, particularly over Iraq. Re-watching the audience's contributions almost twenty years later, they remain powerful. Many people, including those who had supported the war, felt they'd been cheated – and probably still do. That's why any consideration of the erosion of trust and the impact of political deceit must focus on Blair and Iraq.

That it was Blair, a man who had appealed to so many voters as 'pretty straight', only increased the cynicism. In 2005, and ever since, his obsession in these interviews, audience encounters and press conferences has been to counter the charge he finds most damaging and stinging: that he acted in bad faith and lied to or deceived the British people about the reasons he went to war in Iraq. No, he says, I took a decision you may profoundly disagree with, but believe me, I did so honestly. The question, even today, is whether that stacks up. He might not have told a bare-faced lie or have never entirely been caught doing so, but the British people nevertheless felt, and feel, that he deceived them – and they have good reason to.

The women in the audience offer Blair cold fury. They talk about their sense of euphoria when he was elected, believing him to be a new sort of politician. They say he let them down by telling them a story that wasn't true. They evoke the memories of the dead, sacrificed for a flawed case. Blair absorbs it all and offers a justification:

> I had to take the decision in the end about whether it was right to remove Saddam Hussein from power or leave him there. I took the view that in the end it would be safer … if he was removed from power. I know a lot of people disagree with that but I still believe it was the right decision.[15]

Hearing this, the audience audibly groans. A young woman in the front row asks what turns out to be something of a killer question:

> Why didn't you say then, when you went into Iraq, that was the reason? Why was it all about the weapons of mass destruction?[16]

The audience's groans transform into a hubbub of assent.

This exchange is revealing for two reasons: first, because Blair justifies Iraq instinctively in terms of regime change and not weapons of mass destruction, and second because that's not how the audience remembers it. For them, the case was always disarmament. That was what they heard day in, day out. That's why they felt deceived when he invaded anyway before the disarmament process had been exhausted. Blair, remembering himself, clarifies:

> Iraq wasn't in compliance with the UN resolutions, and I didn't believe with Saddam in power, they ever would be, so that's why I felt I had to get rid of him.[17]

Maybe this'll work, he's thinking: regime change as the only way to disarm. After all, after the weapons inspection route had been abandoned in 2003, this had become the position. The other problem, of course, is that there were no WMD. Saddam could not comply because he didn't have the weapons. The only thing that would have averted the war would have been producing the weapons, but that was impossible because he didn't have them.

Now for the forensic questions we hope will tighten the screw on Blair, questions that we'd spent the week working on. Jonathan tells Blair that many are sceptical and don't trust him because they think he promised Bush he'd go to war in Iraq come what may.

To back this up, Jonathan produces a document that became iconic in the post-invasion debate about Blair's road to war. It's a two-page memo written by Sir David Manning, a civil servant who served as the prime minister's foreign affairs adviser. Since 2005 a treasure trove of such documents has entered the public domain, including further memos from Manning, but at the time of the interview this memo was the most damning and difficult for Blair. It was March 2002, before the prospect of war in Iraq was in the minds of the general public but some time after the Americans had renewed their interest in getting rid of Saddam Hussein, and Manning was dining in Washington with George Bush's national security adviser Condoleezza Rice. They were joined by the extrovert, red-socked UK ambassador to the United States, the late Sir Christopher Meyer. The memo details their discussions – over a long Washington dinner – that were, according to Manning, 'particularly frank'. Jonathan read Manning's words to Blair in the studio:

> [I told them that] You, Tony Blair, 'would not budge' in support for regime change, but that you had a press, a Parliament and a public who were a problem for you.[18]

This was dynamite. Blair was set on 'regime change', Jonathan suggests, and everything else was 'moving the goalposts to legitimise an invasion that you were determined to do in any case'.[19]

Irritation flashes across Blair's face. He quibbles about what Manning said, but Jonathan has it in front of him in black and white. Blair says Manning meant something else: that Saddam had to be disarmed. The trouble is, that's not what the memo says, so Jonathan jabs back, forcing Blair to clarify. What did Blair 'not budging' in support of regime change mean if not what it obviously means? Blair looks like he isn't enjoying this, but he makes a stab at explaining himself.

> **Blair:** It's that we would not budge in insisting that the UN resolutions that were outstanding, that had been outstanding for years, were actually enforced, and that was the crucial thing.[20]

Blair is exasperated. That answer was nonsense, and he knows it, so he tries to draw the questioning period to an end. 'Let's take some audience,' he suggests. But Dimbleby isn't having it.

It's up to him to decide when to go to the audience, not Blair. The prime minister is rattled.

No wonder. Here he's very close to an outright lie – maybe that's what it was. Manning's note to Blair is very clearly about regime change and barely touches on disarmament. To the extent that WMD and Saddam's compliance with UN resolutions are mentioned, they are referred to as something that could provide a pretext for regime change rather than being the whole point of the exercise.

How the UK joined the war in Iraq convinced many voters that they could not trust Blair. Here, in 2005, when he's seeking to persuade disillusioned voters that he always acts honestly, whatever you think of his decisions, Blair is misrepresenting the contents of this pivotal memo. The next time he comes before Jonathan, six weeks later, right at the end of the 2005 general election campaign, he will have a new explanation for it. But for now this account will have to do.

In the meantime, the March programme wraps up with Blair at his most compelling and, simultaneously, most hammy. A woman in the audience, more in sorrow than anger, tells him that she will vote for him again if he has the humility to admit he was wrong to go to war. Blair, a little inflection of emotion in his voice, regretfully declines:

> **Blair:** I'm sorry, I can't do that. I'm very sorry, if you want me to say that I regret the decision to go to conflict, I can't do that for you … If you actually want to elect me on my saying, 'I regret going to war,' when I don't, that would be foolish for both of us.[21]

And there, as strings swell and the principals choke back tears, the political romance is over. Blair's just too good a man to pretend that such an arrangement could truly satisfy either of them.

Finally, after the love has gone, Blair makes his final plea:

I can only tell you the truth: the truth is I believe I did the right thing. And I believe also that in time to come, people will see that it was a right decision. All I'm trying to say to you is I don't disrespect you if you profoundly disagree with me, but please don't put it on the basis of my integrity or my honesty. I did it honestly. You may disagree with what I did, but I genuinely believed it and believe it to have been the right thing … I can't tell you I believe I did the wrong thing when I didn't.[22]

Putting aside questions of honesty and deceit, this is Blair at the audacious top of his game. By March 2005 the Iraq war had already killed, maimed and left life chaotic for hundreds of thousands of people, but there's no escaping Blair's sense of personal hurt. It's the same wounded prime minister who protested to John Humphrys that anyone could impugn his integrity over the Ecclestone affair. The political message: a man so affected by accusations of dishonesty cannot possibly have deceived you.

Blair versus Dimbleby 2 – 2 May 2005

In May, Blair was back. He didn't know it then, but as he walked onto the studio floor on the Monday before polling day in the 2005 election, this was the last time he would appeal to the country to lend him their votes. Two years later, he finally relinquished the struggle for power with his Downing Street neighbour Gordon Brown, but that was the unknowable future. For now, Blair had an historic third term to secure, and he still had the same problem: Iraq.

We'd been thinking long and hard about what to ask this time. The disastrous aftermath and faulty intelligence might be in the public mind, but the regime change charge remained the strongest and most fertile line of attack. Blair had misled us in

March about the contents of the Manning memo, suggesting it was all about UN resolutions and WMDs when they barely featured. We felt we were onto something.

So, after the audience had had their say, we returned to the promise, given to the US early in 2002, that Blair would not budge in his support of regime change. But Blair had a plan: if Jonathan raised Manning's damning memo, he'd stop pretending it was purely about UN resolutions and accept that he favoured regime change as an alternative means to disarm Saddam.

Blair, in both interviews, is happy to head into the weeds of the argument. The more complex the issues appear, the more he can convince his audience – in the studio and watching at home – that the straightforward story his assurances to the Bush administration seem to tell is actually a simplistic reading of events.

In a way, Blair's enemy is language itself. His case – and he may well believe it – is that the words in documents like the Manning memo or other contemporary records do not mean what they are commonly taken to mean. He wants people to set aside the obvious meaning that the words appear to convey in favour of alternative, more complex explanations. We see this with his handling of Manning's words across the two programmes in 2005, as Blair interprets and reinterprets the meaning of the text.

In March the Manning memo is represented in one way – it's all about UN resolutions and disarmament, not regime change; and in May it's given a different spin – OK, it *was* about regime change but only as a way to disarm Iraq. There might be aspects of truth in both versions, but the shifting interpretations help create confusion, which might help to get Blair off the hook.

He then moved the goalposts a little further, claiming that whatever he'd said in public or private about the need to get rid of Saddam Hussein, this all changed when he went down the UN route and tried to secure resolutions, which, if complied with, could have saved Saddam's skin. So the audience should ignore all those words about not budging and backing regime change, Blair suggested, because Saddam could have survived if he'd complied.

Blair's true position was that he'd have been alongside the United States to influence their policy and be part of the action whatever happened. This meant, at the very minimum, toying with regime change (an illegal pretext for war) before convincing the US to go down the UN route for reasons of managing the press, public and parliament. The Chilcott Inquiry into the Iraq War, which reported in 2016 after seven years of hearings and delay, revealed further communications between Blair and Bush that cemented this sense of a British prime minister committed to supporting the US under any circumstances.

In July 2002 Blair wrote a memo to Bush that stated, 'I will be with you, whatever.' We didn't know that in 2005, but it certainly would have bolstered the argument Jonathan Dimbleby put. When Jonathan's brother David asked Blair about those words in 2018 in his excellent podcast series *The Fault Line*, Blair denied that 'I will be with you, whatever' meant he would be with Bush, whatever. Blair argued this wasn't the blank cheque it sounded like, just a commitment that was essential if he were to win the ear of the president or, as Blair put it, 'the decision maker'. Alastair Campbell, Blair's director of communications at the time, told the same podcast the words were just 'a figure of speech'. Again, words don't mean what they mean; blank cheques that were cashed were never issued. So it goes.

The audience on that day in May 2005 were on to Blair. They felt the rush to war in early 2003 undermined everything he said. They thought the British and Americans wanted to get on with their war against Saddam before allowing the weapons inspectors or diplomacy time to succeed. Chilcott, all those years later, concluded they were right:

At the end of January 2003, Mr Blair accepted the US timetable for military action by mid-March. President Bush agreed to support a second resolution to help Mr Blair.

The UK Government's efforts to secure a second resolution faced opposition from those countries, notably France, Germany and Russia, which believed that the inspections process could continue.

The inspectors reported that Iraqi co-operation was improving while far from perfect.

By early March, the US Administration was not prepared to allow inspections to continue or give Mr Blair more time to try to achieve support for action. The attempt to gain support for a second resolution was abandoned.

In the Inquiry's view, the diplomatic options had not at that stage been exhausted. Military action was, therefore, not a last resort.[23]

But that damning verdict lay eleven years in the future. During a general election campaign there were other subjects to cover, but towards the end of the programme Jonathan returned to Iraq. Blair immediately returned to his theme: disagree with me by all means, but do not say I took the decision in bad faith.

Then, right at the end, the frustrations start to show. The difference between the Blair of 2005 with Jonathan Dimbleby and the Blair of 1997 with John Humphrys is notable. In 1997 Blair was pleading with the public to credit him with being 'pretty straight'. Eight years on, and that ship has sailed. So much so that Blair sounds as if he's now beyond caring, almost losing his temper and going so far as to say that those who don't trust him shouldn't vote for him.

Blair: I mean, I've had this election campaign where there's been some pretty fearsome attacks on my character, and I'm not gonna stand here and beg for my own character. People can make up their minds whether they trust me or not, and that's a decision on May 5th [election day].

Audience member (shouting): I don't trust you!

Blair: Well, that's fine. That's your prerogative, sir.[24]

Three days later, Blair won Labour a third term, securing 35 per cent of the vote, down from 43 per cent in 1997, losing four million votes.

Two years later, he was gone.

I have never been a Blair hater. Quite the opposite, in fact.

As a Labour supporter who'd grown up in the 1980s, I was delighted to see a Labour government investing in health and education. Blair's electoral achievements were extraordinary. I was enthused by his interventionist approach to foreign policy, I backed him over Kosovo and was willing to give him the benefit of the doubt on Iraq.

Over time, however, I had to admit that there was something flawed about a leader who surrendered British foreign policy to the United States, whatever. There was something dishonest about Blair's protestations that words promised to the president of the United States didn't mean what we understood them to mean. I can't budge on that. And there was something deceitful about setting up a process that could theoretically avert war by allowing the Iraqi dictator to disarm when that process was abandoned before it could work and when the alleged weapons didn't even exist.

That's before we consider the failure to plan for the aftermath of the coalition's intervention and the subsequent cost in human life; before we think about Abu Ghraib, Fallujah, the crimes of ISIS, and children blown to pieces in marketplaces and schools and shopping streets.

Tony Blair still says that history will judge that he made the right decision and the world is safer without Saddam Hussein and the weapons of mass destruction he no longer had. He would have re-armed, Blair says. He would have been as brutal as Assad in crushing an Iraqi Arab Spring.

We don't know what would have happened if Saddam had been left in power. We do know the outcome of regime change. For Blair, the Iraq war cannot be acknowledged as a mistake. It has to be stood by. As Clare Short, who served in the cabinet under Blair puts it, 'If he now said, "You know something? I made a mistake," that would be a crumbling of his persona. So he has to keep going with it.'[25]

Did Tony Blair lie to the British people about Iraq? He insists that he didn't, but perhaps, in private, to get through the day, he has to lie to himself.

6

SIAN HAS GORDON
FOR *BREAKFAST*

'Brown to Brussels after Balls' Triumph',
The Times, **23 June 2016**

Former prime minister Gordon Brown is on course to become
the first British President of the European Commission in over
40 years, claiming a mandate for radical change to hold back
the tide of anti-EU feeling across the continent.

Prime minister Ed Balls congratulated his predecessor, who
will now leave the domestic stage and dampen repeated allegations of 'backseat driving' from the former premier.

Mr Brown will take over the job next month following the
premature departure of Portugal's Manuel Barroso. It was
widely reported that Brown had been agitating for the new role
since leaving Downing Street last year.

The announcement that he had won the backing of the
European Council comes just two days after his protégé Ed
Balls secured a record sixth term for the Labour Party with a
majority of 79 seats. The European Parliament is expected to
approve the appointment next week.

The move is likely to be a double-edged sword for the British
prime minister, who will hope for a powerful ally at the top of
the EU but could find himself clashing with a political big beast
he has worked alongside since the mid-1990s.

Mr Barroso refused to comment on the appointment of his successor last night, but relations between the former Commission President and Mr Brown have been described as 'extremely tense' since Brown left No. 10 and began his search for a new role. One Barroso aide criticised Mr Brown for 'briefing against Manuel and continually calling on him to name his departure date'.

Mr Brown bought a home in Brussels a matter of weeks after leaving the post of prime minister in May 2015 after eight years in the job. He was widely suspected of leading a campaign against Mr Barroso that led to his departure from his post before his term expired.

Brown has always denied any campaign to take Mr Barroso's job, and suspicion of a whispering campaign against the former Portuguese prime minister has centred on Mr Brown's senior aides. Brown paid tribute to his predecessor in a statement last night, describing Mr Barroso as 'the greatest Commission President we've ever had', adding that it would be 'my great privilege to carry on Manuel's work'. These comments were greeted with derision by aides of Mr Barroso, one of whom described them as 'lies'.

Mr Balls came to Mr Brown's defence last night, telling the BBC's Andrew Neil that his former boss would be a 'reforming' leader of the European Commission at a time when the European Union faces a growing wave of Euroscepticism in parts of Europe.

Mr Brown's political career has been glittering despite doubts about his temperament and brooding personal style that date back to his time as former prime minister Tony Blair's chancellor. After taking over from Blair in June 2007, Brown was hailed as a strategic genius when he called a snap election just three months into his premiership and won an impressive fourth majority for Labour.

In the years that followed, Brown claimed credit for 'saving the world' after the 2008 financial crisis but faced several years of economic difficulties and attendant unpopularity before his unlikely 'Olympic bounce' election victory in September 2012. He stood aside in 2015, paving the way for his hand-picked successor Mr Balls.

The former prime minister has been widely seen as a lucky leader, as much because of the calibre of his political enemies as his own political gifts. He ended the political career of short-lived Tory leader David Cameron within a few months of becoming prime minister. Cameron, last seen during a brief stint in the jungle on *I'm a Celebrity … Get Me Out of Here!* in 2008, was the final official Conservative leader before the party split over the issue of European Union membership in 2009. His effective successor, Conservative UKIP leader Nigel Farage, was scathing about Brown's appointment last night, describing him as a 'traitor to his country'.

There was a more measured response from the outgoing leader of the opposition, One Nation's Nick Clegg. Clegg congratulated the former prime minister on the new job but warned that his party, whoever leads it in the future, would urge Mr Brown to stand firm against a 'rising tide of Euroscepticism' across the continent. Boris Johnson, seen as the favourite to succeed Mr Clegg as leader of the right-of-centre Europhile party, used an appearance on the BBC's *Have I Got News for You* to criticise the appointment. Johnson said that while Brown was 'right on Europe', he was 'in it for the job title and the *moules et frites* rather than any more noble political reasons'.

Mr Balls was said by aides to be 'delighted' with Mr Brown's appointment, as much because of weariness about his former boss's domestic interference as the benefits of having an ally at the top of the European Union. One cabinet minister said that Mr Balls believes the appointment will 'underline Britain's leadership of the European Union and mark the final death knell for British Euroscepticism'.

Mr Brown's former colleague and political adversary Tony Blair was unavailable for comment last night. A spokeswoman told reporters that Blair, who Brown allowed to be forcibly extradited to The Hague in 2015, is 'focused on defending himself after his indictment by the International Criminal Court'.

Oh, Gordon, it could have been so different.

But then again, if character is destiny, maybe it couldn't.

Part of the mystery around Gordon Brown, a frontline politician of enormous capabilities, came from his reluctance to be interviewed at length and his aversion to studio audiences. My ITV show, *Jonathan Dimbleby*, comprised both these elements and was a hard sell to Brown. However, in 2005 we made a breakthrough, securing him for a special on the eve of the G8 'Make Poverty History' summit in Gleneagles. Strangely, given his serious and cerebral reputation, I'm pretty sure what sealed the deal was our plan to surround the chancellor with political and showbiz royalty.

Looking back, there's something a little nauseating about the build-up to the G8 that year. The cause, making poverty history, was laudable, but the spectacle – the concert in Hyde Park, repeated appearances by Bono with world leaders, news programmes featuring Elton John offering a pre-recorded message to the world (yes, that was one of mine) – seems incongruous.

The green room we assembled for ITV's 'G8 Debate' was easily the most ridiculous of any I've ever spent time in. Guest of honour was Brown, whose team had been locked in negotiations with us about who would be in the audience and whether he'd take their questions before pretty much agreeing to everything when we confirmed we'd booked Elton and Sting.

The blond ex-Police frontman rocked up early that afternoon wearing a light green vest and a pair of sharpened cheekbones. Somehow, he could talk while simultaneously sucking in his cheeks. This was just a few years after *Zoolander*, and the 'Blue Steel' vibes were strong. I was stuck with the peroxided popster for a few minutes and searched for small talk. I'd loved the Police as a kid but hated the man's pretentious jazz noodling. I tried to be cutting edge: Apple had recently dropped the iPod, and I loved it. So I tried to strike up a chat on the subject with Sting. He was a music fan, after all.

'So,' I said, producing the sleek, silver music player with the iconic headphones from my pocket, 'what do you think of these?'

Sting, who'd been pretty aloof thus far, looked over at me and inspected the device I was holding. His expression was somehow both horrified and bored.

'Have you, er, got one?' I asked him, ploughing on.

'No,' he exclaimed wearily, turning away. 'It's just more noise pollution.'

I wish I'd bravely shot back that you could say the same about his excruciating solo career, but that wasn't really an option. The conversation was over. I went to find him a herbal tea.

A few minutes later I got word that Brown had arrived. He'd swept into the car park at the base of the ITV Tower and had been waiting for a minute or two when I got there. It won't surprise you that he was glowering but it was unclear why, exactly. The journey in the lift was silent apart from the odd grunt from the chancellor. I decided against asking him if he had an iPod, to break the ice, and the bad atmosphere evaporated when we arrived at the make-up room, where Sting was having his already super-sharp cheekbones further accentuated. Brown clocked the rock star – and the cheekbones – and was all smiles. Sting, for his part, immediately warmed up, suddenly becoming more northern and chatty now that the chancellor had arrived. Sting, if you're reading this, it's how you treat the little people that counts.

Next up was Kofi Annan, the UN secretary-general (nice man, no airs and graces), followed by Benjamin Mkapa, the president of Tanzania (also pleasant and jolly), and, finally,

Coldplay frontman Chris Martin (a sweetheart, since you ask). Elton dialled in later from New York. If it all sounds sort of ridiculous, that's because it was.

If Brown enjoyed the stardust, I'm not too proud to admit that I did too. Sting notwithstanding, it was a thrill to assemble such big names, but I was particularly glad to have finally landed Brown himself. His aversion to risk was legendary, but even he felt safe in an environment focused on poverty and climate change. I counted it as an achievement, but it also felt a bit like cheating.

Despite high-profile programmes like the 'G8 Debate', the writing was on the wall for *Jonathan Dimbleby*. Under my editorship, ITV's political show punched above its weight in an unfair fight with the BBC. Budget cuts and endless scheduling shifts had taken their toll. Then, later in 2005, we were cheered when the guest-hoovering machine that was *Breakfast with Frost* was axed by the BBC, although we quickly became depressed again when the Sunday-morning slot was given to the BBC's political editor Andrew Marr, with Frost's editor Barney Jones staying on. By then, Marr's vivid insights into Westminster politics, built on decades at the top of the newspaper business, had made him a household name and a genuine star.

At least we didn't have to contend with *On the Record* anymore. In an act of extraordinary self-harm, the BBC decided to abolish their Sunday-lunchtime political show in 2003. It's a mistake that the BBC are still paying for, and was a hammer blow for the long-form forensic interview from which our political culture has never recovered.

On the Record had started life in 1988, immediately becoming iconic thanks to an extraordinary opening title sequence that transformed the House of Commons into a marauding and deranged crocodile snapping and roaring its way across the United Kingdom. The programme, most associated with presenter John Humphrys, was a combination of policy-heavy films and long-form interviews. This was serious political television, and, as we saw when the Ecclestone affair erupted, it could still attract prime ministers and chancellors because of its reputation and credibility.

Bizarrely, though, and in a depressingly familiar pattern, the BBC decided to throw it all away for reasons that seem incomprehensible today. The problem, as then director-general of the BBC Greg Dyke saw it, was that the BBC was too concerned with the high politics of Westminster and not interested enough in the issues and concerns of ordinary viewers and voters. This problem was particularly acute after the 2001 general election, when voter turnout dramatically decreased.

Dyke decided that the BBC needed to reimagine its political coverage in a way that would reconnect people to politics. In this context, a show so wedded to Westminster that it featured an animated House of Commons disguised as a reptile was not a good look. And so, after a review of the kind only the BBC can produce, BBC bosses decided to axe the best political programme on BBC television. As David Jordan, *On the Record*'s editor who later became the BBC's long-standing head of editorial policy, told me, the decision to axe the programme was 'vandalism'.[1]

Jonathan Dimbleby came to an end in 2006 after eleven years. It was briefly succeeded by a disastrous replacement called *The Sunday Edition*, fronted by Andrew Rawnsley and Andrea Catherwood. The two presenters had many things going for them, but on-screen chemistry wasn't among them. There was also the small matter of a huge cut in the programme budget and a general sense that ITV had lost interest in politics. So, as the Blair years gave way to the Brown era, it was time for me to move on. I left my glass-walled editor's office in the iconic ITV Tower of *Walden* and *Dimbleby*, and walked away.

* * *

In politics, there are lies, and then there are lies. The small fibs – the evasions and petty deceits – are commonplace and politicians usually get away with them, but when the untruth is brazen and contradicts reality, politicians are in real trouble. Mrs Thatcher knew why Nigel Lawson resigned, but her feigned ignorance damned her in 1989. In 2017 Theresa May told journalists 'nothing has changed' on social care policy when something definitely had changed, and her election campaign never recovered. Gordon Brown, in some ways temperamentally similar to May, had his own moment of maximum untruth in the autumn of 2007, and it did for him too.

Three months into his premiership, Brown was popular. A series of crises were well handled in the summer and early autumn of 2007 – flooding, terror attacks and a run on the Northern Rock bank. His status as a serious man for serious times, free of Blairite smoothness and full of reassuring heft, was playing well. Labour's advertising firm was working up a new slogan: not flash, just Gordon. Understandably, talk in Downing Street turned to the possibility of an early general election.

This was always a risky course to take. If it went wrong, Brown would go down in history as the chancellor who agitated for the top job for ten years only to throw it all away after three months. Brown was instinctively risk averse, and senior members of his cabinet were sceptical about the idea, but others in his team argued that he should take advantage of popularity ratings that were unlikely to go anywhere from there but down.

From multiple accounts, there can be no doubt that an early election was under very serious consideration. Polling was commissioned, advertising prepared, election photos taken and the government's public-spending review brought forward to fit an election timetable. Enquiries were even made about the whereabouts of Her Majesty should Brown want to ask for a dissolution of parliament.

Labour arrived at their party conference in Bournemouth at the end of September 2007 with speculation about an early election at fever pitch. The prospect was terrifying for the Tories, who seemed to be facing a devastating defeat just two years after the arrival of their young leader David Cameron. Brown fielded questions on the subject and teased journalists with non-committal answers. The working assumption was that Brown would go for it.

What happened next demonstrated that Cameron and his shadow chancellor George Osborne were a new breed of Tory politician. Unlike their hapless predecessors since 1997, these two were ruthlessly effective operators. Rather than allow the threat of an early election to destabilise or spook them, the young Tories went to their party conference with a plan to regain the initiative.

On Monday morning Osborne unveiled a plan to raise the threshold at which people paid inheritance tax on their estates from £300,000 to £1 million. He'd pay for it, he said, by a new levy on 'non-doms': residents of the UK who paid no tax here. Two days later Cameron took to the conference stage and made a highly effective speech, without notes, goading Brown, daring him to call his threatened election.

These events transformed the political landscape. Fresh polling commissioned by Brown showed the Labour lead evaporating: the inheritance tax announcement resonated with voters, and Cameron had impressed. Brown and his team, having marched everyone to the top of the hill, now decided to march them back down again.

On the evening of Friday 5 October, Andrew Marr's editor Barney Jones got a call from Downing Street. They told him they wanted to offer Marr an interview with the prime minister. The only problem was that it would have to be pre-recorded on Saturday afternoon for broadcast on Sunday morning. That would be fine if the contents of the interview – Brown's decision to cancel an early election – could be kept under wraps, but Jones was doubtful:

I said, 'You're loopy if you think you can hold it.' I can hold it. I can not tell my bosses. I can not tell our political editor Nick Robinson. They'll be really, really pissed off, but I can do that, but I don't think you'll hold it from your side.[2]

But No. 10 were insistent they could, so Jones warily agreed. On Saturday morning he bumped into Nick Robinson in the street. He remembers thinking, *This is really bad news. I know something that you and every political hack is desperate to know.* Later that day the Marr team arrived at Downing Street for the interview, thinking their secret was intact. However, the news had leaked just as Jones had predicted and soon Downing Street was crammed with a very angry media pack. Granting Marr the exclusive in a bungled attempt to keep control of the story had enraged the rest of the media. They were in no mood to forgive Brown.

Watching the Marr interview back, it remains as surreal an experience as it felt on the day it was broadcast. Brown suggests that all the speculation about a general election – speculation he'd fed – was merely party conference overexcitement. He confirmed there would be no election. Instead, Brown said he wanted to articulate his vision for the country and deliver on it. He denied Labour's slump in the polls was the reason for the election retreat. He just wanted to get on with the job.

Jones reflects with some regret on how the programme dealt with what he regards as a lie from Brown:

Andrew should probably have gone a bit further in saying, 'Prime Minister, people listening to this just won't believe you. They will think you are not telling the truth,' and he didn't quite nail that. But he did it better than Frost would have done it.[3]

The interview was a cheap facsimile of Blair's performance over the Ecclestone affair. The two Labour leaders were equally disingenuous in most aspects, but Blair's performance was much more effective. Six months into his premiership, he made a successful personal appeal to voters who wanted to believe the best of him. Four months into the job, Brown could not pull off the same trick with such transparently dishonest answers.

Andrew Marr himself recalls the interview as a 'historic' missed opportunity.

> I remember thinking, 'This guy is making an absolutely massive mistake on television right now.' I thought it was a huge mistake for him. He should have called an election then. I was mystified, really, as to why he hadn't gone for it. Yes, the Conservatives had turned the polls round a bit, but had he gone for it then, then he'd have won.[4]

The following morning Brown stood before the pissed-off press in Downing Street and tried the same unbelievable lines. One journalist asked him whether he would still have rejected the election option if the polls after the Conservative conference had suggested a one hundred-seat Labour majority. Looking distinctly shifty, Brown answered, 'I would have made the same decision.' The prime minister was insulting everyone's intelligence. Arguably, he never recovered.

Ten years later, Brown finally came clean. In his memoir he admits to the 'important error' of allowing early election fever to mount – although it was, he insists, never an idea he personally supported – and accepts that the idea was ultimately abandoned because of polling that was bad for Labour. Recalling the Marr interview, he confesses: 'I went too far when in the face of hostile questioning, I refused to concede that I had seen the public polling that lay behind the final decision.

That was a mistake and much of the criticism was valid.'[5] Better late than never.

I watched all this from the sidelines. I'd left ITV at the worst possible time. Television, like the economy more broadly, started to contract in 2007–08. The financial crisis engulfing Brown's premiership quickly had real-world effects.

Eventually, I got my foot in the door at BBC's Westminster address at 4 Millbank, just across the road from the Houses of Parliament. It was a long way from my glass-panelled office at ITV, but sometimes you have to start again. I swallowed my pride and took all the shifts I could get on programmes like *This Week*, *The Daily Politics* and *Newsnight*. I was no longer a programme editor but, once again, a lowly researcher back at square one.

Eventually, sometime in 2008, I made an impression with the new boss of BBC political programmes, Robbie Gibb. Robbie and I came from very different places politically – he was a right-winger steeped in Tory politics, I wasn't – but he gave me my chance by employing me on a broadcast journalist contract. It was the lowest rung of the ladder, but I was glad to get the chance and remain grateful to Robbie for backing me in the way that he did.

Although I was new to the BBC, I was already passionate about impartiality, which is hugely important but hard to achieve. It meant a commitment to airing all sides of the argument, and doing everything to ensure that all those who paid the licence fee felt heard and represented. This is easier said than done, but I was committed to the effort.

As a right-winger at the BBC, Robbie was in a minority. While some high-profile BBC journalists came from a Conservative background, and others left the BBC to go and work for the Tories, the cultural and political centre of gravity of the BBC is liberal and ever so slightly to the left. This was certainly obvious to me when I started working there as a freelancer.

Many people at the BBC seemed to view public attitudes to issues like the European Union or immigration as distasteful and wrong. I would place myself on the liberal side of these questions, but I didn't think I had the right to impose my attitudes on licence-fee payers. I thought we should take ideas from the right as seriously as those from the left, analyse the issues on our programmes and let the people decide. My personal views were neither here nor there.

Pretty soon I'd established myself, and, against the odds, I was rapidly promoted to assistant editor, skipping a grade on the way. Sounds brilliant, but there was one drawback: the promotion sent me to work way outside my political comfort zone in the domain of Bill Turnbull, Sian Williams and Susanna Reid. I was off to BBC *Breakfast*. Knackering doesn't cover it.

The first thing that shocked me about working on the BBC's hugely popular *Breakfast* programme was that the people who produced the show on a given day literally stayed up all night to make it. I think I'd imagined I might be obliged to pitch up at 5 a.m. or something. In reality I'd arrive at work around eight in the evening and stay awake overnight until it was time to broadcast the show between six and nine in the morning, then head home at about nine-thirty to try to sleep until it all started again. It was an utterly surreal way of life, and I found it very tough.

Exhausted and disoriented as I was, I immediately appreciated the talents of the *Breakfast* production and presenting team. They delivered high-quality and very complex material in the dead of night when, if they were anything like me, they were shattered and barely functioning. The presenters would arrive at around 4 a.m. and did much more than reading scripts off an autocue. They had to be ready to ask intelligent questions across various subjects with minimal briefing. There just wasn't time.

This type of work was completely foreign to my world of polished and prepared political interviews, where there were hours to talk to presenters about interview strategy. Instead, interviews were essentially conducted solo by the on-air journalists. It was, and remains, one of the most demanding jobs in television and I was hugely impressed by them all. Susanna Reid, Sian Williams and Charlie Stayt stood out as the most able on-the-hoof political interviewers.

For politicians, these interviews mattered. *Breakfast* attracts audiences in the millions and is watched by people who don't watch many political or news programmes. It connects politicians with voters like few other programmes, and a bad performance on *Breakfast* can be damaging. While some interviewers are very tough, the *Breakfast* sofa could sometimes be an easy ride. I'd seen Gordon Brown appear a few times, and he'd benefited from an occasionally over-deferential approach.

I was desperate to have my own crack at a Brown interview, so in September 2009 I practically begged *Breakfast* editor Alison Ford – an inspirationally fun and sharp editor who tragically died way too young in 2013 – to take me off the gruelling overnight rota and let me work on the programme's Labour Party conference interview with the prime minister.

Brown had been having a terrible time in the two years since the election that never was. As the Liberal Democrat MP Vince Cable memorably put it, he'd gone from 'Stalin to Mr Bean' in record time. But when things in the global economy got worse, Brown was able to partially recover.

His interventions to shore up and buy out British banks when the storm of the financial crisis made landfall in the UK in the autumn of 2008 averted the genuine risk that the cash machines and credit cards people relied upon would stop working, with unimaginably grim consequences. Brown also won accolades from world leaders, including Barack Obama, for identifying the right international action to take and leading the world in introducing reform.

All this helped Brown at home, but not for long. The deficit ballooned because of the costs of bailing out the banks. This was made worse by the British economy suffering job losses, business failures and repossessions. Brown had boasted of abolishing boom and bust more times than anyone could remember, yet here we were.

By the time he arrived at what would have to be the last Labour Party conference before an election due in 2010, he was in deep political trouble. Bankers' bonuses, the 2009 expenses scandal and Labour Party internal warfare had frustrated all of his attempts to relaunch and get a grip. Before we got to all that – as we would in the *Breakfast* interview – things took a peculiar personal turn.

'Gordon,' writes Tony Blair in his autobiography, 'is a strange guy.'[6]

I suppose it takes one to know one, but maybe political people are strange. Many of the most successful politicians of modern times are more than a little odd. Most of the politicians featured in this book could be described as 'different'.

Back in 2006, when Blair began buckling under the pressure of Brown's relentless agitation for him to set the date of his departure from Downing Street, the veteran Labour backbencher Frank Field came to see him to urge him to stay on. 'You can't go yet,' pleaded Field, 'you can't let Mrs Rochester out of the attic.' At this, New Labour's master chronicler Andrew Rawnsley reported Blair 'roared with uncontrolled laughter'.[7]

This comparison with the mysterious mentally ill woman locked in the attic in Charlotte Brontë's *Jane Eyre* was repeated by Field in public a few months later. He added that Brown had 'no empathy with people'. Field's joke was cruel and displayed an attitude to mental health that feels uncomfortable from today's vantage point.

Soon after Field's intervention George Osborne, then shadow chancellor, even called Brown Mrs Rochester to his face in parliament. Brown, being Brown, ignored the joke entirely, but it teased at concerns that Brown possessed 'psychological flaws' (as one Blairite famously told Rawnsley in 1998), which made him unfit to be prime minister.

And then, in the autumn of 2009, all this resurfaced. Stories of Brown's temper tantrums and his habit of hurling mobile phones across Downing Street offices were well known in Westminster and made their way into the papers, but nobody had asked him directly about them. As Andrew Marr pondered how to approach his conference interview with Brown at the end of September, these stories were on his mind.

> I had first-hand accounts from senior civil servants and senior cabinet ministers of extraordinary displays of intemperance and anger in No. 10. It was building up as a story that everybody was talking about at Westminster, but nobody was directly asking him about. And so I thought, well, this is the moment. I'm going to do it.[8]

Fair game, perhaps, but things were about to get even more personal.

Brown had taken a kick to the head when playing rugby as a sixteen-year-old that had left him blind in his left eye. His manner and appearance were profoundly affected by his disability. The prime minister's friends said at the time that to truly understand Brown, you had to appreciate what he'd been through and know that he still lived in fear of losing his sight altogether. In 2009, attention turned to whether his eyesight was deteriorating further and whether this might explain his reportedly dark moods.

At the same time, the Guido Fawkes website went much further. The right-wing site published rumours – without any evidence – suggesting that Brown was taking antidepressants. These stories would usually stay on the margins, but Marr, who was already interested in asking Brown about his moods and behaviour, took them seriously.

> My big mistake was that I had read, in one of the newspapers and online, references to him using pills and that he was misusing them somehow. And they were making the outbursts worse, not better. Now, I had no evidence of that at all. But I was lulled into it. Somebody online said, 'None of the TV interviewers are brave enough to ask him about that.' So I thought, well, stuff you, I will.[9]

The pre-conference interview starts where you'd expect it to, on the issues that dominate the Sunday papers: public-spending cuts and the size of the deficit. Then, about halfway through, Marr changes tack.

'If you were an American president,' he stated, 'we'd know all about your medical history.'

The temperature in the room immediately cools. Brown is on alert, inspecting Marr warily as he proceeds with the question, allowing himself a slight lip curl.

'Let me ask you,' Marr continues, 'something else that everyone has been talking about out there in the Westminster village,'

Brown is listening and reacting. As the words 'talking about' come out of Marr's mouth, Brown quizzically furrows his brow and raises his hand to his mouth, staring at Marr.

Then Marr goes there.

> **Marr:** A lot of people in this country use prescription painkillers and pills to help them get through. Are you one of those people?

> **Brown** (in a soft, almost sing-song voice): No, I think this is the sort of questioning that, um (looking down and sorrowful), is …

Marr: It's a fair question, I think.

Brown: ... all too often entering the lexicon of British politics ...[10]

Brown turns the subject away from the 'pills question' and talks about his eyesight, which has created 'serious problems' but is stable.

Marr shifts back: 'What about my other question?'

Brown, dismissively and with a flash of understandable anger, says, 'I answered your other question,' then adds:

One of the problems is, you get too much involved in this
Whitehall game. I mean this programme this morning
even though it's in Brighton, it's about sort of Whitehall,
inside politics, as you've just revealed by your questions.[11]

It's hard not to feel sympathetic towards Brown about this. His disability had an impact on how he came across and the media handled his disability clumsily. If he seemed, as Blair put it, 'strange', then maybe some of the reason for that was his partial blindness. As for the rumours that he used antidepressants, these were unsubstantiated stories that probably shouldn't have made it on air. Today, given greater understanding and sensitivity to issues around disability and mental health, they almost certainly wouldn't.

On the other hand, there had been persistent rumours and credible reports of Brown's erratic behaviour and explosive temper that might have led to legitimate questions about his emotional stability. Unsurprisingly Brown, who chatted happily with Marr after the interview, was soon privately fuming about the line of questioning. The presenter was later confronted by delegates in the conference hall and criticised by cabinet minister Peter Mandelson for asking questions based on 'extreme right-wing' smears.

Marr expressed regret when we discussed the 'pills' episode for this book. Given a chance to redo the interview, he told me he would have focused on Brown's erratic behaviour, which was a relevant question, but 'I wouldn't ask the pills question again in the way I did'. He has since apologised personally to Brown.

Three days after Brown's uncomfortable appearance with Marr, it was our turn. Sian Williams was one half of *Breakfast*'s dream team, circa 2009, along with the late Bill Turnbull. Bill was a lovely man. He wasn't remotely grand and was hugely welcoming to me when I joined *Breakfast*, not really knowing what I was doing. Together Sian and Bill had the sort of chemistry and on-screen magic you can't replicate. Working with them at the height of their powers was a privilege.

Sian was a former programme editor and producer at the BBC, so she brought enormous editorial authority to her role on the sofa. Arriving in Brighton in time for Brown's set-piece conference speech on Tuesday, she was very much up for working on an interview plan that the prime minister would not be expecting.

Gordon Brown presents particular challenges as an interviewee. While Tony Blair, Peter Mandelson and Alastair Campbell are most closely associated with New Labour's obsessive media management, Brown should get his share of the credit. Or blame. In 2000 Dave Hill – Labour's director of communications at the 1997 election – proudly explained to Radio 4 the 'on message' interview:

> What it means is that in the course of answering every question, you try and come back to the message that you went on that programme to deliver. The interviewer will try and take you up all sorts of alleyways. Remember, and we go back to the great phrase, that you have to be 'on message' because if you're not on message, then the interview was really not worthwhile because you didn't

get your case across. Probably the model exponent of the on-message interview is Gordon Brown.[12]

This orthodoxy still holds sway with many politicians, and it was always Brown's approach – and the approach he disastrously bequeathed to a generation of Labour politicians who followed him – but knowing about the method and dealing with it were two different things.

Most news interviews take a shopping-list approach: a list of questions designed to deliver clips for the news bulletins across a range of topical stories. That's fine, but news producers are not always programme makers. They will cover the ground, but there won't be much pressure on politicians and we're unlikely to hear anything but the message they want to communicate. This time, however, with the help of producer Matthew Pencharz, I had time to think more deeply and formulate a detailed plan with Sian.

Before we could get started, we needed to answer a question ourselves: what exactly was Gordon Brown's political problem? The answer, listening to his speech, was that he was stuck. Brown saw politics as a choice between spending money and making cuts. Cuts were for the Tories, and they were wrong. The problem was that this was a message for a different time. The costs of bailing out the banks and paying for the recession had led to a ballooning deficit. Brown had to reassure the public – who were concerned about spending more at a time when many believed the government should tighten its belt – that he was being responsible.

The other side of the argument was that government should be spending more money when times were so difficult, even if that meant running a large deficit. Now would be exactly the wrong time to turn off the spending taps. This argument became the central political battleground in British politics, and it was down to Brown to win it. Our job was to put the opposite case and see whether he could find the answers. His conference speech – with very little acknowledgement of the deficit – bulged with new promises. Brown just didn't seem to have a new way to make his case. We planned to expose this.

Then, things were thrown off, partly for us but mainly for Brown, when the *Sun*'s front page dropped at ten o'clock the night before the interview. 'Labour's Lost It' screamed the editorial. After twelve years, Labour had lost the support of the tabloid newspaper that Tony Blair had worked so hard to win around to New Labour. The symbolism was brutal, the timing terrible for Brown. His conference speech was no longer the story.

Early the next morning I sat down with Matthew and Sian to redraw the interview plan, and just after 7.45 a.m. we were under way. Brown and Sian sat across from each other with a sea of empty chairs between them and a stage emblazoned with the very Brownite slogan 'Securing Britain's Economic Recovery'. Sian remembers he seemed 'exhausted and beleaguered'.

We started with the *Sun* because that was where the story was, and it probably set the tone for an irritable interview. When we raised it, Brown feigned indifference and said that newspapers should concentrate on reporting the news, not telling voters what to think, but he was kidding nobody. He was bristling from the start, challenging Sian over the number of readers the newspaper reached.

Sian, who has since combined her television career with a career as a psychologist (she's Dr Sian Williams these days), reflects today on Brown's reaction:

> By the time he was sitting with me doing this interview, I think he'd come off that initial high of the conference speech and come into this environment where a newspaper was saying, 'Labour's Lost It.' That's the place you pick up as a journalist. That's the story. He was under threat, and when you're under threat, it's fight,

flight or freeze. He was fighting, so he was very defensive.[13]

On message as ever, the prime minister turned to the promises he'd made in the same hall the previous afternoon. He said Labour's policies were about investment in health and education. By contrast the Tories could only offer cuts, and let me tell you why … Sian interrupted: all of this came with a price tag, she said, and people were worried that we were spending too much money already. Hearing this, Brown's irritation got the better of him: 'Yeah, we announced how we'd do it yesterday,' he shot back, dismissing her. Sian stuck to her guns, challenging Brown again about spending more money when borrowing was already so high.

Brown made a stab – and not a terrible one – at arguing that the recession was precisely when the government needed to spend more or risk the situation getting worse, but Sian's insistence that there must be some commitment to controlling spending was effective. 'Would there be a pay freeze?' she asked. 'No,' said Brown, as if this was pure crazy. Might he means-test child benefit, targeting it on the worst off and removing it for higher earners? 'No,' said Brown with a tone of 'are you mad?' Refusing to consider such cuts was fine, of course, but Brown seemed incredulous that Sian was asking him to consider painful steps to tackle the deficit and reduce borrowing in an interview he'd expected to be a breeze. As Sian recalls:

To the viewer, what he was doing was snapping at me because he thought, from his perspective, he thought he could get an easy ride on *Breakfast*. I think there was an assumption that *Breakfast* would be a rather light, fluffy PR exercise where you wouldn't get challenged effectively.[14]

Sian Williams is not an aggressive interviewer. She believes in giving politicians a chance to connect with viewers, and *Breakfast* is not *Newsnight*, but Brown couldn't take the opportunity to make a case that morning.

> You are broadcasting to a very mixed audience on *Breakfast*. You are broadcasting to your voters. This was his chance to tell them why they should continue to trust him. But I think he saw it as a combative interview, and he almost didn't look past me to get to the viewer. What the viewers saw was him saying, 'You're wrong, you're wrong, you're wrong,' and that is quite typical of somebody who feels very threatened.[15]

After some questions about his wife Sarah's speech, which had introduced him onto the stage the day before – 'I didn't see her speech before she gave it,' he said, a little implausibly – our twelve minutes were over. Sian began to wrap up the interview and throw back to the studio, but before she could get her words out the ticked-off prime minister was up and out of his seat, blocking the view between Sian and the camera. 'You can stay where you are if you want,' she said as he awkwardly sat back down, mumbling something inaudible, 'or you can move on.'

Eight months later, in an election dominated by the same issues, he did move on. Permanently.

In 2021 BBC Two broadcast the latest in their illustrious line of political documentaries, a series called *Brown & Blair: The New Labour Revolution*. It's a serious piece of work, but watching Gordon Brown's interview, I just had to laugh. The unwritten rule of these retrospectives filmed after the political caravan has moved on, and with the benefit of cooler tempers and calming hindsight, is that the political interviewees offer a candid account of their time in politics.

That's not to say they don't remain self-serving. Those politicians who are best at them – hello again, Tony – manage to combine enough self-deprecation and honesty to come across as authentic and honest while choosing the right moments to lay blame subtly, take credit and burnish their reputation. Not Gordon Brown.

Just as he proved maladroit at political communication when in Downing Street, so he must have missed the meeting on how to handle interviews in the years after leaving office. Perhaps, like Blair, there are certain untruths which he simply has to hold onto. So, in a documentary that centred on the struggle for supremacy between the two men at the top of New Labour, Brown addressed the years of agitation, sulking and brooding like this:

> I was in politics not for what position I held but for what I could actually do, and I wasn't really obsessed with any particular title or anything else. I just wanted to get things done.[16]

Yeah, *right*.

It's easy to condemn and mock Brown. He was such an unhappy prince and came across as such a hopeless king at times, but he was also a serious man of substance and weight. While he was a creature of overbearing and obsessive ambition, he never gave the impression that he was in it for himself or his ego. He wanted to be chancellor, then prime minister, and those titles and the power that came with them did matter to him, but only because they would allow him to do the things he was in politics to do, not because he wanted them for their own sake.

There's also a question for the media about how it covers politicians: do we place too much emphasis on how politicians speak and the image they project rather than what they do? Brown suffered because he wasn't able to connect with voters on an emotional level. Others since have prospered because they can connect emotionally – using, for example, humour – but lack the substance of a figure like Brown. We have to decide which is more important.

Reflecting on Brown, Andrew Marr regards him as a 'great figure. He thinks big. He has an overarching view and a very strong moral purpose.' His problem was that he was really from a different age:

> In a sense, you have to remember he grew up with the old politics. He grew up with the politics of big conference halls and titanic debates and Neil Kinnock at his most operatic. That was his world. He was never a smooth politician of the television age. Tony Blair was completely relaxed in front of the camera. You could see his legs stretching out. He'd lean back. A smile would come to his face. He knew where the lenses were. He liked the lenses. They liked him. And Gordon was never, ever, ever like that. He didn't like being there. He didn't like the TV cameras pointing at him. He found the whole thing awkward, unsettling and generally a pain in the arse.[17]

The most moving moment in Brown's political career came in its final moments when, for the first and last time, Brown and his wife Sarah led their two young boys by the hand down Downing Street and into a car to take them away to start the rest of their lives. This was Brown as we'd never seen him before. He wasn't brooding or jealous or strange but a devoted father. It was a beautifully executed piece of political theatre featuring a leading actor who had previously tended to stumble onto the stage and knock the set over.

It was so compelling and so moving because it was the opposite of cynical. Brown treated his family as people, not as political props. Most politicians wouldn't have passed up the opportunity to use adorable children to humanise themselves in the public eye, but Brown wasn't prepared to, even though it might have helped project a warmer, less 'strange' public image.

In the end – for good or ill – Gordon couldn't and wouldn't fake it.

7

IF YOU BUILD IT, THEY WON'T COME

It's rare that the opening question of a political interview on BBC One – as distinct from one conducted by a police officer at the local constabulary – is 'What is your name, and why do you have so many aliases?' but that's essentially how Andrew Neil opens the *Sunday Politics* on 16 June 2013.

> Welcome to the *Sunday Politics*, Tommy Robinson. Or should I say Stephen Yaxley-Lennon, Paul Harris or Andrew McMaster? Why do you have so many names?[1]

What follows between Andrew Neil (born Paisley, 21 May 1949) and Stephen Yaxley, aka Tommy Robinson (born Luton, 27 November 1982) is a fight but hardly a fair one. Yaxley is the younger man and the one with convictions for violence, but there's only one winner today. Neil relies entirely on facts and controlled and justified rhetorical aggression to take down the leader of the English Defence League (EDL). The far-right organisation has been growing in prominence and menace on Britain's streets since the murder of British soldier Lee Rigby by Islamist terrorists the previous month, and we've decided that an interview with Yaxley – despite his thuggish history – is justified.

This won't be a typical political interview in other ways too. There's no real prospect that Yaxley will offer arguments that require examination. He will deny evidence that the EDL and its followers provoke division, give Nazi salutes and menace the Muslim community with threats – at the very least – of violence. We've spent days reviewing every interview and speech, and we know which way he will jump.

So this is an interview where the questions matter more than the answers, where video evidence of EDL demonstrations and Yaxley's own words build a case, providing viewers with the evidence they need to judge the intentions and methods of the group and the man himself.

Neil has established his real name, but he's not done with the subject.

> The confusion over your names had one advantage for you; it concealed for quite some time that you'd once been a member of the racist British National Party, didn't it?[2]

Yaxley can't deny he was once in the BNP, but tells Neil he was a naive and innocent boy from Luton who made mistakes but who'd moved on. And he had – to the leadership of the EDL.

Neil builds the case from here. He plays Yaxley a clip of a speech he made in 2011 in front of a baying mob. In the speech, Yaxley threatened 'every single Muslim' and 'the Islamic community' that they would 'feel the full force of the English Defence League if we see any of our citizens killed, maimed or hurt on British soil ever again'. Neil wants to know what 'the full force of the EDL' means. Yaxley plays the innocent, suggesting the EDL is just a pressure group lobbying the government for action, not making threats. That's what he means. That's the 'full force'.

Neil can't help but laugh.

> You didn't say you'd raise it with your MP ... 'Full force'
> is a threat of violence in any language.[3]

And so it goes on: Yaxley denies, Neil demonstrates the truth.

Watching from the control room, I offer Neil the occasional prompt in his earpiece (he doesn't need many). I can't deny I feel a little conflicted. Is it right to give Yaxley the status that comes with a slot like this? Well, he's making waves and influencing people, so it's justified to use an interview to show the true face of the EDL to viewers, including potential supporters who need to know the truth about the organisation and its leader. Ultimately, I do think that sunlight is the best disinfectant.

Yaxley was visibly nervous when he arrived for the programme. Stepping into the ring for more than sixteen minutes with the most well-researched and ferocious interviewer on British television must be nerve-wracking. The most I can say for Yaxley is that he showed up.

Not everyone in British politics did that, even those facing the prospect of a far less hostile interview.

By the end of 2009 I was tired. I had to get out of *Breakfast*. Much as I admired the hard-working and journalistically gifted team, I still hated the night shifts. Instead of getting used to them, they started to become faintly hallucinogenic and I'd float around in what felt like an anxiety dream made real. I'd be handling a difficult breaking news story, then wander off and fall asleep on the nearest sofa for a few minutes before coming to with a jolt and realising where I was and what I was doing. When the shift was over, I'd try to sleep through the day but find myself in a strange, restless half-sleep, acutely aware that I'd have to get up soon and do it all again.

As time went on I began to dread work – the feeling of cumulative tiredness had soaked into my bones. I had to get out, but I also needed work. My chance arrived when a job came up at *The Politics Show* at the end of 2009. This was the programme that replaced *On the Record* on BBC One in 2003. The show, given the catchy strapline 'From Downing Street to Your Street', had made very little impression during its six years on air. It was best known for its presenters – first Jeremy Vine, then Jon Sopel – who didn't wear ties, which was pretty radical for political TV. The pastel-coloured open-necked shirts were supposed to signal that this was a modern show, less stuffy than its predecessor and primarily focused on the bread-and-butter issues that matter more to a mythical 'you' than to Westminster politics.

The result was a show that didn't seem to know what it was and was embarrassed that it had to talk about boring old politics at all. The political interview remained at its heart, but it was rarely a particularly forensic one. Losing out on the big guests to Andrew Marr, *The Politics Show*'s USP was its films. These were often beautifully made but tried desperately to make political subjects sexy and exciting. The result was an awful lot of dad dancing, strained televisual devices and faux humour designed to make 'boring' subjects like local government finance interesting.

None of this stopped me from joining the team as an assistant editor as soon as the opportunity arose. I was brutally honest in my assessment of the show in my interview – or 'board', as everyone in the BBC called them – and Gavin Allen, the new editor, seemed to agree. At the BBC an assistant editor takes charge of a given edition of a programme and 'outputs' the show on the day. This means sitting next to the studio director in the control room and leading the editorial content, including giving the presenter guidance in his or her ear. Editors need assistant editors and deputy editors who share their vision. Gavin didn't have that until he hired me and Lizzi Watson – one of the best journalists I worked with at the BBC – at the end of 2009.

There's a lot of talk about 'BBC waste' from critics of the corporation in politics and the media. This narrative gives the impression that the BBC is bloated and is used to help make the case for cutting the licence fee. In my experience it's nonsense. In fact, over the thirteen years I spent working there, cuts to BBC funding became more and more severe, leaving BBC News with the bare minimum of staff by the time I moved on in 2021. *The Politics Show* turned out to be the exception to the rule; it was the only programme I worked on at the BBC that seemed to have more money than it needed. There was a large team of producers and reporters, a dedicated graphics operation and set of edit suites, all servicing a weekly show that lasted little more than an hour. It seemed to me, fresh from the *Breakfast* salt-mine, that *The Politics Show* really was your proverbial holiday camp.

Reporters and producers might deliver a film every few weeks (if you were lucky) and often spent a long time seemingly doing little or nothing. This would make more sense if the films they were producing were the sort of journalism that needed time; things like investigations that required lots of research, fact-checking and legal oversight, or access documentaries that took a long time to film. But the films were largely straightforward. Most of the effort went into crafting them to make them beautiful and coming up with wheezes to disguise the fact that they were about politics. The producers who made them saw themselves as directors, not journalists, and they really belonged on *Countryfile* or *Top Gear*, where gorgeous or exciting film-making suits the subject matter.

Pretty quickly my attitude to all this largesse – I didn't hide my feelings very well – put me on a collision course with the producers who'd ruled the roost on the programme for so long. I don't think the editor was entirely unhappy with my attitude. I didn't want conflict, but I could handle it if it came to that. I liked most of the staff as people a lot and didn't particularly want to be the baddie, but confrontation was unavoidable.

The show mainly hung together because of Jon Sopel, a gifted broadcaster with whom viewers wanted to spend time.

The interview preparation was never detailed or extensive with Jon because he was across the subject matter and used to delivering high-quality interviews on the fly. Nevertheless, there was no question that something had been lost: the BBC had effectively abandoned the long, deep-dive political interview when they'd axed *On the Record*. Twenty years later, people still remember the mad crocodile, but nobody remembers the open-necked shirts.

Fortunately for me, when the time came to put *The Politics Show* out of its misery, I was in pole position to shape and help lead a new political show to replace it. The idea was to emulate and modernise the tradition of Humphrys, Dimbleby and Walden. Who better to front it than the toughest political interviewer in the business: Andrew Neil.

Before he was an interviewer, Andrew Neil was a host. He was one of his generation's most talented and high-achieving journalists, becoming editor of *The Sunday Times* at 34. Neil came to the BBC in the mid-1990s as an established – and controversial – public figure already bigger than the political shows he fronted. These programmes, long-forgotten late-night political chat shows like *The Midnight Hour* and *Despatch Box*, were where Neil cut his television teeth.

Andrew Neil is not your typical BBC man. As the editor who'd taken on the print unions while at News International in the 1980s and then launched Rupert Murdoch's controversial Sky TV at the end of that decade, he was already a hate figure for the left before he arrived at the BBC. As I've said, there's a cultural challenge: most BBC staff, in my experience, tend to be on the centre-left of politics and lean towards liberal. I know, I'm one of them. Anyone who can disturb this cultural orthodoxy is a good thing, which is why Neil was so important to the BBC.

Back in the early 2000s the BBC, as part of that largely disastrous Dyke review, got something right: they created two new programmes as vehicles for Neil. *The Daily Politics* ran Monday to Friday lunchtimes on BBC Two, and the late-night political discussion show *This Week* aired after *Question Time* on BBC One on Thursday nights. These were the programmes where Neil emerged as a modern counterpart of greats like Walden and Day.

The Daily Politics was a solid but relatively traditional political show. It was built on a changing cast of guests, plus the occasional one-on-one interview. It started as an attempt – always doomed to failure – to find ways of making politics relevant to people who don't care about it, but when Robbie Gibb became editor of live political programmes in 2008, he scrapped that, and the show focused unapologetically on Westminster.

Neil flexed his intellectual muscle on the daily show alongside, variously, co-presenters Jenny Scott, Anita Anand and, most successfully, Jo Coburn. But the late-night *This Week* was the game-changer. The programme was built around Neil, seated alone, and his two co-hosts: former Tory cabinet minister Michael Portillo and left-wing Labour MP Diane Abbott, both perching opposite him on a tiny sofa. It's hard to overstate how different this felt in the early 2000s. Until then, politics and political programmes had kept within the narrow boundaries of the traditional rules of engagement. Political opponents weren't supposed to like each other – as Portillo and Abbott seemed to – and they certainly weren't supposed to cuddle up on an intimate micro-sofa.

However fully formed it seemed to arrive for viewers who became avid fans of the show, Neil himself looks back on a more uncertain start:

> The early editions were quite scratchy. That was partly my fault because I hadn't found my feet doing it yet. I mean, I basically approached it, to begin with, as a late-night *Daily Politics* in a hard-interview vein, which was

wrong. It just wasn't working, and it didn't get the vibe
of the show. It lacked humour. It was only as we went on
and we gained in confidence that we began to develop a
sense of humour and didn't take ourselves too seriously,
but it took us a long time to find our feet.[4]

After this rocky start, the show blossomed and something
special emerged. Here was a programme where political guests
were in new territory, as Neil recalls:

Not all of them got it. I used to tell them, 'It's not
Newsnight, have a bit of fun and please don't take
the party line because we've just had an hour of the
party line on Question Time.' Some got it, and some
didn't.[5]

But the mix of celebrities and other non-political guests invited
into the BBC's political space as equals created the real magic.
In this way, Neil and his producer Vicky Flind created something genuinely new: a television programme about politics that
reflected how people are. People can hold more than one idea
in their heads at the same time. They can be serious about the
day's political issues and break off for a joke; that's how they
talk in real life, and this was what was created on This Week. It
was an exceptionally clever thing to have decided to try and a
tricky thing to pull off.

Around this, a This Week sensibility emerged – silly, then
serious, funny, cheesy, welcoming – along with a set of in-jokes
that made viewers feel like they were part of an exclusive, if
slightly naff, club, one whose members quaffed Blue Nun – a
sweet German wine that was briefly cool in the 1970s – and
partied as if they were in London nightclub Annabel's during its
1980s heyday. Peak This Week arrived in 2005. The show's
general election campaign got under way with a remake of 70s
cheesy pop classic '(Is This the Way to) Amarillo' featuring Neil,

Portillo, a feather boa and a pantomime horse. We were not in Kansas anymore.

So far, so silly, but the show mattered because it was also where Neil established himself as an interviewer who could deliver electric television. He was well into his fifties by then, but Neil sees this period as his 'apprenticeship' as a political interviewer. And as for lying – and truth – this was not a programme where anyone with any sense would go in unprepared or try to pull the wool over the viewers' eyes. It was harder to offer up the usual bullshit here precisely because it was so warm, funny and real.

Despite his success in this most unconventional political show, Neil had taken on his apprenticeship with an eye on bigger prizes. For Neil's generation and my own, the lure of the Sunday political show is powerful. Neil is an aficionado of news and current affairs television, particularly from America. To adopt the sort of language of self-actualisation and psychobabble that he would thoroughly reject, I suspect that for him to truly live his truth, he would need to find himself behind the desk of a US TV behemoth like the *NBC Nightly News* or *Meet the Press*.

There's something about Neil that evokes Cronkite, Brinkley and Brokaw: the men – and they were almost always men – who dominated their desks and tables and panels in the second half of the American century. He is a host more than a presenter, an anchor more than a news reader. He is urbane, well connected, global in outlook and remains authentic, even as a boy from Paisley, a small town to the west of Glasgow, who seems to speak transatlantic.

All this fed into the decision to replace the tieless timidity of *The Politics Show* with a new Sunday show. In January 2012 I worked with Robbie Gibb and the exceptional programmes team – since abolished and subsumed into 'news' by the BBC – to launch a new lunchtime vehicle for Neil called the *Sunday Politics*. Our brief: to bring back and update the long-form political interview, offering time and deep analysis comparable to the halcyon days of *Weekend World* and *Walden*. For me this was a proud moment. All my romantic notions of political accountability and drama had brought me from 1989, in that Nottingham student hovel, to this. It was my chance to build something new, my *Field of Dreams* moment in political television.

If you build it, they will come.

So we did.

And, with the notable exception of Eric Pickles, whom we had to beat off with a shitty stick so keen was he to get on the telly, they did not.

Here's something people on Twitter don't seem to know: we cannot force politicians to come on to our programmes. There's no constitutional right or legal imperative that means we can summon whoever we want, whenever we want – or even at all.

The truth is that, over the sixty or so years since Robin Day sat down with Harold Macmillan and invented the modern political interview, politicians weigh up three competing and contradictory factors when they decide whether to agree to be interviewed: opportunity, risk and duty. Actually, let's make it four and include vanity too.

The opportunity is obvious: a television interview can take your message or explain your policy to millions of people watching live or later, and millions more when reported in bulletins, online and in the press. It can also produce short clips that travel on social media, which can be shared and repackaged. They may even go viral! The higher profile the interview – for example, a one-on-one interview during an election campaign – the greater the opportunity to get the message across and attract attention. The fact that a politician has the confidence to put themselves in front of a skilled interviewer can also work in their favour. Who that interviewer will be is part of the equation, but if you can prove your mettle with, say,

Andrew Neil, the opportunity for political reward may be all the greater. You may look cowardly if you opt for an interview on *This Morning* with Phillip Schofield and Holly Willoughby, but you'll also reach a valuable demographic. What an opportunity!

The risk is the other side of the opportunity coin. A television interview that goes wrong, where the interviewee is exposed as ill-prepared, deceptive or stupid, can reach millions of people watching live or later when reported in news bulletins, online and in the press. It can also produce short clips that work perfectly on social media, and that journalists and the politician's political enemies can share and repackage. Oh shit, it's gone viral! The interview that goes wrong is a bigger story than an interview that goes right. The higher profile the interview – for example, a one-on-one interview during an election campaign – the greater the risk all your messages and policies will be overwhelmed by this one moment. This risk is magnified if you go into a room with, say, Andrew Neil. The risk is reduced if you opt for an interview on *This Morning* with Phillip Schofield and Holly Willoughby, but if you screw that up, a whole new audience will see what a disaster you are. Risky business!

I don't know how you're feeling, but this all feels a bit risky to me. So to duty: this is the impulse, found in some politicians, to go onto the media to explain their actions and views, even if the environment is hostile. This impulse becomes much more important during an election or referendum campaign. Until the 2019 election, when Boris Johnson refused, unlike all the other party leaders, to be questioned by Andrew Neil, this sense of obligation when asking for votes, whatever the risks and whatever the rewards, held sway. A sense of duty still counts for something, but it's endangered once the convention has been broken. Proving the point, Liz Truss won the Tory leadership and became prime minister in 2022 by running away from tough interviews, including Andrew Neil.

Finally, to vanity: politicians are vain by nature. Not all of them, of course, but there are plenty of puffed-up blowhards on the front- and backbenches in all political parties. It would be strange if the vain weren't attracted to a job that pays you to express your opinions and gives you the power to vote on the country's future. And after years in the game, that vanity only increases. Like the more noble sense of duty, vanity in politicians is the broadcaster's friend. Add arrogance to the mix, and things are really humming. It's not just politicians either; it's true of celebrities wading into politics or princes trying to clear up a set of nasty allegations. Vanity and arrogance can lead you into a room with lights, cameras, and Andrew Neil or Emily Maitlis.

We designed the *Sunday Politics* to give us a fighting chance of attracting the most significant figures in British politics. We offered a long-form, forensic interview focused on policy and based on facts. This would eschew the cheap thrills of political gossip and Sunday newspaper stories in favour of proper analysis of the policy ideas enacted by the government or proposed by the opposition.

Jeopardy, in the shape of Andrew Neil, would remain. We couldn't eliminate the risk factor, nor did we want to. However, we had enhanced the opportunity for an able politician to explain policy seriously and in detail, and have the time to do it. With any luck, this would encourage those politicians who saw accountability and explanation as essential parts of their duty as elected officials to come on. As for vanity, the glossy set, considerable screen time, and the offer of hair and make-up – hello, Eric Pickles! – offered all the attention any politician could desire.

We wanted to create a modern version of a *Walden* interview, with graphics highlighting quotes, and evidence and clips offering deeper context. And Neil saw the potential:

No one has ever recreated the sweet spot that Brian
Walden was in that allowed him to do his job as well as
he did. Don't forget, *Weekend World* involved a half-
hour introductory film, so the viewer was informed of
the issues at stake and what the arguments were before
you then went to a half-hour interview. No broadcaster,
least of all the BBC, had recreated that sweet spot, and
that is the perfect sweet spot for an interviewer to be in.[6]

So, all was set. Neil was in his sweet spot, and the BBC was
behind us. They commissioned a smart promo video featuring
the presenter going about his daily business while dictating
tough political questions into his Dictaphone, closing with a
final shot of him tucked up in bed in black silk pyjamas on the
Saturday night before the Sunday morning. 'The questions are
ready,' said the voiceover, 'now it's time for the answers.'

So we launched, and from the start we struggled.

This was eighteen months into the coalition years, that now
distant period when Tory leader David Cameron and Liberal
Democrat Nick Clegg came together to form what turned out
to be a stable government. The dominant Cameron drove
through radical and controversial policies: austerity cuts to
reduce the deficit, an inexplicable and disastrous reorganisation of the NHS, and an approach to welfare that could be
seen as 'reform' or slash and burn, depending on your point of
view.

The Lib Dems, meanwhile, came over as bloodlessly mana-
gerial and opportunistic. In choosing to go into government
and provide stability (which many voters thought was a good
thing), they abandoned their principles in the eyes of much of
the electorate. In the 2010 general election campaign, Clegg –
like Ashdown before him – had played the traditional Lib Dem
card of somewhat sanctimonious, holier-than-thou posturing.
In a party election broadcast that resembled a pop video by,
let's say, James Blunt, good-looking Nick strode through the

streets, squares and hills of Britain surrounded by thousands of pieces of paper blowing like dry ice around his feet. These, it transpired, represented the 'trail of broken promises'.

The very first shot featured a broken Labour pledge: No Student Tuition Fees. From there, Nick dialled up the rhetoric. 'Say goodbye to broken promises,' he proclaimed, doing his sincere face for the camera. 'The trail of broken promises can come to an end, and a new road can begin. We can say goodbye to broken promises and welcome back to hope.' Yes, Nick was going big on broken promises.

The party made their own crystal-clear promise on student tuition fees: they would scrap them. Then, with the university vote in mind, they amplified that commitment, the leader and many of his candidates signing a pledge from the National Union of Students that promised they would never vote for an increase in tuition fees. Many of them, including Clegg, posed for photographs holding the pledge up for the camera. Lib Dems in government would abolish fees, and Lib Dems in parliament (assuming they weren't in government) would not support any increase. Comprehensive and clear.

Then they formed the coalition government with the Conservatives and, in a political environment where austerity economics meant big cuts in government spending, the Lib Dems' tuition fees pledge was quickly deemed unsustainable. Within six months, deputy prime minister Clegg had broken his promise and backed a tripling of fees in England from just over £3,000 to a maximum of £9,000. He had his arguments, of course, but they weren't the point. Clegg exemplified the politician who promises one thing and does another. His subsequent party political broadcast, two years later, also resembled a pop video; this time, Godley & Creme's classic 1985 video 'Cry', where a succession of distraught faces weep to the camera. The difference was that Nick was all alone, emoting down the barrel, saying, 'I'm sorry' in a not-sorry way. Nice video, shame about the song.

The episode was not good for truth – or trust – in politics and, along with Clegg's party's transformation from free-spending champions of public services to hard-nosed agents of austerity, thoroughly trashed the Lib Dem brand. They still haven't fully recovered.

In 2012 this should have been fertile ground for a new political show hoping to bring back the forensic interview. The coalition did help us in one way, because Lib Dem cabinet ministers, shocked and delighted by their new status, were more than willing to come onto the programme and explain themselves. Danny Alexander, chief secretary to the Treasury and number two to chancellor George Osborne, was certainly gettable. Facing Andrew Neil, the startled but happy-looking Alexander resembled nothing so much as a child who'd won a prize to come to London for the day and be on the telly. The Lib Dems were ultimately not very exciting, and low-wattage and low-calibre politicians did not make for electric television no matter how elevated their job titles.

As for the Conservatives, the going was tough. More obscure Tories like local government and communities secretary Eric Pickles loved the show. Look up 'gruff Yorkshireman' in the dictionary, and there's a picture of Pickles next to Sir Bernard Ingham. A boyhood communist, Pickles turned to the right after the Soviet Union and other Warsaw Pact countries invaded Czechoslovakia in 1968. He made his name as an enthusiastic budget cutter at Bradford Council in the late 1980s and, in more jovial form, was made for a place in Cameron's austerity cabinet. He was plain speaking yet undeniably plain boring too, but, along with others like Tory Party chairman Grant Shapps and assorted political minnows, he kept the *Sunday Politics* show on the road. Just. Thanks, Eric, and sorry for the gags.

The real frustration about the show's failure to secure the big names – as Robbie Gibb recalls, 'We would never get the prime minister or leader of the opposition' – was that the *Sunday Politics* was precisely the sort of programme politicians said they wanted. Gibb, a former (and future) Tory adviser, under-stood how politicians viewed the opportunity presented by an invitation onto a political interview show:

> All interviews need to work for the audience and for the programme, but they also need to work for the politician. The trouble with some programmes – *Channel 4 News* being the classic example – is that they don't care about whether it works for the politician. It's all about them being rude, and politicians don't want to do it.[7]

With this in mind, Gibb offered the cabinet minister in charge of welfare, Iain Duncan Smith, the lion's share of an episode to lay out his approach to welfare reform. Critics of Duncan Smith and the coalition hated it, but Gibb was willing to offer what critics always call a 'platform' for Duncan Smith to set out plans that would have a huge impact on people's lives, as Gibb recalls:

> In the interview we were able to go through all the issues that the government was trying to address and all the criticisms. Andrew did so calmly and forensically, with no histrionics and no attempt to try and embarrass or trip up the minister for the sake of it. It was an opportunity for the minister to set out what they were doing and time for us to cross-examine it properly.[8]

If this sounds worthy – and it was, but in a good way – there was also the inherent theatre of Andrew Neil in a room with a politician. This was enhanced by the use of a graphics wall the size of a house that allowed us to present evidence, quotes and polling that could create TV magic, as Neil recalls:

I do think we pioneered the forensic and fact-based interview with things up on the wall. One Tory minister said to me during a programme, 'Well, Andrew, polls go up and polls go down.' So we brought the piece of polling up and showed it to him. And I said, 'Well, hold on, let's just have a look at those polls. In which bit does it go up?' He couldn't tell me. The director then cut to his face as they looked at the graph, and you could see him thinking, 'What the fuck am I going to say about this?' It was good television.[9]

In the end, not enough top-rank politicians were willing to risk moments like this, however high-minded the programme's intentions. With the BBC offering an alternative, more convenient, less forensic experience with Andrew Marr earlier in the morning, the *Sunday Politics* was fighting a losing battle. Inevitably, Andrew Neil was left feeling increasingly dissatisfied.

We were handicapped by the inability to get the really top people, who preferred to sit on the Andrew Marr sofa. You can understand that; they're only human like the rest of us. They didn't come, so that's why I stopped doing it in the end. In a way, it was easier for me if I was regarded as an 'A division' interviewer and week after week I was presented with B and C division politicians. It was like shooting fish in a barrel. But that wasn't what I wanted to do. I wanted to be up against the A division politicians.[10]

Neil would stick it out for a full five years before moving on, and during that time the programme had to come up with imaginative solutions. Enter Stephen 'Tommy Robinson' Yaxley in the summer of 2013. The interview ended with Yaxley proudly setting himself apart from the politicians who usually sat in the seat next to Neil:

Neil: I would suggest you are not interested in democratic politics, just street thuggery.

Yaxley: I don't want to be another man putting a suit on sitting there lying and bound by political correctness.

Neil: It's the politics of the street that you're interested in, which is the hallmark of extremism, fascism and communism throughout the ages.[11]

Yaxley half-heartedly protested, and they were done.

A few weeks later, so was I. After eighteen months helping build and devise the *Sunday Politics*, it was time to move on. *Newsnight*, BBC Two's late-night current affairs programme, is the pinnacle of news programming for me and for many who grew up watching it. In 2013 it was still recovering from its worst ever crisis and had a new editor. Its main presenter, however, remained in place. Still the big draw for many viewers, not to mention producers like me, he embodied the brand.

Think *Newsnight*, think Paxman.

8

YOU GET FED UP
WITH THE BULLSHIT

Have you ever wondered what it's like to be asked a question by Jeremy Paxman?

Have you ever wondered how it feels when you haven't got an answer?

Unsurprisingly, as I found out a couple of months into my new job at *Newsnight*, it's very uncomfortable.

When Ian Katz, the *Newsnight* editor, called me one Tuesday in October 2013 to let me know I'd be producing a high-profile interview for the following night's show, I was excited. I'd been establishing myself on the programme and trying to carve a niche as the expert on political interviewing. This is right up my street, I thought. Could it be the prime minister, the leader of the opposition, perhaps even a foreign leader?

'Who is it?' I asked Ian excitedly.

'Well,' he said, 'it's a bit unusual, this one.'

'Oh, yes,' I replied, intrigued.

'It's Russell Brand.'

'Russell Brand,' I said. *Russell fucking Brand*, I thought. Then, unable to hide my dismay, I asked why.

An hour later, Jeremy Paxman asked me the same question. We are interviewing who? And exactly why are we doing that?

For a brief period, Russell Brand's star shone brightly. Originally a stand-up comedian and TV presenter, Brand became even more famous as a bad actor and a drug addict. He was probably most famous for his short marriage to the singer Katy Perry. Perry, who kissed a girl and liked it, divorced Brand, who kissed a lot of girls and liked it very much, two years into their showbiz marriage.

Then, in 2013, Brand took a leftward turn into politics. This interest in inequality and social justice coincided with the comedian's relationship with Jemima Goldsmith, who worked for the left-of-centre political magazine the *New Statesman*. Goldsmith invited Brand to guest edit the magazine and write a cover piece entitled 'On Revolution'.

The episode had a strong revolutionary cosplay vibe, with Brand sporting the metaphorical Che Guevara beret. Predictably, he hit some authentic notes of the sixties macho New Left with his slightly creepy comment that he'd only written the piece because a beautiful woman – Goldsmith – had asked him to. Presumably, if an ugly woman had suggested it, he wouldn't have bothered. The entire enterprise felt deeply superficial.

Katz, however, wanted a piece of it. Ian had previously been deputy editor of the *Guardian* and had no TV experience. He'd taken over shortly after *Newsnight*'s darkest hour. In 2011 the programme had ditched an investigation into the recently deceased BBC TV star and DJ, sex offender Jimmy Savile. Savile's sexual abuse of both children and adults had long been rumoured, but after his death *Newsnight* journalist Meirion Jones and reporter Liz MacKean (who sadly died in 2017) had begun to uncover his abuse, and it was deeply embarrassing to the BBC, where he'd operated for decades. Then, just a week before the film was scheduled for transmission, the editor, Peter Rippon, dropped the story.

ITV picked it up the following year and broke it to enormous acclaim, with *Newsnight* and the BBC left looking incompetent at best, complicit in a cover-up at worst. Rippon stepped down as editor, pending a review into the affair. The review concluded that he'd acted in good faith – there was no cover-up. It also said that the decision to drop the film was flawed and that it should have been broadcast.

If that wasn't bad enough, *Newsnight* then wildly overcompensated for burying a story about a prolific sexual abuser by putting another one on air that wasn't true. This piece made an accusation of child sexual abuse against an unnamed man with links to the top of the Tory party in a way that easily identified him as Lord Robert McAlpine, a former party treasurer. After McAlpine denied the allegation, *Newsnight* returned to the complainant with a photograph of him. The accuser told them that the man in the photograph was not the abuser.

This trashed the programme's reputation, and the newly appointed director-general of the BBC, George Entwistle, himself a former *Newsnight* editor, went onto Radio 4's *Today* to defend the programme. Despite his professional experience of plotting interviews as a journalist, Entwistle was eviscerated by John Humphrys and his reign as director-general soon ended after just fifty-five days.

This was the mess inherited by Ian Katz in the summer of 2013. I was one of his first hires, joining the show as an assistant editor. His vision for the show was never quite articulated, but he wasn't in the business of being boring. When the opportunity to interview Brand about revolution arose, Katz was keen, but he wasn't the one who had to sell it to Paxman. That was my job.

Like a crap contestant on *University Challenge*, I didn't have the answers. Paxman interrogated me about why we were committing his valuable time and the BBC's resources to a vanity interview for a dilettante dipping his showbiz toe in politics. I couldn't convincingly tell him why.

'He's written a piece in the *New Statesman*,' I tried.

'So what?' shot back Paxman.

'Young people like him,' I said, without evidence.

'Do they?' he countered.

Eventually, he stopped arguing. He'd do it under duress, but he still had no idea why. Despite his reservations, the revolution, it seemed, would be televised.

The only question remaining was where it would take place. Perhaps Brand would choose the *New Statesman*'s offices, a working men's club in his home county of Essex or somewhere else that signalled solidarity with the working class? No chance. Instead, Paxman and I walked a few metres across the road from the BBC to the Langham, one of the most exclusive and expensive hotels in central London, where, in room 905, our revolutionary awaited us.

As I boarded the lift with a still fuming Paxman, one of the titans of political interviewing, I wondered how it had come to this. I got the impression he was thinking the same thing.

And now, a coincidence: on Sunday 29 October 1989 – the day Margaret Thatcher's interview with Brian Walden was broadcast on ITV, the day I sat down on my student sofa and watched the prime minister, finally, unravel – on that day, a few hours later on Channel 4's *The Media Show*, Jeremy Paxman said something that has framed the debate about political interviews ever since. So much so that the words he used give this book its title.

The Media Show featured a film about the crisis in political interviewing that had clearly been made some weeks earlier. There was no reference to the Lawson resignation, and it couldn't reflect that day's *Walden* interview, which rendered it hopelessly out of date. If anyone thought the political interview was dead or in crisis before Walden/Thatcher aired, they could hardly think so afterwards.

The film featured interviews with prominent political journalists, including Jonathan Dimbleby (still at the BBC at the time). But the star was thirty-nine-year-old Jeremy Paxman, who'd just started as a presenter on *Newsnight*. Paxman, speaking softly, in a white open-necked shirt and chinos, cut a dashing and youthful figure, languid on a Liberty Ianthe-print sofa that screamed late eighties. He's immediately magnetising, dark and handsome, a presence. He looks like a man who has something to say.

This is a more idealistic Paxman than the jaded, cynical public persona he's now associated with. He says his job is to hold the powerful to account on behalf of those who are 'governed, or poor, or impotent'. He describes the pre-interview 'bullying, blackmail' and 'threats' delivered by politicians – 'If you ask me that question, you'll regret it' – which the interviewer must ignore. As the film goes on, there's more and more Paxman. As it closes, the focus is on political lying and he gets the last word. He starts talking about the advice given to Louis Heren, former deputy editor of *The Times*, when he was a young reporter. Paxman hesitates. 'How best to say this?' he seems to be thinking before launching into his answer:

> He was told that you should always ask yourself when talking to any politician; you should always have the question nagging away at the back of your mind, 'Why is this lying bastard lying to me?' And I think that's quite a sound principle from which to operate.[1]

As Paxman delivers the 'lying bastard' quote – perhaps still a little risqué on television in 1989 – a smile dances across his face, and by the time he reaches the words 'sound principle', he's laughing. He looks pleased with himself. He's labelled the political class as lying bastards, but he's done so in a roundabout way by quoting somebody else. Naughty Jeremy, sailing close to the wind. But he's probably got away with it, right?

No chance. The quote stuck to him – sometimes to his annoyance, sometimes to his amusement – for the rest of his interviewing life.

There was a time, in the decades that followed, when I'd switch on *Newsnight* on BBC Two at 10.30 p.m., not for the news or the analysis, but for the presenter. If Paxman wasn't in the chair, I'd usually turn it off. This was unfair on impressive presenters like Kirsty Wark and Gavin Esler, but it was true. And I don't think I was the only one.

He was so compelling because he was dangerous. Like Sir Robin Day – and I think Paxman has been the most influential political interviewer since Day – he brought jeopardy into the studio. Like Day, Paxman saw himself as a representative of the people, putting their questions to the powerful. Unlike Day, Paxman had never wanted to be a politician himself. The older man had yearned for a career in parliament, and revered the place and its traditions. Paxman, more than twenty-five years younger than Day and a child of the 1960s and 70s, did not.

Andrew Neil detected something close to hostility from Paxman towards the political class.

> Jeremy had disdain for politicians. He doesn't really like them. He doesn't spend any time with them. It's beneath him to mix with them.[2]

I put Neil's comment to Paxman, who suggested he was only half-right.

> I don't have them as friends, but I don't have disdain for them. I have lots and lots of different groups of friends. But I don't have politicians as a group. It was a choice.[3]

But to many viewers, he certainly seemed to hold those he interviewed in delicious disdain. He looked down his nose at Tories and Labour alike, dangling them in front of the viewers like specimens to be toyed with. His apparent contempt manifested itself in looks – haughtily arched eyebrows, rolled eyes, the famous 'sneer' – and noises – the long, strangulated 'Yessssss', the exasperated sigh. The questions were repeated or freighted with disappointment and disbelief at the state of the interviewee and their hopeless position.

No wonder Paxman became a cult hero. Here was a man who gave no concessions to bullshit. What's more, in the early days it felt like *Newsnight* was able to summon the biggest names in politics to come before him. As with much else, when New Labour arrived things changed; big names became harder to come by as politicians asked themselves why they should endure his withering inquisitions. By then his reputation and caricature were well established, cemented by ITV's satirical puppet show *Spitting Image*.

Paxman's tactics put him in the firing line from politicians, commentators and his actual boss in the shape of BBC director-general John Birt. Birt, who'd founded *Weekend World* and helped David Frost interview Richard Nixon in the 1970s, is a behind-the-scenes figure in the history of the British political interview of enormous importance. Paxman and Birt could not have been more different; Birt stood for sober analysis and dry explanation, Paxman delivered television theatre and was allergic to being boring.

Birt spent the early 1970s on *Weekend World* developing the 'mission to explain'. At the heart of it was his view that television is inherently superficial: more about pictures than information, heat rather than light. The result is what he called television's 'bias against understanding', which must be counteracted by information and context. When Birt arrived at the BBC in 1987, he brought the 'mission to explain' with him. Whatever the idea's merits – and there were some – it put him on a collision course with journalists like Paxman. To him, the arrival of Birt with management consultants in tow was like 'an invasion by the Moonies'.[4]

In 1995 the tension between the man who led the BBC and the corporation's star interviewer finally surfaced. Birt made a speech in Dublin that included a pointed sideswipe at big-shot journalists who saw themselves as more important than the politicians they covered. Birt reminded his audience they were not.

> Some journalists sometimes forget that. Reporters who pretend that the answers and remedies are obvious, that everyone but themselves in the world is an incompetent fool; overbearing interviewers who sneer disdainfully at their interviewees ... all exhibit attitudes which are unattractive in a journalist and rarely appropriate.[5]

I asked Birt, now in the House of Lords, which 'overbearing interviewers who sneer disdainfully' he had in mind, but he wouldn't tell me. Paxman, on the other hand, is in no doubt

> It appeared in the *Observer*, and I was told by someone who worked at the *Observer* that he [Birt] had, in terms, been specific about who it was referring to. He named me for guidance to the man from the *Observer*.[6]

Whatever Paxman heard from the man at the *Observer*, when I checked Paxman's story with Birt, the former director-general was adamant someone had got the wrong end of the stick:

> It's absolutely not true. As should be clear from any study of the period, I never indulged in off-the-record briefings. Just not my style, then or now![7]

I'm not going to contradict Lord Birt on that, but it seems likely that when he talked about interviewers who 'sneer disdainfully' he had Paxman in mind, even if he never told anyone so. At this point Birt had been running the BBC for three years and would last another five. He had the power to take Paxman down a peg or two, shuffle him from *Newsnight*, move him on if he really wanted to, but he didn't. Paxman was a star, loved by his audience because he didn't let politicians get away with not answering his questions. By 1995 Paxman was too big to be taken out; two years later came his apotheosis.

Twelve questions without answers, by Jeremy Paxman, May 1997

Did you threaten to overrule him?

Did you threaten to overrule him?

Did you threaten to overrule him?

Did you *threaten* to overrule him?

Did you threaten to overrule him, Mr Howard?

Did you *threaten* to overrule him?

Did you threaten to overrule him?

Did you threaten to overrule him?

I note you're not answering the question whether you *threatened* to overrule him.

I'm sorry, I'm going to be frightfully rude, but I'm sorry, it's a straight yes or no answer:

Did
You
Threaten
to
Overrule
Him?

With respect, that is not answering the question of
whether you threatened to overrule him.

With respect, you haven't answered the question of
whether you threatened to overrule him.

There are political interviews before 13 May 1997 and there
are political interviews after 13 May 1997. Jeremy Paxman's
encounter with former Tory home secretary Michael Howard
changed everything. It doesn't matter too much now what the
interview was about, just what it signalled and where it led.
However, if it helps, all you need to know is this: as home
secretary Michael Howard was entitled to express his opinion
to the head of the Prison Service about whether any particular
prison governor should keep their job, but he was not entitled
to insist. However, the man running the Prison Service at the
time had accused Howard of threatening to overrule him,
which would have been going beyond his formal powers.
Paxman simply wanted Howard to tell him whether or not
that was true.

That's what the interview was concerned with, but it was
really about a politician not answering a question. Not the first,
not the last, but probably the best. Politicians and their advisers
sometimes argue that what the public hates most are interviewers who interrupt too much, preventing them from hearing the
answers. There's no way of measuring who's right, but I disagree. Interruptions may annoy, but politicians who don't answer
the question annoy the most.

The politician's strategy of addressing the question they want
to answer, rather than the one they are asked, was already
long-established. That night Michael Howard adopted a varia-
tion on that strategy, but a flawed one; faced with a question
about whether he had done one thing, he repeatedly fell back
on a form of words concerning something else, something
related, certainly, but something else nonetheless.

This is a ritual the viewer has seen a million times and for reasons of time or politeness or fear of boring the ence it always ends the same way: the interviewer gives up moves on. Not this time. The first eight questions Paxman asks are virtually the same: 'Did you threaten to overrule him?' Sometimes he asks in a purposefully flat voice emphasising the repetition. Sometimes he stresses the word 'threatened' because it's the point of the question, once he adds 'Mr Howard' politely at the end. The last four questions vary, as Paxman laughs at the absurdity of the repetition and adds 'with respect' (twice).

Paxman decided that night to break the unwritten, unspoken rule that you don't do this to politicians. The relationship between the two opposing sides rests on rules of engagement that must be respected. If a politician does not want to answer a question, the interviewer may push back, point it out, rephrase and try again, but they shouldn't make the interviewee look silly. But Paxman won't play the game this time, and his persistence and repetition transform the interview into political theatre. Later, Paxman recalled asking Howard as he got up to leave whether he was 'Happy enough?'

'What do you think?' asked Howard, perhaps more aware than Paxman that the interview was likely to get him on the front pages, and not in a good way. Later Paxman noted innocently, 'The incident dashed Michael Howard's hopes of winning the party leadership in 1997.'[8]

Paxman has always been ambivalent and a little 'embarrassed' about the furore created by the 'incident'. At first he suggested that he'd repeated the same question so many times because the next item had fallen through at the last minute, and he had no other questions to ask. Later he stated that Howard's evasions indicated he was on to something worth pursuing until, twelve questions later: 'I gave up, judging that it would now be clear to anyone watching that Howard had ducked the question.'[9]

When I asked Paxman about it he was more blunt.

'You just get fed up with it,' he said when I asked him about the Michael Howard interview. 'You get fed up with the bullshit.'

'And that was the point you'd reached on that day?' I asked. 'Yes,' he answered.[10]

A weary Paxman has said that he expects the first line of his obituary to refer to this 'notorious' interview, and it probably will. For a generation of television journalists who want to interview the powerful, Paxman set an example: be tenacious, persistent and unrelenting, call out politicians for evasions, deceptions and lies, even at the risk of being rude.

Today, 'moments' like the Paxman/Howard interview are of even greater value because success is measured by clips shared on social media. Twitter clips must usually come in at under two minutes and twenty seconds. Paxman's twelve questions, and Howard's non-answers, took one minute and forty-three seconds to complete. There was no social media or iPlayer in 1997. You'd either seen the interview live or you hadn't, yet it became a sensation based on newspaper reporting and word of mouth. Today it would be everywhere.

Andrew Neil inherited Paxman's status as the toughest interviewer on television in the 2010s. While Neil has never asked a question twelve times – he has a limit of three, after which he thinks the evasion is surely clear to viewers – he shares Paxman's gift for theatre and a determination to call untruthful politicians out. Imitation is the sincerest form of flattery, but Neil acknowledges it has created a problem.

Part of the problem now – and part of a problem I helped to create – is that all interviewers now are trying to be Paxman or trying to be me, but not every interview has to approach it with a 'When did you stop beating your spouse?' sort of attitude.[11]

Many politicians hated Paxman. My old adversary Paddy Ashdown complained about Paxman in his diary, calling him 'indescribably rude'.[12] Peter Mandelson wrote, 'I would come to see him as a bully' and David Cameron, the Tory prime minister, was openly hostile:

> As an interviewer, I thought that most of the time, he was a self-indulgent monster. He wasn't trying to get answers or inform viewers, he was just trying to make his victim look like a crook while he looked like a hero ... I could see absolutely no point in doing an interview with Paxman: it would never be an attempt to examine policies or priorities, just an opportunity for him to show off and try to take me down at the same time.[13]

Paxman calls Cameron's broadside 'rubbish'.[14]

In 2007 Paxman made a speech to the Edinburgh International Television Festival, the August Bank Holiday weekend get-together for UK television's boss class. In it, he took a moment to clarify something:

> I do not, incidentally – and I am heartily sick of this quote being attributed to me – think they're all lying bastards. I never said it. And they're not. Although I do think we should always be very sceptical.[15]

He was heartily sick of it, but when I asked him about it, while he reiterated that they were words he'd quoted rather than originated, he added pointedly, 'I do not resile from them.'[16]

As time passed, the big beasts of politics began voting with their feet, walking away from *Newsnight* and Paxman altogether. All that was left for the old lion by then was the odd innocent gazelle who'd come loose from the pack in the form of a junior minister asked to defend the indefensible.

The most celebrated of these was Chloe Smith, a junior Treasury minister who came on to *Newsnight* in June 2012 to explain a government U-turn on the level of fuel duty. It's become one of Paxman's most famous interviews, cited alongside Michael Howard and Russell Brand as among his greatest hits.

Ten years on, I'm not so sure. It's an unfair fight: Smith is a timid interviewee, and Paxman dominates throughout. He seems preoccupied with whether she influenced the policy change and, knowing she didn't, repeatedly asks when exactly she'd been told about it. This made for good sport but was hardly damning. It just reminded viewers that *Newsnight* didn't have the chancellor. There's also no doubt that Paxman is rude to Smith: 'Is this supposed to be a joke?' and 'Do you ever think that you are incompetent?' are pretty brutal.

Paxman has admitted that the interview was 'unkind' but says 'it would be dishonest to deny an element of pleasure, too … at the realisation that you've been involved in a terrific piece of theatre'. Never underestimate how important that was for Paxman, a man who understood that television thrives on spectacle, however much that might upset John Birt.

But to my eyes, this was more of a late-period exhibition match than a first-class Paxman. The truth is – by the time of the Smith interview – he was contemplating moving on. Only the Savile crisis that engulfed *Newsnight* a few months later kept him on board and set the stage for the encounter at the Langham with Brand.

When I had a bad case of imposter syndrome on my first day sitting in an office talking to Jeremy Paxman, I wish I'd known that he had imposter syndrome himself – he felt it when interviewing prime ministers or foreign secretaries. That's the problem with imposter syndrome. People are so good at hiding it that nobody realises everyone else is in the same boat.

Paxman was decidedly intimidating in person. The mannerisms so familiar on screen were fully present in real life. If you had an idea he didn't like, he would swat it – and you – away like Chloe Smith. The Paxman 'persona' was his authentic self. I remember feeling sure that he didn't like or rate me in the first few weeks. This was imposter syndrome again, but others told me not to worry: He was like this to everyone for the first month, at which point he decided whether you were OK and, if you passed, would ease off. Luckily for me, that moment eventually arrived, and I was in.

Joining *Newsnight* was daunting but exciting. The crisis that had engulfed the programme the previous autumn had left the team demoralised and worried about the long-term future. Ian Katz's arrival with a new management team was a new beginning. Katz was a brilliant journalist. He also had real panache and ambition, and was loyal to his team. He was the sort of editor who could infuriate but was also someone you wanted to work for and please.

Katz saw *Newsnight* as a place for high-quality journalism, discussion and interviews, but he also wanted to bring some light and shade to the programme by adding humour and spectacle. This was fine in theory but led to some moments that, in retrospect, feel a little off to me. They usually appeared at the end of the programme – known as the playout – and would run as the credits rolled.

I had the dubious honour of editing *Newsnight* on the night we carried an interview with the Cookie Monster from *Sesame Street*. There had been a story that the character was coming to BBC Children's programmes, so Ian thought it would be fun for Emily Maitlis to interview him. So that's what we did.

'So why Britain, why the BBC?' she asked.

His answer, delivered down the line onto the big screen, surprised no one:

Cookie! Om Nom Nom Nom.[17]

This was just a bit of a laugh, but the image of Emily Maitlis interviewing the Cookie Monster on set, grabbed out of context, clipped and shared on social media, made people think *Newsnight* had become gimmicky and silly. Maitlis herself is unrepentant about her encounter with the blue furry thing:

> I loved the Cookie Monster. Loved it then and love it now. It was the first time my kids' headmaster ever understood or saw what I did, I think. It helped us reach new audiences, which is something I'd never be sniffy about.[18]

The Cookie Monster episode was followed by Kirsty Wark's extraordinary Halloween playout – which involved a recreation of Michael Jackson's 'Thriller' video, complete with Wark doing the zombie dance across the studio floor. It was brilliantly done, and I thought it was great at the time, but, looking back, it does seem a little odd.

Jeremy Paxman recalls feeling 'detached' from it all. He'd seen this sort of thing before:

> You have to get used to these damn fool editors coming along with one crackpot idea after another that they all want to try out. It's a great toyshop that they all want to play in. [But] I didn't think it worked, really. I thought it was jejune, really.[19]

I had to look 'jejune' up; turns out it means either juvenile and puerile or just plain dull. Perhaps Jeremy meant both. Either way, his views on the most famous moment, our Cookie Monster playout, were not difficult to decode.

'Oh,' he told me, 'it was awful. Awful, awful, awful.'[20]

I think that's a bit harsh – I loved Katz's editorial chutzpah – but I understand where Paxman's coming from.

Katz made some unhelpful headlines himself when, after an appearance by Labour shadow cabinet minister Rachel Reeves, he tweeted that he'd found the then shadow chief secretary to the Treasury 'boring snoring'. I saw his tweet as my train pulled out from Victoria station on the way home to Brighton. Could this be him creating an ill-advised buzz around the programme, or, more likely, was it a cock-up?

'That Reeves tweet you did was a bit candid,' I texted.

A minute later my phone rang. It was Katz sounding a little panicky. Had he really tweeted that? He'd meant to send it in a direct message to a friend. Maybe it wasn't too late to take it down, and hope nobody had clocked it. By the time he'd hung up, Reeves had responded with a sarcastic 'Thanks'. The tweet had been noticed – he'd have to take it down, apologise and take a punishment beating. He later recalled this as a moment of 'bowel-loosening mortification', and I felt very sorry for him, but as I texted later: 'It's not exactly McAlpine.'

While *Newsnight* re-invented itself, Paxman seemed increasingly semi-detached. It said something about his state of mind that he'd returned from the summer break in 2013 still sporting his holiday beard. Such was his celebrity that the newspapers found the presence of hair on the Paxman chin fascinating. That was ridiculous, but it did suggest that he was still on the beach.

He'd stayed on at *Newsnight* longer than he'd planned because he didn't want to abandon the programme and staff after the Savile scandal. For their sake, he remained in place while the Katz era bedded in.

Then, in October, reluctantly, Jeremy met Russell. What followed became one of the most high-profile – and certainly most-watched – interviews of Paxman's illustrious career.

That hotel room was full of charisma. It's an elusive, highly valued quality because it's less common than you might think. It's sometimes found in unexpected places – Sir John Major is exceptionally charismatic in person, less so on TV – but I've encountered quite a few presenters and politicians who just don't have it. On the other hand, Jeremy Paxman and Russell Brand did, in person and on screen. It's a great starting point for any interview because, as a viewer, you want to spend time with these people, even if you don't like them or what they say.

The reason they were sitting in that hotel suite and I was leaning against the wall while Jemima Goldsmith and my fellow producer Natasha Mardikar, who'd fixed the interview, perched on the bed, was Brand's piece in the *New Statesman*. I'd sent it to Paxman and identified some areas we might go into that highlighted the celebrity's inconsistencies and weaknesses. He might have skim-read the article and my list of questions, but he didn't follow any plan (which was unusual for him). He was, in his elegant way, winging it. Perhaps that's why, overall, Brand won the day.

Paxman played into the comedian's hands. He went into the room with one thought: you're an actor with no real authority or track record who doesn't even vote, and you claim to have the answers to the world's political problems.

Brand was more than OK with this. It allowed him to say that he was merely raising issues he felt strongly about that actual politicians were failing to address. The central charge – that Brand was illegitimate because he didn't vote – was effectively swatted away. He didn't vote because he didn't think there was any point when the political parties didn't offer solutions to the environmental crisis, inequality and the exploitation of the poor.

When Paxman came back with variations on the same question, Brand was impressive. He pushed back with growing confidence. He was at his weakest when he tried to be funny – one gag about Paxman's beard was particularly clunky – ironic given his actual job was being a comedian. Paxman responded by accusing Brand of being trivial and facetious. This seemed to get the Brand goat somewhat, and he later admitted that this particular Paxman charge had stung him.

At his worst, Brand projected very strong sixth-form Marxist vibes that day. It was 'pre-existing paradigm' this and 'massive economic disparity' that, lots of 'hierarchical systems' and 'prescriptive parameters'. None of this would butter any parsnips, and it didn't get much better when Brand called for revolution and Paxman, channelling John Lennon, asked to see the plans.

Brand didn't have specifics. 'Cor blimey, Mr Paxman!' went the shtick. 'I'm here to raise awareness, not provide details.'[21] He got away with this because Paxman didn't push enough, which frustrated me. He did ask whether Brand's desire to tax corporations would require some sort of government to levy the taxes. Good question. Brand had a think and said, yes, some sort of government, which he said would be something like a 'centralised administrative system' run by 'admin bods'.

While it was understandable that Brand would be sketchy on these details, Paxman might have been a bit sharper here. He could have pointed out that Brand's 'socialist egalitarian system based on the massive redistribution of wealth' might, in practice, resemble the sort of political experiments parts of the world had tried with pretty disastrous results in the relatively recent past.

Overall, Brand had his lines worked out and provided a message that would appeal to a younger audience, who would come to the interview via social media and YouTube. The impact of Brand's intervention was extraordinary. The number of YouTube views rapidly stretched into millions, reaching 12.8m today. Brand's unapologetic revolutionary fervour contrasted with a Labour Party led by Ed Miliband that seemed scared of its shadow. For a generation who'd lived through the near collapse of the global economic system, the bailout of the banks and the MPs' expenses scandal, Brand's pitch made perfect sense.

It didn't harm his chances that his audience was finding it so hard to make its way in an increasingly dysfunctional property-owning democracy. For them, property-owning was a pipe dream, and democracy seemed to have failed. How significant this constituency was and how influential it was on the broader left was cloaked at this point, but Brand was the canary in the Corbynite coal mine. Within two years of the Paxman/Brand interview airing, Jeremy Corbyn was Labour leader.

As the interview progressed, Paxman seemed to warm to Brand, agreeing that the issues he highlighted were not being addressed by mainstream politicians but excusing them because the scale of these problems was so overwhelming for most politicians. This created an odd moment. Paxman sounded like a man who wanted Brand to vote, engage with the political establishment and make allowances for their failings. Somehow, Paxman had become a defender of the political class he was widely seen to despise – 'That's a fair enough criticism,' he says now. Brand then had his best moment:

> Jeremy, you've spent your whole career berating and haranguing politicians, and when someone like me says they're all worthless, and what's the point in engaging with them, you have a go at me ... Aren't you bored? Aren't you more bored than anyone? Ain't you been talking to them year after year, listening to their lies, their nonsense?[22]

The lying bastards, he might have added.

The success of Paxman/Brand vindicated Katz's judgement, however sceptical Paxman and I had been. His big takeaway from its success was that viewers wanted these encounters: real conversations where the interviewee actually said something and meant it. Brand was the anti-Rachel Reeves circa 2013: not boring, no snoring.

But Katz also knew that Brand was the exception rather than the rule. He could preach revolution, offer no specifics and get away with it. Brand had nothing to lose. He was even seen as a serious and significant player for a while. By the 2015 election Labour leader Ed Miliband was making time to pay a high-profile visit to the comedian's home and win his endorsement. Brand shifted his famous 'no-voting' stance, and the *Guardian*'s Owen Jones proclaimed, 'The Tories should be worried.' That, as Tony Blair said about the intelligence assessments that took us to war in Iraq, turned out to be wrong.

As for Paxman, the Brand interview came just six months before he announced his departure from *Newsnight*. His decision triggered another period of agonising about the political interview and whether it had finally expired. Believing it had, Katz had been ruminating on how to revive it and reset *Newsnight*'s approach. The big question was who should replace Paxman as the main anchor on the show and do it differently.

To many on the programme, the answer seemed obvious: Emily Maitlis. Maitlis, who'd arrived from BBC London in 2006, had established herself as the best interviewer on the programme, particularly as Paxman's energy levels and commitment started to dwindle. I'd classify Maitlis as the most satisfying presenter to work with because you could always see your work on screen. She was like a thoroughbred footballer of the highest quality who could scale even greater heights if coached attentively. She was obviously the woman for the job.

But Katz had other ideas. In an attempt to break away from the tired old format of the political interview – aggressive questions, defensive answers, nobody any the wiser – Katz wanted to bring in a presenter who was the anti-Paxman. His choice was Evan Davis, a mild-mannered presenter of Radio 4's *Today* programme and star of *Dragons' Den*. Evan had a pleasing manner but was an introverted character. But still, Katz's attempt to rescue the political interview was worth a try. Maybe Davis could remake the political interview in his own image: brainy, illuminating, reasonable and constructive.

To cement this idea, Katz wrote an essay in the *Financial Times* on 'The death of the political interview'.[23] Katz argued for an 'updated contract' between interviewer and interviewee, acknowledging that both sides needed to get something from the exercise. This would enable a more nuanced approach that would illuminate the processes and imperfections of policy making. In this way politicians could be more honest, and journalists more proportionate and understanding. It would also allow viewers to learn more about how decisions are made and about those who make them. Finally, Katz said, broadcasters needed to offer these interviews time to breathe so that an honest conversation might occur free of aggression and defensiveness, 'even if that means more boring, snoring bits'.

Shortly after Katz's piece, Davis arrived. While I was definitely a Maitlis man, I was excited to work with him. My greatest pleasure was working with presenters on interviews; a new presenter was a challenge and an opportunity. I'd worked closely with talents like Jonathan Dimbleby, Andrew Neil, Maitlis, Jeremy Paxman and Kirsty Wark. These presenters wanted the best outcome on screen because it improved the programme and made them look good. They understood that television is about collaboration and that experienced colleagues are worth listening to. However, it became apparent pretty quickly that Evan wasn't very interested in my input.

The content of Evan's interviews came from his head, not from briefing or conversations with staff or at least not with me. He had the air of an academic, as befitted a graduate of Oxford and Harvard. But then there's book clever, and there's TV clever. Pretty quickly, it seemed clear to me that his style was sucking the life out of the encounters that made *Newsnight* special. There was a way to retain the drama and dynamics of television while honouring a new push for seriousness and civility, but it had to be discussed, teased out and produced. Instead, Evan did everything his way as if he were some sort of editor-in-chief. My views – by this time I was deputy editor – seemed irrelevant to him. It was pretty demoralising.

I tried to make allowances: perhaps I needed to prove myself to him so that he'd listen to what I had to say and realise that I knew something about this interviewing business. My chance arrived in October 2014 when, you've guessed it, revolutionary dandy Russell Brand danced into view again. He had a book out called (of course) *Revolution*. Where better than *Newsnight* to give a landmark interview to launch the new tome? How better for Evan to prove his worth than an interview echoing one of Paxman's most famous encounters?

The pressure was on. Evan's first few weeks had been underwhelming. Katz's 'updated contract' between interviewer and interviewee was all very well, but there were two problems: first, it produced quite boring, snoring TV, and second, it wasn't clear that both sides – broadcaster and politician – had actually signed on the dotted line. It was unilateral disarmament not a non-aggression pact. The reviews weren't good.

So Brand offered an opportunity. Paxman's interview had reached millions and launched a debate about voting, revolution and beards. Surely a tussle between Evan's undoubted intellect and Brand's lithe, if superficial, mind would be fascinating. Surely Evan would emerge triumphant, teasing out the contradictions and flaws in Brand's pound-shop *Das Kapital*.

When the day of the interview came I was the most senior member of the editorial team in the office. When Evan arrived, I presented him with an interview brief from one of the team and a copy of Brand's book. In his usual way he worked alone on the interview, typing away at his computer. Occasionally I'd try to interest him in a discussion, but he said he was fine. We could talk later. It became obvious he didn't want to discuss the plan. So, determined to contribute somehow, whether he wanted me to or not, I went back to basics. Channelling the TV researcher I'd once been, I decided to read Brand's book from cover to cover in search of a nugget that would lift the interview. If I found something, I reckoned, Evan might realise it was worthwhile paying attention.

It was 384 pages and a slog of a read, but I persevered. Eventually, towards the end, I hit the jackpot. In a chapter focusing on foreign policy, Brand turned his attention to the 9/11 terrorist attacks in New York and Washington. Most people believed that the Twin Towers were destroyed by two 767 jets full of fuel flown directly into the buildings, live on television, by al-Qaeda terrorists. But not so fast. Brand saw the hand of other, unspecified forces at work. He suggested that the collapse 'looked like a controlled explosion'.[24] He didn't say it was, mind you, but he thought it looked fishy.

This was dynamite. Here was Brand entertaining a truly wild conspiracy theory that the American government had carried out the mass murder of its own people. Generally, he'd been seen as a well-meaning, if slightly naive, idealist, but this cast him in a different light, placing him at the crazier end of the political spectrum. Excitedly I rushed from my desk to Evan's office to present him with my interview nugget. He listened politely, and said he'd add it to his plan and ask Brand about it if he had time. Fair enough. Result.

Brand's interview was at the end of the programme, so I went down to the green room, where he was waiting. I found a very wired Brand full of nervous energy, running up and down the corridor outside the studios, desperate to get started. By the time he went on he was distracted and irascible. Evan adopted a slightly obsequious tone, announcing, 'The book's not just an entertaining read, it has a lot to say, and at times you can think he's neither Groucho nor Karl but the new Jesus Christ.'[25] Despite this, the interview quickly became a weirdly tetchy affair. Unlike Paxman, Evan took Brand seriously and deployed flattery, but the comedian was not in the mood to play ball. The interview was going nowhere.

Eventually, with time running out and without much conviction, Evan turned to my 9/11 question. Nothing else had worked, so why not give it a go? He asked Brand whether he really thought the American government was behind 9/11. Brand said he remained 'open-minded' on the subject. Evan said most people would regard such a position as ridiculous. Brand agreed but noted that he found the relationship between the Bush family and the bin Laden family 'very interesting'. Yet again, Brand was making dark hints without owning his insinuations, dropping in conspiracy theories while simultaneously disavowing them. He was on the hook and needed reeling in. But Evan seemed a little embarrassed to find himself in an argument and moved on. I cursed in the control room, frustrated that he had changed the subject when it was getting interesting. It was as if he were allergic to good television. Even so, the exchange was the highlight of the interview, but there was no escaping from the fact that we'd fallen well short of Paxman's encounter the year before. The squib was very damp that night.

However, the next day *Newsnight* was making news. Brand's conspiracy theory moment was something of a sensation. There was some criticism of Evan's failure to pin him down, but my question had ensured that Davis/Brand made waves. I arrived in the office with a spring in my step, convinced that Evan would finally have clocked that I might be able to help him.

As the time came to start preparations for the night's interviews, I hovered expectantly outside the presenter's office. It had been a rocky six weeks or so for me since Evan had started, but surely things were about to change. Finally, I could begin to influence the content and help our new presenter make his mark. I put my head around the door and said hello. Deep in thought, Evan was typing away on the computer, preparing his interviews in his usual intense, private way. He looked up and half-acknowledged me. I think, from memory, he sighed. What followed was a cursory discussion about the interviews coming up on the programme and how he planned to execute them.

Last night was already a long time ago, and I knew then that my *Newsnight* days were done.

Ian Katz's reinvention of the political interview never really flew. I have a lot of time for him and for the ideas in his *Financial Times* article, but ultimately the experiment failed. Paxman himself hit the nail on the head when I asked him about it:

> Of course, one can have a constructive conversation, but you must play by the same rules. There've been thousands of people who've done what Katz did in that article, and it never ever works because you get taken for a ride.[26]

Evan Davis's overly conciliatory instincts didn't help. His style often made for uninvolving television, putting the project on the back foot from the start. It might have been different had he been more willing to at least make a nod towards the gladiatorial style that had made *Newsnight*'s name, but he wasn't. It can't have been easy succeeding Paxman, and maybe the burden of that explains why he tried to do it all himself and, in my case at least, rejected help. A few years later, when he landed at Radio 4's early evening news show *PM*, Evan found a home more suited to his low-key, cerebral style. He's clearly a huge talent, and I'm glad he ended up at the right place in the end.

And what about Brand? Well, let's just say that his tentative embrace of the conspiracy theory was fully and enthusiastically consummated in the years that followed.

As for me, it was the end of 2014, and I was moving on to the biggest and best job of my life.

Thanks for the memories, Jeremy.

As for you, Russell: do one!

9

DIFFICULT CHOICES

There are four things people used to bring up when they found out I was the editor of *The Andrew Marr Show*.

Thing one: What's Andrew Marr really like?

Answer: Very nice, very clever, very funny and really very nice. He's a brilliant writer who knows more about politics and history than you and me put together. He's an interviewer who listens to answers and is very smart. Did I mention that he's nice?

Thing two: My favourite bit is when you have politicians chatting together on the sofa each week. I love that bit. Can't you make it longer? It's the best bit, Rob.

Answer: I'd love to, but it doesn't happen every week, and getting them to do it is really hard. Prime ministers never do it, for example. It's risky, and that's why it makes great television but also why so many politicians say no. People think it's there every week, but it really isn't, and if it lasted any longer they'd be even less likely to agree to it. Sorry.

Thing three: Who chooses the music at the end of the show? I don't know why you have it. Why do you have it? The politicians look really awkward listening to it and clapping at the end.

Answer: I choose it. We have it because I like it, and so does Andrew, and so do lots of other people, I'm sure. It's part of a very successful mix. So no, I'm not getting rid of it. Oh, and the politicians looking awkward is brilliant. Sorry. Again.

Thing four: Is Andrew Marr OK after having that stroke? He seems fine, but I do worry about him.

Answer: He's fine, thanks. I never knew him before he had his stroke, so I can't tell you how much it's affected him. All I can say is he's made of stern stuff and he never complains. He's also, if I haven't mentioned this, the nicest man in television.

For those of us working in the shadow of first Sir David Frost and then Andrew Marr, it looked so easy. The biggest guests had lined up to sink into Frost's generously upholstered sofa. The same applied to Marr's faintly modernist orangey-yellow variety. We watched critically, sometimes appalled by Frost's obsequious approach, often frustrated by the genial Marr. Whether toiling on the long-form interview in the dying days of *Walden* or trying to spice things up with audience questions on *Jonathan Dimbleby*, at ITV we gazed resentfully at the establishment's sofa. It was the same story for those Sunday-lunchtime BBC competitors like the long-forgotten *Politics Show* or the rapidly fading *Sunday Politics*. We even looked on jealously from *Newsnight*'s ivory tower.

I'd worked for them all, and cursed Marr and Frost every Sunday morning. And then, like an upstart football manager defiantly shaking a fist at the giants of the game, the call comes from the bigger club, and you have to ask yourself if you have what it takes to take charge of the thing you defined yourself against.

Barney Jones had made running the most important political interview show on British television look easy, but it had required energy and creativity to define and maintain the two programmes over twenty-one years. It seemed like he'd be there forever, but in 2014, after one of the BBC's periodic brutal reorganisations, he was effectively told his time running *The Andrew Marr Show* was up. It was time for a new editor and a new approach.

So I went for it. I wasn't a sure bet to succeed – far from it – and I had a troubling tendency to let myself down in job interviews, but this time was different. Halfway through the 'board' for the editor of *Marr*, I could tell that I'd done well. I was thrilled – and a little apprehensive – to be offered the job, subject to the seal of approval from Marr himself. I'd seen him around at the BBC, but we'd never met. In theory, he could veto my appointment if we didn't click.

I was nervous as I arrived in Primrose Hill, north London, where the presenter lives with his wife, the journalist and broadcaster Jackie Ashley, a few days before Christmas. It's a neighbourhood that looks like London as an American movie watcher might imagine it: beautiful houses, adorable cafes and spotless streets.

While I had ideas about how to change and improve the programme, this wasn't the time to talk about a revolution. Instead, over a cup of tea I tried to reassure Andrew and Jackie that I understood why the show was a success and could be relied on to take it forward. It was immediately apparent that they did not want the programme to rest on its laurels. Fortunately, I convinced them I had the passion and ambition to take charge. It was also clear that Andrew and I were on the same wavelength and could have a good laugh together. By the end of the visit I was in.

After a few more weeks on *Newsnight*, I was due to start on *Marr*. Over Christmas 2014 I returned home to the house in Sussex where I'd spent my childhood, by this time with two young children of my own. My dad was eighty-six years old and increasingly stuck inside the house with my mum, unable to make his escape into the garden anymore. When I was growing up, I'd spend hours there with him talking about current affairs and history. That was how I'd fallen in love with politics. While he was always hugely supportive of my career, being a Yorkshireman born in 1928 he was never effusive about my achievements at work. Until that Christmas when I got the *Marr* job.

When we talked about it on Christmas morning, he beamed, emerging out of the slightly broken demeanour he'd adopted as age had worn him down. He pronounced it 'smashing' news. This was high praise from Sid Burley, and it felt good to make him proud.

Later, after my parents attempted Christmas dinner (more *Butterflies* than *The Good Life*), Dad and I talked again. This time, more gloomily, feeling his arthritis, he told me that he'd had enough of life.

'Don't be daft,' I said, kissing him on his beautiful brown-weathered forehead, urging him to keep going. But he wasn't being daft. He knew what he wanted. In January he fell out of bed in the night and was taken to hospital. Almost immediately he disappeared into a state of delirium and stayed there.

My arrival at *Marr* was delayed as I watched Dad deteriorate. The hospital could have kept him alive longer if we'd wanted, but after frank conversations between the doctors, my mum, my sister and me, we decided to let things take their course. Finally, at the end of February, I watched Dad fade away, kissing his forehead once again, this time to say goodbye.

Dad never got to see my name at the end of the *Marr* credits listed as 'editor', but it was good to know he was proud anyway. It would never have happened without him.

* * *

Andrew Marr's big moments – with Gordon Brown in the late noughties and countless more in the years that followed – might never have happened if Marr and his first editor, Barney Jones, hadn't saved the show from an early crisis.

Marr came to Sunday morning following a dazzling stint as the BBC's political editor. He joined the corporation in 2000 after a brilliant career as a reporter, columnist and newspaper editor. As political editor, he was the face of the BBC's political coverage and analysis. His job was to make political events explicable and engaging for a diverse range of audiences, from the Westminster obsessive to the casual observer. Whoever's in the role needs political judgement and excellent contacts, but above all they require character and broadcasting panache, both of which Marr had coming out of his famous ears.

Marr was a livewire, bringing excitement and vivid colour to politics at a time when others in the BBC thought, with New Labour's dominance, that politics was somehow over. He was a counterweight to the crackpot idea that people were uninterested in Westminster. Marr was interested in Westminster, and the chances were, if you were watching him, you were too.

Barney Jones wanted to break from the past and thought Marr was the ideal person. Frost was an establishment figure – albeit with a more exotic history than most – whereas Marr was a modern, more disruptive character who could bring in a younger audience. Marr also had a hinterland that Frost lacked. His enthusiasm for the arts was genuine and infectious. Above all, Marr brought political knowledge and judgement, and a gift for analysis. You'll often find Marr talking about a political issue or economic warning sign two or three weeks before the rest of us read about it on the front pages. He has a remarkable gift for knowing where the political ball will bounce next.

The problem came when he arrived in his brand-new studio. The space was complex, with three distinct areas and a set of stairs from which he would launch himself into the show. It was very different to Frost's sedentary style, and it was demanding. The look was very different, too, designed to evoke a 'cool, riverside industrial building with exposed bricks'.[1] All this asked a lot of a presenter new to studio work, as Marr explained:

> It was a much bigger challenge than I expected. I knew I could stand in front of the camera, say what I thought and explain what was going on. What I hadn't realised was that studio presenting is a completely different art, which is about being smooth and easy on a Sunday morning, being able to move between different cameras. And I found that harder than I expected. I could never remember which camera I was supposed to be looking at.[2]

Teething problems aren't uncommon, but this was serious, and as the autumn series ran on, things weren't getting any better. BBC management started to worry. Jones recalls Marr repeatedly getting things wrong on air and 'looking lost again and again and again'.[3] Eventually, the deputy director-general Mark Byford took Jones aside and told him to fix Marr's presentation problems, or 'there'd be a real question mark over whether you can continue with this guy on Sunday mornings'.[4] This was not an idle threat. It had to be sorted, and quickly. What the show needed, Jones realised, was a new director.

It's hard to stress how important directors are in television. You've probably seen footage of them in the gallery of a TV studio orchestrating the cameras, and that is their job. They ensure everything looks as smooth and swish as possible, and that the camera operators get the right shots at the correct times. You might not realise that they are also there to manage the presenter. As Marr struggled with the mechanics of delivering a live TV show, Jones called on Chris Cook to walk Andrew through the process and coax a performance out of him. Cook is not only technically brilliant and unflappable but also emotionally intelligent; he knows how to make the studio crew – including a nervous and jumpy presenter – feel loved and looked after. Cook was the man to fix Marr, and *The Andrew Marr Show* took off once he had.

It wasn't a foregone conclusion that the programme could pick up where Frost had left off. After all, Sir David took his celebrity status and legendary contacts book with him when he left. While Marr knew everyone who mattered in UK politics, Frost had global reach. Over the years, however, Marr racked up interviews with huge names like Barack Obama, Vladimir Putin and, in my time as editor, French president Emmanuel Macron, Hillary Clinton and many more. Frost may have gone, but Barney's hard work, together with the efforts of star producer Brian Hollywood and Jones's deputy Libby Jukes, ensured that the BBC's Sunday show remained the first choice for the world's biggest names.

Domestically, Marr benefited from Frost's legacy. He offered guests a fair hearing at an early hour, freeing politicians to spend weekend time with their families, and guaranteeing them maximum coverage on the news bulletins for the rest of the day and in the Monday morning papers too. The programme reached an audience of one to two million viewers and sometimes hit closer to three. It also attracted big names from the London stage, Hollywood, and pop, rock and classical music, providing your average political ugly bug with the chance to rub shoulders with the stars – don't underestimate the pull factor that exerts. The after-show breakfast was legendary, presenting unbeatable networking and selfie opportunities. *Marr* was the big time. Politicians might turn up to talk about pensions policy or the state of the railways, and find themselves making small talk with a rock star over a plate of black pudding. Brilliant fun. Just don't offer a bacon roll to Chrissie Hynde.

When I finally arrived at *Marr*, I had a lot to learn. The show had its own culture, character, and a special place in viewers' lives. It was summed up for me most vividly a few years later when the wonderfully plummy Sir David Clementi was the chairman of the BBC. Clementi was the kind of cuddly old wet Tory who used to run the country and he loved the show. He told me how he and his wife would stay in bed extra late on a Sunday morning to watch it, Sir David in his pyjamas and Lady Clementi 'in her nightie' – a detail that made me laugh whenever I thought of it. *The Andrew Marr Show* was part of people's weekly routine, and was as British as Marks and Spencer, a Sunday roast or *nul points* at Eurovision.

The show had its own rhythm. The first few weeks of the year meant the set-piece New Year interviews with the prime minister and the leader of the opposition. After the summer break, the show hit the road for the party conference interviews in cities including Brighton, Bournemouth, Birmingham, Manchester and Liverpool. Ensuring these interviews got booked and delivered was the minimum expectation of the editor, and they usually were.

While respecting the show's status and history, I wanted to modernise it gradually. There was a familiar roster of newspaper reviewers that needed freshening up. As for the music, while every political journalist I knew hated it and thought it got in the way of gathering news lines from the political interviews, I saw it as part of a successful mix. I just wanted to improve it and relished the chance to indulge my passion for music. The art elements were an absolute joy.

But I also needed to toughen it up. Years later, at his BBC leaving party, Marr made a speech reviewing his years in the job and the editors he'd worked with. In my case, he told the audience – which included director-general Tim Davie, former prime minister David Cameron and many other luminaries – that I thought his interviews were 'shit' and that, happily, I'd made them better. This was funny, but overstated the extent of my hostility. Before I arrived Marr delivered plenty of tough interviews and landed story after story, but I did think there was room for improvement.

In my view, the programme was in danger of feeling a little stuffy and disconnected from the world outside. Social media meant that viewers could engage with content in a new way, and the show couldn't stand entirely aloof and analogue anymore. There was also a sense that Britain's politics was starting to fracture, something that intensified in the years ahead. The Scottish independence referendum in September 2014 provided a taste of things to come, not least because of the tone of the debate on social media, particularly Twitter. In this environment, an interviewer like Andrew Marr was under extraordinary scrutiny. I thought it was time to make the show a bit more forensic while retaining its Sunday-morning character. It wasn't and shouldn't be *Newsnight* or *Walden*, but it did need to toughen up a little.

This was a culture change for the *Marr* show. The team of producers had been driven by newsmaking more than accountability, and I wanted to tilt the balance a little bit the other way. What I tried to do, gradually, was to apply an approach to every interview that centred on a simple question: what is the truth? This changed the way Marr prepared, as he told me:

> We spent more time briefing. We spent more time on structure going through the interviews. I always liked your basic motto of what's the truth here? How do we get to it? So you sit down, agree on what you think is happening, and try to demonstrate it. That was highly effective.[5]

The idea was to ask what the essential truth of a given interview might be. For example, an interview with chancellor George Osborne might be about him justifying public-spending cuts while refusing to fully acknowledge that they will hurt people in the real world. Or an interview with Labour leader Ed Miliband might be about a contrast between the claims he makes for a future Labour government and the timidity of the party's policy programme. This approach ensured that the interview style moved from simply a list of questions covering whatever was around in the news to a more directed plan that sought to reveal something about the politician or their predicament.

I had to be careful, however. Nobody normal wants to watch that nice Andrew Marr haranguing a politician at nine on a Sunday morning. I had to prove myself to Marr and find a way to bring my experience of forensic interviewing to bear without changing the show's feel too dramatically. When I arrived in early 2015 I was helped by the imminent general election, which required more challenging questions and follow-ups. Political Twitter was watching like a hawk. Over the years that followed, I had to learn the hard way that it's never really possible to please the Twitter mob.

Paying too much attention to partisan political tribalism will distort how you approach the work. Most people are interested in hearing the case the politicians want to make but also want them politely held to account. Many who shout the loudest on social media aren't interested in the content but want the politician they disagree with to be vilified by the interviewer, as Marr knows only too well.

> Sometimes, you look at the criticism on Twitter afterwards, and they would only have been satisfied if you'd actually got up and punched your interviewee. No level of questioning would ever have been enough. And as the country has become angrier and more divided, so an ever larger section of the audience wants confrontational blood-sport interviewing. Not interviewing for enlightening; interviewing for humiliation.[6]

The other strange impulse I detected as, perhaps too obsessively, I trawled through the tweets on a Sunday morning after the show, was the anger people felt about the mere presence of a guest they disagreed with. I really don't understand this approach to politics and political debate. I tend to enjoy interviews with those I disagree with more than those on my side of the argument. Over the years, I've been attacked on Twitter by people furious that I've booked Jeremy Corbyn or Nigel Farage or aired the opinions of an environmentalist campaigner or passionate tax cutter. But as I told them, the reality is that people you disagree with will sometimes be on TV. Get used to it.

As 2015 arrived, the same political argument that had dominated politics for years raged. The coalition government led by Tory prime minister David Cameron and his Lib Dem deputy Nick Clegg had pursued a policy of public-spending cuts – austerity – for the previous five years. Their policy was opposed by Labour's young, slightly awkward leader Ed Miliband, with variable effectiveness. The Conservatives planned further cuts should they win outright in the general election due in May. The central question was straightforward: should the government continue to make cuts in public spending in an effort to reduce the deficit and the level of debt, or were these cuts too deep and too harsh, creating unacceptable immediate human costs and long-term damage to the fabric of society?

It's fair to say that in the previous election in 2010, the Conservatives had won the political argument. Their case was that the Labour government had crashed the economy, and there was no money left after years of profligacy. The Conservatives – with Liberal Democrat support, as it turned out – would have to fix things as usual. Whatever the merits of this argument, either in terms of who was to blame or how to repair the damage, Tory leader David Cameron and shadow chancellor George Osborne played their hand effectively.

Once in government, Cameron and Osborne were initially willing to stick with words like 'cuts' and even 'austerity' itself to describe their project of deficit reduction. But as the process ground on, the real-world effects began to be felt and such stark language wouldn't do. Increasingly, these guys needed euphemisms.

So the two men began reframing the concept of cuts by using terms that softened and disguised. One favourite was 'efficiency savings', which they sometimes shortened to the even more opaque 'efficiencies'. In his New Year *Marr* interview in 2015, Cameron referred to 'adjustments' as a euphemism for spending cuts, but that one didn't fly. The favoured formulations they settled on were 'difficult decisions' or 'difficult choices'. This struck me as particularly sneaky because it implied that the difficult part was the decision itself, the part made by the poor, tortured politician, rather than the outcome of that decision felt by the person affected by the cuts. They sometimes acknowledged that the public were making sacrifices, but more often they stuck to a formulation that seemed designed to cloak the truth.

My first ever *Marr Show* came in March 2015, and Osborne was the main guest. Whatever you think of his politics, he was a brave politician, willing to play the bad guy if he thought he was doing the right thing, even if it made him unpopular, which it did. While he was less slippery than Cameron in his interviews with Marr, he was still more than happy to use the language of 'difficult choices' and 'efficiency savings'. So, before the interview, I encouraged Marr to call him out if he tried to separate the act of cutting from the effect of it.

Osborne went straight there. With the election approaching and the human cost of cuts high on the agenda, Marr asked him whether he thought the deeper cuts in areas like welfare that he had said were on the way could be achieved without causing pain.

'Look,' said Osborne, 'there are going to be difficult decisions ...'

Marr was ready to push back sharply: 'Difficult decisions for you, pain for other people.'[7]

It's a brief moment and a minor point in the grand scheme of things, but I was pleased that Marr had disrupted Osborne's tactic, deployed without challenge so many times before. You might think such formulations are just part of the game, something in the politician's linguistic armoury they are entitled to use. But voters who want their leaders to answer questions honestly are frustrated and alienated by words that obscure and mask rather than illuminate and clarify. You might side with Osborne on the policy, you might not. But spending cuts are not merely 'difficult choices' made dispassionately somewhere in Whitehall by principled ministers at arm's length. They are choices the politician has decided to make, and they have difficult consequences in the real world.

Take, for example, David Clapson. David was a former soldier whose five years in the army included two in Northern Ireland. On leaving the service, he spent twenty-four years in work, including sixteen at BT, until he left his job to become his mother's carer after she was diagnosed with dementia. When she died in 2011 he began to look for work. Fatefully for David, this coincided with the coalition government's new, stricter approach to welfare. Cameron and Osborne knew that if they wanted to reduce public spending, the welfare bill was where they had to find a significant proportion of their cuts. At the same time, they were driven by a conviction that for too many years, too many people of working age had been incentivised to stay idle on over-generous benefits.

The solution was a new approach that toughened up the principle that the receipt of benefits was conditional. Claimants had to attend interviews and training sessions to help them find work if they were to receive their money. Those who missed these appointments were sanctioned: the benefits they relied on to live were stopped.

This was what happened to David Clapson. The strict rules designed to weed out the 'benefit scroungers' of popular imagination caught a man who had worked all his adult life but was now struggling to find work and navigate an online system that baffled him. Two missed appointments led to his benefits being cut for a month. His last payment was received on 2 July 2014. Two weeks later – at the age of fifty-nine – he was found dead in his flat in Stevenage. The coroner found David had no food in his stomach. A diabetic, he needed to keep his insulin in his fridge for it to be safe to use. But with no money, he couldn't top up the credit on his electricity card to keep the fridge running. The cause of death was diabetic ketoacidosis, caused by a severe lack of insulin.

A few weeks into the 2015 general election campaign, the prime minister was back on *Marr*. Cameron – at his worst – was a tetchy interviewee who could come across as irritated that he was being asked to justify his policies and their effects. At this early stage in the election, Cameron was under fire for a lacklustre campaign that wasn't shifting the polls. There was feverish speculation and a fair amount of wishful thinking from liberal commentators that Labour was best placed to emerge as the largest party. Against this inauspicious backdrop, Cameron showed up already rattled.

When Marr – in a move that was then unusual for the show – brought up the Clapson case, Cameron's mood didn't improve. Having already tried the 'difficult choices' mantra, Cameron suggested government hardship funds could have helped David. The problem, as Marr pointed out, was that they hadn't. No, Cameron insisted, while this was a 'tragic case', he could reassure viewers that he looked at 'all of those individual cases' and the hardship fund could have addressed them. Cameron didn't like where the interview was going and was quickly tired of being on the defensive. He shifted to the front foot and reasserted that 'people watching this programme who pay their taxes, who work very hard, they don't pay their taxes so people can sign on and show no effort at getting a job'.[8]

This was doubtless a view widely shared by his voters, but it did not encompass David Clapson, who made every effort to get a job until he didn't have the strength to go on.

This was the most unpleasant side of Cameron: the cold, 'Flashman' part of his personality. It wasn't edifying – and it upset Clapson's family, who later told the press that they felt brushed off by his response. David's sister Gill Thompson has spent the years since her brother's death trying, in vain, to force the coroner to open an inquest. Seven years on, she remains upset by Cameron's implication that her brother was one of those who 'sign on and show no effort at getting a job':

> David was not a scrounger or skiver. David did [unpaid] placements with B&Q and Pound Shop, which he had enjoyed, but there was no job at the end of it. He was unwell with his diabetes. David was really struggling. He was depressed and had problems with his memory. He just hit a time in his life when he needed professional and caring support, which never came. I feel that sanctioning my brother took away his control and resulted in his death.[9]

After we spoke, Gill proudly emailed me a certificate from BT thanking her hard-working brother for his years of service. She also attached a photograph of David's CV. It includes a personal statement in which he describes himself as 'hard-working', a list of his 'key skills' and his employment history. There was a pile of these CVs, printed out and ready for posting, lying next to David's body when he was found dead in his flat. This was not a man making no effort to find work.

There was a callousness to Cameron that I found jarring. Here was a man who was genuinely enthusiastic about social responsibility and helping others, as long as that meant community work or charitable giving. The advocate of the 'Big Society' seemed genuinely compassionate when talking about his grand idea, but uninterested in how the state he ran actually operated in people's lives. He was incurious at best when faced with a real-life example of where it had gone horribly wrong because of – at least in part – changes he had introduced. While he seemed sad about Clapson's lonely death, he gave the impression that it was one of those things any system would produce. He didn't think about how hurtful his matter-of-fact rhetoric would be for families like David's, nor did he seem to consider that cases like David's – and there have been many more who have suffered under the sanctioning regime – were a feature and not a bug in the benefits system his government had built. You could still be in favour of sanctioning claimants who fail to fulfil their obligations when seeking work, while being concerned that things were going badly wrong for people like David Clapson and that hardship funds that were supposed to offer last-resort help for the vulnerable weren't working.

I was pleased that we'd proved that we could effectively point out the real-world impact of policy and transform the programme into a tougher environment. This wasn't us taking a position on austerity – we'd often press Labour politicians on how they would tackle the deficit if they opposed cuts – but was about finding the most challenging territory for a given interviewee to reveal a political truth. However, and perhaps more significantly for the outcome of the 2015 election, Cameron became highly effective when he was able to shift the conversation onto the prospect of a Labour/Scottish National Party coalition. As Cameron pumped out political attack lines about Ed Miliband and Scottish first minister Nicola Sturgeon directly into the living rooms of middle England – or bedrooms in the case of Sir David and Lady Clementi – you could feel them landing with a powerful political thwack.

This was legitimate politics, but there was a problem: Journalists – including broadcast journalists at the BBC, as I was – ballsed up the 2015 general election. After the novelty and excitement of 2010, when a hung parliament led to the first coalition government since the Second World War, commentators became convinced that hung parliaments and deals between parties were the new normal. Collectively obsessed by the polls, we spent much of the 2015 election more interested in (what passes for) sexy process, and neglected policy differences.

The *Marr Show* had taken Cameron on over welfare sanctioning, and early in the campaign the chancellor George Osborne had an uncomfortable time after promising an extra £8 billion for the NHS without telling Marr where the money was coming from. Osborne's stonewalling was so frustrating that Marr transformed into a genial Jeremy Paxman that day, asking where the cash was coming from eighteen times without success.

But after that, the campaign's focus shifted decisively towards discussing which parties would strike deals and who they'd strike them with. This was terrible news for the Labour leader Ed Miliband, who, faced with the collapse of the Labour vote in Scotland, looked like a potential prime minister, but only if he'd do a deal with 'the nationalists', as the Conservatives referred to the SNP. The election became about him and Sturgeon rather than the Labour platform.

As election day drew closer, Marr opened the penultimate show before polling with his usual scene-setting monologue: 'Essential story of the week,' he said:

The Tories changed tactics and went big on the threat of the SNP. Is this cutting through in the English heartlands? If so, it could win the election for David Cameron. That depends, very heavily, on how Ed Miliband responds. It is just possible that this may form part of my conversation with the Labour leader.[10]

Of course, it dominated, and Miliband couldn't shut it down, finding himself trying to reassure viewers that any programme for government he would put forward as prime minister would be a Labour programme and not one 'written by the SNP'. This created an impression that Miliband lacked any real confidence that Labour could win outright. He seemed to be opening the door to a deal with Sturgeon even as he tried to be categorical that it wouldn't happen.

Perhaps Miliband failed because, unlike some other bastards out there, he wasn't much of a liar. He needed to create the impression that he could win the election even though the polls suggested he couldn't. While he said some of the right words, he lacked conviction and, fatally, allowed Marr to lead him down the path to a hypothetical hung parliament. Anyone worried before the interview that a Labour/SNP coalition might happen was convinced it could happen afterwards.

Marr's other guest on the Sunday of Miliband's appearance was Boris Johnson. Johnson was in the last year of his term as mayor of London and was about to return to parliament in the general election. His performance that day anticipated the themes and techniques he relied on in the Brexit campaign and beyond. He blusters, questions Marr's integrity and traduces the BBC – 'You're a lefty BBC journalist' – and attempts to subvert the process of serious accountability. This was 2015, but it could have been from the 2020s.

Years after this encounter, when Marr and I were working on his LBC show, Andrew – now free of BBC impartiality strictures – described Johnson as an 'albino gorilla'. So apt is this description that I can't believe nobody had thought of it before. Johnson resembles a gorilla because he is both physically dominating – prowling the confines of the TV zoo – and because of his ape-like mannerisms. Just as an imprisoned primate will launch his poo at spectators watching through the bars, so Johnson hurls rhetorical crap and blustering bullshit, lobbed to deflect and distract. As for Johnson's blond looks, he's albino-like, and in the flesh the pink beneath the mop catches the eye.

On this Sunday in April 2015, Johnson returned to the *Marr* set after Ed Miliband's interview and sat down next to the Labour leader for what is known as the 'sofa chat'. This section of the programme appeared after the final news bulletin and before the musical act at the end of the show. The idea was for a more informal conversation that might produce moments of TV magic. As I knew because they told me, viewers loved it, and many seemed to think it happened every week. In reality it didn't – many politicians had the sense to turn it down flat. The slot was risky and often turned into a tussle for dominance. For a politician who wanted to look masterful and in control, the risk was a verbal roughing up, which made them look like the smaller person. This is what happened to Miliband that day.

His first mistake was agreeing to it. He was in the middle of an election campaign running to be prime minister. He wanted to be seen by voters as the equal of, and alternative to, David Cameron. Yet here he is, climbing onto the sofa with an albino gorilla who's armed with piles of steaming shit.

The sofa itself is quite small, and Johnson makes it smaller, manspreading from the start. Miliband is pinned a little too tightly in the corner for comfort, and as the conversation heats up he has to turn his body towards Johnson. The two are effectively squaring up, speaking over each other. Johnson shouts, and Miliband tells him not to 'get rattled'. Johnson starts talking about Miliband's brother David, whom Ed defeated in the Labour leadership contest. Johnson has accused Ed of 'back-stabbing' in the press and wants to go there again; Miliband laughs it off unconvincingly. It feels like Johnson has hit a nerve.

Time is running out and it's basically a bunfight now, but with the brown stuff. Johnson continues shouting, warning viewers that Miliband 'would do more damage to this country than he did to his brother'. Marr tells them the programme is over and time is up. Miliband is still pinned in the corner, pretending all this is fine. It's been a bad day for the Labour leader. It's hard to look like a prime minister in waiting when you're covered in gorilla shit.

The following week, the last before polling day, the sofa chat is the campaign in microcosm. Liberal Democrat Nick Clegg, Labour's Yvette Cooper and UKIP leader Nigel Farage squeeze onto the sofa for an uncomfortable game of 'Who'll do a deal with whom?'. Nobody wants to answer the question, and nobody does. It falls to Nigel Farage of all people to call for some higher purpose.

'We have four days to go,' he half shouts in exasperation, 'can we not discuss policy?'

Well, no, Nigel, we can't, it's too late for that now. Which is a shame, and I'll take my share of the blame for it.

The following morning, 4 May 2015, the prime minister took to Twitter:

> Britain faces a simple and inescapable choice – stability and strong Government with me, or chaos with Ed Miliband.[11]

We'll just leave that there for now.

They say writing about music is like dancing about architecture. I'm not sure where that leaves writing about music on a politics show, but I'll try it anyway.

The music on the *Marr Show* irritated the 'lobby': the political journalists who work in Westminster. They're the kind of people who know who the first minister is but don't love First Aid Kit. They revere Michael Portillo but overlook Michael Kiwanuka. They can pontificate about teenage pregnancies but have no idea about Teenage Fanclub, and they think Franz Ferdinand is a duke rather than an art rock band from Glasgow.

This is unfair, I'm sure many of them love music, but most moaned and groaned about the song at the end of the show. Their main argument was that the measly two and a half minutes we allocated to some tunes would be better spent hearing politicians refusing to answer the question for a bit longer.

There was also some discomfort in the juxtaposition of a front-line politician talking about the war in Syria or the effects of austerity only for the programme to make a handbrake turn into Annie Lennox doing a Christmas carol. I understood why that could feel weird, but I also loved the incongruity of David Cameron bopping along to PJ Harvey or Haim.

There were times when the music was more than just an incongruous add-on. For example, in November 2015, two days after the horrific terror attacks on the streets of Paris and at the Bataclan concert hall, I wanted to find a way to mark a sombre moment and convey solidarity. What came to mind was the moment in *Casablanca* when 'La Marseillaise' drowns out the Nazis in Rick's café: defiance in the face of barbarism.

Brian Hollywood, the producer with the best contacts book in television, spent Saturday looking for the answer and finally found it in French opera star Nicolas Courjal. The London-based singer came into the studio the next morning and sang 'La Marseillaise' live and unaccompanied with the Tricolour on the screens behind him. Theresa May, the home secretary, was on set alongside the visibly moved French ambassador to the UK, Sylvie Bermann. It was hugely powerful, and I was proud we'd risen to the occasion with such class.

A few months later, in January 2016, David Cameron was back for his New Year interview. In the end he'd won the 2015 election outright, and all the talk of hung parliaments, political deals and horse trading had been so much wasted breath. Cameron led a Tory government on a Tory manifesto and was at the peak of his powers. The prospect of a referendum on Britain's membership of the European Union loomed, but no date had yet been set.

It was a fairly run-of-the-mill outing, covering the timing of that EU referendum, the economy, foreign affairs, and a plan to knock down and demolish or regenerate high-rise 'sink estate' council housing. As Andrew wrapped up the interview, Cameron, a keen fan of pop music in his youth, settled down to listen to Squeeze play us out. Squeeze, fronted by Chris Difford and Glenn Tilbrook, are one of the best-loved bands who emerged from the punk and new wave scene in the late seventies. It isn't hard to imagine a young Cameron getting down to 'Cool for Cats' at the Eton school disco. He's of the right vintage.

Squeeze started playing their new single as Cameron looked on attentively. The song, entitled 'Cradle to the Grave', was pleasant enough, if not a classic. While its title might have hinted at a political message, the lyrics weren't contentious. Well, not at first. Then about three-quarters of the way into the song, Glenn Tilbrook's golden voice launched into a new verse:

> I grew up in council housing,
> Part of what made Britain great,
> There are some here who are hell-bent,
> On the destruction of the welfare state.[12]

Angered by the prime minister's plan to demolish high-rise council housing, Tilbrook had knocked up a quick verse in the green room while he waited to go on.

As the song ended, Cameron clapped awkwardly from the *Marr* sofa. I don't know if he clocked the pointed lyrics, but the viewers certainly did, and Tilbrook was rewarded with a *Guardian* op-ed explaining the thinking behind his impromptu protest song.

Despite being the target of Squeeze's hasty rewrite, Cameron would be back on *Marr*. Up the junction, as it turned out, but back.

10

BREXIT IN FOUR MONTHS OF SUNDAYS AND A TUESDAY

It's 21 February 2016, and David Cameron is done. He doesn't know it yet, but as he settles into his chair opposite Andrew Marr in Studio B of New Broadcasting House, home of the BBC, he's at the beginning of the end.

There's something different about Cameron today, something less assured. Suddenly everything feels very contingent. Power is no longer his and his alone. He's about to hand it over to the people and to other ambitious, unscrupulous politicians. Just hours ago he returned from Brussels with a deal he says is good enough to make the case that Britain should remain in the European Union.

The prime minister has come onto the BBC's Sunday morning politics show because this is what happens here. *The Andrew Marr Show* is almost part of the constitutional furniture of the United Kingdom. This is where prime ministers come to make their case.

Cameron is often derided as a 'PR man', but I think this is wrong. He was really the first political adviser prime minister. His brief career in public relations merely interrupted his work advising the Conservative Party and its politicians. Cameron saw politics as a profession and eventually he graduated from adviser to professional politician himself. Whatever you think of the emergence of a professional political class dominating the major parties, there's no doubt that it has entrenched an approach to political communications that prizes evasion, deflection and deception. Cameron's early professional life involved briefing ministers for interviews and drumming into them the 'line to take'. This stuff was beyond second nature to him by the time he became a politician himself.

For most professional politicians, this creates a very specific problem: they forget to talk properly. They cannot answer questions in a normal way and default instead to stock phrases or impenetrable speech patterns that leave voters baffled and annoyed. But Cameron was not like most politicians. He was the rare professional politician who could make the bullshit sing.

There's a well-known piece of cynicism often attributed to the French playwright and novelist Jean Giraudoux: 'The secret of success is sincerity. If you can fake that, you've got it made.' George Burns, the cigar-toting American comic who'd wisecrack on British TV in the 1970s and 80s, streamlined it and made it his own: 'Sincerity,' he'd drawl, New York-style, 'if you can fake that, you've got it made.' Well, Cameron could, and he did. He became Conservative Party leader by wowing Tory delegates with an apparently off-the-cuff, no-notes speech and then returned them to power after thirteen years in 2010.

This is not to say that Cameron was never actually sincere or that he was less trustworthy and more deceptive than any other politician of his time. But his political gifts, his *professional* gifts, were so highly developed that he could stick to the lines to take, avoid saying anything interesting and side-step difficult questions while giving the impression of sincerity and candour. If Blair was the actor-politician drawing on an instinct for the arts, Cameron was the professional, trained in the science of effective political communications. The contrast with their respective successors is telling: unlike the actor Blair, Gordon

Brown could not emote; unlike the communicator Cameron, the robotic Theresa May could not connect.

But on that morning in 2016 the old way – the tried and tested, controlled and calibrated professional politician's way – is about to run out of road. Despite being tinged with ideological zeal when cutting public spending, Cameron's politics are strangely bloodless. Politics will now be about passion, instinct and conviction. All the normal rules of professional, predictable politics will be set aside, perhaps forever.

And so, with Andrew Marr sitting across from him, Cameron reaches for the starting pistol on the referendum to decide whether Britain will Leave or Remain. He pulls the trigger and, with a single shot, blows his foot clean off.

Highly unprofessional.

Just as Brexit is the most divisive issue in modern British politics, the BBC's coverage of Brexit is the most controversial period of political coverage of modern times. The Remainers complained that the BBC interpreted impartiality as giving equal weight to conflicting claims from the two sides even when one side represented the overwhelming weight of expert opinion. They also argued that the BBC failed to adjudicate when lies were being told. The Leavers complained about a cultural bias towards Remain at the BBC that came with the corporation's metropolitan worldview.

The daily coverage of the Brexit campaign was run by the BBC Politics team based in Millbank across the road from the Houses of Parliament in Westminster. That team, led by Katy Searle, called out or waved through the claims and counter-claims of the two sides, and decided how much coverage was given to particular personalities and policies. Laura Kuenssberg, the first-class political editor, was the most prominent journalist in the team.

Political programmes were run by Robbie Gibb, who was in charge of the BBC's Live Political Programmes unit. That meant he was the hands-on editor of the *Daily Politics* show with Andrew Neil and Jo Coburn, which was broadcast every weekday from Westminster. He also led the BBC's *Great Debate* extravaganza at Wembley Stadium. Robbie was my boss at *Marr*, but because we had our own editor – me! – we operated at one remove from the rest of the programmes and entirely separately from the news.

As the referendum loomed, I knew what I wanted: the *Marr Show* should be where the biggest names on both sides of the argument came to be interrogated. We'd be fair and impartial to both sides and allow viewers to make a judgement. As a weekly show, we'd be stepping back from the frenzy of the news and daily programmes, and take stock of the campaign as it rolled on. Between that Sunday in February and the last *Marr Show* before the vote in June, there were seventeen editions of the programme across four months, most of which were dominated by Brexit. I was looking forward to this debate: here was an opportunity to tackle a vital question about Britain's future and values in depth and with real seriousness. It would be down to the politicians and the arguments they deployed to determine whether that actually occurred.

Seven years on, it's possible to analyse the tactics politicians used in these charged encounters and detect the errors of strategy and other political factors that led to Leave winning. Returning to them, it's surprising that that victory wasn't more overwhelming. That's not a comment on the merits of the arguments put forward by Leave and Remain – full disclosure: I voted Remain – but a reflection of the nature of the conversation that took place in the referendum from day one. The sense that Remain was on the back foot and Leave on the march was in the air from the very first show.

But did I think this at the time? It's hard to disentangle memory from what I now know and the commentary that I've absorbed since, but from the off I felt this was a moment of political uncertainty. The conventional wisdom was, of course, that Remain would prevail. That's what the polls said, and most commentators thought so too, but it didn't feel like that in Studio B at New Broadcasting House. It felt up for grabs.

The four months that followed were Britain's most consequential political period since the Thatcher years of the 1980s or perhaps even the Second World War. So much hung on what was debated between 21 February and 23 June 2016, and we are only at the start of the process of grappling with the implications. *The Andrew Marr Show* was the most influential political show on British television, and the arguments made there mattered to the outcome. I enjoyed more than a ringside seat; as the programme's editor I was a minor player. What follows is my account of the most significant moments on Marr during that time: Brexit in four months of Sundays.

21 February 2016, David Cameron – When the Deal Goes Down

David Cameron returned from Brussels with his renegotiation of Britain's relationship with the European Union late on Friday night. By Sunday morning, as his car pulls up in front of the BBC's New Broadcasting House in central London, it's already old news, such is the nature of the modern news cycle – online, on screen and on radio. This was billed by the prime minister as a fundamental reset of the relationship between the UK and Europe, so much so that Cameron, a man who had more than flirted with Euroscepticism at times himself, was satisfied that he could now recommend to voters that they should vote to remain in the European Union. However, he's thoroughly screwed up the expectation-management game: the deal failed to deliver on Cameron's explicit promises in his 2015 manifesto.

Cameron met with his cabinet on Saturday to discuss the agreement and seek their support. His senior colleagues were free to weigh up what he'd achieved and then decide whether to back him. Most did, but by Saturday afternoon a handful broke ranks and joined up with Dominic Cummings's Vote Leave campaign. The most prominent cabinet Leaver and most personally challenging for Cameron was his friend, justice secretary Michael Gove. Gove had decided to follow his conscience and back Brexit but, according to Cameron, promised he would make just one intervention explaining his decision and then shrink into the background. In reality, he was soon prominently involved in the Vote Leave operation.

That betrayal is all over the Sunday newspapers and must hurt. In my experience, Cameron is one of life's confident striders, often barely acknowledging those around him as he enters a room. He's the kind of man who shakes your hand while looking straight past you, self-contained and uninterested in pleasantries. But as I greet him this morning he's more open, talking about his exhausting few days. This is a less arrogant version of the prime minister. He seems to know he has a fight on his hands.

I leave him in the BBC canteen with his staff and head back down to the production area for a final chat with Andrew Marr. Happily, the referendum campaign has coincided with the arrival of the best interview producer I've worked with, Jason Keen, who's running through the final details before printing the interview plan Marr will take into the studio. All settled, Marr makes his way onto the studio floor and I head to the gallery. It's one of those mornings when you know the country is watching.

The show opens, and Marr lays it out:

An historic deal by the British Prime Minister transforming our relationship with the rest of the EU or a piece of transparent PR spin which ought to convince nobody? Well, it's one of them.[1]

The deal remains our primary focus but the broader politics operation is obsessed with Boris Johnson, the news bulletins dominated by speculation as to which way he will jump. His people have briefed journalists that he will back Leave, but nobody knows for sure. The papers say he is veering around like a 'shopping trolley' on the issue. The BBC's former political editor Nick Robinson is one of the newspaper reviewers, and he notes that the 'theatrics of the will he? Won't he?' moment will not be lost on the mayor of London. That will play out, but we're here for the real arguments, and they're about to get under way.

The themes and tensions that will recur over the next four months are present from day one. Two other conversations will frame Cameron's interview. Nicola Sturgeon, the Scottish National Party leader and Scotland's first minister, is lukewarm about the deal but is the only person who makes a full-throated case for EU membership, pointing out that she regards EU migration as a net economic benefit. However, Nigel Farage, leader of the UK Independence Party, knows that migration is Cameron's biggest problem. Freedom of movement – the right of EU citizens to live and work anywhere inside the EU – makes it impossible for Cameron to meet his pledge to reduce net migration (the number of those coming to the UK minus the number leaving) to the 'tens of thousands'. He'd first gone to Brussels hoping to win the right to close UK borders to EU citizens if the number of migrants was too high. Had he succeeded in taking back control of the border, it might have been a game changer, but he failed, and Farage is crowing about it.

Finally, Cameron sits down in the chair opposite Marr. In his enjoyable memoir of the referendum campaign, Cameron's director of communications Craig Oliver remembers the prime minister as being on 'top form' that day on the show. I don't know what interview he was watching, but it wasn't the same one as me. I remember a prime minister laid bare, his hard-won renegotiation turning to dust in his hand.

First, Marr invites Cameron to sell his deal and sell Remain. His answer is informed by focus groups and polling. He hits the marks, repeats the lines to take: a reformed European Union, stronger, safer, more effective against terrorism and crime, and then frames the alternative as a 'leap in the dark' in an uncertain world. Stay, he says, as 'we've now got a better deal'.

But how much better? As with all our interviews, we have a carefully structured plan of questions and follow-ups, plus a 'quote sheet' containing all the evidence Marr needs. This includes Cameron's manifesto pledge that 'if an EU migrant's child is living abroad, then they should receive no child benefit … no matter how long they have worked in the UK and no matter how much tax they have paid'. Would he concede that he hadn't delivered what he'd promised in his manifesto?

'Well,' he begins, 'what we've achieved, which I think is a big achievement …'

That's not a good start.

> … is to say that for new arrivals they will get child benefit not at British rates but at a rate that reflects the cost of living in their country, and for existing people here, over the next few years, we'll move to a system where they get that lower rate of child benefit too. Now, these are things that many people thought were impossible to achieve.[2]

Perhaps so, although Cameron promised something different. It's predictable but disappointing that he can't adopt a more self-effacing tone and acknowledge the truth; this, however, is the special adviser prime minister, trained not to concede the point. He claims victory thanks to the more general restrictions he's secured on welfare eligibility for EU migrants, but it's not working. Cameron has two big problems. First, this stuff is too complicated: levels of child benefit that reflect the costs of living in other countries, four-year tapered benefits, a seven-year mechanism – it all makes your head hurt just thinking about it. Second, those paying attention to the detail for the first time are reminded that migrants receive welfare and send child benefit home, and it's clear that this won't change under Cameron's deal. The message is: it's bad, but a little bit less bad than before.

The other win in the renegotiation is the explicit removal of the goal of 'ever closer union'. This destination is definitely part of the problem for British Eurosceptics; it set the UK on course for somewhere they didn't want to go. The problem is that it's too abstract. Perhaps those who understood the importance of the concept might be reassured by its removal, but most people wouldn't have the first idea what it meant or why it mattered.

Marr presses Cameron on the other vital issues, including Michael Gove's criticism that being in the EU means sacrificing control over our own laws. The prime minister, unwilling to make a more positive case for Remain, talks about the 'illusion of sovereignty' that leaving the EU promises and makes the negative argument for boring reality over the magical thinking that will serve the Leave campaign so well:

> I am passionate and love the institutions and the constitution we have in our country. I do not love the institutions of Brussels, but I make a clear-eyed determination of what will make Britain stronger, what will make us safer, what will enable us to protect our people in this world, and it's to get the best of both worlds in this amended EU.[3]

And that's very nearly that. There's just time for Cameron to promise, twice, that he will stay on as prime minister if Britain votes to leave. He doesn't want this to become a referendum on him personally, but he knows it's not true. Cameron's charmed political life hangs on the outcome.

The rest of the day is all about Boris Johnson. It takes the mayor of London until five o'clock in the afternoon to come out of his house to greet the press pack and declare for Leave, and when he does, Cameron's renegotiation quickly fades into obscurity. But the arguments sketched out on *Marr* on day one prove a decent guide to how it will go from here.

6 March 2016, Boris Johnson – Ball of Confusion

I'd been pushing for Boris Johnson's first big sit-down interview since he'd declared his hand, but it took two weeks before he was ready for it. Expectations were high. This was Johnson's first chance to show what he could do as the putative leader of the Leave campaign and our opportunity to show that we could hold the trickiest interviewee in town to account.

Sunday comes – two weeks in – and Leave has a problem. As voters contemplate what Cameron calls a 'leap in the dark', the focus is on what will happen to jobs and the economy if we vote to leave, both in the short term and in relation to our future trade relationship with the EU. Clearing this up is supposed to be Johnson's task, but that's not quite how he sees it.

As the interview starts, we give Johnson, as we gave David Cameron, the chance to set out his stall for Leave. He immediately becomes dewy-eyed about 'a once-in-a-lifetime opportunity which will not come again to strike a new series of relationships, free-trade deals with the growth economies around the world whilst maintaining … our free-trade advantages with the European Union'.[4] We are a great and proud country, and we can take back control.

This done, Marr wants to drill down just a little bit into the specifics. But Johnson waves this away as so much negativity, then reaches for a pre-prepared soundbite. 'Do you know what this is like?' he asks before answering his own question:

> This is like the jailer has accidentally left the door of
> the jail open, and people can see the sunlit land beyond
> ... and everybody's suddenly wrangling about the
> terrors of the world outside. Actually, it will be
> wonderful. And it would be a huge weight lifted from
> British business.[5]

This is the mirror image of the Cameron interview. While the prime minister offered an uninspiring plea for voters to make a hard-headed decision to reluctantly stay, Johnson asks Britons to follow their hearts and leap with him into the sunlit uplands. And, of course, he does so to avoid answering a specific question about the real world beyond the Brexit vote. It's breathtaking.

In Johnson's world, the only thing worse than not answering a question is answering one. Marr asks whether the sense of dislocation and uncertainty that would follow a vote to leave the European Union would mean a period where 'people would lose their jobs'. Johnson nonchalantly answers, 'Well, it might, or it might not.' Hang on, this is a story, thinks Marr, who starts to tease at the implications of this admission. Johnson doesn't like this, so he decides to change the subject. The real problem with the EU, he starts, is democracy.

Marr tries to take back control, pointing out that he's still got a lot of ground to cover:

Johnson: Well, I'm going to tell you what I'm going to cover.

Marr: No, it's not the Boris Johnson Show. It's *The Andrew Marr Show*. I get to ask the questions.

Johnson: All right, you have sovereignty.

Marr: Thank you. I have complete sovereignty over this programme.

Johnson: Unlike the UK.[6]

The audience at home probably laughs at that; Johnson has done the distraction job and got a laugh. He loves a laugh, but Marr won't give up. He's won an important admission that Brexit might hit jobs in the short term and pushes on to try to get some clarity about what Johnson thinks the future will look like if we leave. This is where the interview gets really weird.

Johnson doesn't want to answer the question. Leave aren't ready to argue that Britain should leave the Single Market after Brexit, but if we are to end freedom of movement and avoid paying into EU coffers, we'll have to. So Johnson has to sow confusion and muddy all available waters. He launches into an extended and impenetrable riff about the Single Market. When Marr tries to pull him back, he's accused, in a familiar tactic, of 'BBC claptrap'. Translation: asking a difficult question. Marr, exasperated, asks another one: 'Just tell me, are we going to be in it or not?'

Johnson won't say, but he does promise a fantastic free-trade deal that will 'give us access to the European Union'. Marr wants to know whether that can happen without freedom of movement, because this is the crux of the question, but Johnson takes that as his cue to confuse the viewer once more and muddy this puddle too. He muses about what freedom of movement, in a very real sense, actually means. The critical questions about the Single Market and freedom of movement are avoided, meaning is obscured, and so it goes until it ends.

The reviews are bad for both men. Vote Leave spinners text me and call the interview 'disgraceful'. They tot up the number of interruptions by Marr and come to fifty-seven, compared with just twenty-three when he interviewed David Cameron. I point out that the number of interruptions depends on whether the guest answers the questions or not. From the programme's point of view, and certainly from the presenter's, interviews full of interruptions are as frustrating as they are for viewers. They only happen because interviewees will not answer straight questions with straight answers. That was Johnson's choice in his first set-piece interview of the referendum campaign.

On Twitter, *GMB* presenter Piers Morgan comes to our defence. 'People criticising Marr for constantly interrupting Boris,' he tweets, 'need to understand that if he didn't, Mr Johnson would never stop talking.' One Twitter user, representative of furious, BBC-hating Leavers, offers her verdict: 'Marr really has it in for Boris Johnson, furiously jealous, forever trying to derail him, spiteful little pinko.'

The campaign, the most important political campaign in living memory, already feels like a car crash, but today I'm at least confident that it was Boris, and not Andrew, who grabbed the steering wheel and smashed us into the central reservation.

24 April 2016, Theresa May – Find the Cost of Freedom

If you want to know where the 2016 referendum was won and lost, I'd say it's here. I obviously don't mean that voters saw this programme in isolation and then made their decision – they didn't – but no interview on *Marr* in those four months so starkly demonstrates Remain's failure to find an answer on immigration. Of course, it may have been different if they'd attempted – with all the difficulties involved – to change the conversation around freedom of movement, emphasising its benefits for the UK and UK citizens, but that was probably impossible at this stage. So, instead, a party that wanted to be tough on immigration, embodied by a home secretary who had made it part of her brand, had to argue against the one thing that would give her control over a significant swathe of immigration: leaving the European Union.

May's appearance on *Marr* had been a long time coming. The home secretary had not been quick to woman the Remain barricades. She'd made her position public but didn't want to be seen as too enthusiastic a Remainer, presumably with an eye – correctly, as it turned out – on the leadership should this all go wrong for David Cameron. When she did show up, it was on what might traditionally have been her strongest political ground: immigration.

Theresa May is an extraordinary communicator, but not in a good way. This morning in April, however, with two months left before referendum day, she starts well, offering some relatively straight answers relatively quickly. Marr opens with a simple question, asking whether immigration will go up or down if we stay in the EU. After a preamble about how controlling immigration is always difficult, she answers:

'Yes, freedom of movement makes it harder to control immigration.'

'Ah,' says Marr.[7]

Ah, indeed.

Marr says staying in the European Union would mean another three million people coming from the EU by 2030. He's using government statistics, and she doesn't challenge them. She doesn't address the point directly but tries a new approach. She says that if we were outside the EU, we'd still have to accept free movement, assuming we wanted 'the sort of access to the Single Market that people talk about'. She doesn't say which people she means, but Boris Johnson's ears are burning, which is how he likes it.

This could be effective, but it's slightly disingenuous. As Johnson's interview in March demonstrated, at this point senior Leavers are being less than open about what sort of relationship they envisage with the European Union. They're not saying they're willing to pay the price of uncontrolled EU migration that Single Market membership would involve, and it feels as if they're much more likely to jump the other way. In any case, May's deflection doesn't help. Nothing really does. Marr persists: staying in the EU will mean more migration. May can't quite agree but accepts that immigration is too high, and the public is correct to be unhappy about the effect on jobs and public services. The trouble is there's only one way to do something about it, and that's to leave the EU.

No, there's lots that we've done, she says. She means stricter restrictions on non-EU migration and new rules on student visas. Again, not really the point, so she switches tack, suggesting that we already control EU migrants coming in because we can turn away criminals at the border. That's true, but, Marr says, that's not the point either. He returns to the projected three million people coming in from the EU as of right if we stay, and asks if she thinks that would be a good thing or a bad thing.

'I think immigration is too high,' she says.

We're getting precisely nowhere, but that tells its own story. Nothing is working.

As if in recognition of that truth, May comes across as the world's most reluctant Remainer. Towards the end of the interview, she says, unprompted, that while she thinks Remain is the better course, we will 'survive' outside the European Union, and she closes with this underwhelming rhetorical flourish:

> When people look at this, the question is what is right
> for Britain's future. Where will our prosperity best be
> most secure? I think that is inside the European Union.
> And this is not a black-and-white decision.[8]

You wouldn't put that on the side of a bus ...

As I watched that morning, I realised Remain was in deep trouble. Here was a campaign led by politicians who'd spent their political lives criticising the European Union and presenting freedom of movement as a problem. Many of their voters felt the same way. And now they're recommending that the same voters vote Remain.

That morning, Christopher Hope, from that most Tory of newspapers, the *Daily Telegraph*, said it all: 'Not a good #Marr interview for Theresa May. No answer to migration question at all. Risks ridicule.'

8 May 2016, Michael Gove – True Colours

If you push me – oh, go on, push me – my favourite interviewee of the era of Tory government is Michael Gove. Johnson offers the pyrotechnics, Theresa May the almost hypnotic boredom, but Gove gives the best quote. He's witty, funny and surprising. He also has something about him of the nutty inventor who shrunk the kids. He's a scream. It's great TV. Whether he's good for the country I'll leave you to judge.

Best of all, Gove sometimes says things he shouldn't, he sometimes goes there when others will not, and so it proves six weeks out from referendum day, on *Marr* in early May.

> **Marr:** Let me ask you a very simple question I have tried to get an answer to from various people on your side – should we or should we not be inside the Single Market? Do you want us to stay inside the Single Market? Yes or no?

> **Gove:** No. We should be outside the Single Market. We should have access to the Single Market, but we should not be governed by the rules that the European Court of Justice imposes on us, which cost business and restrict freedom.[9]

In the gallery we do a double-take. This is a significant development, and after the obfuscation of Johnson on the same subject, almost unreal. They've noticed over on ITV too, where Robert Peston's new show is a Sunday-morning competitor to *Marr* (it isn't long before they move, successfully, to Wednesday nights). The chancellor George Osborne is their guest, and he's ready to jump on Gove's admission.

Osborne says leaving the Single Market would be catastrophic for people's jobs, incomes and livelihoods. He focuses on Gove: 'Some people might think that wrecking the economy is a price worth paying. I absolutely reject that.'[10]

In a way, Gove's candour is a win for both sides: there can be no doubt now that a vote for Leave will mean an end to free movement; there can be no real doubt that a vote for Remain is better for the economy. Immigration versus the economy. You choose.

On Twitter, the *Financial Times* editor Lionel Barber applauds Gove's honesty: 'Gove admission on #marr that #Brexit means UK leaves Single Market is intellectually honest but economically v damaging – big moment.'

Took them long enough …

22 May 2016, Penny Mordaunt – Little Lies

In the list of political heavyweights who appear on *Marr* during the EU referendum campaign, Penny Mordaunt doesn't feature very near the top. A month and a day before the Brexit vote, Vote Leave has nominated the obscure minister of state for the armed forces to go on television to talk Turkey. Today's skirmishes on immigration will focus on a country that's not in the European Union and has no real prospect of joining. But Mordaunt starts the interview with a warning that Turkey *will* join the European Union within eight years. This claim is – and I'm using a technical term here – utter bollocks, as we now know. For Mordaunt's clairvoyance to be correct, they'd be joining in 2024. As I write, that deadline is just around the corner, and the Turkish application process has gone backwards. Still, when Marr challenges her in 2016, she's confident: 'I think it's very likely that they will.'[11] Just don't ask Mystic Mordaunt to help you with your lottery numbers.

But back in 2016 she has a reason to believe: if she can convince voters that Turkey is on the brink of EU membership, she can tell them that 76 million Turks will soon have the right to move to the UK if we stay in the European Union. What's more, Vote Leave has published a new 'analysis' pointing out that a) the Turkish birth rate is so high that there'll be one million more of them by the time they join, and b) that's bad because the crime rate in Turkey is very high and we'll end up with a lot of Turkish criminals here. The dog-whistle is so aggressively blown that canines all over Britain, rudely awakened from their Sunday-morning slumber, are now suddenly bolt upright and attentive. This campaign is descending into somewhere unpleasant, fast.

Turkey applied to join the European Union in 1987. So, in theory, they might be granted membership one day. But here's the critical fact: Britain, like all existing member states, has a veto on any new country joining. In other words, as Marr points out to Mordaunt, they can only join if we let them. 'No,' she answers. 'We are not going to be able to have a say.'

This is untrue, but Marr moves on. Later, communicating with him through his earpiece, I ask him to return to the veto issue. What she has said is demonstrably untrue, and we need to make that clear and give her the chance to clear it up. Maybe she misspoke. Marr tells her he's sure that the UK does have a veto, asking, 'Are you sure that we don't?'

Mordaunt (doubles down): Well, we haven't ... We'll be unable to stop Turkey joining.

Marr: But if we don't want Turkey in, we can stop Turkey from coming in?

Mordaunt: I don't think that the UK will be able to stop Turkey joining.[12]

Mordaunt must know that the UK, like all EU members, has a veto on Turkey or any new country joining the EU, but she clearly says we don't have a veto, we're not going to be able to have a say and we won't be able to stop Turkey joining.

Over on *Peston* on ITV – and this is becoming a habit – our story dominates their main interview, this time with David Cameron. He's categorical: 'She [Mordaunt] is absolutely wrong. Let me be clear. Britain and every other country in the EU has a veto on another country joining. That is a fact.'

Mordaunt is doing politics, not facts. It's very naughty behaviour but there will be a price to pay for Penny a few years down the track. Stay tuned.

5 June 2016, Sir John Major and Boris Johnson – Mess of Blues

It's hard not to find this moment depressing.

Before the interviews start, things kick off in the newspaper review. The Greens' Caroline Lucas and Vote Leave's Suzanne Evans get into a spat over the most prominent piece of Vote Leave deception: the £350 million they promise for the NHS if Britain leaves the EU, which they have put on the side of a bus. It's a lie, says Lucas, because it ignores the rebate and other monies that come back to the UK from the EU, which make our net contribution much lower. She's right, of course, but Evans has her comeback. She highlights George Osborne's warning that the average family will be £4,300 a year worse off if we vote to leave. That's not true, she says. The reality is that forecasts do say households will be worse off, but this figure feels like a con. It's too precise. It's a guesstimate. So it goes, the most consequential decision the British people will make for decades, and this is the level of debate: lies, dog-whistles and scare stories.

Sir Robbie Gibb – he was just plain Robbie Gibb at the time – was my boss at the BBC during the Brexit campaign. He later left the BBC to work as Theresa May's director of communications in Downing Street before joining the BBC board where he sits today. Looking back on the claims and counter-claims of Leave and Remain, he does not accept that Leave were lying:

> It's just not true that politicians lie all the time. £350 million was not a lie at all. It's just campaigning. Nobody ever says, 'What about Labour saying, "You've got 24 hours to save the NHS."' Nobody ever picks that up, but when it's about Boris Johnson they do. So I just have no truck with it. The reason why the £350 million was taken apart was because the methodology was transparent because it was based on something. Osborne's £4,300 figure was based on some bizarre Treasury econometric modelling that was built on the premise that leaving the EU would be a disaster. Shock horror – it said it would be terrible![13]

The real news this particular June morning is dominated by the death of the greatest: Muhammad Ali. The scripts write themselves. The show is a heavyweight contest between Sir John Major, the former prime minister, and Boris Johnson, leader of the Leave campaign. The contrast between their two versions of Conservatism – the old-fashioned, slightly dreary but dependable variety, and the populist, broad-brush, edgy remake – is stark.

But it was a long and challenging road to get here. It seems quite quaint now, given the way the Conservative Party has torn itself apart in years of argument over Brexit and repeated leadership elections, but during the 2016 referendum the Remain side – led by David Cameron, a Tory – was very worried about what we in the trade called 'blue-on-blue'. That's code for Conservatives debating against Conservatives. They were so concerned because they thought they'd win, and when they did, they'd have a hell of a job putting the band back together.

As soon as David Cameron returned with his deal, I wanted Sir John Major on the programme. The former prime minister had negotiated the Maastricht Treaty and got it ratified in the face of the 'bastards' – as he famously called them – in his cabinet and beyond. Leave or Remain, you couldn't deny he was a significant voice in the debate.

At the end of March 2016 I was delighted to learn from producer Libby Jukes – a skilful negotiator – that Major was available to come on and talk about the referendum. Major had a long-standing relationship with the programme, mediated by his formidable chief of staff, Dame Arabella Warburton. The former prime minister's political operation has its own unique character. It seems to exist in a world of old-fashioned Tory decency marked by courtesy and caution. I confess that every time I encountered Major – first as prime minister in 1997 and later as a grandee – I was impressed. He was charismatic in person and a compelling, if understated, performer on television. I'd been desperate for him to give way to Blair in the 1990s, but by 2016 he seemed like a class act to me.

So all was set for Sir John to come on and give his verdict on Brexit and the Cameron deal. Then on the Thursday before Major was due to appear, former Tory leader Iain Duncan Smith, the welfare secretary, resigned from David Cameron's government. In the wake of the budget, IDS, as everyone in Westminster called him, had discovered a previously undetected aversion to welfare cuts and walked out. As soon as I heard, I called his special adviser. A fresh resignee was bread and butter to the *Marr* show, and I got the exclusive. Great news. There was only one problem: there was no way Major would come onto the same show as IDS. Brexit would come up, and we'd be in 'blue-on-blue' territory. We'd have to choose, and we did: IDS was the story, and I had to tell Dame Arabella, who's no pussycat. As we feared, she wasn't happy, and Major pulled out.

Then, in early June, we went back to Major and asked if he was ready to weigh in on immigration, Turkey, the Single Market and all the rest. His office sounded keen. Their assumption, and it was a fair one based on experience, was that as a former prime minister he'd be given the final interview of the programme. That was where the biggest, highest-status guest appeared and where they could have the last word. Also, his office wondered, if Sir John does come on, could you tell us who will be on from Leave?

The answer, problematically, was Boris Johnson, back for his second campaign interview. The problem was that this was the ultimate blue-on-blue clash, and there was no way we could give the main interview slot to Major over Johnson. Johnson was a frontline politician and the leader of Leave. He was simply the bigger name in 2016. Finally, it would be better for the programme to let Major say his piece – we expected him to be highly critical of Johnson himself – and to then put those words to Johnson.

So we told Dame Arabella, and she said no.

I can't really blame her. The risk for former prime ministers is that they become ubiquitous. Rather than 'rare', their interventions become commonplace, and they find themselves drawn into the fray of daily political argument. Major, in particular, was careful to curate his image and ration his interventions. So I wasn't surprised, but it did seem short-sighted: it was obvious that Leave had all the momentum. Now that Major had declined, the best Remain could offer was Hilary Benn. Benn's a nice bloke, but not much of a match for Johnson. I went to the Remain campaign to make the case and ask them to see if they could persuade Major to go for it. 'He can lay down the challenge,' I texted Craig Oliver, 'understand why he cares about order of play, but these are strange days.'

Oliver was only too aware of how precious the Major team could be and didn't sound optimistic, but the following day he texted again. This time the news was good: Major would do us, but I needed to talk it through with Dame Arabella and, crucially, not let on to her that I already knew he'd agreed. This felt weird, but I still needed to hear it from the horse's mouth, so I called. She was clear that he was minded to do it but was worried about Johnson. Could we ensure that there was no interaction between Sir John and Johnson at the studios on the day? I assured her we'd ensure the two men's dressing rooms were as far apart as possible and that they didn't bump into each other in the make-up room. The Dame was trepidatious but happy. It was on.

Oliver texted again later: 'You're going to have quite a show,' he said, adding that Marr should 'feast on the story.' It struck me as a strange word to use, but he was clearly excited. Finally, the gloves were coming off, and after being pretty comprehensively outplayed so far, Remain was going to try to up the stakes on our show. This was to be the most prominent blue-on-blue encounter of the campaign, and I was delighted to have it.

The only problem was Johnson. When the morning came, he was determined to find Major in his dressing room, somewhere in the bowels of the BBC. We'd gone to elaborate lengths to separate the two guests and choreograph their movements to avoid a pre-show meeting. This had been Major's stipulation, and it seemed a fair-enough request, but there wasn't much we could do about a marauding Johnson intent on finding the mild-mannered former prime minister. Eventually, he knocked on the right door and Major, unruffled, invited him in and closed the door.

There were no raised voices, and the meeting was brief. Johnson seemed to want some sort of psychological victory by forcing Major to see him. I was puzzled by this. I hadn't told anyone outside a small circle inside the BBC that Major had asked to be kept from Johnson, but he seemed to know. This worried me. Was someone feeding information to Johnson? I was never sure.

Whether he was tipped off or not, if Boris hoped his ruse would throw Sir John off his game, he couldn't have been more wrong. In the interview, Major is a study in controlled fury and precision, as close as he gets to incandescent: 'I think throughout the whole of my political life people have regarded me as being guilty of understatement,' he says. 'I am angry at the way the British people are being misled.' The Leave campaign is 'fundamentally dishonest'. They've led a campaign on immigration that 'borders on the squalid'. Major predicts chaos if we leave and economic damage when the economy shrinks. There won't be extra money for the NHS. There will be less:

> The concept that the people running the Brexit campaign
> would care for the National Health Service is a rather
> odd one. I seem to remember Michael Gove wanting to
> privatise it. Boris wanted to charge people for using it.
> And Iain Duncan Smith wanted a social insurance
> system. The NHS is about as safe with them as a pet
> hamster would be with a hungry python.[14]

He sums it all up in his quaint English way: 'People are being invited to vote for a pig in a poke.'

Enter the pig salesman.

Boris Johnson doesn't have too much trouble in this final campaign outing on the *Marr Show*, but nor does he get into his stride. Given its political efficacy, Johnson is probably delighted when Marr brings up Turkey, but he can't accept it when Marr drops the 'L' word.

Marr: You're responsible for this poster that goes up saying Turkey is joining the EU. That is a flat lie.

Johnson: It's the government's policy that Turkey should join the EU.

Marr: That's a different poster.[15]

The encounter is tetchy, but we have held both sides accountable for their spin and deception. That's our job, but it doesn't mean it will make any difference.

Tuesday 21 June 2016 – Two Tribes

The Great Debate, Wembley Arena

And so it went on for another two weeks on *Marr*. The fundamentals didn't shift, even after the tragic murder of Labour MP Jo Cox briefly heralded a more considered and less hysterical tone. Hostilities paused for a few days, but in the home straight, the immigration-versus-the-economy referendum rolled on. The TV campaign culminated in an event that felt in tune with the disappointing, messy and depressing campaign: the BBC's *Great Debate*. It was two days before polling day.

Like Jeremy Corbyn at a wreath-laying ceremony, I was present but not involved.

The set-piece event was held at Wembley Arena in front of more than six thousand people. I was only there for the ride on the night, watching the event from one of the green rooms with a beer.

The show – and it was a show – pitted a team of three Leavers against three Remainers, led by Boris Johnson and Scottish Tory leader Ruth Davidson respectively.

The only new and interesting dynamic was created by the Remain team finally deciding to make some sort of positive case for staying in. From David Cameron's appearance in February onwards, Remain had been grudging about a future in the EU. Fair enough, that's who the Tories were, but it was a terrible way to run a campaign. At Wembley, Davidson, London mayor Sadiq Khan and Trade Unions Congress general secretary Frances O'Grady offered a glimpse of how things might have been: a passionate debate about what sort of country we wanted to be, rather than a nasty argument over bogus buses, dodgy Treasury projections and lies about immigration.

So that was the upside, but it was largely drowned out by the dynamics of the spectacle the BBC had built. It was all heat and no light. Now, I'm not a boring fundamentalist on this kind of thing – conflict and passion can create TV moments that sweeten the pill – but they were the pill at Wembley.

The evening ended on a jarring note. Mingling with the production team, I'd overheard the result of the pre-show coin toss: Remain was to give the closing speech. That might be important in a close vote. But then, as the programme drew to a close, Remain's Ruth Davidson was invited to make her final pitch first. Inexplicably, the coveted closing peroration had been handed instead to Boris Johnson, the man with the pig in his poke, Dr-Everything-Will-Be-All-Right, the human embodiment of Brexit, and he was spectacularly effective:

> If we vote to leave and take back control, I believe that this Thursday can be our country's Independence Day.[16]

The crowd went crazy, and on 23 June snake-oil sales were through the roof. In the immigration-versus-the-economy referendum, immigration won.

And the day after that, the special adviser prime minister, despite his promises to stay, come what may, walked.

* * *

I have two notes to conclude this chapter.

The first concerns my admission earlier that I voted Remain. For some readers, this will be the slam-dunk evidence that the BBC was – and is – full of Remainers whose coverage of the Brexit campaign was coloured by their own opinions. When they read my admission about my Brexit vote they may well have thrown this book across the room so won't even be reading this sentence, but I'll press on anyway. Whatever I say from here will be dismissed by them because of my status as a card-carrying member of the Remainiac media-elite. Forget the fact that the likes of Johnson and his crew are more privileged than I've ever been, my card is duly marked.

The truth is that most people working in political television have political views. In fact, they all do. There were very prominent people I worked with at BBC Politics who were Conservatives and Leavers, but I think it's probably true that, just as the BBC is a little bit left-leaning, it was a little bit Remain-leaning too. The most serious criticisms of the BBC's handling of the referendum actually centre on the false equivalence between, for example, the body of opinion on the economic impact of Brexit that said it would be negative and the handful of pro-Brexit economists who shared Boris Johnson's faith there would be a Brexit boom. So, if anything, Leave benefited from the BBC getting it wrong, not Remain.

I can only answer for what we did on *Marr*. I'm content that our work – demonstrating the weakness of the Remain position on immigration or exposing lies about Turkey from Leave – was fair and impartial. Reliving those weeks confirms, if anything, that Leave had the more effective answers and the better strategy, which says a lot for the self-inflicted failures of Remain. It's also hard to avoid concluding that Leave was cynical and often outright deceptive, and that BBC Politics more broadly didn't do a great job of calling that out.

The day after the referendum in 2016, I remember talking to my boss at the BBC at the time, Robbie Gibb, who ran the political programmes department. I told him that in my view we needed to interrogate the veracity of the Vote Leave claims that had won them the referendum, claims like that '£350 million a week' for the NHS on the side of the bus. Robbie was horrified. All that was done, he told me. It was now time to move on. Robbie thought that anything that looked back at the referendum would look to voters like an attempt to re-run it. It risked giving the impression that the BBC couldn't accept the outcome and wanted to discredit the result.

I understood the argument, but didn't see it like that at all. It was part of the Vote Leave strategy to close down any discussion of their own claims and ask everyone to move on. Journalists who refused to comply were then smeared as 'remoaners' who couldn't accept the result. I didn't think the BBC should be intimidated. We needed to stand up to the pressure. Holding the Brexiteers to account for their claims was, and remains, completely justifiable journalistically. It's not an attempt to re-run the referendum but to test the claims made in the campaign. It's the same principle as judging a general election-winning government against their manifesto promises once they're in power. We don't say that to do so is an attempt to re-run the election. Robbie was my boss and he was entitled to tell me what editorial approach he thought I should take, but I thought he was wrong on this and I ignored the instruction.

Interviews are about accountability, and those who claimed the sunlit uplands awaited us if we voted to Leave should be accountable for the reality. I don't think they should be held accountable because I voted Remain; I think they should be held accountable because they won. That's also the reason I personally thought trying to re-run the referendum was wrong. It's true that we didn't know what Brexit really was when we voted for it, and there was an argument that this meant a new vote was required, but Leave won, and the vote had to be respected.

There will never be a settled view that allows us to judge Brexit as a success or a failure. Nobody will agree on the criteria to be applied to make that call. How can you quantify the value of restored sovereignty and measure it against lost GDP? You can't, so the argument will rage on, and the Brexiteers will always claim that the real Brexit is just around the corner if only those awful Remainers, the European Union and bloody journalists would allow it to emerge. In that way, Brexit is never achieved, only betrayed, so it can't be regretted.

My second point concerns Jeremy Corbyn. The truth is he barely features in this account of the most significant political debate in recent British political history. Why? Because his impact on the referendum was negligible, and his campaign appearances on *Marr* were so low-wattage that I struggled – and then gave up trying – to find anything to say about them here.

But he is, of course, interesting in other ways. So now, over the page, we'll go back to the land before Brexit and the emergence of Labour's unlikely leader.

11

JEREMY IN THREE PHASES

Summer 2015, BBC canteen

How do I broach this?

I'm sitting next to a member of the shadow cabinet who's running for the leadership of the Labour Party. We're having breakfast in the BBC canteen. They've just appeared on *The Andrew Marr Show* on BBC One and, with unfortunate timing, have forgotten how to speak. The trouble is they don't seem to have noticed. After all, they've been like this for years, and it's all been fine, but in a leadership contest people demand vision, inspiration and solutions. What's more, you'll be open to ridicule if you can't answer a straight question with a straight answer. If you want to make a pitch to the country, you need to know how to speak.

So, what do I say? I feel myself pulled into their world of woolly obfuscation as I reach for words that will convey my meaning without offending them. I say something about communication. I talk about choice of words. I hint but don't make my meaning clear at all. I think I'd expected they'd get my drift immediately, and we'd have a frank conversation about the downsides of New Labourspeak, but it doesn't happen. So, after a conversation between two people who can't speak, I give up and eat my bacon and eggs in silence.

In my experience, politicians are not the most self-aware group of people in the world. While everyone else sees and hears a malfunctioning robot, they just think this is how it is supposed to be. They have learnt to ignore the blank looks of the electorate as they spout the party line or dance around a simple question. These tactics have stood them in good stead so far. Why change now?

They're about to find out.

Later in the summer, the wildcard candidate for the leadership, left-wing rebel MP Jeremy Corbyn – who only made the ballot because indulgent MPs lent him their nominations to ensure a 'wide-ranging debate' – arrives on the *Marr* set with opinion polls pointing to his near-certain victory.

Corbyn has not forgotten how to speak. Not as scruffy as he used to be (there are images of him from the eighties in unspeakable jumpers) but still untouched by image consultants, Corbyn is relaxed, confident and expansive. He answers questions about Marxism happily, unconcerned they might be some sort of trap. All the candidates that arrived on *Marr* that summer were asked where they stood on austerity. All, to some extent, leaned into the government's argument that savings – cuts – must continue to be made. All except Corbyn, who rejects Cameron's austerity and Labour's failure to effectively oppose it. He's compelling in a low-key, refreshing way. He seems to be enjoying himself. The *Marr* studio has never heard so many clear answers and so much unapologetic radicalism.

As I watched that Sunday morning, my mind returned to the conversation with his Labour rival. Their safety-first politics and inability to articulate any compelling vision for fear of upsetting someone looked politically suicidal. The Corbyn bandwagon was rolling, and it was going to run them down. No matter how hard they cried out to halt it, no noise came from their mouths. That's what happens when you've forgotten how to speak.

11 June 2017, BBC canteen

I'm back in the canteen at the BBC after an edition of *The Andrew Marr Show* just three days after the dramatic 2017 general election. This is an environment where you might find yourself chatting to a major rock star, a senior member of the government or the editor of one of the national newspapers. It's fun, relaxed and usually very interesting.

There's also the danger that you draw the short straw and find yourself sitting next to the slightly whiffy drummer of a heritage rock band who wasn't in the original line-up and didn't have time for a shower before rocking up to the studio. Worse, you might be cornered by a slightly unhinged pundit there to do the newspaper review who is decorating your lapels with spittle as they bang on about the benefits of Brexit or local government finance. Who you get is the luck of the draw.

Today, the conversation is far from scintillating. It's low energy and essentially banal. There's something about potatoes, something about leeks, and I think onions come up. I start looking over my neighbour's shoulder, hoping somebody might rescue me. It's not unpleasant, just a bit boring.

Then, salvation! A member of BBC staff – not one of the journalists, but one of the hundreds of support staff – catches sight of my conversation partner. Then something unusual happens. He bounds towards us, smiling, waving his phone in the air.

'Jeremy! Jeremy!' he cries.

The leader of the opposition looks up and smiles, quickly swallowing down a last mouthful of veggie sausage. He starts to get up. He knows what's required. The selfie is delivered quickly and with genuine warmth. He gets this all day, every day, but he's gracious, kind and uncomplaining. The picture is taken, another staff member sees him and comes over for their selfie moment. Before long, a small crowd has gathered. A chant of 'Oh, Jeremy Corbyn' goes up, and he smiles, basking in it.

No wonder, as Andrew Marr had put it to Corbyn on air a little earlier, the Labour leader 'looks pretty chipper': three days previously, this radical politician outperformed all expectations and deprived Theresa May of her majority. The Corbyn chant is never sung with more gusto than in the summer of 2017. It will ring out across the fields of Glastonbury in a few days when Corbyn 'plays' the Pyramid Stage. The accidental leader is now a rock-star politician.

Eventually, he sits back down next to me to finish his breakfast.

'Now, where was I?' he asks.

'You were talking about your allotment,' I say wearily. 'Please do go on.'

23 September 2018, the Museum of Liverpool

It's the Labour Party conference in Liverpool. Marr and Corbyn are having a long and unproductive discussion about Brexit and Labour and Theresa May's attempt to find a deal. Sitting next to Corbyn on the *Marr* sofa in our makeshift studio at the Museum of Liverpool, with its views of the Liver Building and the Ferry Across the Mersey, is an enormous elephant. It's spent the first eight minutes or so of the interview examining its nails, staring out of the window and, now and again, trying to attract Marr's attention. Eventually, he decides he cannot ignore its presence anymore.

'Jeremy Corbyn,' he asks, 'are you an antisemite?'[1]

Corbyn looks exhausted and haggard, his eyes baggy, his face creased. Accusations of personal and institutional antisemitism in the Labour Party have dominated the summer of 2018, taking their toll on him. This is the first time he has sat down for an extended interview since the furore began, his first chance to properly make his case.

'No,' he insists, 'absolutely not. I've spent my whole life opposing racism in any form, and I will die fighting racism in any form.' (Corbyn never talks directly about antisemitism alone. He always talks, instead, about 'racism in any form'.) 'I completely and utterly reject the idea that I'm any kind of racist,' he continues.

As the conversation goes on, taking in antisemitic murals, controversial commemorations and comments made about 'Zionist' Britons who didn't understand 'English irony', Corbyn sighs. He seems wounded, and it must be tough. He confesses that comments by the former chief rabbi Jonathan Sacks comparing him to Enoch Powell are hurtful. How has it come to this?

Although he can't say it today, Corbyn's honest answer is that he believes it's come to this for political reasons. He believes that the accusations of antisemitism, whether directed at him or Labour members, have been exaggerated by his political enemies inside and outside the Labour Party and by the print media, whose lead is so often followed by the broadcasters. The fact that *The Andrew Marr Show* is choosing to talk about it only feeds this suspicion, and his team are furious that the subject dominates the interview.

Before he moves on, Marr invites the Labour leader to look into the camera and express remorse to the Jewish community for the summer's revelations that have upset so many. He won't do that. In fact, it seems he can't. All he can offer are his convoluted formulations that create more problems than they solve. Perhaps this is Corbyn's curse, the flip side of what used to be his appeal. He can't defuse this crisis by saying something he doesn't believe to be true, so he ties himself in knots.

On antisemitism, it seems Jeremy Corbyn has forgotten how to speak.

Phase one: The end of the innocence

Here's the truth: we need Jeremy Corbyn more than he needs us.

It's Saturday 12 September 2015, and the longest long-shot candidate of them all, veteran Labour lefty, serial troublemaker and all-round naughty boy, has been hailed as the Messiah. His initials are even JC.

Corbyn has brought thousands of disciples into the Labour Party and created more fervour and excitement than any other British politician in living memory. He has managed to smash the centre and right of his party with a thumping 59 per cent of the vote. Labour MPs are horrified, while huge chunks of the party membership are delighted. It's a massive story, and it's perfect for *Marr*. The result was announced on Saturday evening, and we have a comfortable chair waiting for the new leader's bottom on Sunday morning. *Marr* is what you do when you win.

Until it isn't. I've spent days trying to reach Team Corbyn, finally speaking to Carmel Nolan, his 'head of broadcast', to arrange the traditional post-victory leader's interview. Nolan couldn't be more helpful, but there's something wrong. Corbyn has won despite, not because, of what his supporters invariably call the MSM – the mainstream media – and he's not about to dance to our tune, even if it will connect him with more voters than he could possibly meet in a year of public meetings. He just won't confirm.

And who can blame him? Earlier in the campaign, when everyone saw him as an irrelevance, Nolan contacted *Newsnight* to ask if they might be interested in interviewing candidate Corbyn. When she got through to a producer there, her suggestion was greeted by actual laughter from the person who picked up the phone. She was eventually referred to the work experience. People remember things like that.[2]

All that changed when, in July, the *New Statesman*'s political editor Stephen Bush dropped a bombshell: he'd seen polling suggesting that Corbyn was miles ahead of his nearest rival, Andy Burnham, and on course to become Labour leader. This was reinforced by news reports of Corbyn's public meetings, with queues around the block. The sense was that a significant chunk of the existing Labour Party membership and a wave of new members were sick and tired of triangulating, mealy-mouthed Labour politicians who couldn't answer a question and were too scared to do anything but ape the Tory government. The years of New Labour messaging and policy discipline once deemed essential were shrugged off like a winter coat in the sunshine. The party could finally be itself again: gorging at Jeremy's socialist buffet, getting hammered at the Bennite free bar and dancing with Dennis Skinner all night long like nobody was watching.

Let's be honest about how the journalistic and political establishment greeted this. They were shocked and, in large part, horrified. For many like me – Labour supporters of the Thatcher generation who grew up in the 1980s – this seemed like a route towards inevitable political failure. There can be no doubt that this scepticism infected coverage of Corbyn from the beginning.

For my part, I tried consciously to resist it, and Marr agreed that we needed to be scrupulously fair to Corbyn, whatever the Westminster consensus. Our job was always the same, whomever we interviewed: probe the weaknesses of their arguments and explore the political challenges they faced. We always took Corbyn, his policies and his achievements seriously, and it was our job to test him. But first, he had to show up, and on that Saturday afternoon in September 2015 the word finally came back: Corbyn was a no. Instead, we'd have to make do with the slightly larger posterior of Tom Watson, the newly elected deputy leader.

The following day, you could tell we were in a new era. Alongside journalists from the *Sun* and the *Guardian* on the

Marr sofa for the newspaper review sat the editor of the *Morning Star*, once the organ of the British Communist Party. Suddenly, publications and pundits that had existed at the margins for decades were slap bang in the middle of mainstream discourse. A new dawn had broken, had it not?

When Watson appeared – looking as dazed as anyone by the events of the previous twenty-four hours – he was jovial enough, but from that first morning there were conflicts and contradictions to probe that had been left undiscussed in the leadership contest. At their heart was the division between the leadership and membership on one side, and the majority of Labour MPs on the other. In a sign of what was to come, Watson walked softly but carried a big mandate of his own, and he reminded Marr of it more than once. The message was clear: you won, Jeremy, but you won't have it all your own way.

Party conference interviews are a big deal. If I ever felt jaded by the weekly repetition of covering politics as *Marr* editor – which was rare, but could happen – the juices would start flowing again when conference season came around.

Labour's party conference in Brighton in September 2015 comes just a couple of weeks after Corbyn's unlikely election, and it's a genuinely exciting moment. The media and the Labour establishment remain discombobulated by Corbyn, and the conference really brings it home. This is his party now, and all the rules and norms are out the window. Except one: Corbyn has decided he'll do the traditional set-piece leader's interview with Marr on the opening Sunday morning. The MSM are back, baby.

We are broadcasting live from a cafe overlooking Brighton seafront, and the political atmosphere is charged. This is our first chance to interview Corbyn in power – well, Labour power, at least – and it's a test for us both. On a beautiful September morning Corbyn appears, without an entourage but with one lowly press officer, pursued by numerous film crews. He's early

and seems relaxed, happy to read the papers and eat BBC crois-
sants. Nobody's briefing him and he displays no pre-show
nerves. Corbyn the candidate is now Corbyn the leader, which
means Corbyn the potential prime minister.

But he makes no concessions to this. Refreshingly crumpled
in a linen jacket that may be brown or perhaps grey – it's hard
to tell – he's not a lying bastard. He acknowledges differences
in his party and shadow cabinet over the renewal of the Trident
nuclear deterrent. He remains opposed to renewing Trident,
consistent with his lifelong position on these issues, but, well,
disarms the situation by asking whether it's really 'so disastrous' that there are some disagreements in political parties. Of
course, such decisions will ultimately have to be made, but his
relaxed attitude to internal dissent is refreshing.

This is straightforward, unruffled Jeremy. He sometimes
resorts to fake bonhomie to get through the interview, but he's
not dishonest. Although he isn't a funny man, he uses humour
as a rhetorical weapon, and it's only the sarcastic edge to these
jokey responses that suggest something else is going on. He's
technically honest but holds something back, not quite revealing his authentic self when under a little bit of pressure. Finally,
bridling about questions on his view of the monarchy, he lets a
little annoyance show.

'I understand your irritation,' says Marr, and Corbyn,
remembering himself, snaps back into friendly mode.

'Oh, no, no, no,' he replies, smiling. 'I don't do irritation.'[3]

That turns out to be a lie, but perhaps an understandable one
for now.

But it couldn't last. The simple, unaffected, home-spun
wisdom of allotment-man could only take him so far. The leadership was an enormous step up for a politician who'd been on
the back benches for thirty-two years and spent much of that
time opposing the Labour leadership of the day. Now he is the
Labour leadership. Help arrived in October 2015 in the wiry
form of Seumas Milne, a long-standing comment editor at the

Guardian who became Corbyn's executive director of strategy and communications. He recalls the scale of the challenge that faced the sixty-six-year-old rookie:

> Jeremy's situation was very particular and unusual. He'd not been a frontline politician, so he wasn't used to doing mainstream frontline media in a way that most politicians who get to that position have. It was the paradox of Jeremy: it was part of his appeal and why he was elected leader of the Labour party – but also meant it was a very fast learning curve.[4]

Milne remembers the early months of 'car crashes and problems', and that's what it felt like. That autumn Corbyn told an interviewer that he'd never fire nuclear weapons, in which case there really was no case for renewing Trident. Later he questioned the legality of the drone strike that killed ISIS murderer Mohammed Emwazi, aka 'Jihadi John', confirming his critics' worst fears about his instincts on terrorism. Many of those who were worried about his leadership, but who also thought they should give him a chance, concluded that he was as bad a leader as they'd feared he would be.

'He was in an extraordinary position,' Milne says, 'being elected leader of a political party where a majority of his MPs didn't just not vote for him, but many of whom were actively opposed to him from day one, or actually before day one.'[5] This dynamic made it difficult for Corbyn and his small, embryonic team of media advisers. They were up against the Conservatives, many of their own MPs, the staff in the Labour press office – 'They were not working for us,' recalls Milne sardonically[6] – and, they argued, the press and broadcast media.

When it came to the BBC's political news operation, Milne is damning. From the start, he says, BBC Politics would 'take their political agenda very heavily from the press', which was largely Conservative, right-wing and very hostile. 'That's a problem for most Labour Party leaders,' he concedes, 'but it was on steroids for us.'[7] The problem was compounded, he believes, because the political journalists and correspondents at BBC Westminster had little or no relationships with the Labour left or the trade union movement, but were often close to the 'Labour establishment'.

> The mentality of the Labour establishment, which is largely the centrist framework of accepted political debate and contest from the early nineties until at least the crash of 2008, is also the mentality of a lot of people working in broadcasting. They regard that as the centre ground and the mainstream. And that was where they were coming from themselves. They saw that as common sense rather than a political position – while Jeremy Corbyn and his supporters were regarded as somehow illegitimate.[8]

That autumn Corbyn, newly fitted out in – and somehow boxed in by – a dark blue suit and red tie, is back on *Marr* amid the first stirrings of an anti-Corbyn putsch, but he keeps his chin up, telling his host, 'I'm not going anywhere. I'm enjoying every moment of it.'[9] But by January 2016 Labour gloom has deepened, and as the leader of the opposition's traditional New Year's interview arrives, Marr introduces him as 'on probation'.[10] Corbyn cuts a beleaguered figure in a light brown suit and scruffy let-the-side-down shoes. His mojo has largely deserted him.

This is Corbyn in the intermediate state between the candidate leader and the later, fully developed, more guarded version of himself. He retains an open approach to questions but allows traces of irritation to surface. His go-to method of closing things down – insofar as he can be bothered to do so at this point – is to hammer the interviewer with industrial quantities of boredom. And so the interview that day – 17

January 2016 – veers between empty waffle, mild annoyance and careless blundering into unwise news-making territory. In those moments, Corbyn is like a tourist in the Everglades, disregarding the warning signs and going for a dip with the crocodiles.

This interview marks the high point of Corbyn's naive willingness to take requests and play the political hits of the 1970s and 1980s without the slightest concession to modern production techniques. Nuclear disarmament? You hum it for me, Andrew, and I'll pick it up. Secondary picketing? I'm pretty sure I know the chords to that one. Acknowledging Argentinian sovereignty over the Falkland Islands, or should I say Las Islas Malvinas? I probably shouldn't, but I can't resist a tango.

So after a preamble where Corbyn deals well enough with the ongoing chaos inside the Parliamentary Labour Party, Marr asks about Trident. Corbyn isn't here to recommission nuclear weapons systems, and that's fair enough, but he has to think about the jobs that depend upon building the *Dreadnought*-class submarines that will carry the nuclear warheads. Luckily, he has a solution: we build the submarines anyway, thereby retaining the jobs, but we don't put the nuclear missiles on them. The navy can do patrols without the beastly things.

There are gasps in the control room.

Marr wants to know where Corbyn stands on other touchstone issues that have defined his political attitudes. What about the trade union laws introduced by Margaret Thatcher to restrict secondary picketing, sympathy action and flying pickets? Corbyn indicates he is open to reversing these measures. Twitter catches fire.

And then there's the Falklands. Maybe my own memories of the controversies around the conflict in the 1980s influenced this line of questioning, but the arrival of a new Argentinian president keen on opening a fresh dialogue on the future of the islands gives the question currency. Corbyn talks about the need to find some sort of accommodation with the Argentinian government. While he says that the islanders must retain an 'enormous say' in the islands' future status, he doesn't think they should have a veto. The press starts writing the interview up.

To Corbyn's credit, he answers all these questions. He doesn't evade or obfuscate or deflect. And here's the problem: all three answers create a blizzard of bad press in almost every paper. 'Off His War Head!' screams the *Sun* next to a picture of Corbyn topped with his trademark Lenin cap superimposed on an image of a nuclear missile. The interview has compounded Labour's problems, in what even the *Guardian* calls a 'mind-blowing 15 minutes'. The consensus is clear: this is a triple gaffe and a disaster.

For Corbyn's friends, the interview and the reaction to it were absolute evidence of the way the mainstream media was determined to gang up on and discredit a good man. The BBC was as bad as the *Sun* for asking these questions in the first place. John Prescott, the former deputy prime minister, blogged his outrage:

> I thought Andrew Marr's interview this morning with Jeremy Corbyn was a disgrace … Why did he ask about Flying Pickets and the Falkland Islands? Are these really the big issues of today?
>
> Forget Deutschland '83 – today's Corbyn interview was more Marr '82.
>
> If Marr wants to make headlines in the Daily Mail, he should go and join them.[11]

After the show I sought out Seumas Milne. I always got along well with Seumas, who was thin as a rake – despite putting away vast quantities of full English over the *Marr* breakfast table – and weirdly ageless. I half expected a furious reaction, but he seemed more bemused than unhappy, though probably fully aware it had gone badly for his man. Talking to him for this book, seven years on, he is characteristically polite and good-humoured about it, and much less sanguine.

> The Trident questions were legitimate because that was a controversy and an internal tension in the Parliamentary Labour Party at the time, but the questions about flying pickets and the Falkland Islands? That was just sort of a *Daily Mail* agenda, really. What has the Falklands War in 2016 got to do with the price of fish?[12]

Milne thinks our choice of questions revealed an attitude towards Jeremy Corbyn that was quite different to how we perceived other senior politicians, because Corbyn's views went against the received wisdom that underpinned all of our coverage.

> I think that's why he was interrogated about it, because he was an outsider and he was supporting, and had supported, things which were regarded by the political mainstream as wrong and beyond the pale. It just felt like, 'OK, this guy is outside the mainstream. This is like a repeat of Michael Foot. So let's talk about Michael Foot's time to show that this is all hopeless nonsense.' So John Prescott was absolutely right, though we didn't put him up to it![13]

This is a powerful challenge, and however hard we all tried to set aside the influence of the orthodox political view, it must have played its part in some of the choices we made in the early days of the Corbyn leadership.

But let me put the case for the defence. It's true that some of the questions were about the past, focusing on what might be seen as ancient history: 1980s union laws and the Falklands War in particular. But the truth is that these issues were salient for three reasons: first, they spoke to what you might call

Corbyn's 'worldview' – one of his political challenges was countering criticisms of his particular outlook and set of values; second, because Corbyn was telling the country he ought to be prime minister one day, his historic views were relevant since he might have the power to reopen those issues (what would he say as prime minister to an Argentinian leader who asked for a reopening of talks on the status of the Falklands, for example?); and third, because Corbyn's politics derived from the 1970s and 80s, and seemed not to have changed very much since then. Had Labour elected a leader from the left of the party with a new, modern and distinct agenda, the accompanying intellectual energy would have made its way into interviews. Without that energy, we were drawn to issues from the era that defined Corbyn's politics.

When it came to the most eye-catching policy he dropped that day, the idea that Labour might spend billions on new submarines capable of carrying missiles but not deploy actual missiles on them, as Milne concedes, this was far from backwards-looking. Again, it showed that Corbyn had stuck to his views on nuclear disarmament, but it also raised many questions about the wisdom of his approach.

Perhaps we did more readily question the underlying worldview of Corbyn because he was outside the political mainstream. It was part of his job as an outsider leader to deal with that political problem and convince viewers to give him a chance and reject the orthodoxy. Ultimately, the situation he found himself in by early 2016 resulted from his understandable inability to manage what was a difficult situation inside his party, together with a series of unforced errors that only made things worse.

Over the next few months, *Marr* focused on the Brexit referendum. Corbyn was a bit-part player, only showing up late in the campaign to give Remain a languid and half-hearted endorsement. When Leave won, anger and frustration with Corbyn's performance boiled over and – the night before the first post-referendum edition of *Marr* – a coup against Corbyn was under way.

It had been a dreadful first nine months in the job for the Labour leader. He could have been forgiven for walking away, but he was far from finished.

Phase two: Glory days

The atmosphere at the *Marr* breakfast on 11 June 2017 is giddy. With the arrival of shadow chancellor John McDonnell, it only gets giddier. Now there's a sentence nobody's ever written before.

'Britain's next chancellor of the exchequer!' calls out one of Jeremy Corbyn's entourage as he spots McDonnell sloping across the canteen floor towards us. McDonnell is a man whose idea of getting a party started is formulating a composite motion on the plight of Bolivian sugar cane workers, followed by a little light insurrection, but today the shadow chancellor is smiling, which only makes him look more sinister than usual. He has the air of a quiet, apparently conventional suburban man who blends in perfectly with his fellow residents, only to be unmasked as a goat-troubling Satanist, the kind of man neighbours say 'always kept himself to himself'.

But he's all right, really. Having met him on many occasions by now, I'd say he mainly comes across as shy. Today, though, he's positively jolly. He's pitched up at the BBC to do an interview for another programme later in the day but has come in early to join the celebratory breakfast.

This is Jeremy and John's finest hour. Three days after their 2017 election defeat, the two men are on their victory lap. Theresa May has cobbled together an arrangement with Northern Ireland's Democratic Unionist Party that she hopes will keep her in power for a while longer, but the Labour leader and his advisers are confident it won't last and that power is within their grasp. As far as they're concerned, McDonnell and Corbyn are, respectively, chancellor and prime minister-elect.

The maths doesn't lie, though, and that seems a distant prospect to me, but they're not in the mood for realism. A leader who, twelve months earlier, lost scores of his shadow team in a mass resignation that triggered a leadership contest has now emerged stronger than ever.

Brexit left Corbyn in deep trouble. His most memorable contribution to the Remain campaign came on Channel 4's satirical comedy chat show *The Last Leg*. The Labour leader inexplicably arrived at the studio in a Bentley, sporting a floor-length white fur coat for one of the programme's skits. But that wasn't the worst part. Asked by the hosts for a mark out of ten to describe his personal enthusiasm for the European Union, he manages a reluctant 'seven or seven and a half'. It was far from a clarion call for Remain.

By the early hours of the Saturday night/Sunday morning after the referendum, Corbyn was in crisis. Hilary Benn, his shadow foreign secretary, called him that night to tell him he'd lost confidence in his leadership, leaving Corbyn with little choice: he had to fire him. Benn was the star of *Marr* that Sunday, booked by producer Jason Keen literally in the middle of the night. After Benn came the deluge and a formal leadership challenge from plucky Owen Smith, the erstwhile shadow work and pensions secretary.

Corbyn's victory was never in doubt because he retained the enthusiastic support of the Labour membership, if not the MPs. However, a second leadership election in less than a year and the spectacle of Her Majesty's Opposition barely able to cobble together a credible shadow cabinet left Corbyn battered. There was even speculation that he wanted a way out.

He remained tetchy throughout the leadership election process, becoming particularly prickly when Marr asked whether he'd really voted Remain in 2016, as he always insisted he had. It was a fair question, given his years of Euroscepticism and his lacklustre performance in the campaign, but he insisted he had voted to stay in the EU. Later, in the same interview, he denied considering walking away from the leadership. 'There's no wobbles,' he insisted, 'There's no stress. There's no depression.'[14]

But then came Theresa May's announcement of what turned out to be a disastrous snap election for the prime minister and her party, but which was greeted as smart politics at the time. 'Blue Murder' screamed the *Sun*'s front page the following morning, adding 'PM's Snap Poll Will Kill Off Labour'. *The Times* backed this up, stating baldly: 'May Heads for Election Landslide'. Nobody gave Corbyn a chance. Seumas Milne recalls that the consensus from the 'huddle' of political journalists from the press and broadcast media gathered around him after Prime Minister's Questions that day was that Labour would be 'massacred'.[15]

Milne was not so sure. He told the Westminster lobby that he was confident the gap between the parties would shrink much more quickly than expected. A large section of the public would like the Labour manifesto because it would be full of policies that had been excluded from the mainstream but which polling showed were popular. Furthermore, he was confident that the election rules requiring equal coverage of the political parties in the campaign would allow the public to 'hear Jeremy and the Labour Party, speaking in their own voice', without the distraction of the 'white noise' that had focused on 'internal clashes, personalities, attacks and controversies' rather than Labour's policy agenda.

Those election rules changed things, but the Labour message was still communicated to the public via the beastly MSM, which meant a 'framing' of their positions that, Milne believes, revealed a bias towards the 'received wisdom' of the Blair and Cameron years. It was in evidence, he says, at the launch of Labour's manifesto in Bradford:

The manifesto had been leaked the previous week, and the right-wing press had attacked it as the extreme return to the 70s, extremist left-wing Corbyn madness. I was standing next to Laura Kuenssberg, and the moment Jeremy finished speaking, she turned to camera and started her live broadcast, along the lines of: 'There you have it. The Labour Party has launched its manifesto, and it's more spending, more taxes, more borrowing.' The immediate framing of our manifesto was from the perspective of the political establishment consensus from the Blair period through to 2008, and that had been broken by what would be proven to be a popular manifesto.[16]

Milne didn't say anything to Kuenssberg at the time – he's not a ranter and raver – but I now need to come to her defence. That day in Bradford – not for the first, or the last, time – she was hissed and booed menacingly by Labour Party members whose hostility was fed by the interpretation Milne articulates (if you watch the clip back, you can see Seumas behind her when this is happening). The truth is that it's the media's job to question the claims of political parties sceptically. Laura's 'framing' of the manifesto was both factually correct and the central charge against Labour: to pay for their ideas they would tax, spend and borrow. This isn't Kuenssberg agreeing with that charge but identifying the political problem Labour had to overcome. Her film about the manifesto explained why they wanted to spend more – on hospitals, education, police – and left the voter to decide whether they should.

I don't mean to imply that Milne in any way encouraged this hostility towards Kuenssberg. In fact, Corbyn himself stepped in and told the crowd to stop the abuse, but while we can talk about framing and discuss bias, we shouldn't forget it's often the partisan prism that supporters, advisers and politicians see through that detects unfairness when what's actually happening is impartial journalism – with all the difficulties that entails – in this case embodied by Kuenssberg.

After speaking to Seumas about all this, I sought out the equivalent coverage of Theresa May's manifesto launch in 2017. Kuenssberg was equally pointed, equally focused on the weaknesses of the Tory offer. She called May's offer 'bleak' and included prominently the voices of protestors outside the Conservative Party bubble who wanted to highlight the cost of austerity. The unfair and untrue presentation of her work as biased is unsupported by the evidence. The demonisation of the BBC's first female political editor would culminate in the corporation hiring bodyguards for her when she attended the Labour Party conference later that year. It was a shameful episode.

But on the campaign, Milne was proved right. Corbyn was personally appealing, reaching beyond his activist base to speak to the country. He galvanised young voters and offered angry Remainers the chance to register an anti-Brexit vote, however incoherently. The campaign truly blew the blues away in every possible sense. Corbyn reduced a Tory majority of twelve to a hung parliament, gaining thirty seats in the process. Labour's vote share had increased by the greatest amount since 1945. The whole underlying basis for the 2016 coup – that Corbyn was essentially unelectable – was blown out of the water. He'd almost won power with an unashamedly left-wing programme after a highly effective campaign. When the exit poll landed at 10 p.m. on election night, centrist Labour was stunned and bewildered.

So we arrive at this unusual breakfast, a triumphant Corbynite occasion. That morning's programme had been a little bizarre, with the election loser at the top of the bill. As he bent my ear about his allotment, it struck me this was the happiest I'd seen him after a show – and he was Marr's most regular guest of that period, so I saw him up close a lot.

This already surreal scene was topped off when Corbyn was further interrupted – I think he was talking about his home-made jam at the time – by the most gobsmacking selfie request in the history of Jezzamania. Here, proffering his phone and leaning in towards JC, was the father of austerity, former chancellor George Osborne. Osborne said it wasn't for him, you understand, but for his Jez-curious son. Whatever. Corbyn was delighted to oblige.

Osborne had been on the programme to give his verdict on Theresa May's disastrous election, memorably calling the prime minister – who had sacked him the previous year – a 'dead woman walking'. Now, even he was caught up in the Summer of Jeremy.

As for Corbyn's own interview that morning, he was a man transformed and at his most comfortable in the job. A little cocky, perhaps, but with a right to be, he was genuinely enthusiastic and hopeful for the future and relished Marr's closing question:

Marr: Is Jeremy Corbyn in this for the long term?

Corbyn: Look at me. I've got youth on my side![17]

Sixty-eight years young, candid, straight-talking candidate Corbyn was back. Not lying, not a bastard, Jeremy unspun.

After overperforming in the 2017 election, Corbyn's team describe a relative 'honeymoon period' for the leader where his traditional enemies – the Parliamentary Labour Party, the press and the broadcasters – treated him more fairly. When I recalled those days with Seumas Milne, Corbyn's closest adviser, he sounded almost wistful.

The honeymoon did not last.

Phase three: Free fallin'

The version of Jeremy Corbyn that came to dominate, which he largely settled on in the last two and a half years of his leadership of the Labour Party, was always there. Martyn Sloman, a veteran of Labour Party work and organising, came into contact with Corbyn in Islington North in the 1980s. Sloman wasn't an ally, but the personal traits he recalls from those days do chime with the Labour leader's public persona thirty years later. He doesn't say Corbyn was aggressive or rude but that he bridled at criticism or challenge:

> He was absolutely convinced he was right. When challenged, he became petulant. That was his weakness. Any criticism and the tone was: 'How dare you criticise me? I am destined for sainthood.' He resented any criticism whatsoever.[18]

Before he won the leadership, this irritability made occasional appearances, most notably on *Channel 4 News* in July of 2015 when presenter Krishnan Guru-Murthy asked Corbyn why he'd called terrorist groups Hamas and Hezbollah 'friends'. The candidate seemed to be on a hair trigger as far as this issue was concerned. After nineteen seconds on the subject, he exploded into incandescent anger in the face of a gentle interruption. 'Can I finish!' he half-yelled, rolling his eyes. 'CAN I FINISH?'

After that, he really lost it, jabbing his finger at Guru-Murthy, gesticulating furiously. For a while he calmed down as Guru-Murthy sought to lower the temperature and move on. Not so fast, Krish, Corbyn wasn't done: 'Well, thanks for the tabloid journalism,' he interjected with a hefty dose of snide. He wanted the last word.[19]

As the summer of 2017 faded, tetchy Jeremy started to reappear. Theresa May's doomed attempt to find a way out of the

Brexit mess, with no majority and a rebellious party, consumed British politics. Labour endured their own agonies on the biggest political issue of the day, caught between metropolitan Remainers who wanted a second referendum and traditional Labour voters who'd backed Brexit and, understandably, wanted it to happen. As a result, the party pleased nobody. Nor was Brexit Corbyn's comfort zone, his promise to broker a better deal with the EU than the Tories could manage not convincing anyone. The Labour leader seemed semi-detached from the argument.

Corbyn and his team were determined to avoid making the mistakes they'd made in their turbulent first nine months. Gone was the free-wheeling Jeremy, willing to answer any question, however treacherous. Making news from a Jeremy Corbyn interview was no longer like shooting fish in a barrel, but there was a cost: the Labour leader was now prone to evasion like other politicians and, perhaps frustrated that he'd become one of them, irritation was often close to the surface.

His party conference interview in 2017 was a case in point. Still in good spirits post-election, Corbyn was pretty comfortable until Marr turned to a suggestion from Unite leader Len McCluskey that he'd be willing to defy a new law requiring a 50 per cent turnout threshold for industrial action. Did Corbyn back McCluskey's willingness to break a law he thought was wrong? Corbyn didn't answer. Corbyn deflected. Corbyn accused Marr of blaming the unions rather than the government. Finally, Corbyn suggested that the new law was unfair. Progress! So would he back trade unions like Unite if they decided to defy it? Corbyn wasn't ready to say yes, so he launched into a history lesson, criticising the Heath government (!), attacking Mrs Thatcher, anything but answering the question. Finally, Marr called it out, exasperated:

Marr: What has happened to Jeremy Corbyn that you can't answer my questions?

> **Corbyn:** What's happened to Jeremy Corbyn is he's the leader of the party and determined to lead this party and this country in the direction of social justice and equality.[20]

There was passion here, tinged with finger-pointing irritation, but it was as clear a statement as it could be: Corbyn wanted power, and if he had to play the game, he would. This was the new, serious version of the man, no longer candidate Corbyn but a contender for power.

He didn't know it yet, but the writing – or, more accurately, the painting – was already on the wall for the Corbyn project.

If Corbyn's opponents in the Labour leadership contest in 2015 could not speak, then in the summer of 2018 his problem was that he could not see or understand. Here was a man who seemed blind to antisemitism, and the problem was not new.

It's hard to imagine how, six years earlier in October 2012, Corbyn – an obscure Labour MP but a man with decades of political experience – could have looked at an image of artist Mear One's mural *Freedom for Humanity* and missed what everyone else could see. The mural was about to be removed from near Brick Lane in East London because of complaints about its antisemitic content, content it was hard to miss. Yet Corbyn just couldn't see it, even when it was pointed out to him.

At the centre of *Freedom for Humanity* was a depiction of a group of six suited businessmen playing a board game resembling Monopoly. One man with a full beard is counting money. The men have exaggerated features: hooked noses, bushy facial hair and evil expressions. They look, if not exclusively, then mostly Jewish and evoke the caricatures of Julius Streicher's Nazi hate sheet *Der Stürmer*.

The board game is supported on the backs of four black men who appear semi-naked as slaves. Above the heads of the predominantly Jewish oppressors sits the Eye of Providence, a Masonic symbol associated with conspiracy theories about a secret network that allows the Jews to control the world. Subtle it ain't.

Still, back on 2 October 2012 Jeremy Corbyn couldn't see any of this. The artist, angry at the decision of Tower Hamlets council to paint over the offensive artwork, posted the image on Facebook and messaged Corbyn to tell him it had been banned. With *Freedom for Humanity* right in front of him, Corbyn responded with a question: 'Why?'

The answer should have been obvious, but Corbyn couldn't see it. Instead, he sympathised with the artist and compared his situation to that of the great Mexican muralist Diego Rivera, whose works had also been torn down by powerful interests.

Six years later, in March 2018, Jewish Labour MP Luciana Berger – already familiar with resurgent antisemitism in the Corbyn Labour Party – saw the image and Corbyn's troubling, supportive response. She had the same question, but this time for her leader: 'Why?'

Thus began what turned into a summer dominated by Labour's antisemitism problem. The mural controversy was followed by a stream of stories that alleged antisemitism not just in Labour's ranks but specifically on Corbyn's part. These included his attendance at a wreath-laying ceremony in Tunisia in 2014, which involved the commemoration of two Palestine Liberation Organisation officials with alleged links to Black September, the group responsible for the brutal murder of Israeli athletes at the Munich Olympics in 1972. Corbyn couldn't deny being there – there were pictures – but said that while he was present, he was 'not involved' in laying those wreaths. He was there to commemorate the victims of the 1985 Israeli bombing in Tunis.

Then, in August, footage emerged of him at a meeting in the Houses of Parliament in 2013 talking about 'British Zionists' who did not understand 'English irony'. Corbyn appeared to be implying that these British Jews – people who were born and grew up in the UK – were somehow different from more authentically British citizens in that they didn't understand cultural cues obvious to most Britons. Many people – including those in Corbyn's party – felt this was barefaced antisemitism. Corbyn denied any such implication. The clip, he argued, had been wrenched out of context and distorted.

Throughout that summer of 2018, the row over Labour anti-semitism raged on, but beyond a few short clips and newspaper pieces Corbyn himself was absent. So, as the Labour leader sat down for our traditional conference interview at the end of September, Marr was the first serious interviewer to ask Corbyn himself if he was an antisemite.

Corbyn visibly winced. He saw himself as a campaigner against racism. To him, the suggestion that he was racist was ridiculous and offensive, yet he couldn't neutralise the situation. He just couldn't see it. As ever he insisted on his usual formulation that he was against all forms of racism, when he should probably have focused entirely on the matter at hand: antisemitism. On this he couldn't help himself. He was soon listing other sorts of racism – Islamophobia, 'far-right racism', never just antisemitism.

This partly reflected a view at the top of the Labour Party that those other forms of racism weren't talked about as much, not least because they were Tory problems rather than Labour ones. Whatever the reason, this rhetorical tick undermined his response.

The same was true of his handling of the argument around which definition of antisemitism Labour should officially adopt as it grappled with the crisis. Corbyn had reservations about the International Holocaust Remembrance Alliance definition but had accepted it in 2016, although the party had not signed up to all of the examples attached to the IHRA definition.

Corbyn was particularly worried about the party officially agreeing that saying 'the existence of the State of Israel is a racist endeavour' was antisemitic. The Labour leader was reluctant to endorse any definition that, he felt, would inhibit the party's ability to criticise the Israeli government's policies and the occupation of Palestinian land. Colleagues such as shadow chancellor John McDonnell told Corbyn in private that he needed to adopt the definition in full – and that meant all the examples – straight away if he wanted to close the row down. Instead, because of his real reservations, he allowed it to rage for weeks until he finally bowed to the inevitable and signed up anyway.[21]

Every answer he gave that morning undermined efforts to deal with this corrosive issue. Shown the mural again in all its horrendous glory live on television, Corbyn couldn't bring himself to acknowledge its use of antisemitic imagery. He merely conceded he might have made a 'rush to judgement' in supporting the artist on freedom of expression grounds – not the point now, but OK. But he couldn't offer a proper apology or even accept that the mural was antisemitic. Instead, he said he wished it hadn't ever been put up (I bet he did) and was glad it had been taken down. It was hopeless. He still just couldn't see it.

And so he went on from there: failing to apologise for the 'English irony' comments; refusing to agree that if he'd known about the alleged links between those being commemorated in Tunisia and Black September, he wouldn't have attended; refusing to offer remorse or apology for any of it.

After the interview, Corbyn and his team were furious. 'We felt that it was over-the-top, wrong and disproportionate,' Seumas Milne told me when we spoke, almost five years on. Milne and his colleagues had several objections. Their main beef was the length of time we spent on the subject, which is a pretty subjective question. In a twenty-five-minute interview, we focused on antisemitism for eleven minutes. That's about forty-five per cent. It's a lot. They thought it was too much; I thought, given this was the first time anyone had had the chance to talk to Corbyn about the events of Labour's troubled summer, it was justified. The issue was consuming Labour, and we wanted to conduct the definitive interview on it. I stand by it but Milne is not having it, detecting again a willingness to follow the lead of the press and apply a double standard:

> All the lines were coming from a press campaign which had been running all summer, and from our political opponents, internally and externally. Nothing of the kind was done to hold the Tories to account, even though Boris Johnson, who was then the Foreign Secretary, had a pretty extreme record on issues around racism and Islamophobia in particular, which was rampant throughout the Conservative Party, according to the polling.[22]

I can only answer for the *Marr Show*, but it's wrong to say that we ignored allegations of Islamophobia in the Conservative Party. We interviewed former Tory chairwoman Baroness Warsi, who raised the issue powerfully. We put allegations of Islamophobic behaviour by Conservative Party members to numerous Tory politicians including home secretary Sajid Javid three months before Corbyn's grilling on antisemitism. And as we'll see in later chapters, I didn't shy away from questions about Boris Johnson's comments about Muslims and ethnic minorities, even when it enraged Johnson's media handlers.

In any case, from then on, the Corbyn/Marr vibe was gone. Corbyn's anger and suspicion seemed to harden. By the time he appeared at the following year's party conference back in Brighton, the leader was avoiding straight answers about a move to topple his deputy Tom Watson, the man who'd stood in for him on that distant Sunday in 2015 after he'd won the leadership. The leader was often a tetchy and sarcastic interviewee, who could be as evasive as anyone else who'd sat in the *Marr* chair. A politician very much like all the rest, after all.

He didn't stay for breakfast.

12

NOTHING HAS CHANGED

One of the less enjoyable duties of the editor of *The Andrew Marr Show* was what we called the 'meet and greet' shot each Sunday morning. This involved standing outside the front door of the BBC's New Broadcasting House in all weathers with a camera crew and a bank of press photographers waiting for the arrival of the big guest of the day.

It had been pioneered by my predecessor Barney Jones – a gregarious and enthusiastic presser of the flesh – and was designed to provide some extra pictures for the team making the political news piece that day. I would appear on the news bulletin most Sunday evenings grinning while shaking the hand of the prime minister or the leader of the opposition. When the guest was that senior, the ritual added to the sense of theatre around the show, but it could feel faintly ridiculous bringing the camera out for Grant Shapps, whoever might happen to be leading the Liberal Democrats or someone nobody had heard of from the shadow cabinet. Hello, Barry Gardiner! The only person who really enjoyed it was my mother, who saw me on the news every Sunday night.

So why did I hate it so much? Two words: small talk. After the initial 'Good morning, Chancellor' or whatever, and a reference to the weather or expression of hope that they hadn't had to get up too early, I'd run out of material fast. Whether this mattered or not depended on the guest. Some, like former chancellor George Osborne, were happy to help smooth out the moment, filling the awkward silences and asking questions about who else was on. Others, like former prime minister David Cameron, were aloof, eschewing eye contact and exuding the sort of self-importance that discouraged too much engagement. Fair enough, he was the prime minister. But there was no need to be a dick about it. Jeremy Corbyn was different: he'd say hello to me before immediately shifting his focus to the most junior member of staff he could find, usually one of the security guards or receptionists. This delighted them and took the pressure off me. I think Corbyn enjoyed it too.

The worst meet and greet of all was Theresa May. The three or four minutes it took to greet the then prime minister, take her through reception and down in the lift to the deep basement of the BBC felt like an eternity. May had no small talk. None. Beyond an awkward 'Hello', we would walk together in exquisite silence. Occasionally I'd dredge up a reference to cricket, knowing that she liked the game, and she would hold her fixed grin but offer no response. Nothing.

Only once did I succeed in making some sort of conversation with her, but even that was weird. We were interviewing her in Birmingham ahead of the Conservative Party conference in 2016, the broadcast coming from the BBC headquarters in the city. The journey from the front door to the location was short, but each step was freighted with the usual, painful silence. Then, about halfway up a flight of stairs, I spotted an opening: a sign reading 'Welcome to Ambridge'.

I coughed lightly to attract the attention of the prime minister, whom I guessed would be a fan of the Radio 4 rural soap opera, and said:

'Of course, we make *The Archers* here at BBC Birmingham.'

She half-glanced at the sign as she walked up the stairs and looked back at me blankly.

'Yes,' she began, uttering the only sentence she ever said to me, 'you make *The Archers* here at BBC Birmingham.'

Who said the art of conversation's dead?

Looking back, it might have been better if the Conservative Party had skipped the May premiership altogether. Electing a pragmatic Remainer – albeit one who'd flirted quite extensively with Euroscepticism down the years and kept her head down during the referendum – was an exercise in putting off the inevitable when it came to Brexit. It was also an outward expression of the confusion that gripped the riven governing party when it came to the defining question of the moment: what does Brexit mean?

The 2016 leadership race came down to May versus Vote Leaver Andrea Leadsom. Leadsom came a cropper after giving an interview to *The Times*'s Rachel Sylvester in which she said, as a mother, she had a 'real stake' in the country's future, referring, at the same time, to the fact that Theresa May did not. Leadsom was very upset by the story and tweeted that the headline that accompanied it – 'Being a mother gives me an edge on May' – represented the 'exact opposite of what I said'. Which was fine, but it didn't. Here was a politician brazening out controversy in the face of clear-cut evidence in the form of her own words. When *The Times* released a recording of the interview confirming Sylvester's report, Leadsom's position and campaign became unsustainable, and she withdrew.

Perhaps the Conservative Party would have benefited from a contest, though. It may have exposed the fissures over Brexit that would hobble May from the start. It would also have revealed May, the communicator and campaigner in action. Even in the blink-and-you-missed-it thirteen-day campaign, the signs were there that May was the queen of clunk. In her launch speech, she tried to answer that pesky question: what does

Brexit mean? She needed something snappy, something meaningless: 'Brexit,' she said, 'means Brexit.' The only sensible response is, 'Yes, but what does Brexit mean?' Unable to answer the question meaningfully, May repeated the formulation ad nauseum.

Of course, this wasn't entirely May's fault. She had to speak like this because her party remained split between Leave and Remain, and 'soft' and 'hard' Brexit. The late Colin Powell, former US Secretary of State, had a famous 'pottery shop rule' – 'you break it, you own it' – which he applied to foreign wars, but it could equally apply to Brexit. It would have been better if the job of fixing the broken relationship between the UK and the EU had immediately fallen to one of those who smashed it in the first place. Instead, they were free to heckle as May tried to assemble something new from the shattered pieces.

May was focused on getting a deal done with the European Union that could minimise the economic damage of leaving while honouring the intent behind the Brexit vote (itself a contested question). This was a responsible position to adopt but was doomed from the start. It would be impossible to keep everybody happy. May would ultimately need to be able to push her version of Brexit through once it emerged. The problem was that David Cameron's thin majority was insufficient. The political maths must have been playing on her mind from the start.

For now, stuck with the parliamentary numbers as they were, any May deal would need the support of all the factions, from the Tory Remainer rump to the European Research Group massive. The battle for Brexit was being fought post-referendum, and Mrs May's admirable pragmatism was the political equivalent of taking a knife to a gunfight.

The dawn of the May era was strange from my perspective. The prime minister was the interview everyone wanted, but she also made for dreadful television. For years she'd played a cautious game, keeping her head down while running the Home

Office. They called her 'the submarine', and you could see why. But this meant she offered a blank canvas to her party, which served her well. The trouble was when she became prime minister and had to decide what to paint on it, it was not to be a masterpiece.

Theresa May and Andrew Marr had history. It was painful, but there's no use crying over spilt milk.

In 2010 when she was home secretary, May made a rare appearance on the *Marr Show*. It was a tetchy affair. Still, after much post-show persuasion from Marr, the small-talk-allergic home secretary agreed to come to the famous *Marr* breakfast.

Around this time, I was banging my head against a brick wall at the *Politics Show*, trying desperately to get an interview with May for the programme. I eventually managed to secure a meeting with her steely aide Fiona Hill who, along with policy adviser Nick Timothy, was May's gatekeeper. We sat down for a cup of tea in the Home Office, and after a brief preamble she told me to stop bothering her with interview requests.

'She doesn't do many interviews,' Hill said with a dose of Glaswegian brutality, 'and when she does, she does Andrew Marr.'

'Oh,' I said.

'Yes,' she said, standing up to leave, her tea virtually untouched. 'She likes Andrew Marr.'

But for how long? That morning at breakfast with Marr, May had turned up in a brand-new silk trouser suit that was reportedly worth £4,000. A 'full English' is a challenge in silk, or so I gather, so she must have been trepidatious about the risks of an errant baked bean or a squirt of yellow from a nearby fried egg. As it turned out – the food wasn't the problem, the presenter was.

As they sat down, Marr, playing host, offered May a cup of coffee. She accepted, and he offered to pour her some milk. The milk jug that confronted him that morning was enormous. I remember noticing the two-pint monsters when I first went to the BBC canteen. They were a struggle to lift and a bugger to pour. Marr didn't get that far. Leaning over the table to grasp the hefty jug, he clipped it with the side of his hand, sending it flying and dousing May in freezing cold milk. This took place five years before my time on the show, but I'm still gutted to have missed it.

'She was aghast,' Marr remembered, 'and very angry.'[1] So bad was the drenching that May had to return home to Maidenhead, delaying her arrival at the Home Office – where she had the aftermath of a foiled terrorist plot to deal with.

Marr spent the next few years regularly apologising, but his messages, flowers and offers to pay the dry-cleaning bill were to no avail. May occasionally appeared on the programme but never acknowledged the incident or signalled forgiveness until after Marr had a stroke in 2013. Finally, May yielded, sending the stricken Marr a note that contained a rare example of a Theresa May joke:

> I do hope you're back on television soon. Whatever that might do to my wardrobe.[2]

Absolutely hilarious stuff. By the time she'd become prime minister in 2016 the milk incident was forgotten, and May's renewed love for Marr made him favourite to land her first major 'sit-down' since she'd moved into No. 10. So it was, in September, that the call came from May's director of communications Katie Perrior telling us we had the interview. I liked Katie. She was one of the only senior people I encountered in politics who spoke like an ordinary person. So I was delighted when she told me we had the interview, but there was a catch: it would not be live in the *Marr* studio on Sunday morning but pre-recorded on Friday afternoon. In a hotel. In Maidenhead.

It became a feature of the May premiership that more and more interviews were set up like this. They're not ideal: they put the interviewee on home turf and can go out of date quickly when events move stories and political arguments on. Saturday pre-records are risky, and Friday ones are reckless in today's news cycle.

These interviews offer an advantage to the guest: they subtly change the dynamic and lower the intensity. Crucially, they protect politicians from unhelpful stories in the Sunday newspapers that might otherwise raise difficult questions. Live interviews are just better, and viewers are rightly unhappy when they get pre-cooked, sedate encounters instead. The chance of that happening increases when your guest is as low-octane and risk-averse as Theresa May.

Having said that, this was the short-lived, relatively sunny iteration of prime minister May. We showed up at the slightly shabby five-star hotel in her constituency on Friday afternoon and waited for the prime minister. When she arrived, she was more smiley than usual and greeted Marr enthusiastically. He didn't spill milk all over her. Things were looking positive.

Then the interview began.

I can only describe it as upbeat but platitudinous. She stone-walled every attempt to put flesh on the bones of her vision for the country or Brexit. Marr asked how she planned to address the 'burning injustices' she'd talked about on the day she arrived in Downing Street.

She told him she wanted a country that works for everyone. Which was nice – I mean, who doesn't? – but didn't tell us anything about how. We asked about education and immigration; she said nothing meaningful. I wondered why she'd agreed to the interview when she had nothing she wanted to say.

Talking to Katie Perrior about her time working for Theresa May is revealing. Katie had plenty of run-ins with May's two advisers, Fiona Hill and Nick Timothy, mainly because they controlled access to May. Looking back, Perrior is more sympathetic to them these days. She describes what she calls a 'Wizard of Oz scenario'. 'They were protecting the world and me from knowing that she [May] was lacking in so many skills that were needed to be prime minister,' Perrior says today.[3] Chief among these were communication skills.

May was inherently uncomfortable being interviewed because, as Perrior told me, she was essentially 'an introvert'. She was also suspicious of journalists and didn't understand the purpose of journalism. Her attitude was that she was a committed and honourable public servant who was impervious to corruption. So there was no need to interrogate her about her decisions. As Perrior recalls:

> When she's come to the conclusion that something is the right thing to do, she can't understand why people might question that because it is a selfless act. 'Why would you even question me on it?' On an individual policy, after question three, she'd be rolling her eyes thinking, 'I don't understand why you haven't got it yet,' and she'll come off air and say, 'They're obsessed.'[4]

It's scandalous: journalists in a democracy obsessed with bloody questions.

Back in Maidenhead, Marr asked one, and May actually answered it. He wanted to know whether she might be considering a general election, as the polls were showing a significant bounce for the Tories since she'd taken office. It made sense – it could secure her own mandate and empower her to find a way through the Brexit tangle – but she told him she wasn't keen. There'd been too much instability, and there was no need for an election. Pretty clear, but Marr wanted a receipt:

> **Marr:** Let me make this very clear because, again, it's very important. Under current law, the next election will be in 2020: no ifs, no buts, no snap elections, no changing the law. Under you, is that absolutely certain that we're not going to see an election before 2020?

May: I'm not going to be calling a snap election. I've been very clear that I think we need that period of time, that stability to be able to deal with the issues that the country is facing and have that election in 2020.[5]

There it was. Finally. A straight answer we could take to the bank. 'No snap election' was the story, and given how little she engaged with any other question, it seemed like a significant answer.

The following month, in October 2016, May was back, this time at the Tory Party conference in Birmingham. The same pattern of question and non-answer followed, but May was thriving. Her no-frills offer was popular with the public, and the madness of 2016 politics seemed to subside a little. She was at the peak of her powers, while *Marr* retained its constitutional role as the biggest political show on television.

But then, suddenly, we had competition.

You may have noticed by now that the story of the political TV interview is dominated by older white men: Day, Walden, Frost, Humphrys, the Dimblebys and Paxman. Laura Kuenssberg became the BBC's first female political editor in 2015, and Emily Maitlis had to wait until 2018 to take the lead anchor role on *Newsnight*. Meanwhile, women like Sue MacGregor, Sarah Montague, Mishal Hussein, Martha Kearney and Carolyn Quinn were present on big Radio 4 shows like *Today* and *PM* but too often were expected to play second fiddle to male colleagues.

So, when Sky News launched a new Sunday-morning political interview programme in January 2017 fronted by thirty-two-year-old Sophy Ridge, it immediately felt significant and different. Ridge had enjoyed a meteoric rise through the ranks, and now she'd landed her own show. Sky, as usual, had serious ambition for the programme. When I first saw the simultaneously youthful and commanding figure of Ridge on her sleek set at Sky HQ I felt impressed and intimidated. Maybe we were the dinosaurs now.

If that was a worry, the next development was a punch in the gut. For years *Marr* had been able to bank on the presence of the prime minister of the day on the first Sunday back in the New Year. Along with the party conferences, it was one of two fixtures in the diary you could build your year around. On 8 January 2017 May was due in the *Marr* studio because that was how it always was. You didn't want to be the editor to screw that up.

I'd contacted Downing Street before Christmas to tie up the formalities. Perrior and co. had been slow to respond. It nagged at me as I helped demolish the turkey, but I still had the first week of January in which to sort things out. When I returned to work in the new year my calls went unanswered. Eventually the phone rang. It was Katie Perrior. She was very sorry, but the prime minister would not be on *Marr* on the 8th. Instead, she would mark the first edition of *Sophy Ridge on Sunday* by appearing as their main guest.

Was this about the milk?

No, as Katie explained to me:

> I said to the prime minister, 'Sophy Ridge has got a new show. I think she's an excellent journalist. I think we should give it a chance. We should support a female in her new endeavour. Let's do something different. This is a Sunday-morning kind of monopoly. Let's put some competition in it, and let's have a woman doing it.'[6]

All this was completely understandable, but it hurt. We took the low road that weekend – booking Nicola Sturgeon, the party leader we thought would most irritate May – and quietly fumed. Could this signal a shift in the balance of power on a Sunday morning? The fact that it didn't was thanks, in no small part, to Donald J. Trump.

The Ridge/May interview itself was impressive. With quotes on a video wall for the politician to read, clean lines and a modern feel, *Sophy Ridge on Sunday* had adopted the best bits of the *Sunday Politics* and updated them with a touch of American television panache. Ridge is a proper anchor, and a very clear and precise interviewer too. She possesses an unusual combination of tough, forensic interviewing with a disarmingly casual and conversational style. She was effective that morning as she pushed May on immigration and Brexit.

Perrior was with the prime minister at Sky HQ in Osterley in west London that day, and she'd made sure May was well-briefed and ready. Perrior had spoken to her contacts in the Sky newsroom in the run-up to the interview. They told her stories of arguments between senior Sky staff over how to maximise the impact of the encounter. According to her sources, they wanted to 'catch May out' with some sort of Trump-related question. Arguments or not, that seemed to be the plan.

That January in 2017, the world was trying to come to terms with Donald Trump's imminent arrival at the White House. With inauguration day just a week away, the British government needed to establish a close relationship with the new administration. There were plans for a meeting in Washington between May and Trump later in the month. Perrior did not want to jeopardise that and warned May to be ready, telling her:

'They're going to be doing close-up shots. They're going to stick it out on Twitter saying, "This is the moment I asked her about Trump," and then you pull a face. That's going to get across the world in seconds. I do not want that.' And so Theresa was briefed to literally not move a muscle, answer the questions and just get out of there.[7]

With two minutes left of the interview, Ridge finally turned to the subject of Trump and, referring to May's record on promoting women's equality, brought up some of the nastier things he'd said about women:

> **Ridge:** I really feel slightly awkward reading this out, but I do think it's important to re-hear what Donald Trump was recorded saying in the past about women: 'When you're a star, they let you do it, you can do anything, grab them by the pussy.' I mean, forgetting the fact that you're prime minister for the moment, how does that make you feel as a woman?[8]

It was an effective question and one that male interviewers had avoided. While listening to it, May tried to remain expressionless as instructed. Inside, she can't have been happy, and who can blame her? These were vile words, and they weren't hers to answer for, but she did need to develop a relationship with the man who'd said them. She responded by saying she found the comments unacceptable but noted Trump had already apologised for them, before she turned quickly to the importance of the 'special relationship'.

After the show, Perrior was furious with Sky. She felt the question – which was justified and legitimate – had been demeaning and embarrassing. She didn't think you should say 'pussy' to the prime minister at any time, but certainly not at eleven in the morning when children – including Perrior's own – would be watching.

Perrior blamed Sky executives eager to make a splash with the first show. 'I was so fucking furious,' remembers Perrior, who had stuck her neck out by opting for *Ridge* over *Marr*. 'That interview didn't do me any favours.'[9]

I love Ridge's Trump question because it refuses to accept the narrative that if you say something as vile as Trump did, you can wash it away with a quick apology and the legitimacy you attain by winning power. The president's conduct in office demonstrated that Donald Trump was exactly who he said he was when he'd made those offensive statements, however much he'd offered sorry-not-sorry apologies. So that truth justifies Ridge's question in retrospect. But it was also legitimate at the time and was all the more potent because it was put to someone who had no choice but to overlook the nasty truth about Trump because she had to build a relationship with him.

On the other hand, there was something unfair about the question being put to May but not, so far as I can remember, to others like her then foreign secretary, Boris Johnson. The implication was that only women would be offended by nasty boasts about sexual assault. Equally, it fell to Ridge, the new woman on the block, to put the courageous question to May because the ranks of male interviewers felt somehow inhibited or embarrassed to discuss this stuff with a woman. Or perhaps they didn't think it really qualified as a political question.

The question – ridiculously, in my view – damaged May's relationship with *Sophy Ridge on Sunday*. A few weeks later, May was back in the *Marr* studio. We also asked about her relationship with the new president – she paid a visit to Washington the following week – but there were no fireworks this time. Come to think of it, I have no memory whatsoever of what she said, which for Theresa May represented a job well done.

It's a Saturday night in a slightly crappy Holiday Inn in Salford's Media City. This is the hotel where ITV puts up guests appearing on *The Jeremy Kyle Show* and where the BBC stick their star presenters – or some of them – when they're working out of the corporation's North West HQ. This made for strange bedfellows or, at the very least, lift mates. It's October 2017 and I should be in bed myself, but I've still got work to do. The nine months since Theresa May's belated and uneventful 'New Year' interview in late January have nearly, but not entirely, destroyed her political career. I'm still up, drinking white wine and plotting an interview that will force May to acknowledge the depth of the hole she's in.

Tory activists and MPs have arrived in Manchester feeling wounded. In April the prime minister had broken her solemn and repeated pledge not to call a snap election. She wanted to capitalise on her lead in the polls and the perceived weakness of her opponent, Labour leader Jeremy Corbyn. Katie Perrior quit as director of communications – her relationship with Hill and Timothy had completely broken down by then – and it was downhill from there. May's appearance on *Marr* during the campaign was typical. At the start of the interview Marr tried to set rules of engagement that would discourage her from resorting to robotic soundbites like 'strong and stable', which she'd spent the entire campaign parroting.

May seemed to sign up to Marr's plan, and things got under way. He raised the scandal of NHS nurses resorting to food banks to survive. 'That's not the kind of country that you want to run, is it?' he demanded. May looked him in the eye and answered: 'I want a country that works for everyone, not just the privileged few.' In the control room we howled – so much for no soundbites. What was the point?

By election day on 8 June May had blown it. The more that voters saw of the wooden leader, the less they liked her, and overnight the Tories' small majority had been wiped away, resulting in a hung parliament and a prime minister clinging on to power thanks to Northern Ireland's Democratic Unionist Party.

May had looked broken on election night, and things went from bad to worse the following week when she mishandled the aftermath of the tragic fire at Grenfell Tower in west London. The fire, in which seventy-two residents died, held up an unflinching mirror to the inequality of modern Britain, and May – despite her genuine distress about the tragedy – had come over as remote and uncaring.

Party conference set-piece interviews were the biggest moments in the *Marr* political year, and this one – her first major sit-down since that cruel summer, and the one I was busily prepping for – felt huge. For the editor, prime ministerial appearances, in particular, were a bit like Cup Final weekend: pre-match pressure, a high-stakes game and lots of people titting around in suits.

The build-up has been under way for more than a week, but come Saturday night I'm still talking tactics with Marr. After a slightly boozy team meal in an Italian restaurant, we have a nightcap in the hotel bar and run through the interview plan. Again.

Unlike most interviewers, Marr chooses not to take a list of questions onto the studio floor. As mentioned, he thinks that if he's focused on reading questions from a piece of paper, he'll break eye contact with his guest and the interview will suffer. He also fears that a list of questions might make him too inflexible, stopping him from really listening to what's being said and tying him to a rigid plan. Both good points, but ultimately I disagreed; without a road map on paper, it was very easy for an interviewee to drag us away from our carefully prepared plan and take control of the agenda.

So we compromised. There would be no list of questions, but I would drill him on the interview plan so that every question and planned comeback was etched into his brain before the programme started. It was our version of the *Walden* question map, and we were still practising as Saturday night came perilously close to Sunday morning.

'Main headings?' I asked.

'Apology. Tuition fees announcement. Capitalism. Brexit. The election. Truth,' said Marr without hesitation.

'Break them down,' I said

'Say sorry, express contrition,' said Marr.

'Great, what's next?'

'Tuition fees, failed system, Corbyn's policy banquet, May's thin gruel.'

'Great. Capitalism?'

'Falling wages, low growth, time to renationalise the railways?'

No wonder he knew it off by heart. We'd been working on the interview together for more than a week, sharing drafts with each other and with talented producer Joel Massey. As with all the interviews I worked on at *Marr*, I started the process with my trademark question: 'What is the truth?'

In the run-up to the interview I formulated a thesis – just to help organise my thoughts – to guide me as we started to think about what we wanted to cover and how to come at the interview. Here's what I wrote in October 2017.

What is the truth?

The prime minister is diminished. She went to the country when she did not have to and led a disastrous campaign that wiped away her majority. She cannot bring herself to say sorry. Her party and cabinet are angry and deeply split over the Brexit negotiations. She's now trying to change the subject with meagre policy offers, but these inadequately address the inequality and injustices she claims to care about and which increasingly concern voters. Can she use this interview to reset by offering some honesty, or will she continue to deny and deflect?

From this proposition, we assembled questions – lots of them. From the NHS to HS2, we started with maybe thirty to fifty possible options and then worked to whittle them down to the best twenty-five. By the time Sunday morning came we had just twelve. Now to see whether, in only twenty-two minutes, they could travel successfully from our elaborate interview plan, through Marr's brain and onto the telly, revealing something truthful about the predicament of this inscrutable prime minister.

* * *

The look on May's face on election night had stayed with me – hunted, brittle, a sort of political death mask – and I recognised it again on Sunday morning. Her demeanour was dark and fearful, and it was no wonder. That cruel, graphic description of May by George Osborne on the *Marr* sofa as a 'dead woman walking' came back to me as she approached for the 'meet-and-greet' shot. This time, beyond wishing her a happy birthday – she was sixty-one that day – I didn't bother with the small talk.

In the election wreckage, May's advisers – Hill and Timothy – had resigned, and she had appointed a new director of communications: my boss at the BBC, Robbie Gibb. Robbie had clearly been working hard with the prime minister, and it showed as she sat down on set, not because of what she said – we'll come to that – but because of how she looked and what she sought to project. Gone was rigid do-it-my-way Theresa. In her place sat a more sympathetic figure, someone warmer. Robbie, a TV man to his bones, had clearly told the prime minister, whatever the truth of her dark mood this difficult morning, to try to project contentment, look happy and put on a brave face.

She wasn't a natural smiler. Too often, her grin came over as a grimace, a fixed effort that conveyed how uncomfortable she felt, but clearly, she'd been practising. Katie Perrior was watching from home:

> You can see the cogs turning in her brain. And at some point, she's like, 'Oh! I've forgotten to smile.' And then she flashes on this kind of Cheshire Cat grin, which looks weird.[10]

Weird as it was, this was the May 'twinkle'. More than just happy or resolute, she was delighted to be here, however sticky the wicket.

Marr opened the show with the prime minister by his side. This was the shot where the guest looks into the camera as we sell viewers our line-up of the biggest guests of the week, and, depending on Marr's script, it could be excruciating. This particular opening was decidedly odd, a jarring mismatch between his words and her face:

Marr: Good morning, and as the Tory conference opens in a rain-swept Manchester, the prime minister arrives to headlines describing her as 'broken' and facing a battle with other Tories for her very survival.

May stares at the camera. She is smiling broadly, too much, and it looks a little forced.

Marr: Here, she has to stand and fight or surrender office to her critics.

May, still smiling, cocks her head slightly and makes a minor attempt at the twinkle.

Marr: Happy Birthday, Prime Minister!

May takes a deep breath and then offers a fake, jolly half-laugh. Wasn't Marr *funny* with his birthday joke?

And then we were off to the news, the paper review and the line-up of other guests before the main event: twenty-two minutes with Theresa May. It would not be a laugh a minute.

This is May's chance for a reset. This is her opportunity to acknowledge the dreadful election result in an honest, fulsome way and pledge to show the country that she could change. Instead, besides the smile, nothing has changed. She goes straight to the politician's playbook. The first exchange embodies her techniques of evasion.

Marr: Last time you were here, you had a lot of authority … ahead of a general election campaign, which you didn't need to call. Can you apologise to the Conservative Party for the way you handled that campaign?

May: Well, Andrew, it's great to be back here at the party conference in Manchester.

OK, it may well be, but that wasn't the question.

May: And this week's going to be a really good opportunity for us to show the mission of this government, which is …[11]

May heads straight to her overall message, ignoring the question and downplaying the election debacle. Marr tries to interrupt, only too aware of where she wants to take the conversation, but May ploughs on. She returns to her 'mission' to fight 'burning injustices' and build a 'country that works for everyone'. She might have been able to get away with this guff in that dreary hotel in Maidenhead a year ago, but now it sounds ridiculous. With this in mind, she promises to heed the 'message' of the election and calls in evidence some meagre policy announcements.

But none of this is working, and the moment of truth arrives; it's time to say sorry to her party and country for creating more of the instability she promised to avoid when she ruled out a snap election a year ago. Here it comes at last:

I've been very clear that I called the election, I led the campaign, I take my responsibility, and I'm sorry that some very good Members of Parliament lost their seats and some very good people who were candidates didn't gain those seats. But what you'll hear from us this week, as a Conservative Party and a government, is how we are going to move forward, how we're going to address the issues that are of real concern to people, and we're going to build that country for everyone.[12]

Oh.

It's a classic non-apology apology. May says she's been very clear about things that cannot be denied: she called the election, she led the campaign. The best she can summon up is 'I take my responsibility,' a strange construction. She's sorry about some specific things but not the defeat itself. She moves on. She's smiling. Marr isn't having it:

Marr: You and I know there's a difference. If you bump your car into somebody else's car, you may be sorry the accident has happened, but that's different from apologising to the driver of the other car. So can I ask you again, can you apologise to the Conservative Party for what happened in that election campaign?

May: Well, I've already spoken to my Members of Parliament. I'll be speaking later today to the party activists. Look, throughout my entire life, I have worked for the Conservative Party, and I know people who went out during that election who worked really hard, and I'm sorry that the result wasn't the one that all of us wanted.[13]

Again May is sorry, but not for the conduct of the election or for throwing away her majority, but that the result wasn't what she or her fellow Conservatives had wanted. But wait. Enough contrition. Maybe this election was more of a triumph than everyone thinks it was. May brightens, she starts talking about the total number of votes the Tories won and unexpected victories in Scotland. Maybe she can spin this:

May: What I'll be saying to people is, yes, we've got to look at what happened during that election. We've got to listen to the electorate, listen to voters … I think one of the things they were telling me was that some of those issues that I addressed when I first became prime minister, that I identified –

Marr: You completely forgot about them.

May: No – I think we didn't get that message across sufficiently during the election campaign. But I think what voters were saying was that they felt those even more keenly than perhaps we'd realised. That's what we're addressing at this conference.[14]

And there it is: people have got this all wrong. Dig a little deeper and you'll see the real story of the 2017 election: a Tory victory, more votes, a greater vote share and some seats they could only dream of, including in actual Scotland. Why, she seems to be asking, is everyone being so negative?

But that's not enough. May says the real lesson is that the issues she identified when she first became prime minister just a year before were the ones the voters most cared about. She seems to be saying she spotted the big problems the country faced, devised a plan to deal with them – and pushed large numbers of voters into the arms of the most left-wing leader in the history of the Labour Party. But the problem wasn't her or the policies, but a failure to 'get the message across sufficiently during the election campaign'. It's like one of those awful job interviews where the boss asks what the candidate's biggest weakness is, and they answer, 'If anything, it's that I care too much.'

These exchanges epitomise how often political discourse is a charade that insults the public's intelligence. It's hard to imagine any other setting – from a classroom to a business to a kitchen table – where anyone could get away with such a breathtaking refusal to respond to concerns straightforwardly or honestly. But politics – which should prize honesty and openness – so often operates to a different, lower standard.

And so the interview goes on, a twenty-two-minute tussle between reality and unreality: proposals on tuition fees and help for home buyers that fly in the face of May's previous positions; a review of the new Universal Credit system without acknowledgement of the hardship created by the long waiting times; the refusal to accept that average wages have fallen under the Conservatives; a discussion about whether capitalism itself is failing people and, of course, cabinet division over Brexit.

Here at last the mask slips for a moment. The cabinet is bitterly split over negotiations with the European Union. The foreign secretary Boris Johnson is barely pretending to be loyal anymore, publishing his 4,000-word Brexit vision and helpfully offering May his set of 'red lines' for the talks. Marr invites the prime minister to acknowledge the reality. This is a cabinet, he says, 'fighting like rats in a sack'. 'No,' May offers weakly, 'what I have is a cabinet that are united.'

Marr: No, they're not.

May: No, united in the mission of this government, Andrew, and that's what you will see this week.

Marr: A nest of singing birds?

May: United in a mission to build a country that works for everyone …

Marr: If it's a nest of singing birds, it's a nest with at least one enormous cuckoo and several vultures sitting in it as well.[15]

So far, so routine for May, denying a rift everyone knows is there, ignoring open treachery.

I make a suggestion to Marr via his earpiece, and, conscious of time, he goes to the nub of it: Boris Johnson.

Marr: Is he unsackable?

May's response can't be transcribed. Unable to find a way of avoiding a truthful answer, she makes a sort of guttural noise, somewhere between a snort and a laugh, which translates as 'yes'. It's the most honest moment of the interview. She's left speechless. Eventually, unable to come at it directly, she resorts to cliché, prepared lines and meaningless slogans.

> **May:** Look, let's be very clear about what we have here
> in this government. We have a government that is
> determined to build a country that works for everyone.[16]

It's time, for a moment, to offer some mitigation for Theresa May and politicians in general. In an environment where the broadcast and print media are always seeking a story, a mistake, a gaffe, something embarrassing, it's easy to see why May and her colleagues so often play it safe. They use techniques of evasion and deflection, and deliver pre-scripted lines, whatever the question might happen to be.

It's also true that a female prime minister has to operate under different rules. Lack of visible empathy – which damaged May after the Grenfell tragedy – can be fatal for women and forgiven or even ignored in men. Equally, Mrs May's no-nonsense and taciturn style was less readily accepted in a woman than a man, and may have been an approach she adopted as the only way to make it to the top in the male-dominated world of politics.

This may also explain her slightly beleaguered air and carefully constructed insularity. For years it was Theresa and her loyal aides against the world. Perhaps that made sense to a woman fighting against the odds, and it had succeeded while May was home secretary. In those days her interviews were similarly dire, but it didn't matter so much. Perhaps, given her limitations, her mistake was to want to be prime minister when more is expected and more required. However you judge her, it's understandable that a woman in her position should have developed such impenetrable armour, which, in the end, hindered more than helped her.

Hence the advice to smile, appear breezy and laugh it off. But May just wasn't very good at it. That she ended up having to prove her humanity and good humour later by dancing onto the 2018 party conference stage to the strains of 'Dancing Queen' is evidence that something had gone very wrong indeed, and it probably wasn't only her fault.

Still, however much sympathy one has for May, it's no exaggeration to say that she had a problem with the truth. Marr returned to that issue as the interview neared its frosty conclusion in October 2017.

I wanted to use the interview to remind the prime minister of the most extraordinary moment of the 2017 election campaign. The Conservative manifesto was a serious document designed to address the 'burning injustices' May had listed outside 10 Downing Street on the day she became prime minister. It was detailed, and it was bold. It contained a policy that aimed, once and for all, to address social care funding, an issue all previous candidates for prime minister had chosen to dodge and fudge. Not Theresa May.

The May plan required those who needed care in their own homes – for example, those with dementia – to pay for that care unless they had assets (including their homes) that amounted to less than £100,000. This meant that the costs of providing care for a person who needed to be cared for at home would be recouped from their estate until they reached that £100,000 floor. So there was a floor but no cap on costs. That might mean hundreds of thousands of pounds coming off the estate's value at death.

Here was a policy that seemed designed to terrify Tory voters in the Home Counties, who saw their hard-earned house-price inflation disappearing beyond the grasp of their children's inheritance. This complex (and arguably sensible) policy, which grappled with the difficult question of how to pay for social care in an ageing population, was quickly boiled down to two words: 'dementia tax'.

The issue came to a head three weeks before polling day, with pressure growing for the policy to be junked after days of disastrous headlines. On Sunday 21 May Damian Green, the hapless work and pensions secretary, was on the *Marr Show*. Asked whether the prime minister might consider changing the policy, Green made a passionate defence of it and gave a straightforward no. The answer could not have been clearer. The following morning the prime minister junked it. She'd torn up the manifesto she was standing on.

That morning in front of the political press pack, May was peppered with hostile questions about the screeching U-turn. She could have said that she had 'listened to concerns' before acknowledging that she was simply stopping to think again, but that was not in her nature. Instead, May stared the assembled journalists down and insisted, arms spread wide in exasperation, 'Nothing has changed, *nothing* has changed.' This made Andrea Leadsom's denials about her comments to *The Times* look positively candid. Everyone knew that something had changed, not just with the flagship care policy but also in the general election campaign.

As the interview at conference draws to a close, we want to remind May of the social care debacle because of the wider truth it reveals about political honesty. It's time to call her out.

Marr: Can I put it to you that I'm asking you very straightforward questions, and you're not answering them? And this happened during the election campaign as well, which is why you got into so much trouble. Can we just remind ourselves what happened when you did another U-turn on the so-called 'dementia tax'?[17]

We play a clip of that famous moment, and the prime minister has to watch herself back. Unlike the viewers, I can see her reaction from the control room as she relives the worst moment of a dreadful campaign: 'Nothing has changed, nothing has changed.'

May's face remains impassive: she does impassive very well. There's no reaction, not even a wince.

Marr: But we all knew something had changed, and that was a pivotal moment in the campaign … Wouldn't you be better off actually just looking people in the eye and telling them the truth?

May: No …[18]

And on she goes until we run out of time. She has chosen her path as a politician with limited communication skills: never give way, plough on, invent your own reality and smile through it.

She continues as best she can to stay cheerful, but once the programme credits start to run and the theme music plays, the smile slips. Most guests share a post-interview word with Marr, conscious that they're still on air during the credits, but not Theresa May. This time Marr tries to instigate conversation, just as I'd done so many times myself, but the prime minister looks past him in silence.

As ever, no small talk.

* * *

In early 2018, after three years as *Marr* editor, my time was up. Robbie Gibb's departure opened up the top job running the BBC's Live Political Programmes department. That meant overseeing all the content from the programme team at BBC Millbank. Shows like the *Daily Politics* and *Sunday Politics*, *This Week*, and radio programmes like *The Westminster Hour*. But I would still be closely involved with *Marr* as an actively engaged executive producer, building on the work we'd already done to improve and toughen up the show's political interviews. I'd also be in line to lead any special programmes during elections and leadership elections. But that seemed a distant prospect. Theresa May was in trouble but hadn't been Tory leader long and was busy with Brexit, and the next general election wasn't due until 2022.

I could put my feet up. Couldn't I?

13

PARAGRAPH 5C

12 July 2019, Westminster Studios, Albert Embankment, London

Boris Johnson wants to be Britain's next prime minister, and he's taking a beating. Andrew Neil, the toughest interviewer on television, is in charge, blocking every escape route Johnson tries to bolt down. Neil's themes are character, trust and fitness to lead the country. This is close combat, and he's landing rabbit punches that bruise Johnson's soft, pink underbelly.

Early in the interview Neil asks a question about trust, so Johnson changes the subject. He proudly points out that he cut crime in the capital city by 20 per cent when he was mayor of London. It's a standard Johnson deflection. He's used it repeatedly in the hustings, TV debates and interviews of the 2019 Tory leadership election that followed Theresa May's resignation as prime minister. But there's a problem. Neil knows he'll go there, we've discussed all that, and he's ready.

'How much did crime go down at the same time in the rest of the country?' he asks.

Johnson is silent, caught out. He waves a hand towards Neil and can only say, 'Well, you know.'

Oh, we do know, don't you worry.

'It went down by twenty-six per cent,' Neil points out, 'so you were behind the rest of the country.' Johnson's gambit has failed, and his irrelevant boast has backfired. The average voter watching might conclude that trust is an issue, but the average voter doesn't get to choose. The only voters that matter are the 150,000 Tory party members who will choose between Johnson and foreign secretary Jeremy Hunt. Perhaps they are lapping this up at home. *Classic Boris.*

It doesn't get much better for the would-be prime minister.

He blocks and distracts and won't answer questions properly about the resignation of the UK's ambassador to the United States, Kim Darroch. Johnson half-denies that Darroch quit, at least in part, because he refused to support him in a recent TV debate, but the evidence suggests he did. Johnson ignores the question and tries to answer a different one.

Then Neil turns to Johnson's disastrous mistake of blurting out that British hostage Nazanin Zaghari-Ratcliffe was in Iran teaching journalism and not on holiday as she had told the Iranian authorities. Her captors seized upon the comment to justify her continued incarceration, which had been going on for more than three years. Johnson dubiously asserts that his loose words in no way harmed her chances of being reunited with her husband and young daughter. Then he deflects, accusing the interviewer of blaming him when he should be blaming the Iranians. Neil is not having it:

> **Neil:** You're doing what you've done throughout this campaign. You get asked a question, and then you go on to something else, which is a sideline to the actual issue … This bluster may get you through the hustings, it doesn't work with me. I'm trying to pin you down on some facts.[1]

It's a masterclass from Neil. Nobody is better at calling Johnson out. And then we turn to Brexit.

Johnson famously wrote two dummy newspaper columns – one for Leave, the other for Remain – each bursting with assertions about what was true and what was good and what he believed. All he had to do was choose which truth to embrace and which one best served his interests. He chose Leave and he led the charge, convincing enough of the country to follow him. Since then, things have become complicated. His task in this race is to make them simple once again. He says only he can get a deal with the European Union agreed and through the House of Commons. And only he can do so by the end of October 2019 and on terms that will satisfy the ultras in his party, deal with the Northern Irish border problem and deliver favourable terms with the European Union.

Neil asks Johnson whether he can really guarantee his timetable that the UK will leave by Halloween, Johnson's promised departure day. Oh yes, says Johnson, you can bank on it. (Spoiler alert: In reality, he will miss that deadline by three months.)

Neil asks whether he might consider suspending – 'proroguing', in the jargon – parliament to allow him to wrest control of the Brexit process from MPs. He says he doesn't want to, he doesn't think it will be necessary and in any case it wouldn't be sensible. A little over a month later – unlawfully, as it turns out – he does it anyway.

The interview has been unrelenting and damaging to Johnson, but he has just about survived the onslaught. Brexit is home territory, and this is the home straight. There are ten minutes left. Neil continues to press him about what would happen if there were a 'no deal Brexit' – a UK departure from the European Union without an agreement on our future relationship.

This question has dominated the campaign, and Johnson loves talking about it. He says he'll get a deal, but that 'no deal' would be just fine for the UK. He's confident that things will continue as usual if that happens. Johnson even has a way of explaining how. This explanation allows him to present himself as a man across the detail, in contrast to his image as a sloppy chancer whose dog invariably consumes his homework.

Johnson's eyes light up when Andrew asks him to elaborate. His answer is confident and well practised. Under the 1947 GATT agreement – full name, the General Agreement on Tariffs and Trade – the UK and the European Union could, if they wished, carry on trading without imposing damaging tariffs. It was all there, said Johnson – and please forgive him for getting technical – in Article 24, paragraph 5b of the seventy-two-year-old treaty. As he finishes, Johnson resembles a student in an early-morning seminar who has successfully regurgitated a pre-planned answer despite a raging hangover.

Then things get even better when Andrew Neil makes an uncharacteristic error. Reflecting Johnson's words back to him, the esteemed interviewer gets his article and paragraph numbers mixed up. It's just a slip of the tongue, but Johnson smells blood. Here's Andrew Neil, the great man, pulling him up on his grasp of the detail and getting it wrong. Johnson decides to put Andrew in his place.

'Paragraph 5b. Article 24,' he crows. 'Get the detail right.'

Johnson is brimming with hubris as he jabs his finger at the BBC's toughest nut. It's his turn to browbeat now.

'GET the detail right!' he repeats, his voice rising to something approaching a shout. Fucking hell, he's thinking, the old bastard wants to show me up on the detail, and I'm knocking this out of the park.

'Andrew,' he concludes with a weary flourish, 'it's Article 24, paragraph 5b.'

The interviewer waits for Johnson to stop talking and looks across the studio at him. Neil wants further clarification from our unlikely expert.

'And,' Neil begins steadily, assured in the face of Johnson's grandstanding, 'how would you handle paragraph 5c?'

For a moment the world stops. The birds stop singing. The cars driving up and down the Albert Embankment outside the studio pull over silently and wait. Only the clock keeps ticking. Tick, tock. Just a beat.

5c? Johnson registers.

Oh shit.

I love it when a plan comes together.

I believe that the BBC is one of Britain's greatest assets. It brings the British people together – whether through national crises, celebrations or shiny-floor entertainment – like nothing else. It can reach into the world like no other broadcaster on the planet. It is, at its best, a source of enlightenment, joy and comfort. So, when I was given the chance to run the BBC's political programmes department at Millbank in Westminster, I did so with enormous pride. My connection to the BBC, made through that black-and-white portable in the 1970s, was just as powerful more than forty years on.

Working for the BBC is more than a job. It's a mission. At least, that's how it is for the vast majority of staff I encountered during my thirteen years working there. Where you work inside the huge, global organisation defines precisely what that mission is for you. But the famous statement of the BBC's purpose by its first director-general, John Reith, that it's there to 'inform, educate and entertain', remains a decent starting point. The provision of 'impartial, high-quality and distinctive output' stands alongside those words in the BBC's current mission statement.

The 'inform' bit of the BBC's mission is not simply about being told that things have happened. It's about understanding and debating why they happened, whether they are important and what happens next. That's particularly vital in politics and is exactly where political programmes come in.

Historically, there has been a healthy divide between the news – bulletins like the *News at Ten* – and the programmes that analyse that news deeply. Some journalists at the BBC are good at both, and most are better at one than the other. Those who prosper in news like, more than anything, to cover a story as it breaks: 'This has just happened!' 'Oh, look, and now this!' In politics, 'news' often relies on intelligence, which is a posh word for gossip. For political journalists who report the news – whether in print, online or broadcast – relationships with the powerful and their people are vital. But this need for access is also the most serious impartiality risk: the risk that politicians, in general, and the incumbent government, in particular, will have undue influence over the BBC's political stories and how they cover them. Why does this happen? First, because journalists can become too close to those they cover and their staff, and second, because journalists want things that politicians can give, things like access to the prime minister and juicy stories. The majority of excellent BBC journalists – whether on screen or behind the scenes – try to resist 'incumbency bias', but it is a real problem.

How real was laid bare in an investigation by Rowena Mason in the *Guardian* in March 2023. Mason revealed WhatsApp messages and emails from senior BBC executives to BBC journalists that made them aware of the government's view and appeared to encourage them to reflect Downing Street's perspective in their coverage. For example, when Covid restrictions were introduced in March 2020, No. 10 urged BBC executives not to use the word 'lockdown' to describe them. This was then passed on to journalists. Despite staff protests, BBC coverage omitted the word 'lockdown' in those initial reports even though everyone from Sky News to the *Daily Mail* was using the word.

This does not reflect political bias – I don't for a moment think BBC executives were doing this because they necessarily support the Conservative Party – but a tendency to give undue influence to those in Downing Street, whether Tory or Labour. They do so to gain access to senior government ministers and to get stories ahead of rivals. They are also affected by the fear of political reprisals against the BBC from those who ultimately control the purse strings. These reasons, and the allure of power, are seductive. BBC executives should be expected to demonstrate the judgement and integrity to resist them.

My goal was to promote programme culture. I had come up through the *Weekend World* and *Walden* tradition. I was interested in testing politicians and their ideas, holding power to account and trying to help viewers understand the intellectual ideas that drive the policies that affect their lives. I did not particularly want to cultivate relationships with politicians or their staff but to stand back from all of that and ask questions on behalf of the public. In the programmes department we were less exposed to the risk of incumbency bias because we kept the parties and their people at arm's length.

This was all good, but there were problems. Years of savage cuts to the licence fee were being felt at the BBC. The financial pressures only got worse, and I knew from the start that there was an opportunistic argument being made that the BBC news machine should swallow up political programmes to save money. This empire-building would be bad for the quality of programmes and potentially expose us to the same impartiality risk. I had to fight for our very survival from the start.

The licence fee is extraordinary value for money – it's currently just under forty-four pence per day – but the Conservative government had been clobbering the BBC for years with cuts and freezes and new responsibilities. And now, the libertarian and populist forces on the right were organising against it. At the same time, the left – finally in charge of Labour after all those years in the wilderness – regarded the mainstream media as the enemy. As the ultimate establishment institution, the BBC was in the sights of both disruptive extremes. To add to the toxic mix, Brexit had created a sort of mania on both sides. The defeated Remainers blamed the BBC for the referendum result. The suspicious Leavers thought the BBC wanted to promote a second referendum and steal their precious Brexit away.

For these actors, the BBC was just collateral damage in their political war. The important thing was to give the impression that they were hard done by, as the BBC did its best to deliver impartial coverage in a toxic political culture. They didn't care about the damage done to public consent for the licence fee by their point-scoring. Sometimes it felt that whatever bitter arguments raged between the different political tribes, they all agreed on one thing: they hated the BBC.

I had a job to do as I took over Live Political Programmes. Morale was low. Staff felt that management ran cliques and excluded diverse viewpoints. So I worked hard to open up the culture, allowing opinions and fresh thinking to develop. I thought naively that the best way to protect the political programmes department was to make great ones. This desire to remake the department and culture fed into the concept for a new sort of political discussion programme to replace the *Daily Politics*. I wanted a more free-flowing panel show that broke away from the stuffy traditions of political programme presentation but which, at the same time, committed itself to serious, in-depth and unexpected coverage.

Politics Live – presented by Jo Coburn and Andrew Neil – launched in September 2018. From the start it worked. The first edition featured an entirely female panel of high-quality guests and was fronted by Coburn. As that first line-up started to shape up, I could see that it would draw attention to the programme and make a powerful statement. I was very proud of *Politics Live*. It felt modern, with a distinctive set, swish graphics and high-quality films designed for social media. It worked from the start.

Andrew Neil was never really suited to the show's style, which didn't play to his strengths as a tough interviewer. *Politics Live* was about discussion and direct engagement between the panellists. Jo Coburn was willing to unlearn the more stuffy style of BBC presenting and thrived as a freewheeling host who got out of the way when things were going well and moved things on when needed. It wasn't long before we saw the audience numbers increase, eventually reaching 30 per cent higher than the *Daily Politics*. For their part, the *Politics Live* films clocked-up millions of views online, reaching new, younger and less male-skewed audiences. All the things the BBC said they wanted, we achieved.

The show landed in the middle of the Theresa May Brexit shitshow. As the prime minister tried in vain to secure a deal with the European Union that could command the support of both her party and parliament, we charted every twist and turn. The details of backstops, Brady amendments and all the rest are lost in the mists of time, but the visceral divisions Brexit revealed in the country are never far below the surface. The vast majority of these discussions were civilised and serious, but the programme could also deliver social media 'moments' that exploded into the culture. The most memorable came when the author Will Self – the embodiment of the metropolitan Remain 'elite' – was sitting next to Tory MP Mark Francois – the Brexit ultra – on the *Politics Live* set in March 2019.

The needle between the novelist and the Brexiteer had started as they made their way into the studio, before they'd even sat down. What the argument was about is disputed. Some say they argued about who had the bigger set of balls, others over who possessed the larger penis. An all-female panel it wasn't.

Once on air, the two men seemed fine, if a little wary of each other. Then after about forty minutes, a discussion about political populism heated up rapidly when Self went for it:

> **Self:** Your problem, really, Mark, is not that you have to be a racist or an antisemite to vote for Brexit. It's just that every racist or antisemite in the country did.

Francois: I think that's a slur on 17.4 million people, and I think you should apologise on national television. I think that's an outrageous thing to say.[2]

From here, the two went at it, Self repeating that racists support Brexit, Francois telling him to say sorry. Coburn tried to move on and bring in the other guests – political strategist Jo Tanner and comedian and campaigner Grace Campbell – but the two men continued shouting as the women tried to make themselves heard.

At this point, something extraordinary happened, which you rarely see on television outside of a boxing weigh-in. The two men, just centimetres apart, fell silent before squaring up and staring directly into each other's eyes, daring the other to be the first to break eye contact. The intensity of the stare-off was palpable as I watched from my office. This was real. This was hatred that you couldn't confect. As the discussion continued, I called the director and asked her to keep the camera on the two men for as long as this went on. The spectacle was simultaneously utterly compelling and totally pathetic.

Meanwhile Matt Booker, the journalist running the show that day, was worried. He had a question for Jo Coburn.

'What,' he started over the studio talkback, 'are you going to do if this turns into a fight?'

Jo couldn't answer with words, so she glanced down at the two *Politics Live* branded mugs on the desk. Matt thought for a second and then got her drift.

'You're going to throw water over them?'

Jo nodded. That was her plan.

Mercifully, it never came to that. The credits rolled, and the two men walked off set together. Will told Mark he could have him in a real fight. Mark told Will to 'fuck off'.

Matt Booker was one of the nicest men in television, but shortly after the Francois/Self stare-off he departed for a career in education. He now teaches history at a comprehensive school in London. I like to think he throws water over unruly school-boys if they start scrapping about who's got the biggest balls.

For my part I was happy. This wasn't a confrontation we'd engineered or provoked. The genuine animosity between the two men – the luvvie and the Leaver – told a true story about what the Brexit debate had done to us. It was hard to know which man was worse. But it was terrific television.

Back in the more sedate surroundings of Sunday mornings, I'd recruited John Neal as my successor as *Marr* editor. John had lots of interview experience working with Mishal Husain and John Humphrys on *Today* on Radio 4. He also brought an excellent grasp of foreign affairs to the mix. He cared about the programme and understood the show's brand. Moreover, he was willing to ask for help, and wanted me to continue to influence the programme and help shape the interviews.

In May 2019 elections took place to the European parliament. These elections wouldn't have been necessary if the UK had left the European Union. Almost three years after the referendum, that we hadn't was political gold for Nigel Farage's new Brexit Party. The former UKIP leader had founded the party to campaign for the hardest of hard 'no-deal' Brexit. Frustrated Leave voters were ready to back the new party in enormous numbers because of Theresa May's failure to get Brexit done.

When Farage launched the party in April he got a bit carried away. Rather than presenting the Brexit Party as a single-issue party only concerned with getting the UK out of the Brexit impasse, Farage aimed higher. 'Our task,' he said, 'and our mission is to change politics for good. To change all aspects of politics in this country.'

I saw an opportunity. Farage wanted to launch a new right-wing party that aspired to be a force in British politics akin to Marine Le Pen's National Rally or other populist right-wing parties in Europe. This meant that Farage would have to answer questions beyond the single issue of Brexit, given the scale of his ambition. I urged the Marr team to plan an interview with Farage – covering Brexit and examining the leader's broader political positions – for the European election campaign.

When the interview came, in the middle of May, Marr spent ten of the fifteen allocated minutes on Brexit. Then, towards the end, he turned to Farage's views on other issues: the NHS (he'd backed a private insurance system), measures to deal with global warming (he was a sceptic), immigration (he'd been famously troubled by foreign languages being spoken on trains, despite having a German wife at the time), the size of the state (he thought it was too big), gun control (he's supported liberalising the post-Dunblane restrictions) and Vladimir Putin (he'd expressed admiration for the Russian dictator). These were all legitimate areas to cover, given his desire to remake British politics, but as soon as we went there Farage squealed like a baby.

The questions were 'boring' and then 'ludicrous'. He'd never seen a more ridiculous interview, he said. Farage couldn't stop bleating. He told Marr he wanted to talk about democracy, ignoring the fact that a free media asking tough questions was a vital part of any democratic society. 'What's wrong with the BBC?' he complained. 'It's in denial.' I'd never seen Farage more rattled and angry. He then went outside and told any camera he could about the dastardly BBC. It was pathetic.

The BBC often gets attacked by the more unhinged wing of the Continuity Remain campaign for somehow 'creating' Nigel Farage by putting him on television and radio. They are particularly cross about the number of times he has appeared on *Question Time*. The truth is that UKIP's electoral performance drove these appearances. Since their founding in 1997, UKIP were able to benefit from voters' real concerns about the European Union. As this message became more widely heard, their support increased, and as the rules dictated, they appeared on the BBC more frequently. It's true that they were largely a one-man band in the shape of Farage, which explained his personal ubiquity as the UKIP representative, but they won millions of votes and even came first in the 2014 European elections. If angry Remainers want to blame someone for Farage's success and his influence on British politics, they should focus on the politicians who failed to counter his messages on the EU and immigration, and stop shooting the messenger.

Anyway, Farage's 2019 rant against Marr and the BBC didn't do him any harm in the European elections of 2019. Maybe it helped him. That's usually the game he plays. Come election day, the Brexit Party triumphed, coming first with more than 30 per cent of the vote. The Conservative vote cratered to a little over 8 per cent. Incredibly, they came fifth. The following day Theresa May, a good woman unsuited to be prime minister, scuppered by Brexit, quit No. 10.

The chancer's chance had finally come.

Boris Johnson's chequered history of fabrications, infidelities and betrayals is long. I don't have time to rehearse it all here. That's another book. Literally. Quite a big one, too.

Here we're concerned with Johnson the communicator, and how he behaved when selling his ideas and the 'Boris' persona to the public on television. You should always be suspicious when someone goes by an assumed name. Johnson's family, Paul Simon-style, call him 'Al'. 'Boris' is his stage name. So it's ironic that Johnson's mastery of television was built on his apparent authenticity, an authenticity established primarily on *Have I Got News for You*.

Johnson used the BBC's topical comedy panel show to project an image of himself that was almost exactly the opposite of who he really was, coming across as bumbling and self-deprecating when he is really calculating and vain. When invited to discuss his mastery of light entertainment on *Kirsty Wark Talks to Boris Johnson* in 2005, Johnson didn't bother to hide his strategy. He talked about his 'carefully constructed veneer of a blithering buffoon' and made an explicit admission that his goal was political:

> There is a point to going on these shows … maybe there's
> a logic to going on a show where you can subtly, in a
> weasely, stoat-like way, insinuate some political point
> into the discussion and sugar the pill in that way and
> who knows, the audience might swallow it.[3]

Sonia Purnell worked with Johnson in the 1990s as he emerged as a national figure. She knew him in Brussels, where he spent his time writing often fictional anti-EU stories for the *Daily Telegraph*. In her biography of Johnson she writes that his 'brilliant act' on *Have I Got News for You* marked the moment when he morphed into 'Just Boris' (also the title of her book). He was an unlikely man of the people, but he became one because he seemed real, a more open and engaging politician than anyone could remember. His reward was a rare status enjoyed by Madonna, Beyoncé and Che: refer to 'Boris' and everyone immediately knew who you meant.

For political interviewers, the *HIGNFY* legacy was a difficult one. If they weren't careful, Johnson could sucker them into his clown act, and everyone would end up covered in custard pie, allowing serious political questions to go unanswered. But then came Eddie Mair.

It's March 2013 on the *Andrew Marr Show* set, but Andrew Marr is not the man in the chair. He's still recuperating from a serious stroke and Radio 4's Eddie Mair is standing in for him. His main guest is the mayor of London, Boris Johnson. Mair's style is utterly individual and completely fearless. He resembles a polite but sadistic surgeon who wields a scalpel while telling his victims precisely where he plans to make his next very painful incision. By the time he came off air that morning, blood was pooled on the carpet, splattered on the sofa and smeared on the walls. Mair seemed pleased with his work. After all, it wasn't his blood.

The interview had started conventionally enough, with Johnson adopting his usual persona while dealing with questions about immigration and the Olympic legacy. Then Mair, having lured Johnson into complacency, got on to the main event.

The interview came the day before the BBC broadcast a film about Johnson made by the eminent documentarian Michael Cockerel. Mair had viewed a copy of *Boris Johnson: The Irresistible Rise* in the days before the interview and was struck by its portrait of a man willing to lie and cheat his way to the top of journalism and politics. Mair had seen many interviews with Johnson before and, according to *Marr Show* boss Barney Jones, felt that even the most rigorous interviewees were 'sucked into Johnson's bonhomie'. Not this time.

Mair had agreed with Jones that he'd pick out three of the most indefensible Johnson episodes from the documentary and 'lay them out forensically, without sneer or spin'. He begins his questioning gently but ominously. 'I want to talk about you,' he says. Johnson laughs and confesses, 'Well, that's exactly what I'm trying to avoid.' It's a joke, but it's true.

Mair moves on to the trio of troubling episodes in Johnson's past: his sacking for faking a quote while a journalist at *The Times*; his removal from the Tory front bench by Michael Howard for lying about an affair; and a phone call in which he was recorded offering help to an old friend who wanted to assault a journalist. Johnson splutters, jokes, huffs and scratches his head while Mair runs through all this. 'Why don't we talk about something else?' he pleads. At one point, he puts his hand up and asks Mair for 'permission to obfuscate'. Eventually, Mair sums up the charges:

Making up quotes, lying to your party leader, wanting to be part of someone being physically assaulted; you're a nasty piece of work, aren't you?[4]

In the gallery, Barney Jones is watching. He's horrified. When he rehearsed the interview with Mair, Eddie had used the same phrase, but Barney had assumed that, on air, he'd modify the sentiment. He expected Mair to say viewers might conclude Johnson was a nasty piece of work, but he'd gone with a wording that sounded very much like Mair's personal judgement on the mayor of London's character. After the show Jones sought out Johnson and apologised, but he found him in a forgiving mood. It was his fault, he confessed. He hadn't expected such a rough ride at nine in the morning and wasn't prepared.

Asked about the interview by the press later that day Johnson said something very interesting that reveals he used to understand what accountability and a robust BBC were about:

> Somebody said Eddie Mair was too hard on me; you cannot be too hard on politicians. It is the function of BBC journalists to bash up politicians, particularly people like me. Fair play to Eddie, he landed a good one.

At the time, Mair's charge sheet felt brutal, and his verdict extraordinarily rude. Viewed from today, it seems prescient: Johnson's character was an issue and has remained so. The question in the summer of 2019, six years after the Mair dissection, was whether it should stop him from achieving his ultimate ambition and becoming prime minister.

Before we get back to the Albert Embankment and paragraph 5c, I have something painful to deal with: the 2019 debate between the final five contenders to replace Theresa May as Tory leader and prime minister, broadcast on Tuesday 18 June 2019 on BBC One. Host: Emily Maitlis. Guests: Boris Johnson, Michael Gove, Jeremy Hunt, Sajid Javid and Rory Stewart.

If there's a moment I could go back to in my career and change, it would be the afternoon of Saturday 15 June, three days before showtime. It was my sister's birthday, and I was out having lunch with her and my nephews and niece when my phone rang. It was Chris Cook, the BBC's star news director, who, if you recall, saved Andrew Marr from disaster in 2005 when he was struggling to get the hang of presenting. As it turned out, Chris was offering to save me, too. I just didn't know it.

'Chris,' I answered, walking away from the noisy pub into the garden, 'how are you?'

Chris was fine but busy. He was rehearsing for the five-way leadership debate and had a question for me. 'Rob,' he asked, 'are you sure about the stools?'

With the approval of BBC's Head of Newsgathering, Jonathan Munro, I'd decided to break with tradition and take away the lecterns that were generally used in debate programmes like this. Influenced by the success of *Politics Live*, I was interested in breaking down the usual artifice and grandeur of political programming to facilitate more free-flowing and engaging discussion and debate. I wanted the debate to be serious, but I wanted to encourage a more open conversation. I tended to trust my instincts for this stuff and be brave but not reckless. This time my instincts were wrong.

'I'm sure,' I told him.

'OK,' said Chris. I should have been more alarmed by the worry in his voice, but with a dash of hubris I stuck to my guns.

'You see, we still have the lecterns from the last debates we did,' Chris tried again, 'and it wouldn't take long to bring them out of storage, tart them up a bit and use them. I'm on set staring at these stools, and I just wonder.'

I let Chris's words hang there. I questioned myself one more time to check. Again, the answer came back to me: stick with it, and do something different.

'I'm sure,' I said to Chris. 'Let's use the stools.' And that was that. He hung up and I went back into the pub. Johnson, Gove, Hunt, Javid and Stewart would be on stools, not behind lecterns.

Thus was born the worst boy band in history.

* * *

In the run-up to the programme, Johnson was the prize. Channel 4 had held a debate the previous week without the front-runner, and his absence made a mockery of the whole thing. This was an early sign that, as Downing Street finally came into view for Johnson, he was willing to ignore democratic norms and avoid scrutiny. The overwhelming message from the managers at the BBC – Munro, the newish Head of News Fran Unsworth, and the manager that ran political news, Katy Searle – was that Johnson had to be there come what may. I agreed he was vital to the show's success but was worried we were too willing to bend over backwards to accommodate him.

Political debate shows need an audience to ask questions and create an atmosphere. My idea of using high stools rather than lecterns was inspired by town hall debates in American elections. The absence of physical barriers between the candidate and the questioner could create an interesting dynamic.

The problem was that the BBC managers suspected Johnson would use the audience as an excuse not to participate. Munro – a veteran of these sorts of negotiations – was worried that we'd end up in an endless dialogue about the precise make-up of the studio audience. He feared we'd get bogged down in circular discussions around how big the audience should be, the balance of party-political opinion within it and where people stood on Brexit. That risked the whole enterprise collapsing, or individuals – including Johnson – walking away. Munro then had a brainwave: we could avoid all that by bringing members of the public into the debate remotely from BBC studios around the UK. This would allow us to hand-pick ten to fifteen people and avoid a tortuous conversation about who was in the audience.

This made the negotiation easier but sacrificed the atmosphere and chemistry of a studio audience because of fears – real or imagined – that it would spook Johnson. I could understand the logic, but this was troubling. It seemed to me that the tail was wagging the dog. It tells you a lot about where the balance of power between politicians and the broadcasters had got to that we decided to go with this plan. I should have voiced my concerns and not been so timid on the issue.

This decision also left the stools without a leg to stand on. As soon as there was no audience, I should have dropped the stools and gone back to the lecterns. After all, they were designed to encourage the candidates to engage with a physical audience, and there wasn't one. But I stuck with them.

My main job was talking to the candidates' campaign teams and confirming them for the show. The only difficult team was Johnson's. Lee Cain was his loyal communications guy. He'd seemed like a nice enough bloke when I first encountered him in 2016. We'd got chatting over a *Marr* breakfast during the referendum campaign when he'd been in charge of booking Vote Leave's TV and radio interviews. Lee was from an ordinary working-class background, and I recall him saying how most of his London friends couldn't understand how he could be a Brexiteer. I got the impression he liked his status as a Brexit renegade. He was perfectly pleasant. I liked him.

By the time we met at the St James' Café in central London, Cain had changed. He was keen to wring out every advantage from Johnson's front-runner status and knew the BBC needed his participation, so he wasn't quick to confirm. The most jarring aspect of our meeting was his habit of referring to Johnson not as 'Boris' or 'Johnson' but as 'The Boss'. In my world, that sobriquet only applies to Bruce Springsteen or Jürgen Klopp. When applied to Johnson by Cain, it came over as sinister, pseudo-gangster schtick. It was also a little too ingratiating for my taste, as if he knew his place when it came to Old Etonian Johnson. At this stage at least, Cain was a deferential and unashamed Johnson fanboy.

As such, he was very sensitive to the charges of racism that were levelled at 'The Boss' in the leadership campaign. He did not want them to feature in the upcoming debate. Cain knew that this was not an undertaking I could give, so he had another gambit. He assumed, he said, that any question asked of one candidate had to be asked of all of them. I agreed that this would generally be the case but that a rigid rule to that effect would kill the flow of the programme and that Emily Maitlis was free to make her own points. I was happy to agree that, in principle, this was a reasonable rule of engagement when it came to audience questions. Cain was trying to set the terms, and I didn't mind him feeling he'd done so, even though I'd kept the necessary wriggle room. I wasn't going to give him an easy excuse not to show up. It was important for Johnson to face scrutiny.

Cain was specifically trying to prevent questions about some of Johnson's newspaper columns that many people saw as racist. You'll remember them: the one saying Muslim women in burkas resemble 'letterboxes' and 'bank robbers'; the description of the 'watermelon smiles' of Africans. Cain's logic was that we could hardly ask everyone a question about Johnson's offensive columns, which meant we couldn't ask Johnson either. I took a different view. It seemed to me that as long as we were asking all five candidates about race, we could reasonably refer to Johnson's comments in the programme. I was careful to use a form of words that left that option open.

While all this was happening, the BBC political programmes team was putting the 'audience' of remote questioners together. This was a Tory leadership election to be voted on by Conservative Party members, but whoever won would get to govern all of us. I told the team to pick the best questions that reflected the wider public's concerns, not just the attitudes of Tory members and voters. The spectacle of the country's prime minister being hand-picked by a tiny rump of Conservative members has been repeated since 2019 and has not become any more attractive. I'm glad we included concerned non-Conservatives in the audience in 2019, despite the battering we were about to take for it.

After further telephone conversations with Cain seeking ever more precise assurances about the nature of the questions,

Johnson was on board. When the night arrived, Emily Maitlis opened the show in dramatic style.

'Five men,' she announced, 'one job.'

What followed was a debate that should have been an embarrassment for the Conservative Party but which, thanks to the *Daily Mail*, was used as a stick to beat the BBC with, presumably egged on and briefed by Team Johnson.

The first problem was the stools; as we've established, that was my fault. The five male politicians perched awkwardly on the white leather upholstery like a twisted Westlife. Far from improving the nature of the debate, the lack of a more formal lectern seemed to encourage the candidates to behave badly because they were unanchored.

The first few minutes were fine, but then, about fifteen minutes in, Johnson started throwing his weight around, talking over his fellow candidates and completely ignoring Emily Maitlis as she attempted to steer the programme. In the end, faced with Johnson's selective deafness, she resorted to asking Johnson whether he could hear her. Pretty soon, the others followed suit, creating a cacophony of Brexit chat. Their fantasies about the wonderful Brexit deal that only they could deliver and their hi-tech solutions to the Irish border sounded like so much wishful thinking.

The only candidate who rejected these fantasies entirely was former international development secretary Rory Stewart. He cast himself as a Brexit realist, a position that misjudged entirely where his party stood in the summer of 2019 and perhaps forever. His arguments died on contact with the unreality of the Tory moment, and he seemed to visibly despair, at one point removing his tie in a gesture that felt both weary and louche. Here was a man simultaneously running to lead the Conservative Party and decisively falling out of love with it.

As the debate moved on to education, Rory made one more stab at elevating matters, introducing AI and robotics and their potential impact on the world of work into the discussion. At this, there was a collective groan from the other candidates, who quickly shut boring Rory down for talking about real things that might actually matter. They had platitudes to deliver and wanted to get back to them.

Then came what was to be the most controversial moment. Maitlis called on Abdullah Patel, a Bristol-based imam. His question was about Islamophobia, which he regularly saw in his community. 'Do the candidates agree,' he asked, 'that words have consequences?' Maitlis turned to Johnson, repeating the question and then adding examples of his incendiary comments about Muslim women. Johnson took the opportunity to half-apologise for any offence his words might have caused. For that, he was sorry.

Lee Cain, watching from the green room, wanted to try a little intimidation, and my phone lit up with a text:

This whole line of questioning was aimed at Boris –
totally unacceptable. We were told no questions aimed at
specific [sic] – no doubt they was [sic]. Very unhappy.

'Totally unacceptable' is telling. It betrays an attitude. Johnson is, literally, 'The Boss', and he gets to say what's allowed. Somehow I'd failed to operate on this basis, and Cain was pissed off.

Abdullah's broad question was followed by specific points from Maitlis to all the candidates about their record on race. This led to a reasonably constructive discussion about racism and a commitment from all the candidates to an inquiry into Islamophobia in the Conservative Party.

The final audience question came from Aman from London. He expressed the reasonable view – which has only grown in resonance over subsequent years – that prime ministers elected by Conservative Party members do not have a mandate. It was obvious that Aman was not a Tory when he asked the candidates, 'When will you do the right thing and call a general election?'

Johnson responded by ruling out an early election – he would call one four months later – and the rest of the candidates engaged happily with Aman's question in the little time left.

As the show ended, I was concerned that my decision to stick with the boy band seating had made the debate more difficult for Maitlis. Five politicians on one stage for just an hour would be a challenge for any presenter. But I thought the negative elements reflected more on the candidates than on Emily or the BBC. Watching it back now, this was right, but a wounded Johnson campaign, angry that we'd done our job, was about to activate its social media and newspaper assets.

My phone lit up again. It was Cain. 'The event wasn't as agreed,' he texted. 'Noted and very disappointed.'

Noted.

Menacing stuff, and he meant to deliver on it.

The next day right-wing website Guido Fawkes began digging into the questioners' lives and social media backgrounds, and they quickly struck gold. Abdullah – the imam from Bristol – had a Twitter timeline full of offensively antisemitic and sexist comments. How could the BBC have been unaware of the kind of man they were putting on air on such a high-profile programme? Didn't they check his Twitter account?

The answer, of course, is that we did. But Abdullah had told us he had closed his Twitter account. We checked, and he had no Twitter presence. We asked him whether he had deactivated his account to obscure controversial tweets, and he assured us he hadn't. We also checked numerous other sources for any red flags. None appeared. Perhaps the fact he told us he had closed his account should have troubled us, but it didn't.

The trouble was that the account was only deactivated temporarily so we couldn't see his offensive tweets before we put him on the show. After the programme ended it reappeared, and the world, including Guido Fawkes, was able to see his Twitter history.

As if that wasn't enough, Guido also established that the final questioner, Aman, was a Labour supporter. He'd done some paid work for the Labour Party when engaged by them as a lawyer, although Guido presented him as Labour 'staff' …

All this thrilled the culture warriors who were out to get the BBC. Lynton Crosby, the Australian election specialist running Johnson's campaign in the background, texted Emily Maitlis with links to the Guido stories. 'That's why I don't engage with the BBC,' he said. 'Sorry.' Crosby's 'sorry' was really a thank you. Our audience troubles were a godsend for him as he could use them to distract the media from the real stories – Johnson's apology to Muslims and other news lines out of the debate – while firing up the party base who hated the BBC.

The Daily Mail followed up with a front-page story that screamed: Biased, Brazen, Contemptible. The hysterical piece featured a parade of outraged Conservative MPs attacking the BBC, alongside 'sources' from inside the Johnson campaign complaining about the stools, the questioners and the pressure put on Johnson.

The furore lasted several days and had Tory MPs calling for an Ofcom inquiry. The BBC had become the story. The Abdullah Patel tweets were embarrassing, but such relationships are built on trust and we had no idea about the contents of his (reactivated) Twitter account. As for Aman, we weren't hiding that he wasn't a Conservative. He was someone, quite justifiably, calling for a general election to establish a mandate for whoever became prime minister. So outrageous was this idea that Johnson later did exactly that.

The stools were a mistake, and we should have booked a studio audience in the usual way and let Johnson walk if he didn't like it. But watching the programme back today, these aren't the issues that jump out at you. Instead it's Johnson and his colleagues and their glib assurances. Within a few years

Johnson was out of office in disgrace and Britain was in an economic crisis in the wake of yet another fantastical Tory leadership race.

Still, after trashing the BBC, things were on track for Johnson and his menacing advisers. Before long, the race was whittled down to a straight fight between Johnson and Jeremy Hunt – the best performer on boy band night. Team Johnson only had one major hurdle to overcome: half an hour with Andrew Neil in mid-July.

Nothing for 'The Boss' to worry about.

Neil (innocently): How would you handle paragraph 5c?

A beat.

Johnson (Half-smiling, knowing he's been exposed but pushing on regardless): I would confide entirely in paragraph 5b because that is …

Neil (not about to let this one go): How would you get round what's in 5c?

Johnson (stumped): I would confide entirely in paragraph 5b, which is enough for our purposes.

Neil (reeling it in): Do you know what's in 5c?

Johnson: (with nowhere else to go) No.[5]

For some reason – perhaps to try to convert the situation into a joke, which usually works for him, Johnson pointed for emphasis as he said 'No.' Then he laughed weakly and without conviction, but it's not funny. At least not for him.

Preparing for a big interview is fun. You get to role-play the questions with the interviewer, help hone the questions and make sure the presenting talent is match-fit. Sometimes in these sessions, you'll stand up to the challenge of Andrew Neil's questions, but more often, you end up having to fold, backed into a corner by the power of his logic. Rarely, when the real interview happens, does it go exactly, or even to a significant degree, the way it does in rehearsal. And it never goes the way you imagine it might when you're lying in bed, the night before a big interview, dreaming of how it could play out if all goes to plan. Until it does. On 12 July 2019, it happens.

There's good-natured disagreement in the team about whose idea it was. Andrew Neil maintains he came up with it. I think it was me. Programme editor Andrew Alexander credits producer Adam Donald, but nobody really cares. All we know is that in the run-up to the interview, somebody suggested we entice Johnson into a discussion of his favourite clause of his favourite paragraph of his favourite treaty, let him grandstand and then go one step deeper into the detail. If we did, we were confident he would be exposed as the Brexit bullshitter he truly was. So we did, and he was. The credit for the flawless execution is Neil's.

Johnson spent what was left of the interview trying to regain the initiative. In one of his standard moves when in trouble, Johnson started BBC-bashing. His only response to Neil's inconvenient mastery of the detail was an accusation of 'BBC-generated gloom'. It's pathetic, and Neil is withering. 'Yeah, OK,' he says, 'let's get back to the facts.'

That's the last place Johnson wants to go.

Watching from the green room, Johnson's media adviser Lee Cain must have been horrified by his man's performance under Neil's questioning. He wasn't going to make that mistake again.

14

GAFFE MACHINE

It's 5 December 2019 and the prime minister's team of media advisers have finally stopped stringing me along. Now even they have stopped pretending they'll allow Boris Johnson back into the TV studio with Britain's toughest interviewer, Andrew Neil. It's been a bruising few weeks. I've been called every obscene name going on social media. I've been branded a corrupt liar who has dragged the BBC's reputation for impartiality through the mud. At least one MP has called for my resignation. And yet, through all this, I haven't been able to defend myself. To do so I'd have to expose Downing Street's dishonest behaviour, which isn't an option in my position as a BBC manager. So I've had to suck it up.

Until now. Today, the fightback begins. We are back in the Westminster Live studios on the Albert Embankment. It's the same location where, a few months earlier, Andrew Neil exposed Johnson's flimsy grasp of detail during the Conservative leadership election. Neil is here today. Johnson, now prime minister, is not. Neil may be alone, but he's about to deliver a moment of powerful television. I'm in the tiny control room, watching him on a monitor. The director counts him in, and he wraps up the final interview in the series of BBC specials with the party leaders:

> There is, of course, still one to be done. Boris Johnson. The prime minister. We've been asking him for weeks to give us a date, time and venue. So far, none has been forthcoming.[1]

Neil is calm. There are no histrionics, although he's as disgusted by the prime minister's cowardice as any of us. No broadcaster can force an interviewee into the chair, but the BBC has scrutinised the leaders of Britain's main political parties for decades, in prime time during general election campaigns. Jeremy Paxman and David Dimbleby are among those who've sat where Andrew Neil sits in 2019. None before him had to explain to viewers why these interviews matter to our democracy:

> We do them, on your behalf, to scrutinise and hold to account those who would govern us. That is democracy. We have always proceeded in good faith that the leaders would participate. And in every election, they have. All of them. Until this one.[2]

Many of those viewers who engage with politics on Twitter (and several senior Labour politicians) don't believe that we – that I – have acted in good faith. Many think the BBC is in some way in cahoots with Johnson and the Tory Party, and has let him get away without doing an interview. The truth is that we're more desperate than anyone for it to happen. We have important questions for Johnson. We also want to protect the BBC – an institution we believe in – from the battering it's taking.

There's a reason why passions are running so high. Just over a week ago Jeremy Corbyn, the Labour leader, sat down on the set of *The Andrew Neil Interview*. Many believe that his general election campaign hasn't recovered from the bruising encounter, which was broadcast to an audience of three million at 7 p.m. on BBC One, just before *EastEnders*.

The left smell a rat. They believe that the BBC – that I – tricked Corbyn's team by telling them that Johnson had confirmed he'd be taking part when he hadn't. The result was an outrage – one candidate eviscerated by Neil, the other avoiding him altogether. How could the BBC let that happen?

So, as Neil delivers his monologue, he makes one last plea. He knows it's in vain, but is it possible that Johnson could be shamed into appearing?

'It's not too late,' says Neil, not really in hope, definitely not in expectation. 'We have an interview prepared.'

2019 was when things started to go weird at BBC News and when the seeds of my departure from the corporation were sown.

The first weird thing was the demise of *This Week*, the popular late-night politics and laughs show fronted by Andrew Neil. The programme had a loyal audience that watched in impressive numbers on Thursday nights, despite the show sometimes starting just before midnight and finishing at close to 1 a.m. No wonder Neil and the *This Week* team joked they'd become 'the lead-in to Breakfast TV'.

The BBC's relationship with Neil was bizarre and contradictory. On the one hand, he was highly valued because he had a rare background at the corporation: he came from the right and he understood business. This made him a one-man riposte to charges from the Tory government and critics in the press that the BBC was exclusively populated by liberals. Neil gave an equally hard time to everyone, but his mere presence helped make our impartiality case to those who held the BBC's future in their hands.

Despite this, he was under-valued by the executives who ran the BBC's channels. The schedulers were allergic to politics. This was understandable. After all, it will never rate as well as drama, comedy or factual entertainment. But their attitude was also short-sighted. Ultimately, politicians determined the very existence of the BBC, and Neil needed to be valued, encouraged and recognised because he strengthened the BBC's case immensely and was the best forensic interviewer in Britain. Instead, the 'suits', as he calls them, failed to nurture their asset:

> Throughout the sixteen years that I did *This Week*, I never once met or heard from the controller of BBC One. Never once. If I, when I was the editor of *The Sunday Times*, had the equivalent columnist, or journalist that was as valuable and did as well, I can assure you they'd be getting herograms from me. And they would have been called in to have a cup of coffee or even a drink to let them know how happy I was, but I never got that at all. The schedulers always denigrated *This Week*.[3]

By 2018 he'd had enough. He wanted a better slot for the programme and made it clear that if one wasn't found, his days of staying up into the early-morning hours were over. If the BBC had wanted to save *This Week*, they could have. If they'd offered to bring the show forward to 10.30 on those Thursday nights when *Question Time* was off air, that might have sweetened the pill, but they wouldn't even do that. By 2019, Neil believes, the decision was made to axe the show for financial reasons, despite its modest budget. 'The show cost peanuts,' he recalls. 'The annual budget was smaller than David Dimbleby's fee for doing *Question Time*.'[4] I can't confirm the exact accuracy of his assertion here, but the point is clear: *This Week* was *cheap*.

The final edition – a star-studded outpouring of affection for the show – went out in July 2019. Appropriately enough, it fell on a week when *Question Time* was not on air. Surely, BBC schedulers would bring *This Week* forward by an hour to give it a fitting send-off? Don't be silly. Instead, the 10.30 slot was taken by a one-off documentary about male circumcision. *This*

Week, getting dicked around by the schedulers to the very end. Bizarre.

Having axed his main show and with fewer days on *Politics Live* – not necessarily the best vehicle for Neil – the BBC had very little planned for the presenter. On the face of it, they just weren't that into him. But Neil was in demand elsewhere, and he might walk away altogether. That he didn't was courtesy of our old friend, paragraph 5c.

After recording that interview with Boris Johnson, Neil headed to the airport to fly home to the South of France – yes, that's how he rolls. The interview was going out on BBC One while Neil was kicking back in Business at 35,000 feet, basking in the afterglow of a job well done. When he landed at Nice his phone buzzed with multiple messages congratulating him on the Johnson interview. But the real test of success or failure awaited him at home. Neil regards his wife Susan as his 'sternest critic', so he was relieved to find her beaming at him when he walked through the door. Then, as the couple shared a nightcap after a long day, the phone rang.

> It was the director-general of the BBC, Tony Hall. He'd seen the Johnson interview and said, 'It's just brilliant and exactly what the BBC should be doing. It's great that you're with the BBC!'
>
> I said, 'Well, I'm not sure I really am anymore because *This Week* is over. I still do the odd *Politics Live*, but other than that, I haven't got anything planned.'
>
> And he said, 'That's outrageous! Leave it to me.'[5]

'Outrageous!' Hall was right, but this was an extraordinary way to run things. The DG was outraged that the BBC had just axed Neil's main outlet, and he ran the BBC. Of course, you couldn't expect him to be across every piece of output, but *This Week*'s demise was high profile. Still, the brilliance of the Johnson interview got us around the suits and gatekeepers direct to the most powerful person in the corporation. The result was a new, prime-time political interview programme on Wednesday nights on BBC Two, *The Andrew Neil Show*. Thank you, Lord Hall.

The format was simple: a snazzy title sequence, followed by a swish bit of film on the political week in the style of an American current affairs show. Then Neil, behind an impressive desk, questioned politicians and other figures in public life. There was often just a single guest, sometimes two. It was heavyweight and, going up against *Channel 4 News* at 7 p.m., usually won the ratings battle with Jon Snow and the rest.

My favourite interview was not with a front-rank politician – although there were plenty of those – but with a campaigner called Zion Lights. Lights represented Extinction Rebellion, the high-profile campaign group whose acts of civil disobedience regularly closed streets and disrupted daily life in Britain. XR, as they were known, took direct action to advocate for radical policies to combat climate change. They wanted to rein in what they saw as destructive capitalism driven by profit, which they said threatened the mass extinction of life on the planet in short order.

The interview, masterminded by the programme editor Hugh Milbourn, took as its starting point the fact that human-made climate change is real and that dealing with it requires urgent action. Neil's focus was the hyperbole employed by XR, including claims that 'billions' would die in the decades ahead and that 'our children will die in the next ten or twenty years'. Lights briefly tried to defend these exaggerated claims but quickly accepted that much of the rhetoric used by XR was alarmist. She suggested that exaggeration might be permissible given the scale of the real crisis but seemed uncomfortable with it.

As Neil moved on and asked her about the XR target for reaching net zero by 2025 – just six years in the future – she wilted. She had no solutions to offer, and you could tell that troubled her. Neil's forensic questioning had exposed her, but I remember being impressed by how she handled it. She'd found herself in a deep hole, but unlike most, stopped digging.

A few months later, Lights appeared in the comment pages of the *Daily Telegraph* – an unlikely location for a left-leaning environmental campaigner – where she recalled the interview and the predicament she'd found herself in.

> I found myself forced to defend statements by one of XR's founders that 'billions' of deaths would happen soon because of climate change. I couldn't defend those numbers because they didn't have a basis in science. So I was faced with an awful choice on live TV: either I could stand up for science or I could defend XR. I had to choose the former, because for me, sticking with the evidence is the most important thing of all. As a result, I looked bad.[6]

Lights's candour on *The Andrew Neil Show* didn't go down well with some of her comrades in XR, who were angry that she'd chosen not to defend their counter-productive hyperbole. Before long, Lights left the organisation and was mulling science-based solutions to the climate crisis, solutions she couldn't offer Neil. Ultimately, that led to her becoming a prominent advocate for nuclear power. It was quite a journey for an XR activist and one that started in our studio. I enjoy this story because it affirms one of the principles of political interviewing: facts matter. Watching the interview back today, it's fascinating to have a sense of Lights's inner dialogue as she realises she can't do this anymore. It's to her immense credit.

These were positive developments, but in the background all was not well at the BBC, and my department was in the firing line. I could feel it.

In October 2019 I was called to a meeting. I was told it was nothing to worry about, just a chat with a guy called Jon

Zilkha. Zilkha was one of those pleasant but slightly faceless BBC types who were moving to centre stage under the new director of news, Fran Unsworth. To be fair to Fran, she'd taken over at precisely the moment when huge cuts to the BBC could no longer be put off. As ever, the first place the accountants looked was BBC News. Fran had a remit to deliver them, and nobody would thank her for it.

The Zilkha meeting took place in a subterranean room in BBC headquarters in New Broadcasting House. Jay-Z – as my deputy Will Boden and I came to dub the unexciting manager – was flanked by two young, smooth-looking men in sharp suits who made notes as we talked. Zilkha had a breakdown of staff in the political programmes department and a detailed set of questions. It was clear that the purpose of the conversation was not simply to identify cuts but also to gather data. They wanted to codify every journalistic action, as if producing programmes could be boiled down into a series of mechanical processes whereby they could convert what is essentially an art into a science. The smooth young men were management consultants. Thanks very much, they said at the end, all helpful stuff and nothing to worry about. I worried anyway.

But the implications of that would have to wait. Boris Johnson and what was left of the Remain wing of the Conservative Party were at loggerheads over Brexit. Civil war was breaking out, the whip was removed, and the prime minister needed a majority to push his Brexit plan through. That meant a general election. All he needed was the Liberal Democrat and Labour turkeys to vote for Christmas. Eventually, festively enough, they did. There would be a December election.

The prospect of the traditional series of thirty-minute election interviews with the party leaders and Andrew Neil was exciting. Neil versus Corbyn and Neil versus Johnson were mouth-watering prospects for me. I couldn't wait to get started.

It wasn't to be that simple.

* * *

After an election is called, the broadcasters get busy. The logistical side is a matter for the news teams and has usually been in the works for some time just in case a snap election arrives, which it regularly did. This is the complicated and crucial business of ensuring that there's coverage of all the events on the campaign trail and, most importantly, that there's a plan to cover election-night counts from the Oasis Leisure Centre in the badlands of Swindon to the Magna Science Centre in downtown Rotherham.

I was only really concerned with the special BBC election programmes. As a sign of how things were going at the BBC, these were controlled by the news executives, but my department would be heavily involved in some of them. In 2019 the BBC proposed four programmes involving the party leaders: *Question Time*, two election debates and *The Andrew Neil Interviews*. There were, of course, other outlets, including *The Andrew Marr Show*, who might ask for interviews, but these four took precedence. In late October all this was put into a letter and sent to the political parties. I was named as the point of contact for the campaigns for *The Andrew Neil Interviews*.

It was down to me to make the interviews happen, so I contacted the parties to nail down the details of content, format and logistics. The first thing to make clear is that these are interview *requests*. No broadcasters can make politicians take part in these programmes. There's no electoral commission rule that can be invoked, nor even an officially endorsed set of expectations for party leaders to follow. It's up to the party what they choose to do. There are two reasons why, until 2019, you could expect them to agree to participate even though they didn't have to: first, because the interview is an opportunity to explain your views and prove your mettle to a large TV audience in prime time; second, because most politicians thought accountability in a general election was important in a democracy. Ultimately, the enterprise rested on trust and adherence to democratic norms.

The other important thing to understand is the logistical aspect. We had bids with five party leaders: Conservative Boris Johnson, Labour's Jeremy Corbyn, Jo Swinson of the Liberal Democrats, Nicola Sturgeon of the Scottish National Party and big baby Nigel Farage from the Brexit Party. Negotiations started in late October for a half-hour pre-recorded interview, preferably in our studio in London but potentially anywhere in the UK (we recorded Sturgeon in Edinburgh). In previous campaigns I'd negotiated these sorts of programmes for ITV and the BBC. Dates are never agreed upon and nailed down in the campaign's early days. Negotiations are usually frustrating and slow, and political parties tend to keep broadcasters guessing when or whether they're taking part. In reality this means you have to take them as you get them and start getting the programmes out as soon as you can.

Early on I spoke to Labour's director of communications Anjula Singh and she was pretty quick to agree a date for Jeremy Corbyn to sit down with Andrew Neil. In my discussions with all the parties, I was accurate with my language. Singh asked about Johnson and whether he'd agreed to take part. I said that a Neil/Johnson interview was definitely the plan but I didn't have a date yet. This was true; it *was* the plan and we were working hard to get it over the line. I did not tell Singh or anyone else that a date was set for Johnson or that he'd explicitly agreed to the interview, as to have done so would have been to mislead her. We were in negotiations.

Anjula and I agreed on Friday 26 November as the date for the Corbyn interview. If, in the interim, one of the parties had made it clear that they would not be taking part, I'd have told her so. In past elections everyone had eventually agreed to be interviewed, whether by Neil, Paxman or Dimbleby. The norms had always been adhered to. The honourable thing had always been done. I was satisfied that I was being straight up but conscious that I was walking a tightrope as I tried to nail down a date for Johnson.

The first *Andrew Neil Interview* of the campaign was with the Scottish first minister and SNP leader Nicola Sturgeon. It was a tough encounter – as Neil/Sturgeon interviews usually were – and was recorded and broadcast on 25 November. In the run-up to the Corbyn interview the following day I continued to discuss the show with Johnson's team to try to make progress. I was frustrated not to have moved very far forward, but not overly worried given my past experience.

As I left for home on 25 November, the night before the Corbyn programme, I went over the interview plan on the train. I'd been involved in many interviews with the Labour leader, and after his first accident-prone year he'd generally been able to stay on his feet. What came next was a knockout, with a backlash not far behind.

Tuesday 26 November was already one of the worst days of Jeremy Corbyn's political life, and sitting down in a TV studio opposite Andrew Neil didn't improve things. The day had started badly when *The Times* splashed with news of an article that they were publishing in the paper by Ephraim Mirvis, the UK's chief rabbi. The headline screamed, 'Corbyn not fit for high office'. Beneath that were the words '"New poison" in the party has been "sanctioned from the top"'.[7]

This intervention put Corbyn's antisemitism problem at the heart of the election campaign. In the article by the chief rabbi, his words were devastating. He talked about a community gripped by anxiety and wondered, 'What will become of British Jews and Judaism if the Labour Party forms the next government?' That he was even asking the question was shocking.

He said the Labour leadership was 'utterly inadequate' in handling the abuse suffered by Jews and described the party's claims that they were dealing with the problem and had 'investigated every single case' as 'a mendacious fiction'. The chief rabbi did not hold back:

> The party leadership have never understood that their
> failure is not just one of procedure, which can be
> remedied with additional staff or new processes. It is a
> failure to see this as a human problem rather than a
> political one. It is a failure of culture. It is a failure of
> leadership. A new poison – sanctioned from the top – has
> taken root in the Labour Party.[8]

He concluded by asking voters to vote with their conscience.
'Be in no doubt,' he wrote, 'the very soul of our nation is at
stake.'

This was powerful stuff, and Neil and the team – including
Jason Keen, who produced it – got stuck into rewriting the
opening questions and reframing the interview immediately.
The section on antisemitism was always part of the plan, but
now it had to come first. We weren't short of ammunition, but
I felt we needed a sharper focus and a central question. Then it
came to me: given what the chief rabbi had written, would
Corbyn say sorry to British Jews?

By the time Corbyn arrived at the studios on the Albert
Embankment at half past four that afternoon, he looked
hunted. I'd seen him many times down the years, but this was
the worst shape he'd been in before an interview. These stinging
accusations of racism hurt, and whatever he did they wouldn't
go away. Now here he was, in the belly of the mainstream
media beast once again, and they had a new stick to beat him
with, courtesy of the chief rabbi.

From the start, Corbyn exuded a sense of exasperation and
frustration. His reaction to the chief rabbi's critique was defensive and defiant. He demanded evidence for the claims that
Labour had not effectively dealt with antisemitism. This was
understandable – he was under attack – but his demeanour was
politically unhelpful.

As Neil dug in to specific examples of antisemitism from
Labour members, Corbyn got bogged down in defensive quib-

bling. Rather than condemn firmly and quickly, he gave an impression of scepticism about the allegations. When he did condemn them, he was low energy and often referred back to his unhelpful standard line about his opposition to racism in 'all its forms'. He was only animated and passionate when losing his temper.

Then came the apology question. Would he say sorry to British Jews in the light of the chief rabbi's unprecedented intervention? Corbyn ploughed on with his mantra that all racism was wrong and that he was sorry for anyone who'd experienced it. He did not say sorry to British Jews. This was odd because at other crunch points in the Labour antisemitism crisis he *had* said sorry. He wouldn't this time. Unsurprisingly, in the aftermath of the interview, he did apologise the following day.

This couldn't have gone much worse for Corbyn. Yet the problem here was not that he was lying. He wasn't. The problem was that the political moment demanded something from him that he didn't want to give: an apology he didn't believe was fair or necessary. He couldn't lie about his feelings.

A year later, when he was no longer leader, the Equalities and Human Rights Commission found that under Corbyn, Labour was guilty of breaking equality law in its handling of antisemitism in the party. Corbyn's response was candid. He said that 'the scale of the [antisemitism] problem was dramatically overstated for political reasons by our opponents inside and outside the party, as well as by much of the media'.[9] That statement lost him the Labour whip in parliament. His performance in the interview with Neil in the election campaign was consistent with that viewpoint. But this is not to say Corbyn's attitude was pure defiance. He seemed to me to be genuinely stung and upset by the charge.

Back in November 2019 the conversation moved on to Labour's uncomfortable Brexit position. Boris Johnson promised to 'Get Brexit Done'. Labour's policy was less pithy. Corbyn told Neil he'd go to Brussels to negotiate a new exit deal with the EU and then let the people decide whether to adopt that deal or Remain after all. This would mean a second Brexit referendum and – a bit like the first one in 2016, really – Jeremy Corbyn would stay out of it:

> **Neil:** What would you do during the referendum campaign? Would you go on holiday?

> **Corbyn:** No, I'd be running the government.[10]

If you wanted to move on from the Brexit nightmare, this was not an appealing way forward, and Corbyn's position just seemed a bit silly and unserious. His agonies over Labour's tortuous Brexit formulation were a dramatic contrast to the straight-talking Jeremy of 2015. Arguably, for the public, they were even more damaging than the antisemitism accusations.

The interview rolled on and didn't get any less tetchy. Corbyn hissed and spat – 'Can I finish, please?' – and nothing went right for him. He couldn't mount a credible defence and Neil seemed to win every argument. As the programme ended and the credits ran, Corbyn took off his microphone while speaking intently to Neil with what looked like anger. He was ready to get out. He wouldn't have long to wait.

The thrill of the political interview is the opportunity to test a politician's ideas and arguments, and occasionally watch these collapse under scrutiny. It happened with Boris Johnson in July over GATT, and on that November evening with Corbyn over antisemitism and the rest. It's not the only purpose of political interviews, but credibility is the hurdle that has to be overcome before the interview can be about anything else.

The headlines were brutal. The *Daily Mail* screamed 'Torn Apart' on their front page, and all the broadsheets led on the story. Stupidly, and with a touch of hubris, I tweeted something celebrating a clean sweep. This just came over as crowing and was a mistake. The reaction from Labour supporters on social media was predictably hostile. They thought it was an MSM interview designed to bring down Corbyn; the truth was that he'd failed to deal effectively with legitimate questions about his record and his manifesto. But the Corbynite outrage about the interview wasn't the problem. The problem was the next question. When is Boris Johnson going up against Andrew Neil?

The answer was that I didn't know. Although I'd been trying to fix a date with Johnson's team, who consistently told me they wanted to do the interview, they fell short of saying it was definite. So I focused on the logistics, trying to make progress on dates. After the Corbyn blowout my questions became more insistent and for the first time I started to worry: was it possible that Johnson would be too cowardly to take part, even after Corbyn had done the show? Then, suddenly, Lee Cain, the man who calls Johnson 'The Boss', made it known to the BBC that he would only talk to Katy Searle, the head of BBC Westminster, from now on. Although I was the designated point of contact, the BBC didn't push back. Searle was close to the Johnson team and spoke with them most days – it went with her job. This closeness between BBC Westminster and the government was something I was personally uncomfortable with, but given the situation I thought maybe it could help, so reluctantly I accepted it. In reality I had no choice. The BBC had agreed to allow the government to choose whom they wanted to deal with at the BBC and there was nothing I could do about it.

Andrew Neil is scathing about this development. 'That was just mad,' he says. 'They can't dictate that. And we now know that was all just part of their kicking it into touch, play them along, let Andrew do the others. He'll give them all a kicking. Let him do all that and still hold out the hope and just run out of time. It's duplicitous and dishonourable.'[11]

On Thursday 28 November Cain stirred the pot. He called *The Andrew Marr Show*'s editor John Neal to offer Boris Johnson for the following Sunday. Cain knew that *The Andrew Neil Interview* took precedence over *The Andrew Marr Show*, so this was calculated to cause trouble. It became obvious then that they had been stringing us along, using the assumption of decency that had held sway for decades to run down the clock. They were not so crude as to lie outright – not to me anyway – but they deceived us by pretending that they wanted to do the interview and were looking for a date. Now they wanted to provoke an argument inside the BBC, force Johnson onto the *Marr* show and then use that as an excuse – having done a big BBC interview – not to do *Andrew Neil*.

Searle spoke to Cain. He said, implausibly, that no decision had been made and that doing the interview was still a real possibility, while simultaneously pushing for an answer on the *Marr* bid. Shortly after, the *Marr* offer was leaked to the press by No. 10. This kicked off a media storm pitting the two Andrew's – Neil and Marr – against each other, spicing up the familiar tale of Downing Street and the BBC at war.

In the face of all this, and the understandable outrage from the Labour Party, the BBC took the position that *The Andrew Marr Show* could not accept the offer of the prime minister unless he also agreed a firm date to do *Andrew Neil*. This was very tough on Marr. The implication was that Neil was the more challenging interviewer, which put Marr in a very difficult position, one he was not going to take lying down:

> The BBC announced that if Johnson wasn't going to be interviewed by Andrew Neil, he couldn't be interviewed by anybody, including me. And so they wanted me to refuse to have him on the show. And I'm afraid I thought F— you. It's my show. I do my kind of interviews in my way. We have an agreement that Boris Johnson is going to come on the show and do an interview, and I would

have walked out of the BBC had they not allowed that to happen. So I had very, very difficult conversations with BBC managers about that. I made it pretty clear how angry I was.[12]

Marr's position was understandable, the BBC's impossible: go ahead with the ban on the *Marr* interview, and Andrew Marr would have walked, and that would have been the story; back down in the face of Marr's ultimatum and allow the prime minister onto his show, and play into the hands of Johnson, who would use it to justify not appearing on the Neil programme.

Ultimately, events intervened. On Friday lunchtime there was a terrorist attack at Fishmongers' Hall, close to London Bridge. The attacker, Usman Khan, murdered two young people – Saskia Jones and Jack Merritt – before being restrained by brave members of the public and then killed by armed police officers. The following morning Tony Hall, the director-general of the BBC, decided that public concern about the national security situation made it impossible for the BBC to turn down the offer of an interview with the prime minister. The *Marr* interview would go ahead.

This piled pressure on Andrew Marr. The result was a very tetchy and argumentative encounter that he does not remember fondly:

It was a car-crash interview. Now that he had agreed to be interviewed by Andrew Marr rather than by Andrew Neil, I had to demonstrate that Andrew Marr could be as aggressive as Andrew Neil. What I hadn't quite appreciated was that Johnson was in a one hundred miles an hour, never going to shut up kind of mood by the time he arrived in the studio. Johnson just decided to talk right over me, to refuse to answer the questions and to be irate that questions were being asked at all. We both ended up shouting at each other for a quarter of an hour, and it was not an edifying, useful exercise on either side.[13]

Uncomfortably, Marr had no choice but to ask Johnson about the Neil programme. 'Why are you avoiding being interviewed by Andrew Neil?' he asked. Johnson joked that he was already being interviewed by a 'perfectly brilliant Andrew'. Marr pressed him. 'Everybody else has done it. Why won't you?' Johnson tried his gag again. 'I'm perfectly happy to be interviewed by any interviewer called Andrew from the BBC,' he said, closing the matter with a lie. He should have added 'as long as his surname's not Neil'.

Johnson's team went through the motions in the days that followed and pretended for a bit longer than they were still considering the bid. Meanwhile, we decided that the best way to mark Johnson's cowardice was to put a monologue at the end of the final interview programme with Nigel Farage – who might be a cry baby, but wasn't scared of Neil – which would throw down the gauntlet to Johnson. We knew it wouldn't convince him to come on, but it would mean he paid some price for cheating.

When the moment came, Neil handled it beautifully. He told Johnson he had an interview 'oven ready', repurposing Johnson's famous Brexit slogan, and then said this:

The theme running through our questions is trust – and why at so many times in his career, in politics and journalism, critics and sometimes even those close to him have deemed him to be untrustworthy.[14]

I sometimes wonder whether we were onto something ...

The monologue was provocative, but we ran the risk of looking entitled by running it. Despite that risk, it only seemed fair that Johnson should face some prime-time grief after what had happened to Corbyn. Neil's extended piece to camera reached more than seven million viewers on Twitter. It's hard to know what else we could have done.

I can understand why Labour were so furious. Their man had gone into the lion's den and been mauled. Johnson had run off scared and got away with it. I became a hate figure for the angry Twitter left and even had former Labour culture secretary Ben Bradshaw calling for 'personnel consequences', a posh way of saying I should be fired. These critics thought it was pretty straightforward where we went wrong: we should have lined all the interviews up before proceeding with them. It sounds simple. The truth is if anyone adopted this approach in 2019 or previously, these interviews would never have taken place. Party X would say we'll only agree once Party Y has, and vice versa. It would make it easier for reluctant politicians to avoid difficult interviews.

The main charge was that the BBC had tricked Labour into taking part by telling them Johnson was in the bag when we knew he wasn't. This wasn't true. I'd told them that we were planning to do a Johnson interview at a time when the Conservatives were telling me they wanted to take part, and I was trying to establish when. My language, as always in these negotiations, was careful; I wanted to persuade everyone to sign up, but did not tell Labour that it was agreed when it wasn't. To say this position was greeted with disbelief was an understatement. Understandably angry Labour supporters went after me for the rest of the campaign. Wading through the vitriol on my timeline was gruelling and upsetting. I took the heat and I can't deny it took a toll. I put up with it, however, because I wanted to defend the BBC from the allegation that Labour had been tricked into appearing because I'd led the negotiations and knew what had – and hadn't – been said.

Three years on, I'm no longer as confident about the BBC's defence. Why? Because it turns out I wasn't the only person conducting the negotiations. I now know that, according to senior Labour staff, other conversations – the details of which I wasn't told about at the time – provided the reassurance Labour needed to go ahead with the Neil/Corbyn interview. While I was writing this book, Corbyn's closest adviser, Seumas Milne, told me there was a pivotal conversation *before* I even spoke to anyone from the Labour Party. This conversation on 30 October 2019 between Milne's colleague Anjula Singh and a senior BBC executive concerned the complete package of four election programmes that the BBC was proposing to the parties, including *The Andrew Neil Interview*. According to Milne, Singh came away from that conversation with the very clear understanding that Johnson had signed up for the entire package of BBC election programmes, including *Neil* and that – on this basis – Labour signed up too. This is backed up by a WhatsApp message from Singh to Milne sent a week or so later, on 7 November 2019, when Singh states that the BBC 'say that the Tories have agreed to Andrew Neil'.[15]

After the Corbyn interview had aired, Singh remained in touch with the same BBC executive. On 27 November she reported to her colleague James Schneider, Labour's director of strategic communications, that she'd been reassured that a Neil/Johnson interview would take place 'next week at some point'.[16] This is astonishing and troubling. On that November day there was absolutely no indication from Lee Cain of a date for a Johnson interview – if there had been I'd have known about it. The government was still pretending it could happen, but dates were not being discussed. Yet again, the Labour Party were coming away with an incorrect understanding from their conversations with the BBC.

When, shortly afterwards, it became clear that Johnson had no intention of doing the interview, Milne met with the head of BBC News, Fran Unsworth, to discuss a range of complaints they had about the BBC's coverage of the general election, including the handling of the *Neil* process. Two days after the meeting, they followed up with a detailed, written complaint:

We agreed to Jeremy Corbyn's participation on the clear understanding that Boris Johnson had agreed the same terms ... It was made clear to us that all parties had to sign up to this arrangement as a whole and that it had been carefully constructed with legal oversight ... We were told that the Conservative Party had agreed to the four-programme package, with only the dates of the Neil interview to be settled from specified days. We were never given any indication that Boris Johnson and the Conservatives had reneged on this agreement (or indeed never agreed to the arrangement in the first place) which we entered into in good faith.[17]

It's clear from this contemporaneous complaint that Singh had sought explicit assurances that Johnson was fully signed up and that she came away with exactly that impression at least twice (30 October and 7 November 2019). There are two possible explanations for this. The first is that the Conservatives *did* tell the BBC explicitly that they'd do the interview as part of the package and this was passed on to Labour, only for Johnson to renege on it. If so, I was never told this as I carried the bid forward. I made sure that I never told anyone that Johnson had signed up because I knew he hadn't (although I believed he ultimately would).

The second explanation is that the senior BBC executive told Singh that Johnson had signed up for the full package of shows knowing that he hadn't or, alternatively, gave the impression that this was the case without saying it as clearly as Singh remembers.

We may never know what was said and by whom. The BBC executive involved will not talk about their conversations with Labour officials, apart from to say that they did not mislead anyone. If they were lied to by someone inside No. 10, they could clear up any suspicion that hangs over the BBC, but they've chosen not to engage. Team Johnson still maintain today that they never made an explicit commitment to take part in *The Andrew Neil Interview*.

Does all this matter anymore? Yes, it does. Labour understandably feel cheated by what happened in the middle of a general election campaign, and until we know what they were told there are question marks over the BBC's conduct. In response to Milne's complaint in December 2019, Fran Unsworth reassured him that, 'We did not tell the Labour Party that an agreement had been reached for the Prime Minister to take part.'[18] Milne sees this as a 'classic civil servant's answer'[19] and notes it is not a denial that Singh *was* told that Johnson was fully signed up to the full package of shows. There's no doubt that the whole affair was damaging for the BBC and consequential for the election campaign.

As for Johnson's team, we now know that they were operating in bad faith from the start. The prime minister's 'chief adviser' Dominic Cummings eventually turned on 'The Boss' – as has been well documented – after leaving Downing Street in November 2020. The following year Cummings revealed the truth about his attitude to the *Neil* interview when he tweeted about it:

Pundits: not doing Neil 'a huge campaign blunder'

Me: why the fu*k wd we put a gaffe machine clueless about policy & government up to be grilled for ages, upside=0 for what?! This is not a hard decision …

So there it is. The man who, more than any other, made Boris Johnson prime minister, saw him as a 'gaffe machine clueless about policy & government' who could not survive being 'grilled for ages' by Andrew Neil. Cummings said the decision was effectively a no-brainer: he knew from the start they wouldn't do it. There was no agonising, just game-playing. The election campaign was an exercise in getting away with it, avoiding the scrutiny that might reveal to the world what Cummings already knew about 'The Boss'. The cynicism is breathtaking.

If Cummings was the organ-grinder, then the communications monkey was Lee Cain, the stringer-along in chief. Cain also went public about the *Neil* interview in 2021:

> **Cain:** It's a classic example, the Andrew Neil situation, of being able to separate what Westminster thinks is important and what actually is important.[20]

> *Translation: I'm an extraordinary political strategist operating on a different level. I knew the Neil interview was unimportant rather than terrifying. Honest. That's why I carried on pretending we'd do it long enough to ensure that Jeremy Corbyn did do it.*

> **Cain:** Most people have no idea who Andrew Neil is … we're all in this bubble, and we're all obsessed politicos. We sort of assume that everyone else carries that same knowledge.[21]

> *Translation: The little people haven't heard of Andrew Neil. That's why we wouldn't do his show, not because we were terrified of him. And definitely not because of the three million viewers.*

> **Cain:** We knew at that point we were ahead. We knew our message was landing and if Westminster wants to go off talking about interviews that aren't happening, great because that isn't going to impact on our campaign.[22]

> *Translation: We repeatedly strung the BBC along about doing the interview because we wanted to create as much distraction from the substance of the political debate as*

we could. We could have told them at the start that we
wouldn't take part like decent human beings, but, you
know, fuck doing the right thing.

The contempt for the voters and democratic accountability is unapologetic.

Apart from Cain and Cummings, there's another dissenting voice on all this. Sir Robbie Gibb – my former boss at the BBC, Theresa May's director of communications and today a member of the BBC board. He thinks Johnson and his team have no case to answer.

> They made a legitimate choice that that approach [not doing the interview] worked better for them. It's up to the public to decide whether they think things are fair. It's entirely up to political parties to choose who they are interviewed by. I would agree if a politician was hiding from journalistic scrutiny, but I don't think that's ever been the case. Boris Johnson did an interview with *The Andrew Marr Show*, so it's not that he wasn't making himself available.[23]

Robbie and I go back a long way, and I love debating these issues with him, but I can't agree with his assessment here, because to my mind it puts politicians first. I believe that what should determine what happens is not what works better for Boris Johnson but what serves the interests of the public. It also ignores the way Team Johnson manipulated the situation to ensure that Corbyn faced Neil and 'The Boss' didn't.

So what of Johnson himself? He's never said anything about ducking the interview, but I have spoken to one person who discussed it with him in Downing Street after the election.

According to this source – one person, but someone I trust – Johnson said he had wanted to do the interview and didn't like looking like a coward running scared from Andrew Neil.

So why didn't you do it? my source asked him.

Johnson, with some embarrassment, confessed that 'Dom and Lee' – Cummings and Cain – wouldn't let him.

But why? my source asked again.

The reason, Johnson answered weakly, was because they couldn't trust him not to screw it up.

Of course, this version of events makes Johnson look slightly less cowardly, so it would be wrong to rule out the possibility that Johnson invented it. Others I have spoken to – again well placed to know – suspect Johnson flip-flopped on the question but ultimately chose to stiff Corbyn and the BBC in an 'adolescent' flounce. I approached Johnson's office to see whether, all this time later, Johnson would offer his side of the story. Fittingly his answer was 'No comment'.

We had no God-given right to interview anybody, but Johnson's team wanted to make sure that Corbyn faced questions and that they didn't, and they exploited the assumption of good faith to cheat. After these people, good faith is dead.

Finally, as we consider the questions of trust that we didn't get to put to Johnson, I have a new question for you – posed by Neil – about what happened next.

Neil: What came back to hit Johnson like a wet sock filled with marbles?[24]

The answer? Trust.

So Boris won his election, Jeremy Corbyn departed and Brexit got done. Sort of.

I was left bruised at the end of 2019, sensing that I'd been somehow damaged by the fallout from the interview that never was. In a way I had – on Twitter I was the public face of the debacle, which is ironic given that I now know I'd largely been sidelined. Inside the BBC, things were shifting. After months of gestation, Jon Zilkha's plan for the future of BBC News gave birth to a truly ugly child called News 2020 – a crap plan for a crap year, as it turned out – which involved a downgrading of individual programme editors and a huge centralisation of power in the hands of a small number of news executives.

Zilkha had been told what he needed to deliver and it wasn't his fault. The head of News, Fran Unsworth, had to present the Jay-Z blueprint to staff as a moment of exciting modernisation. Some senior managers I've spoken to question whether she really believed in it. In reality, it was a cuts exercise that would bland out the content and reward the most adept empire builders. As the implications – and opportunities – of the plan sunk in, office politics began to matter just as much as the Westminster variety.

Once the plan was announced, there was an invitation from BBC management to engage in a consultation process of conversation and interrogation to really kick the tyres on the plan, as a management consultant might put it. The only unwritten but understood rule was that you shouldn't question anything – quite a proposition to a team of journalists.

I've spoken to former senior management at the BBC who acknowledge the mindset that held sway amongst the 'suits' at the time. One who has come to see 'News 2020' as a 'mad plan' was candid about how the disastrous scheme was nodded through.

> There becomes a collective mentality among management that you're either with us or against us. Only we truly get it, and anyone who disagrees are just Luddites who are stuck in the past. Whereas, in reality, the 'opponents of change' also want the best for the BBC and simply had a better view of what might be lost.[25]

Then came Covid, and everything stopped. Most of my programmes, including *Politics Live* and *The Andrew Neil Show*, stopped being broadcast. This was supposed to be a temporary measure but the longer these shows were away, the less likely they were to come back. Just before he officially started as the new director-general in late summer 2020, I met with Tim Davie to talk about the future of political programmes. It seemed *Politics Live* was safe, but he couldn't give the same assurance about *The Andrew Neil Show* or much else. I tried to engage him in a conversation about the importance of Neil to the BBC, but he wasn't receptive.

There was one moment of gold in the gloom: *The Andrew Marr Show* stayed on air throughout the pandemic. Marr, alongside editor John Neal and brilliant producers Jason Keen and Hannah Wilkinson, made it count. They really got to grips with the politics of Covid. They didn't need much guidance from me on a story they'd made their own from the start. However, in June 2020 John told me they'd landed an interview with the Chinese ambassador to the UK, Liu Xiaoming, and I wanted to be more closely involved.

Liu had been on the *Marr Show* before, and while we'd asked him difficult questions about the Chinese government's brutal repression and persecution of the Muslim Uighur people in northern China, we hadn't laid a glove on him. John and I agreed that we needed to go further and do better this time. We both wanted this to be a landmark interview that made an impact. The ambassador should not be able to get away with his usual dismissive denials.

Central to the interview was new, shocking footage of what appeared to be blindfolded prisoners surrounded by guards loading them onto trains, apparently for deportation. The gravity of this had to register with Liu and with *Marr* viewers. The team drew up a powerful interview plan to do precisely that.

On air, the plan came together because of Marr's controlled and quietly devastating performance. The two men watched the chilling film in silence. John Neal had briefed Marr to stay quiet while it ran to ensure it landed powerfully. This was very smart.

Eventually, Marr calmly demanded an explanation. 'What is happening here?' he asked. 'How do you explain it?'

Liu could only deny. He could not explain. At this point, Neal made a courageous call. The interview was scheduled to run for twelve minutes and time was running out, but he told Marr to keep going, to finish the job. The effect was to shrink back the size of the other interviews scheduled for the show that day, but this was more important. The interview ran for more than twenty minutes in the end. It's that commitment to depth that marks out a serious political programme.

Through all this, Liu was flailing. Faced with interview testimony about the forced sterilisation of Uighur women, he said it must be an isolated case: Uighurs were very happy with their lives under the Chinese dictatorship. Then Marr, having waited to go there, named it:

When we see interviews like that, and we see people blindfolded and led off to trains to be taken to re-education camps, it reminds people in the West what was going on in Germany in the 1930s and 1940s.[26]

Liu denied the existence of any camps detaining Uighurs, despite the evidence that more than a million had been imprisoned in them. But his denials were unconvincing. Marr just kept going, suggesting the Chinese may be perpetuating genocide. All Liu could offer was the chilling response that 'people in Xinjiang enjoy a happy life, you know. They enjoy good order.' It was important journalism and powerful TV.

As Britain's stop–start lockdown went on, the BBC's centralising plan – now renamed Modernising BBC News – was reactivated. Then, in the summer of 2020 new, Covid-related cuts were announced. I had to reapply – successfully – for my job, but that didn't mean I was safe. I hadn't hidden my feelings about the 'mad plan' in conversations with senior colleagues. I regarded it as a guaranteed way to remove all the texture and flavour from BBC content, stripping away healthy competition between programmes and reducing everything to a vanilla mush where news was king. I never expressed this view externally, but it was enough to get you put on the naughty step if you questioned the management orthodoxy.

Senior management I've spoken to since acknowledge that the scale of the reorganisation was seen by the better-connected, more sharp-elbowed BBC News executives as a chance for empire-building. 'Too many people,' one told me, 'cared more about their stupid empires and status than about the change itself.' These skills – office politics, empire building and toeing the party line – had become paramount. Creativity and doing the work well came a distant second.

Tim Davie meanwhile had arrived as director-general trumpeting the importance of impartiality. He was right to do so, but wrong to immediately lose Andrew Neil and undermine his point. *The Andrew Neil Show* had been taken off air when the BBC scaled back during Covid, but if Davie wanted to keep Neil on board he needed to manage the talent. Instead, Neil was ignored by the organisation he'd spent decades working for.

> I was left in limbo. None of the suits in the BBC
> contacted me for weeks. The BBC never made any
> attempt to involve me in its programmes. It shows that I
> was always on the periphery. I wasn't central to BBC
> programming. It was easy for me to slip off their radar.[27]

So I asked for clarity about the fate of *The Andrew Neil Show*. It became clear pretty quickly that it would never return. The channel controllers didn't want their more popular programming in the early evening on BBC Two disrupted on a Wednesday night. The more I think about this, the crazier it seems. Ratings are important, and the BBC has to make sure it competes for audiences in prime time, but the BBC is facing an existential crisis. *The Andrew Neil Show* showcased BBC impartiality and seriousness, engaging directly with the politicians who held the BBC's future in their hands. The idea that the director-general of the BBC caved in – to echo Sir Robin Day – to a here today, gone tomorrow channel controller over some here today, gone tomorrow piece of factual entertainment and lost their star political interviewer beggars belief.

Neil did have FaceTime discussions with Davie in the back of his car as the DG was chauffeured around London that summer, but nothing changed. Neil told me that if he did want to save the programme or Neil's presence on the BBC, 'Davie didn't feel strong enough to push it through.'[28] Instead, there was a half-baked offer of a show without a fixed number of episodes and no channel to call home. It was an insult. In June, I made one last appeal to Davie. In the name of impartiality, I urged him to save *The Andrew Neil Show* as the only way to keep Andrew Neil. But he insisted he was handling it. Within days, Neil walked.

It's clear now that the director-general doesn't handle 'the talent' well. He has overseen an exodus of some of the biggest names in BBC News and, in March 2023, badly mishandled the row over Gary Lineker's tweets about the Conservative government's asylum policy. His decision to suspend the *Match of the Day* presenter gave the impression that the BBC was bowing to political pressure. Then, when a show of solidarity from Lineker's colleagues at BBC Sport brought sports coverage to a halt, Davie was forced into a humiliating climb-down.

The signs were there when he underestimated – and lost – Andrew Neil in 2021, but his role in that failure wasn't widely understood. His botched handling of the Lineker debacle was there for all to see and left the previously cocksure director-general seriously damaged.

In February 2021 came a proud moment, when Andrew Marr's interview with Chinese ambassador Liu won the prestigious Royal Television Society Interview of the Year Award. The judges described it as a 'masterclass in technique' that was 'gutsy' and 'went for the jugular'. In 2015 I'd come in with a plan to toughen up Marr's interviews. Before then, the show had been robust and news-making but the interviews weren't winning awards. Jugulars were rarely gone for. Changing that took years of hard work from all of us – most of all Marr – and the RTS award felt like the final recognition that the show had really delivered.

The award ceremony was on Zoom. Andrew Marr, John Neal and Jason Keen – who collectively deserve the lion's share of credit for the interview itself – were all on the call. They were joined by an assortment of 'suits', including Fran Unsworth, Jonathan Munro and other senior figures. After we won, there were a few minutes of virtual backslapping and congratulations. None of them said a word to me. It didn't affect my pride in winning, but I remember thinking, 'That's weird.' It felt awkward. I could start to see the writing on the wall.

After that, things quickened. I was inexplicably excluded from a meeting with Tim Davie and Katy Searle. Unsubtly, my deputy was asked to go instead. It didn't take a genius to figure out what was coming. A few days after that, the final version of the 'mad plan' was unveiled: a fundamental reorganisation and centralisation of BBC News and brutal job cuts. Soon there was a meeting they wanted me to attend, this time with HR.

And so, on Zoom, like many others at the BBC that day, I was told that my position was being terminated. The Westminster news machine had finally swallowed programme-making and I was one of the savings they were making. A few days later I told my shell-shocked team, many of whom also faced an uncertain future.

The following day I emailed the director-general. I wanted my concerns about the risk to BBC impartiality from these changes at BBC Westminster on the record:

This means your most sensitive area – politics – is managed by one person. This is so unwise I can't believe it's made the cut. It means one person gets to decide how the BBC does politics. No corrective, no editorial figure with any power to offer balance or a range of views. It exposes the BBC very badly.[29]

In response Davie, echoing the rhetoric of Tory prime minister David Cameron, talked about 'tough choices' and said that while he understood the risk I outlined, he basically thought everything would be fine. Davie's glib assurances haven't aged well. The perception that the BBC is too close to the government has only grown under his leadership, and troubling allegations about how BBC Westminster responds to pressure from the government have added to those concerns. The BBC is a wonderful institution that we need to cherish but sadly, in 2023, it's not a happy ship.

The break was tough and took some getting used to, but despite the way it ended I was proud of what I'd achieved in my time at the BBC and honoured to have had the opportunity.

And, whatever was next, I wasn't done yet.

15

AFTER THE CLOWN SHOW

Tuesday 5 July 2022, Westminster

It's the most sweltering British summer since 1976 when Margot was living *The Good Life* and Margaret was on the march. LBC's Westminster studio is crowded and sweaty. There's no natural light, just the brash LBC branding and the harsh glare of the fully 'visualised' radio studio. Everything that happens here is on camera: a radio show that's a TV show too.

LBC – owned by Global, the company whose portfolio includes Capital, Heart and Classic FM – is in the big league these days after a series of high-profile poaches from the BBC. The latest – Andrew Marr – is on air, and he's loving it. I'm at his side again, this time as the executive editor of his new show, *Tonight with Andrew Marr*. Tonight, Boris Johnson's premiership is on the verge of collapse.

It's been two and a half years since Johnson hid from Andrew Neil and crushed Jeremy Corbyn at the 2019 election. A series of scandals have led him to the brink. The most damaging became known, inevitably, as 'Partygate'. Brilliant reporting by Pippa Crerar at the *Daily Mirror* and ITN's Paul Brand in late 2021 produced a series of revelations about partying – often very boozy partying – in Downing Street during the Covid-19 lockdown. These included events the prime minister himself knew about or attended.

In terms of political lying, Partygate is a particularly dark chapter and one that illustrates the risks of political dishonesty. In early 2023 Brand released a podcast series – *Partygate: the Inside Story* – which revealed that the No. 10 whistle-blower who blew the story wide open was motivated to act by the spectacle of government ministers going on air to deny the existence of illegal Downing Street lockdown parties he knew had taken place:

> By the time I got to the second minister on the second day who went on the radio and television to say there was no party here that was enough. The frustration turned to anger and disappointment that we had a government that was now lying bare-faced to us in public. We were being led down the garden-path with a line from these ministers that was clearly false, and someone was telling them in government at a top level to say that there were no parties. Yet I knew, they all knew, that that was wrong, and it was time to do something about it.[1]

What he did about it was leak a video to ITV News of Downing Street aides, including Johnson's press secretary Allegra Stratton, laughing about the lockdown parties. The video was a game-changer, ending any doubts about whether the parties had taken place. It also gave the story what political commentators call 'cut through' – what had started as a Westminster story had entered the mainstream.

The sense that, during the painful lockdown, there was one rule for the powerful and another for the rest of us enraged the public. For months further revelations, a police investigation and the promise of a report from senior civil servant Sue Gray kept the story fresh and on the front pages. In an ignominious first, the prime minister was issued a fixed penalty notice by the Metropolitan Police, but he hung on. Gray's report in May was strongly critical of the culture inside Downing Street, but Johnson survived. As the parliamentary recess loomed there was even the prospect of a reset in Johnson's fortunes. But then came Chris Pincher.

Pincher was Johnson's deputy chief whip until late June, when he resigned after allegations that, while drunk, he had groped two men at the Tory Carlton Club in central London. When it emerged that this wasn't the first serious accusation against Pincher, Johnson had questions to answer. How could this man have been appointed to such a senior and sensitive role? Had the prime minister known about the previous allegations, and if so, when?

By Monday 4 July Downing Street was telling reporters that, as far as Johnson knew, all historic allegations against Pincher had been 'resolved' and were not the subject of any 'formal complaint'. They added, with a whiff of hubris, that it would have been wrong to block Pincher's appointment as deputy chief whip based on 'unsubstantiated allegations'. And so – in an echo of Partygate – a procession of ministers went out to answer the media's questions about what the prime minister knew and when he knew it. Their answers loyally reflected Johnson's account.

The former permanent secretary in the Foreign Office, Lord Simon McDonald, had seen enough. Early on the morning of 5 July he intervened with devastating precision and blew Johnson's account out of the water. The former civil servant tweeted, 'No 10 keep changing their story and are still not telling the truth.' He attached his letter to the parliamentary commissioner for standards, which explained that there *had* been a formal investigation into Pincher in 2019 when he was a Foreign Office minister. His boss at the time – then foreign secretary, er, Boris Johnson – was briefed about it 'in person' and was told that the complaint had been upheld. So Johnson knew all this when he appointed Pincher as deputy chief whip. The prime minister was in deep trouble.

By the time we are finalising the scripts for Marr's programme in the early evening of 5 July things feel precarious, but we haven't reached the point of no return. If we've learned anything about Johnson, it's that he won't do the decent thing until he absolutely has to. As we go on air we aren't there yet.

Our show starts at six, and the idea is to offer listeners and viewers analysis, not just news. But news is coming at us fast. At two minutes past six, Sajid Javid, the health secretary, resigns. He no longer has confidence in the prime minister. This is very serious, but it's still not quite the point of no return. Yet. For that we'll have to wait another nine minutes. At eleven minutes past six, Rishi Sunak, the chancellor of the exchequer, announces his resignation via Twitter. I'm not sure whether he did so simultaneously on Instagram and TikTok, but I wouldn't put it past him.

As the Sunak news appears on my Twitter feed, Marr is in the middle of a conversation with Jess Philips, one of Labour's most engaging front-bench performers. She is having a fine old time watching the government implode, and she most definitely has the gift of the gab. I am on the other side of the glass and need to tell Marr the momentous news. Philips is in mid-flow, so I am very clear and precise.

'Rishi. Sunak. Has. Resigned!' I say loudly through his earpiece.

Marr hears me and, for a second, visibly registers the news. He looks through the glass into the control room for a split second and then, involuntarily – and rather wonderfully – half-yells a one-word question that somehow speaks for us all:

What?!?!

Nobody could have blamed him if he'd added 'the actual fuck' at the end of the sentence, but he restrains himself. It's not the smoothest presenter reaction to a piece of significant breaking news, but when has smooth ever been better than real?

'I'm terribly sorry,' he tells Phillips. 'We have to stop there.' He pauses. 'Rishi Sunak has just resigned,' he announces. 'The chancellor has resigned.'

'Oh, my God,' blurts out Phillips, open-mouthed.

Then Marr says what he could never have said on the BBC in the same situation. 'That is it! That is it!' he declares. 'The Boris Johnson government is over.'

It's wonderful radio, and the video clip of Marr's 'What?!?!' explodes on social media. Marr, aged sixty-two going on sixty-three, is wowing the kids on TikTok. It's human, honest and dramatic, and a world away from the cautious, controlled and couched language of BBC impartiality. It works.

Marr is back, and he's in possession once again of a fully operational mojo. As for Johnson – the man who ran from scrutiny, bluffed and distracted, and clowned his way to the top – the endgame is approaching.

Andrew Marr's decision to leave the BBC was big news. After sixteen years hosting the biggest political interview show on TV, his departure was the end of an era. Marr is much more than a political interviewer and presenter. He is the broadcaster you turn to when significant events requiring context, analysis and vivid language take place. A walk down the street with Marr brings home to you just how much the public loves him and how significant his work has been to so many. You shouldn't lose someone like Marr from your organisation lightly.

Marr was restless and, to put it bluntly, bored after so many years on the Sunday-morning beat. BBC impartiality rules were also beginning to weigh heavily on him. He always understood why they mattered but felt BBC impartiality was becoming 'a kind of pickled creed or cult'. And Boris Johnson was presenting problems too: 'I became increasingly concerned,' he told me, 'about the issue of calling out lying during the Boris Johnson years.'

> You ought to be able to say on the BBC, 'The prime minister said this to the House of Commons. We've checked it, and it's not true.' But it would have been very, very controversial.[2]

But it wasn't just on air that Marr felt hemmed in: 'I found I was talking to friends over a beer and was self-censoring,' he remembers. 'I felt I wasn't being the real me.' It was time for a change.

LBC was not an obvious fit. It had made its name with opinionated presenters hosting phone-in shows. Marr wasn't sniffy about that, but it wasn't the right format for him. He wanted to free himself from the shackles of BBC impartiality, but he didn't want to shout his mouth off:

> I'm not interested in being a shock jock. I'm not interested in ranting or tearing people down. What happens is you say something shocking or something that people are really gripped by, and you think, 'Oh, that's good. I'll do it again tomorrow.' Then the next day. It's like a drug. To get the hit, you have to be more extreme. You have to have more loaded into the syringe, and very soon, you become just another bright-red shouting face of which there are more than enough.[3]

But LBC was changing: the arrival of Eddie Mair from Radio 4 in 2018 began a new era there. While the phone-ins and barked opinions remained, Mair's classy presence created room for a less didactic voice like Marr's. The channel is full of compelling presenters from across the political spectrum – from Iain Dale to Shelagh Fogarty and James O'Brien – and Marr would not be slumming it on that roster. Talks advanced quickly and Marr soon agreed to an hour-long show with no phone calls and no pressure to mouth off. It would be, he hoped, 'Public service broadcasting outside the public sector.'

The last *Andrew Marr Show* on BBC One aired on 19 December 2021. Marr signed off, channelling Ron Burgundy, like an absolute anchor: 'You stay classy, San Diego,' were his final words to a grateful nation.

A few weeks later, in January 2022, I arrived at LBC to build the new show with the help of a crack team of producers. Before we had a programme, we had a slogan:

Marr's got his voice back!

And he had. We opened the show with a monologue. This helped get the audience up to speed with the day's events while offering a balanced assessment. Marr's approach – and I agree with it – is that it is important to try to reflect the range of views on an issue because not everything is as clear cut as those who carry megaphones – both literal and metaphorical – like to make out. Nuance is important, and so is recognising that solving political questions is not always straightforward. This is not to let politicians off the hook – they have sought power and must be judged on how effectively and humanely they use it – but it's important to be grown up about it.

Faced with incompetence, deceitfulness and cheap populism, Marr now had the freedom to express his own views. In the past I'd been the voice of BBC restraint, suggesting he tone down analysis that strayed too close to personal opinion. But at LBC I often encouraged him to go further. It wasn't long before his brilliantly written monologues were doing well on social media, but he hadn't compromised his insistence on nuance and fairness.

After Sunak's resignation on 5 July, Johnson hunkered down in Downing Street, desperately trying to figure out how to hold on to power. In the end, however, a tsunami of ministerial resignations left him with no choice but to resign. Marr is scathing about the effect of Johnson's brief, turbulent premiership on British politics:

> He's done immense damage. The combination of the Iraq war under Blair and the two or three years of Johnson announcing boldly that blue is green and Tuesday is, in fact, Sunday means that an awful lot of voters assume that politicians lie almost all the time.[4]

Once Johnson had quit, *Tonight with Andrew Marr* had a Conservative leadership campaign to cover. Among the field of eight contenders was our old friend Penny Mordaunt, she of the Turkish pork pie during the EU referendum campaign in 2016. As you may remember, in that interview she told Andrew Marr clearly that the UK did not have a veto over Turkey joining the European Union when it did. Six years on, as she runs for the leadership, her tall tale comes back to bite her.

My LBC colleague Iain Dale invited Mordaunt onto his show and brought up the dodgy Turkey claim from the referendum. 'Why,' he wondered, 'won't you apologise for saying something that was untrue?' This was Mordaunt's chance, if not to apologise, then to accept she'd given a false impression that there was no veto when there was. But Vote Leave habits die hard:

Mordaunt: I actually stand by that, Iain …

Dale: It wasn't true to say that we didn't have a veto. We did.

Mordaunt: There is a provision for a veto, but we could not have used it because David Cameron gave an undertaking that he would support their accession and having given that undertaking to a NATO country, he would not have been able to walk away.[5]

This is, of course, a different argument. She's talking about whether a veto would be used for political reasons, not whether it exists. Here she says there was a 'provision for a veto', which is progress from 2016 but not much. Later she accused David Cameron of being 'disingenuous' in relation to Turkey, which was bold in the circumstances. This issue, and the impression she gave of shifting her position on trans rights, damaged Mordaunt's 2022 leadership campaign because she looked less than straightforward and honest.

I'll leave the last word on Penny – insert trigger warning to sensitive Brexiteers – to Michael Lake, former EU ambassador to Turkey, who wrote to the *Guardian* on the subject in July 2022.

> Britain always had a veto over any aspiring member, and if Mordaunt had previously had any credibility, her infamous dishonesty about Turkey destroyed it. I thought part of the reason for ditching Boris Johnson was his habit of lying.[6]

After Mordaunt dropped out, the field narrowed to the final two, Liz Truss and Rishi Sunak. Truss refused all our invitations to be interviewed. In contrast, Sunak came on for a testing half-hour with Marr. He was impressive, warning very precisely that Truss's plans to borrow billions to fund tax cuts would push up inflation and increase the cost of mortgages.

After that, Marr came off air for the summer break, and the Tory leadership contest moved from Westminster to the Conservative Party in the country. What could possibly go wrong?

As I started my summer holiday I was proud of what we'd achieved at LBC, but I was restless. My passion was the political interview, and there wasn't time to craft them on a fast-moving news show. I was looking to team up with a talented interviewer who could help bring back the forensic interview I did best.

People often say that Boris Johnson has no shame, but thanks to an interview with Beth Rigby, political editor of Sky News, we know that's not true. It may be hard to believe, but in January 2022 Beth was able to coax the lesser-spotted-Johnson shame out into the open. It didn't stay long before scurrying off into the undergrowth, and it's not been seen since, but it's real. I know, because I saw it on Sky News. This was an achievement, and in the hundreds of ministerial interviews on 'Partygate' that clogged the airwaves, it was perhaps the only one to stand out, to tell us something and ultimately to be remembered.

The encounter took place in a hospital in north London where Boris Johnson, up to his neck in Partygate pain, was scheduled to provide what's known as a 'pool interview'. This arrangement allows senior politicians to give one single interview, which is then shared with all outlets. On this particular morning it was Rigby's turn to ask the questions.

Starting as a print journalist at the *Financial Times* and later *The Times*, Rigby joined Sky News in 2016, becoming political editor in 2019. Her impact was immediate. She was fearless and gobby, with a line in blunt but crafted questions. Her voice was a talking point – particularly her tendency to drop her 'g's – and her look was instantly recognisable: bright red lipstick, blocky, bright-coloured trouser suits or jackets and killer heels. Whether by accident or design, she had a brand.

Rigby does not treat the January encounter like a normal pool interview. She has a plan she wants to work through and she catches the prime minister off guard from the start. Rigby is the exacting headmistress – off-camera but in command – Johnson is the disgraced schoolboy called to her office. He's wearing a light blue protective mask, with only the top half of his head visible. The effect draws the viewer to his eyes – watery and down-turned – and they give him away. The shame lies just below the surface.

Rigby starts with the famous party in the Downing Street garden in May 2020 that Johnson thought was a 'work event'.

> You walked into the garden. There's forty people there, the tables are laid out with food and drink, and there's alcohol being served in the middle of a lockdown, and you think that's a work event? That is just ludicrous, isn't it? You are just taking the mickey out of the British people by suggesting that. You know how silly that sounds, don't you?[7]

Johnson's demeanour suggests he does, but he holds the line: he hadn't known any rules were being broken and, contrary to various claims carried in the press, nobody had warned him that the 'bring your own booze' event was not allowed. All he can do, his voice wavering, is say how deeply and bitterly sorry he is. He's not on *Have I Got News for You* anymore.

As the interview progresses, Johnson deploys some of his usual tricks, but Rigby will not be thrown off. She is firm and stern, and there's no way out for Johnson today. The prime minister holds it together for the first nine minutes or so and even seems to grow in confidence a little. He's still uncomfortable but finds his groove of regret, denial and delay ('I think it's very important we wait and see what Sue Gray has to say ...').

Then Rigby ups the emotional ante. She brings up two more parties, boozy ones, from the evening of 16 April 2021. Johnson wasn't involved in these get-togethers, but they're evidence of a shocking culture inside Downing Street. This was the night before the funeral of the Duke of Edinburgh. The nation was in mourning. The drunken antics of Downing Street staff that night – and things got messy by all accounts – contrasted with the dignity of the Queen the next day in St George's Chapel, Windsor. She wears a facemask during the service, and sits alone and forlorn in a sea of pews. She's observing the Covid rules, like countless others across the country who'd lost loved ones during the pandemic.

At this point, Johnson can't hide his shame any longer. As Rigby starts the question he sighs and looks down at the floor. Maybe he's hoping it will swallow him up. It doesn't. He shakes his head. As she continues, he closes his eyes in despair, then opens them and takes another long, hard look at the ground. She concludes with a direct question that stings:

> Was having to apologise to the Queen about those
> parties the night before she laid her husband of over
> seventy years to rest a moment of shame for you?[8]

In truth, she doesn't have to ask. Even with a mask on, the shame is written all over his face. It's a devastating moment, perfectly constructed and delivered. Johnson looks broken. Rigby is in complete control. It's a brilliant interview.

All of this came back to me in the late summer of 2022, a couple of weeks before *Tonight with Andrew Marr* was due to return from its break. I was in Dorset visiting a friend when I got a call from Sky News. Beth Rigby needed a new editor for her interview show, and they wanted to sound me out. Television and the big political interview were calling me back.

Meanwhile, the Tory party membership was leaning towards Liz Truss and her plan to boost growth by borrowing to cut taxes. Sunak never let up, but his more cautious, orthodox message was boring them. The Tory members just weren't that into him, but they found Truss's plan for a low-tax, low-regulation post-Brexit Britain alluring.

All the more so because it hadn't been tested properly. This was not accidental. Except for an early, tricky outing with Nick Robinson on Radio 4, Truss continued to turn down interview requests. She wouldn't do Marr. She refused Andrew Neil's new Channel 4 programme and abruptly pulled out after saying yes to a TV encounter with Robinson on BBC One. Sunak did them all. There were debate programmes and hustings, but they made no real headway in exposing the dangers of her economic plans.

Andrew Neil, hoping she might relent, had started planning questions for a Truss interview that never happened (sound familiar?):

> I was going to concentrate nearly all of my interview on the economy because it was clear to me that she didn't know what she was talking about. She guessed that the interview would be overwhelmingly about her economic policies. She knew that I was likely to zoom in on that. She also knew it was my area of strength above all, and it was her area of weakness, so she decided that she better not go there.[9]

She wasn't just cowardly. She was also contemptuous of the media. In one party hustings chaired by Talk TV's Tom Newton Dunn, Truss accused the host – once political editor of well-known left-wing rag the *Sun* – of framing a question 'in a left-wing way'. 'I'm afraid the media do this all the time,' she went on. 'Drives me mad.'

Then, in a Trumpian moment, after Newton Dunn asked Truss about the downfall of Boris Johnson, the crowd started booing. But they weren't booing Johnson, they were booing Newton Dunn, who was a proxy for 'the media'. Seeing a chance to ingratiate herself with the Tory crowd, Truss joined in. 'It sounds like you're being blamed, Tom,' she said, 'and who am I to disagree with this excellent audience?'

Yeah, it's not like you're trying to be prime minister or anything.

And then, apropos of nothing, she declared, 'I believe in Britain,' and gestured towards the host, 'unlike some of our media who choose to talk our country down.' The crowd loved it. The cynicism was bad enough but what happened as the event ended said it all.

Truss thought she was off mike, but she wasn't. 'I'm sorry I was mean about the media, Tom,' she said as she hugged him.

Newton Dunn wasn't in the mood to laugh it off. 'It's cheap,' he said.

Cheap won.

The early weeks of autumn 2022 in Britain belong to two women with the same Christian name but not much else in common. The first – and by far the more significant – was Her Majesty Queen Elizabeth II, whose death on 8 September ended the longest reign by a monarch in British history. She towered over post-war Britain and will be long remembered, studied and revered. The second, Liz Truss – became prime minister on 6 September and resigned on her fiftieth day in office, making her the shortest-serving prime minister in British history. She is likely to be studied as an extraordinary failure whose demise was largely self-inflicted.

The weeks that followed were the most surreal of all the surreal political weeks we'd endured since 2016. My position was also a little weird. Sky News had offered me the job with Beth Rigby, and I'd decided to take it. I didn't want to let Marr down, but the chance felt too good to miss, and with my friend Matt Harris in charge, I knew *Tonight with Andrew Marr* was in good hands. When I told my LBC bosses that I wanted to move on, they decided to take me off the show and sent me home to 'put my feet up' for a month or so before I started with Rigby. Everything stopped after the Queen died, but when the political drama restarted, I was consuming the coverage from home, not shaping it.

Well, that's not entirely true. As the Trussterfuck unfolded, I was in regular contact with my soon-to-be-colleague. In her job as political editor, she covered the story every day. Rather than twiddle my thumbs, I would suggest questions when Rigby had big interviews, such as the one with Liz Truss during the Conservative Party conference in early October. The Tory get-together was supposed to be a showcase for the shiny new leader, but by the time she arrived in Birmingham, Truss was already in very deep shit.

On 23 September the chancellor Kwasi Kwarteng delivered what he called a 'fiscal event' – it was really a budget, but calling it that would complicate his mission. He didn't want to have to consult the wonks at the Office of Budget Responsibility who forecast the impact of changes. The rules allowed them to be ignored because it was only a 'mini' rather than a full-fat budget. Sneaky and, as it turned out, too clever by half.

Kwarteng announced a huge raft of tax cuts worth £45 billion – the biggest reduction in fifty years. Measures included the complete abolition of the 45p rate paid by those earning over £150,000. Later that day, the government's Debt Managing Office slipped out a modest little press release with a clue as to how all this would be funded. With bureaucratic dryness, they announced a 'revision' in borrowing 'rising by £72.4 billion to £234.1 billion following the publication today of the Government's Growth Plan'. Blimey. And that only covered a portion of it. It would mainly pay for the widely welcomed energy price freeze. The tax cuts, which would arrive in April 2023, would require more borrowing. The markets were immediately concerned. The pound plummeted, and the cost of government borrowing went up.

Two days later, Kwarteng remained blissfully blithe on Laura Kuenssberg's new Sunday-morning programme that now occupied the Frost/Marr slot. The chancellor spent most of the conversation ignoring the substance of the questions about the mini-budget. And then, emboldened, he told Laura that he'd only just begun. 'There's more to come,' he said. 'We've only been here nineteen days.'[10]

He had nineteen more days to run.

'Spooked' – as only markets and horses ever are – doesn't cover the market reaction. By the middle of the week Truss was floundering. The Bank of England had to intervene to save UK pension funds. Lenders removed some mortgage products from the market, and fears grew that interest-rate rises would inflate mortgage bills horribly. For most of the week Truss stayed silent. Then, on Thursday 24th, she ventured onto BBC local radio for a round of car-crash local-radio interviews where she failed miserably to reassure anybody.

Truss is not quite a robot like May – she has recognisably human traits such as vanity, ambition and the occasional flash of humour. Nor is she an introvert like Brown. As her Instagram addiction demonstrates, she enjoys the limelight and craves attention, but the trouble is that when she's on stage she appears weirdly uninvolved. She came across as someone playing the role of prime minister rather than actually being prime minister, and she was playing it badly. She seemed unable to recognise or digest others' experiences and feelings, and even had trouble registering her own. As her premiership descended into an irreversible crisis, she floated through it all with a half-smile occasionally arriving on her face, apparently oblivious or unconcerned about her own precarious position.

On the Sunday before conference Truss appeared on Laura Kuenssberg's show insisting she planned to push ahead with the entire package in the disastrous mini-budget. On the same programme, former cabinet minister Michael Gove made it clear he wouldn't be able to support the abolition of the 45p top rate of tax. The implication was that he wasn't alone in the parliamentary Conservative Party. The next day, the retreat began and the policy was abandoned just hours after Truss had told Kuenssberg that it would stay. On Tuesday, Beth Rigby had ten minutes with Truss only twenty-four hours before her conference speech. This was too short a time to really get anywhere but Rigby wanted to try, and we discussed questions over WhatsApp and on the phone. Her opener was a summary of Truss's terrible tenure to date, which concluded brutally with the question, 'This is surely the worst start ever for any prime minister?'

'Well, let's remember what we were facing,' Truss responded, ignoring the question and steering determinedly towards the freeze on energy bills she'd introduced. No wonder – it was the only thing she hadn't screwed up. Rigby persevered. Did Truss accept she'd had a 'rocky start', she wondered. 'What I am saying,' answered Truss in her trademark monotone, 'is we have acted decisively.' She was talking about the freeze on energy bills again. She didn't bother to pretend to answer the question.

'Let me put it another way,' said Rigby, with the patience of a saint. 'Do you think your personal authority has been enhanced or reduced in your short time in office?'

Truss looked at her blankly, then started up again.

What I have done is I have delivered in very difficult circumstances for the British people ...[11]

It was pitiful. Truss was the worst sort of politician: she stuck to her pre-prepared lines and was entirely inflexible. Fundamentally, she was unable to rise to the occasion. People were worried, and needed reassurance and leadership. Instead they got dead-eyed deflection.

As I watched, it felt like all these years of lying, evasion, deception and distraction had culminated in the Truss premiership. From the refusal to involve the OBR to keeping the Bank of England in the dark about her plans and her contempt for the media and accountability, Truss was as bad as Johnson when it came to sweeping away democratic norms. It was the triumph of ambition over ability and revealed a complete failure to explain, persuade or engage with the public. Imagine Sir Robin Day presented with *this* charade. For her part, Rigby offered quiet despair. Wearily, she told Truss voters were tired of dishonest answers.

Ten days later Truss fired her friend Kwarteng in the demented conviction that this might save her own skin. After the sacking, Truss called a press conference at Downing Street. This was the last chance to grasp the narrative and take as many questions as the journalists in the room wanted to ask. Instead, Truss delivered a performance of such rhetorical inadequacy that it made Theresa May look like Barack Obama. She took questions for just six minutes. As she hurried away from the podium, Rigby, whom she'd ignored, shouted a question anyway: 'You're out of your depth, aren't you, Prime Minister?'

Eleven days later, she went under. Reports later emerged that, as the axe fell, Truss expressed relief the ordeal was over and cheered herself up by declaring 'at least I've been Prime Minister!'[12] Like taking a bungee jump or climbing a mountain in Peru, for Liz 'being a world leader' was just another experience to tick off the bucket list.

That mad autumn of Truss landed perfectly for Emily Maitlis, Jon Sopel and Lewis Goodall when they launched their new blockbuster podcast *The News Agents* in September for Global. It was nice to have them as colleagues once again. I'd known Lewis when he was a producer on *Newsnight* and had worked with Jon on *The Politics Show* ten years previously. Of the three I'd spent most time working with Emily on *Newsnight*, and I rate her very highly.

After a career in political television, I'm used to getting asked who the best interviewer I've ever worked with is. The answer depends on what you want: Andrew Neil is the most precise, well briefed and lethal. Paxman is a rock star interviewer and the king of TV theatre. Jonathan Dimbleby is an outstanding forensic interviewer, and Andrew Marr knows how to gently skewer a deceptive politician. Beth Rigby is a *very* tough customer, and Evan Davis isn't. But if I were launching a new TV show and wanted the fullest possible range of presenting and interviewing skills – precision, toughness, breadth of interest, sense of humour and a sprinkling of indefinable, unteachable TV magic – I'd go with Emily Maitlis.

I worked with Maitlis for two years at *Newsnight*, and I loved it. She has a combination of skills and attributes that contradict and complement each other in a way that creates the perfect interviewer. She is intellectually impressive but refuses to take herself too seriously. She is precise in delivering an interview plan but sufficiently curious to listen to the answers and junk it if appropriate. She is deadly serious when the situation demands but brings a sense of humour to the studio that lifts everything. She is tenacious but not niggly. She is interested in politics, but less for the game and much more for the impact on people. She knows her own mind but also knows she relies on a team. She blooms in the spotlight but shares credit. You can't be as talented, driven and successful as she is and not possess an ego, but I've never seen her be overbearing or pull rank.

Like Marr, for Maitlis 2022 was about moving on from the BBC. In the post-Paxman era, she was the undisputed star of *Newsnight*, a reputation secured by her stunning interview with Prince Andrew in 2019. But things rapidly soured between her and the BBC. She found the strictures of impartiality increasingly demanding in the age of Brexit, Trump and Johnson. When populist presidents and prime ministers were tearing up norms, peddling untruths and attacking the media, how could journalists act as if it were business as usual? Maitlis later compared journalists in the age of populism to a frog in a pan of cold water who doesn't notice the temperature creeping up to boiling point until it's too late.

In May 2020 came the turning point, when Maitlis found *herself* in hot water. The problem came after she introduced an edition of *Newsnight* about Boris Johnson's then chief adviser Dominic Cummings's lockdown drive to Durham. Downing Street – presumably in the shape of our old friend Lee Cain – were outraged at what they saw as clear anti-government bias and let the BBC know. This was not unusual. The BBC's response – a swift public rebuke to the presenter for 'giving the perception that the BBC was taking sides, and expressing an opinion, rather than being impartial' – was. Maitlis was shocked and upset. Due to present the following evening's programme, she pulled out.

That affair was the beginning of the end for her time at the BBC. In February 2022 – sporting a sweater with the word 'Oh!' written on it – Maitlis announced her departure to Global, following in the footsteps of Mair and Marr.

The News Agents is conversational and analytical in style. It's more about illumination than *Newsnight*-style accountability, and I love it. Maitlis is too brilliant at political interviewing to be on the accountability sidelines for long, but her break from the cut and thrust of the *Newsnight* interview allows her to reflect and take a step back after a dark and extraordinary period in British political life.

Now I had some distance from it, I wanted to reflect on the Tory leadership debate that I edited and Maitlis presented in the summer of 2019. At the time, we beat ourselves up about the things that went wrong: the boy band stools, the decision by BBC News managers not to have a studio audience and the cacophony of shouty Tory candidates. But now, Maitlis sees it as a sneak preview of the Johnson premiership that followed (for me there are also echoes in the Truss debacle that came next):

> The programme was an almost exact microcosm of the style in which Boris Johnson would choose to govern over the next few years. On stage, I remember seeing him obfuscate, divert, make light, avoid eye contact or a direct response to direct questions. At times I remember him acting like he hadn't even heard what I was asking. We saw all this pretty close up and pretty early. It took his party another three years.[13]

She suspects that the outrage stirred up against the BBC afterwards came from Johnson's team, who wanted to distract from his poor performance. 'He hadn't covered himself in glory that night,' she recalled, 'and they wanted to throw shade back on the broadcast arrangements and the audience questions. It was all too convenient.' The administration that followed did not last long. But however brief it was, I wondered how much damage she thought it had done.

It's hard to know. My worry at the time was that we got used to so much: a leader willing to change the rules to avoid scrutiny and/or help his mates, a politician who believed that ethics or standards in public life were both unhelpful, old fashioned and beneath him. A prime minister who had so little belief or faith in the electorate to make choices that he had to reduce policy to three-word slogans.[14]

I wanted to focus on one part of that: avoiding scrutiny. For me, this is the most worrying aspect of the Johnson legacy and Maitlis was clear about what it signifies. 'It tells me,' she said, 'they lack either confidence, conviction or the maturity to handle debate about the issue they appear to espouse.' That about sums up Liz Truss's failings, and I suppose her rapid fall from power must be evidence of a system, however imperfectly, working.

After the politics of the last decade, Maitlis could be forgiven for being cynical about the political class, but that's not how she sees it. 'I would never characterise my own style as "Why is this lying bastard lying to me?",' she says, but:

It would be naive to pretend I wasn't acutely aware I was being lied to. This is where knowing your facts comes in. I would happily use past quotes, past examples to let the interviewee see that I'd done my homework and wouldn't be whitewashed into accepting stuff that was blatantly not true. I much prefer an incredulous raised eyebrow to a hot shouty rant. I've always found that ridicule is much more effective on liars than moral outrage.[15]

In the end, Maitlis is an optimist. The glass is half full. She thinks the removal of Johnson and the delayed arrival of Rishi Sunak might turn out to be a sign that politics is taking a 'different path'. She doesn't say so, but I sense she's reassured that Sunak – wherever you stand on his policies – is a more traditional politician who is less likely to disrupt norms and entirely disregard truth. Which takes us back to Johnson – the dominant figure in British politics of the last decade – and a cheery thought. 'Ultimately,' she says, 'I'm not sure Boris Johnson will have left as big an imprint on British politics as we all assumed.'

On his first day as prime minister, Rishi Sunak made a promise to the country. He said, 'This government will have integrity, professionalism and accountability at every level. Trust is earned. And I will earn yours.' The meaning was obvious: the days of Johnson and Truss are over. It was the UK's modern-day return to normality.

But after the damage that's been done, it's not enough to go back to business as usual. And politics on television – whether live in the moment in a set-piece event, or diced and sliced on social media – remains the most vital method of political communication. We need to renew political television and the political interview. That will depend on the politicians and the broadcasters deciding it's time to recommit to serious interviews that take us beyond the soundbites towards accountability and real depth. That's what Beth and I are trying to do with *Beth Rigby Interviews* on Sky News. The show's purpose is simple: a return to the long-form interview.

That means something more considered and serious than the ten-minute news interviews that dominate today. Rigby has decided to leave Paxman's 'Why is this lying bastard lying to me?' approach to her political editor day job. For the interview show, she prefers to embrace Brian Walden's more positive question: 'Imagine this person's telling the truth. What follows from that?' Which is the more appropriate response to British politics in the post-Johnson era will become apparent in time. But our programme will only work when the interviewee is prepared to engage truthfully and in a more considered and open way. This was not quite how it turned out when the chancellor, Jeremy Hunt, sat down with Rigby in November 2022.

Hunt, in his first act as chancellor of the exchequer, had delivered a gloomy autumn statement that hit taxpayers with significant tax rises and set out future public-spending cuts. Hunt wanted to reassure the markets that the grown-ups were in charge again after the Kwarteng/Truss clown show. He'd also been presented with depressing forecasts about the UK economy from the Office for Budget Responsibility (OBR), which, he argued, gave him no choice but to take drastic action. What's more, Hunt emphasised that this was the only way to bring down inflation. And it would work, he said, because the independent OBR had confirmed as much.

But there was a problem: Brexit. The OBR said the effect of Brexit would be a 4 per cent reduction in the size of the UK economy over the next decade. Sunlit uplands it wasn't. The following day Hunt spoke a little wistfully on the radio about how 'unfettered trade with our neighbours' tended to help economic growth.

Two days later, the *Sunday Times* front page announced, 'Britain mulls Swiss-style ties with Brussels.' The paper said 'senior government sources' had suggested that Rishi Sunak might seek a new relationship with the European Union resembling Switzerland's arrangements. That meant frictionless trade based on more liberal migration policies, payments to the EU and the possibility of greater oversight from the European Court of Justice. As the story landed, you could almost hear

Brexiteer Britain choking on its full English. This was betrayal on toast to the Mark Francois tendency. The man in the frame for floating the idea was obvious: incorrigible Remainer, Jeremy Hunt.

The following day the government set out to kill the story. The prime minister declared 'I believe in Brexit!' the way some people – young children mainly – talk about Father Christmas. Brexit would be a huge success – already was, to be honest – and any trade arrangement with the European Union could not jeopardise that.

As Rigby and I prepared for the Hunt interview, we were clear that the most fruitful area for discussion was Brexit. This wasn't an easy choice because, for journalists, Brexit often resides in what Emily Maitlis calls the 'too awkward' box. Since 2016 Brexiteers have presented any attempt by journalists to explore the difficulties or cost of Brexit as the 'elite' trying to undermine or overturn the democratic will of the people. It was a highly effective way of shutting down discussion and intimidating interviewers.

But enough was enough. More than six years after the referendum, and with the UK facing recession, it was time to go there again. The OBR had quantified the cost of Brexit and it was steep. This might be a price worth paying for breaking free of the European Union – that's a legitimate position – but politicians needed to start being honest about the cost and decide whether they would do anything about it.

As Rigby sat down with Hunt, she had an open mind, anticipating a nuanced discussion. In my experience, Hunt was one of the more thoughtful and straightforward people in politics. It wasn't impossible that he'd choose to speak honestly and engagingly about the costs of Brexit and the options for dealing with them.

Rigby began with the 'elephant in the room'.

It's almost become a taboo subject. Journalists aren't even allowed to really ask questions about it without feeling like you're somehow attacking Brexit. But it's hurt the economy. What do you think the hit to the UK economy will be because of Brexit?[16]

Hunt started with an important truth. 'Well,' he said, 'Brexit was a change in our trading relations with our biggest single trading partner.' This wasn't a direct answer to the question, but it suggested Hunt was ready to be a grown-up and address the challenge. Then he went on:

> **Hunt** (sunnily): I've always believed, in fact, I believed even before the Brexit vote, that we could make a great success of Brexit.

> **Rigby** (puzzled): You weren't a Brexiteer.

> **Hunt** (seemingly trying to convince himself): I was worried about the constitutional risks, but economically, I've always believed we can make a tremendous success of it.[17]

This statement is very easy to disprove. Here's Hunt on 18 April 2016 on Twitter:

> Lots of support for HMT [Treasury] analysis that every household would be £4,300 worse off if we left the EU.[18]

Yes, you read it right. During the referendum campaign, when cabinet ministers were free to speak their minds and share their true feelings, Hunt endorsed Remain's most contentious claim about the cost of Brexit. And that wasn't his starkest warning. On 15 June 2016, just before referendum day, the then secretary of state for health was apocalyptic about the dangers of a

Leave victory. 'Chancellor right,' he tweeted firmly. 'NHS funded through tax revenues that would disappear following Brexit.' These aren't 'constitutional worries'. This is poorer households and disappearing tax revenues. It's full-fat Project Fear. This is not a man who 'always believed we could make a tremendous success of Brexit'.

Or, to put it another way, pull the other one, Jeremy, it's got bells on.

From there, things deteriorated. Hunt said that the OBR's prediction that the economy would shrink by 4 per cent was wrong because he was introducing policies that would make the UK 'the world's next Silicon Valley'. This was an unprovable claim – just a slogan, essentially – but it was all he had, and he repeatedly deployed it. Rigby wasn't buying.

Rigby (unperturbed): How much lost income and tax revenue does that 4 per cent over the medium term add up to?

Hunt (irritated): Beth, I don't accept the 4 per cent.

Rigby (not having it): But you accept the OBR figures sometimes when you like them, such as falling inflation. You're happy to take that one.

Hunt (aware this is ludicrous but sticking with it): Yes, I don't have to accept all of them …

Rigby (smiling): So you accept the ones you like?

Hunt (too late to stop now): Well, I accept the ones I agree with, and I don't accept the ones I don't agree with and that one I don't agree with …

Rigby (done with it): As a journalist, all I can work on are independent forecasts by the OBR rather than the promises that you're making about Brexit.

It's an extraordinary moment and, at the risk of sounding pompous, a sad one too. Here's a man with a reputation as a relatively candid politician trashing his brand. His decision to pretend he always thought Brexit would be marvellous was bizarre and inauthentic. Picking and choosing when to accept the verdict of the independent OBR was chilling. Suddenly, six years after the vote, Jeremy Hunt had had enough of experts.

As the interview wore on, Hunt became more irritated. He started to complain that Rigby had spent too much time on Brexit – in fact, it comprised around eight minutes out of twenty-four. He topped it off with some light menace. 'I'll answer your question,' he said, before adding darkly, 'but let's make it the last time.' I can only explain his behaviour as defensive overcompensation for his comments on 'unfettered trade' and the widespread view in Westminster that his department had briefed that *Sunday Times* story about a Swiss-style deal for the UK. To be interviewed is to choose. Hunt chose to insult everyone's intelligence, including his own. I look forward to seeing the real Jeremy Hunt again one of these days. Maybe he was just having a bad day.

So much for Sunak and co, but Sir Keir Starmer has his own challenges. There will be tricky interviews ahead as he seeks to make the transition from Labour leader whose party is ahead in the opinion polls to prime minister in waiting.

Starmer remains associated with the Corbyn years despite moving decisively against his predecessor and his acolytes since becoming leader. As the party's shadow Brexit secretary, Starmer was the public face of post-referendum Remain. He's associated in the public mind with the attempt to re-run the referendum, which played its part in Labour's devastating defeat in the 2019 'Brexit election'. Starmer is terrified of reigniting Brexit passions in the former 'red wall' seats that abandoned Labour for Boris Johnson. In order to inoculate himself from the 'Remainer' charge, the Labour leader increasingly tries on Brexiteer garb. He talks about making Brexit a success and has laid down a personal 'red line' against any return to freedom of movement. These may be the right political calls, but Labour's Brexit position risks looking more and more absurd as time passes. It's also, to be blunt, intellectually dishonest and, as we saw with Jeremy Hunt, that can be a problem.

Starmer also has trouble accounting for how he ran for Labour leader in 2020. At the time he presented himself as a radical, as Corbynism in a better suit. He made ten pledges designed to convince members that he'd be a continuation rather than a repudiation of the previous five years, judging that a membership that had elected Corbyn twice would need reassurance. In the years since, he has abandoned many of these promises, including the pledge to nationalise 'mail, energy and water' and the commitment to stop private provision in the NHS. This is a well-trodden path – Neil Kinnock ran from the left but took the party to the right – and these may prove to be the correct policy choices, but pledges are pledges and breaking them is not a good look. It's perfectly legitimate for the Labour left to feel they were conned, and interviewers will continue to challenge him about it.

Whatever the risks of the long-form and serious political interview, I'm encouraged that Sunak, Starmer and their colleagues have generally chosen to show up. It didn't go well for Jeremy Hunt, but I'm grateful that unlike Johnson and Truss, he seems to understand that scrutiny and accountability are at the heart of our democracy.

Andrew Marr, like Emily Maitlis, is optimistic about the future. He believes that Starmer versus Sunak is, and will continue to be, an 'absolutely gripping, serious, grown-up political argument of the kind we haven't had for a long time'.[19] But can it live up to that billing? Politicians will need to change to make it possible.

As we've seen, politics on television has always involved deflection, distraction and sometimes outright lying. Politicians have always tried to rig the game by setting the rules of engagement and threatening reprisals for perceived unfairness. There has always been a lying bastard tendency. However, the Brexit referendum campaign marked a new era of dishonesty. The £350 million on Boris's Brexit bus was a lie. The scaremongering numbers and threatened 'emergency budget' of Project Fear were fiction. None of the real choices were illuminated. The conversation was rhetorical, not rational, and was essentially dishonest.

Since then we've had the toxicity of the post-referendum reckoning, the debacle of the 'nothing has changed' election of 2017 and the gross simplicities of the Get Brexit Done bulldozer. The Johnson and Truss administrations that followed plumbed new depths. Dishonest political communications became standard operating procedure, as did contempt for truth and for the public itself.

Boris Johnson's interview with Andrew Neil that didn't happen feels like a critical moment in that deterioration. It's not because it upset over-entitled BBC journalists like me that it matters. It's the fact that a deliberate, cynical choice was made to avoid accountability and gain an unfair advantage, and to do so by lying about your intentions. That cynicism was internalised by Liz Truss, who took the same route to Downing Street. As a country, we must learn this lesson and be forever wary of the politician who doesn't have the decency and courage to do proper interviews. Soft-soap outings on *This Morning* or short Sunday morning soundbites are not enough, nor are the TV debates during general elections that excite much interest but often reward Johnsonian showboating. It tells you everything you need to know if a politician is running scared of the forensic interview. As Neil, the modern-day master of the form, says:

If you haven't the confidence to be interviewed, there's a question mark over whether you've got the ability to run the country. The fundamental issue is – do you know what you're talking about? And quite often, as we found with Boris Johnson, and as we found with Liz Truss, they actually don't know what they're talking about and yet they want to run the country and take decisions that will affect all of our lives. It's only the robust, long-form interview that can reveal this.[20]

The danger is that – however badly their periods in power ended – avoiding scrutiny worked for Johnson and Truss. As Neil puts it, 'They just want to win; they'll worry about screwing things up afterwards.' It's encouraging that both ultimately paid the price, but we need politicians to renew their commitment to proper scrutiny, particularly at election time. And voters should punish those who refuse.

One way forward would be a more formal process – as exists in America – where an independent commission is established to set out the rules of the game in general elections. Neil backs the idea of a body that 'takes charge of the debates, determines the number of debates, where they are and the format and also stipulates that the main national party leaders have to do a prime-time one-on-one interview'.[21]

BBC board member Robbie Gibb disagrees. 'I'm against it,' he says. 'There's a terrible sense of entitlement there. There are lots of programmes, lots of journalists and they've all got to make their pitch to get the interview and it's absolutely fair enough for a politician to make a judgement about where best they can operate.'[22] In reality, the status quo works better for politicians than for the public. For me, it's not about broadcasters with a sense of entitlement, as Gibb puts it, but about the public being entitled to effective journalism. The free market in political interviews is not working for anyone apart from the politicians, client journalists in the press and soft interviewers.

It's too important to leave in the hands of the Dominic Cummingses and Lee Cains of this world. Good faith has gone. We need rules.

It's more than forty-five years since I first started watching political interviews on that tiny black-and-white television in the 1970s. Something about them drew me in, and I was hooked. They were important, real and, at their best, powerful drama.

After more than twenty-five years of making political programmes and plotting political interviews, I still get excited when a politician sits down in front of a skilled interviewer and has to deal with an interview I've devised. The thrill lies in the possibility that something will happen out there. There may be a revelation, an error or even – as with Walden and Thatcher – an electric encounter that seems to signal the end of an era.

Most of the time the interviews will be less dramatic, but they all play a vital role in our democracy. They give the people to whom we grant power over our lives the opportunity to truthfully answer the questions that ordinary people want answering. Whether they take that opportunity or choose to lie, deflect or in some other way be less than honest is down to them. Ultimately, history tells us they will pay a heavy price for choosing to deceive.

It's over to you, then, politicians. Try not to be lying bastards. We deserve better.

AFTERWORD

November 2021

Me: 'Doctor, my arm feels like a dead fish.'

Doctor: 'That sounds worrying. How are your mussels?'

OK, I made that up. It's not actually what my GP says when I describe my symptoms in the dingy consulting room.

She's a doctor. She doesn't do comedy. She knows her plaice.

Instead, she asks me a perfectly reasonable question: 'How do you mean your arm feels like a dead fish?'

'Well,' I explain, 'it just sort of hangs there. I can't really feel it.'

'You can't feel *anything*?' she asks, sounding concerned for the first time.

'Not much, no, just some stiffness and a tingly feeling. And the dead fish.'

She pauses, weighing up what to say. She doesn't mention any scary conditions or name any diseases. She thinks it might be a good idea to see a neurologist about the dead fish, get it checked out.

'OK,' I say, with heroic stoicism, 'and when can I do that?'

'Well, there's a waiting list,' she says in a sad voice.

'Yes,' I say quickly, signalling that I'm not the usual middle-class wanker who expects to be seen *now*. 'Covid. Of course,' I say bravely. 'The *backlog*.' Then, leaning in a little, I ask, 'How long do you think it will be?'

'A year,' she says bluntly. 'Minimum.'

I'm taken aback. Can I carry this dead fish around for a year without knowing why it's there?

The doctor says the only way to be seen more quickly is to go private and then head back into the NHS with the same consultant once I've been 'assessed', which already feels like a euphemism for 'diagnosed'. It seems wrong, like cheating, but I say I'll think about it. She looks at me with a concerned face. She's excellent at compassion.

'Well, thank you, doctor,' I say, getting up to leave. I don't know what else to say. I clam up. I flounder.

I'm sorry for the fish jokes. I'll get my coat. But that won't be so simple. As I try to extricate my raincoat – blue, but not famous – from the back of the plastic chair I've been sitting in, I realise I'm making more of a meal of it than usual. Presumably, a fish supper.

The doctor must notice my clumsy fingers and lack of general dexterity. As I head for the door, she'll have clocked the slightly shuffling gait that's sometimes noticeable, something my partner Holly first remarked on back in the summer. A quick google of my symptoms could point me to the troubling truth, but I'd rather remain in denial until I can see a specialist, and that will take a while, it seems. It's been a shit year. First Covid dragging on, and then having to leave a job I loved at the BBC. I'm not sure I can take any more bad news in 2021.

I used to go around asking, 'What is the truth?' but I don't want to know anymore.

'I'm sure it's nothing to worry about,' I say breezily to the doctor as I open the door. 'I better get my skates on.'

Do you think I might be using fish jokes to distract myself from how terrifying all this is?

I don't go private in the end. Instead, as the dead-fish blues worsen, and the stiffness and tingly feeling in my arm start to morph into the shakes and a tremor, I go to A&E. The first nurse wonders whether I might be an alcoholic – not yet, I think – then a young doctor says she's worried about 'Parkinsonian' symptoms.

That's not quite the same as branding me with the 'P-word', but it's getting closer. Then good news! They do some scans and tell me that I'm 'all clear'. I'm either never told what this means or misunderstand it entirely. It turns out that 'all clear' means the scans have revealed no other terrifying explanation for my symptoms, like a brain tumour, but that means the most likely possibility is the 'P-word' itself. The trouble is that I understand the 'all clear' message as a clean bill of health.

So, gripping happily to the wrong end of the stick, I tell myself it's something benign. When my follow-up appointment to see a neurologist arrives a week later, I head to the hospital a few miles from my home in Hove, curious but not particularly worried. After an hour's wait I see a junior consultant, who, with brutal efficiency, takes me out with a three-word cosh to the back of the head.

You. Have. Parkinson's.

I don't remember getting out of her office or much else until I find myself standing on a grass verge in the hospital grounds calling Holly to tell her the news. My memory of this is weird: I can see myself standing there as if I'm watching a film. The mobile phone is in my hand, and it's definitely me, but then the next image that flickers into my head is of the consultant – shoulder-length frizzy hair, and a dark tweed jacket and skirt – standing on the verge in my place. In my memory, there's some strange association between the person who delivered the shitty news – the doctor – and the person whose shitty news it was. Me.

I'd been so confident that everything would be all right that I told Holly she didn't need to come with me to the appointment. So now I need to drive home alone. The steering wheel feels unfamiliar and awkward. Nothing seems real now. 'I can't fucking believe it,' I say out loud as I join the mid-afternoon traffic on the A27. I'm convinced there's been a mistake. I've never really been ill. I'm only 52. I can't have Parkinson's.

A week or so later I'm in a posh London hospital for an expensive second opinion from a Parkinson's specialist. Any qualms about going private belong to the life before diagnosis. This will be money well spent, I think, because this is bullshit. The doctor is Northern Irish, no-nonsense and business-like. She asks me to do some exercises: walking up and down, writing my name on a piece of paper – it looks terrible, but then I've always had dreadful handwriting – and then she asks me to wiggle my fingers. I grow even more confident that this is all a mistake. My fingers are brilliant, I'm thinking, I'm really great at wiggling them. Nobody with Parkinson's could possibly wiggle like this. The neurologist observes me quietly, making notes, and then asks me to sit down. She doesn't bother to sugar-coat it. Maybe sugar-coating costs extra.

'Well, Robert,' she says. 'You've got Parkinson's all right.'

Holly is with me, which helps, but it's a brutal blow. I resent the £350 bill I have to settle on the way out. That sort of money should buy you a treat, not a life sentence.

Parkinson's is scary. It's caused by nerve cells dying off in a small area in the middle of the brain called the substantia nigra. That's bad news because it reduces dopamine in the brain. Dopamine is a neurotransmitter that fine-tunes the signals your brain sends to your muscles when it wants them to move. Lack of dopamine slows down movements and causes shakes and a tremor. When you have it you can feel that something's wrong, but its effects are not just physical: lack of dopamine can also cause depression and hallucinations, and make it harder to sleep.

Parkinson's is a degenerative brain condition. That means it usually gets worse over time, but how it will play out will differ with every individual. Being diagnosed at fifty-two is early, but others have it worse. Those who develop it when younger often have it for genetic reasons. As for the rest of us, the condition is blamed on 'environmental factors'. The cause is a bit of a mystery, to be honest, and so is the reason the number of cases keeps growing.

There's some good news: the drugs *do* work. They can make you feel like they've stopped the bastard in its tracks for a while, but unfortunately they're only masking the condition's onward march and become less effective over time. New research and clinical trials are happening all the time, but so far there's no cure. Parkinson's won't kill you itself – it just makes it easier for other things to get you because the condition puts a strain on your body and means you're more likely to succumb to serious infections. In other words, it's shit. I can't pretend I don't feel bleak.

> **bleak**, (*Alburnus alburnus*), small, slender fish of the carp family, Cyprinidae, found in rivers and lakes of England and Europe. A silvery-green fish, it grows to a maximum length of about 20 centimetres (8 inches).[1]

January 2023

I'm in west London on a train from Clapham Junction to Syon Lane near Osterley, and it's a bad day. One of the worst things about Parkinson's is its unpredictability. Mostly I sail through it. The medication is highly effective, and as long as I get the dose right, life feels normal most of the time. Only those with a trained eye would know there was anything wrong.

But some days it's different. The shakes and the tremor are there and, you feel sure, they're visible. Then there's the exhaustion that comes at you from nowhere, a wave that carries you off your feet without warning. For me there's also an internal sensation, a sort of fizzy feeling of something like nausea that makes me feel 'off', unsteady and unanchored. Stress can magnify all these symptoms and trigger more stress, locking me in an inescapable loop. This can be tricky when you're making live TV or radio.

I've been managing this for more than a year – first at LBC, then at Sky News – but haven't mentioned it to anyone outside a small group of family and friends. From the start my instinct was to hide my diagnosis. Outside the embrace of the BBC I felt vulnerable to discrimination and being written off as an old fucker, a has-been and an object of pity. Maybe that's what I used to think when I heard people had conditions like Parkinson's. I'm pretty sure that even though most people wouldn't admit it, in reality that's what a lot of them still think.

Parkinson's? Burley?

The poor bastard.

But secrets eat away at you. I want to be able to say if I need to stop for ten minutes to take the edge off the symptoms or, rarely, if I need to go and have a little lie-down. Parkinson's may be a brain disease, but it doesn't affect your mental faculties. If anything, it motivates you to do what you do well, creatively and with commitment. A Parkinson's diagnosis is a pretty effective way of making you realise it's later than you think. So I've decided I'm done with worrying about discrimination, pity and the fear of being written off.

I'm heading to Sky News HQ to tell my boss Cristina Nicolotti-Squires, the director of content, about my diagnosis. As luck would have it, I can tell her about my Parkinson's in the middle of what you might call an 'episode', probably partly caused by the stress of the meeting itself. This is as bad as it gets – so far – and she can see as we sit down to talk that I can still conduct a conversation and use my brain. Working with Beth Rigby and the Sky News team on her interviews has been a joy from the start, and I've been able to do the job to the highest standard without my Parkinson's interfering. Still, it only feels fair to let Sky know about the diagnosis. Cristina is the definition of a 'no-nonsense' news boss, but she's entirely supportive and reassuring. The message from the meeting is that when it comes to my work, my Parkinson's is pretty much irrelevant. As with any disability, there will be accommodations when needed, but essentially we crack on.

As I head home after the meeting, the relief washes over me, and what comes next is easy. I'd noticed a tweet from the Cure Parkinson's charity a few days earlier that shared news of a promising treatment that was entering further clinical trials. I'd planned to retweet it without comment, but instead I decide to share the story at the same time as telling my 41,000 Twitter followers about my diagnosis.

The sense of relief I feel as friends and Twitter followers get in touch to offer support, love and congratulations for sharing is overwhelming. I'm called 'brave' and told I will help others by being so open. To be honest, I haven't done this for praise or even to help anyone else. I've done it to make myself feel better by lifting the burden of secrecy. I've done it so I can escape being defined by a medical condition, and keeping quiet about it gave it too much power to do exactly that, at least in my own mind.

I've spent many hours in my first year or so with Parkinson's writing this book about lying politicians. When or whether to be honest about a medical diagnosis is a personal choice and there are good, justifiable reasons for telling the world or keeping quiet about it, depending on your circumstances or mindset. It's very different to the moment when a politician chooses to be less than honest when answering a question. However, in my case at least, I'm certain that telling the truth is good for your health. Some politicians – you know the ones I mean – might want to think about that and try it some time.

Rob Burley, March 2023

EPILOGUE
Keep Hope Alive

On page 386 of the hardback edition of *Why Is This Lying Bastard Lying to Me?* Hope, as she tends to, springs eternal. For almost four hundred pages, the abstract noun has been taking a beating: first a gentle pummelling, then an unforgiving kicking as the story of my search for truth in political TV hots up. By the time we reach Liz Truss, Hope has crawled into a corner to die, defeated by the lying bastards and by leaders who run from scrutiny. Hope, it seems, has drowned in a sea of political bullshit. Which is a nasty way to go. RIP, you poor bastard.

But then page 386 arrives, and we're with Emily Maitlis. The former *Newsnight* presenter, who now fronts the hugely successful *News Agents* podcast, is optimistic. 'Ultimately,' she tells me, 'I'm not sure Boris Johnson will have left as big an imprint on British politics as we all assumed.' The implication is clear: post-Johnson and post-Truss, our politics might return to truthfulness, acceptance of scrutiny and respect for boring old democratic norms. As the words sink in, Hope sits up, warily at first, still dizzy from Partygate, Pinchergate and one hell of an almighty Trussterfuck. It's been a rough few years, but Hope's not dead yet.

By page 392, Andrew Marr – the man who made politics sing on a Sunday morning and who's now smashing it out of the park at LBC through the week – is getting excited. He sees an edifying contest of ideas between the new prime minister Rishi Sunak and Labour leader Sir Keir Starmer, a 'serious, grown-up political argument of the sort we haven't seen in a very long time', which will reach its denouement in a general election no later than January 2025.

As I wrote those pages I too allowed myself to believe in Hope, and that the conduct of political conversations on TV, radio and online might improve post-Johnson/Truss. At that, Hope stood up, kicking away her crutches, buoyed by the prospect of a return to honesty and integrity in British politics.

That was a year ago. I wonder how Hope's doing today?

Has anyone seen her?

It's five in the morning on 11 May 2023 and I've given up trying to sleep. The car taking me to *Good Morning Britain* will be here in an hour. I'm in the nondescript Hilton in Shepherd's Bush, and I feel weird and worried. Weird because after more than twenty-five years on the other side of the camera, I'm about to make my on-screen debut. It's publication day, and I'm promoting *Why Is This Lying Bastard Lying to Me?* on live TV. I'm worried because this is the big league: millions of viewers, Susanna Reid and a live 'segment' on political interviewing. This is *GMB*, not *Today* on Radio 4 (those bastards never called), and not the natural home for this discussion. I must strike the right tone: serious but likeable, warm but authoritative, not boring, not snoring.

The first hurdle is two words: 'Good morning!' And that's what keeps me awake. I lie in the darkness, practising how to greet the hosts – Susanna alongside Adil Ray – in a suitably upbeat manner. I'm more of a dry-wit man, to tell the truth, but it's better not to try to be dry on *GMB*. This is the place for broad brushstrokes and affability, creating the possibility that those watching might think what they need in their lives is a book about how and why politicians lie. I eventually manage about two hours of shallow, irritable sleep before waking at half past three, telling myself it will all be fine as long as I can get the greeting right. So I get up and go to the bathroom for a pee and a practice.

'Good morning!' I say to myself in the bathroom mirror. Too much emphasis on the word 'morning', I think, and a slightly creepy facial expression at the same time. Keep practising.

'Good morning?' I say brightly, but I've lost control of the intonation and made it sound like a question, and that won't do; the goodness of the morning on *Good Morning Britain* is not up for debate.

After that I try to sleep again, but it doesn't happen. I may be overthinking this, but it's too late now, and before long I'm up, showered and waiting for my six o'clock ride.

On arrival I'm offered a coffee and a seat in the chair of joy where the make-up artist/hair stylist works. Twenty-five years' experience has taught me that there are few more important people in television. Mostly women, almost always kind and reassuring, they work magic on nervous and knackered interviewees. And so it proves this morning. I stare in the mirror at the bags around my eyes. They're always there, but the anticipation and nerves as I approach the day of publication have carved deeper lines and puffed up puffier eyes than even I'm used to.

Putting me at ease with her chat about football – like me, she's a Liverpool fan – the stylist skilfully applies foundation and teases my lifeless hair. I'm transformed. Or passable, anyway. A few minutes later I'm found in the green room by a friendly sound woman who – as Sir Cliff would have it – wires me for sound and utters the fateful words, 'You're on …'

When it came to it, my 'Good morning!' was fine. The knack is smiling at the same time as you speak. That way I sounded delighted to have washed up on Susanna and Adil's glossy set with a book to flog. Thanks to a first-class production team and presenters who care about holding politicians to account, the discussion was excellent. In fact, all the essential themes in this book – themes I've been banging on about ever since – emerged that morning on *GMB*.

Lying Bastard is about the mighty rise and depressing fall of the political interview on British television – from the end of the age of deference courtesy of Sir Robin Day in 1958, to the golden age of the TV interview that began with the arrival of ITV's *Weekend World* in 1972 and peaked in the late 1980s when Brian Walden completed his final interview with Margaret Thatcher. These interviews allowed politicians and their interviewers time – forty minutes plus, sometimes – to develop ideas and demonstrate credibility. They were much more effective than parliament at holding power to account and helped viewers understand the ideas that drove the political giants of the day.

After that, things went downhill. Politicians became more risk-averse and controlling. At the same time the broadcasters lost their nerve, worried that political interviews didn't rate well enough. As a result, as we come to terms with the seismic political events from Brexit and Trump to Johnson, Covid and Truss, viewers are lucky if they get to see their political masters explain or justify themselves for more than six or seven minutes. All too often they get away with saying next to nothing.

I argued that as we struggle to distinguish between truth and lies, we must return to the long-form interview. If we can devote the time to understanding what politicians believe, we can also reveal, through that process, whether they're being truthful. If this sounds earnest, then it is. I think we've thrown away a great tradition of democratic accountability, and that's a serious loss.

This is not to say that no interviewers are doing excellent work today. From Beth Rigby to Mishal Husain, Nick Robinson to Sophy Ridge, Victoria Derbyshire to Susanna Reid, the talent is there. And Andrew Neil hasn't entirely left the scene either.

But they're being wasted on short, sharp, quick-and-dirty interviews with increasingly dead-eyed politicians sent on to the airwaves to say absolutely nothing – and usually succeeding.

In the spring and early summer of 2023 I appeared on TV, radio and countless podcasts talking about the long-form interview, and I was grateful for the opportunity. Not just because people read and enjoyed *Lying Bastard* but because, as Neil put it in a piece he wrote about the subject for the *Daily Mail*, the book had prompted discussion and brought 'renewed prominence' to the question of how we do political interviewing in Britain.

I have reason to be grateful to Sky News. Not only have they been hugely supportive since my Parkinson's diagnosis (see Afterword), when you can imagine that many companies would quietly let someone with such a condition go, but they've also given me the chance to work with Beth Rigby.

Beth, Sky's political editor, is one of the best political interviewers I've worked with. She's bold, precise and utterly fearless. The only way to counter political lying is to have the courage to call it out, and – to misappropriate Carly Simon – nobody does it better.

All that crazy optimism about the state of the discourse post-Johnson/Truss just about survived 2022. But then the longest election campaign in history got under way at the start of 2023 (estimated election arrival time autumn 2024, although in the event of cataclysmic by-election results, by January 2025), and the early signs weren't good.

Rishi Sunak is an intelligent person who's enjoyed a meteoric rise. Relatively recently he was so C-list that he was seated next to me at a *Spectator* Awards dinner in a posh hotel in central London. He nursed a Coke while I got lightly hammered on free champagne. He was reserved but likeable, and polite enough to talk to someone he didn't know and with whom he had little in common. I liked him.

Four years on, and – on television at least – the real person has disappeared behind his over-rehearsed speaking style and use of words that obscure conviction and feel inauthentic.

Like so many politicians on all sides, Sunak either doesn't have the emotional intelligence to know how to communicate or has subcontracted that part of his brain to the advisers who are supposed to know how to do this stuff. The crisis in trust and the need to maintain the credibility of politicians in the public mind should tell clever people like Sunak that these advisers don't always know what they're doing. Instead, scared of losing power, more interested in other aspects of the job and lacking the imagination to do things differently, they remain in thrall to an approach that doesn't work, leaving the relationship between the elected and the electors in disrepute.

The problem here is politicians' defensive approach to political communications (a dry way of saying how those who seek to rule us explain themselves to those whom they seek to lead), which prizes the repetition of core messages and the sort of dead-bat approach to answering difficult questions that would make Sir Geoffrey Boycott look like a slogger.*

This is not only the politicians' fault – I'll come to the role of journalists later – but those who have governed since Boris Johnson have also doubled down on the techniques that have left many alienated from politics. Sunak's chosen technique is, in lieu of any attempt at real conversation, to repeat the same pre-prepared answers irrespective of the question being asked – and to do so clumsily.

In his case this has meant relentlessly drumming in his 'five pledges' – which, off the top of my head, are: 'stop the boats', something, something, 'halve inflation', something – in every interview. It may work to land the message with voters

---

* I was going to use Chris Tavaré rather than Sir Geoffrey here, but it felt too niche; no offence, Chris.

(although they'll do well to remember it), but they'll also notice that he ignores the question.

On those rare occasions when Sunak doesn't mention the five pledges, he'll deploy a pre-scripted series of words on any subject, from Covid to the war in Ukraine. Combine this with a speaking style that can resemble a peevish children's TV presenter, and you've got problems.

In early May 2023 the reckoning began. Council elections gave the first verdict on Tory government: Sunak edition. It was bad news. The Conservatives lost more than a thousand councillors, and Labour became the biggest party in local government. The experts analysed the results and concluded that Keir Starmer was on course for, at minimum, the most seats in the next parliament. When asked about the results, Greg Hands, the then Tory Party chairman, reached for the bullshit: 'What I'm hearing on the doorstep,' the MP said, 'is that people are giving Rishi Sunak a chance.' As we used to say in the playground in the 1980s while stroking our chins to imply scepticism, 'Jimmy Hill'.

Part of Beth Rigby's job as political editor of Sky News is to follow the prime minister as he travels the world for meetings with other world leaders at events like the G7 in Japan in May 2023. It's a gruelling schedule, but these events ensure regular opportunities to interview the prime minister of the day. The encounters are short – usually seven to nine minutes – and the only way to get anything out of them is either to focus most of the interview on one topic and hope to make progress, or to cover a range of issues but come up with at least one question that produces a 'moment' in the encounter. These questions work best when they address an essential truth the politician might prefer to ignore. They are also a way to disrupt the artificial world of such encounters.

And so it went in Japan, not that I was anywhere near the place. When Beth called from Hiroshima, I was sitting on a park bench in Westminster between media appearances. Beth wanted to talk about the interview. She's the kind of interviewer who's self-confident enough to ask for ideas or help, and she wondered if I had any questions or ideas.

So I asked myself, 'What is the truth?' about Sunak and his bad night at the polls. It struck me that he'd enjoyed a gilded life and career that had left him rich beyond his imaginings, and, one could argue, with a very different view of the world to most voters, not just materially but psychologically. It also struck me, as Beth and I talked, that there was a contrast between Sunak's life, luck and hard-won achievements, and the reality of his political position. He'd been head boy at Winchester. He got a first in philosophy, politics and economics at Oxford and an MBA at Stanford, before earning millions at Goldman Sachs and several hedge funds. He also married the daughter of a billionaire, became an MP, and found himself chancellor before his fortieth birthday and prime minister at just forty-two (after a brief, Liz Truss-shaped bump in the road).

In other words, he was one of life's winners. But now, things were different. Sunak's brilliant career was in the hands of ordinary voters, and they did not much like the Conservative record over the last thirteen years nor in his first months in the job. He'd faced his first electoral test and lost. It felt like the window of opportunity he'd had to break free from the mess he'd inherited was closing.

And that's where Beth and I found the question.

Rigby (smiling, breezy): Prime Minister, you're one of life's success stories.

Sunak doesn't react; he can hardly disagree but wonders where she's going with this.

Rigby (still smiling, still breezy): You were head boy at school. You had a career in finance that made you very wealthy. Now you're prime minister.

Sunak is in the room but perhaps switches off a little, thinking he's bound to have some time to work out what she's asking him and reach for the most appropriate set of pre-planned lines.

But then Beth grinds to a halt and, with barely a pause, drops the question.

Rigby: How do you feel when you lose?

Sunak says nothing for a very long second. Beth waits. He has no idea what she's talking about and appears bamboozled by how quickly the question comes at him. The prime minister leans forward in his seat towards Beth, searching for a clue.

Sunak: Sorry?

Rigby (deadpan): How do you feel when you lose?

Sunak (none the wiser): How, how do you mean, Beth?

Rigby (trying to be helpful): Well, you're a winner in life. How do you feel when you don't win?

Sunak (unsure what's going on but remembering the advice from the comms guys: when in doubt, read them out! It's pledges time): Well, look, my, my, my focus in this job is to deliver for the country. I set out five very clear priorities to halve inflation, grow the economy, reduce debt, cut waiting lists and stop the boats.[1]

Give me strength.

Beth attempts to return Sunak to the question: how does losing feel for a man who's enjoyed such success. If Sunak were listening – really listening – he could engage in what was an interesting question. His inability to understand, let alone answer, looks aloof and speaks to a singular inability to perform outside his comfort zone. The answers he gives are depressingly familiar. Three times he pivots to his five pledges, all topped off, as ever, with the slightly silly-sounding 'stop the boats'. I hoped 'How do you feel when you lose?' might elicit something interesting or revealing. And, although he doesn't answer the question, it does.

But this isn't just about the Tories. Labour is also prone to doublespeak and enters the home straight towards the general election in defensive mode. The position the Labour leader Sir Keir Starmer, consistently ahead in the polls, finds himself in is often compared to a man carrying a Ming vase across a shiny wooden floor; one misstep, one slip, and the priceless pottery could smash into a thousand pieces.

So, Labour plays it safe and spends time criticising the Conservative government with rhetoric that doesn't match their puny spending commitments. Unlike New Labour, there's no big, bold promise equivalent to 1997's New Deal to tackle youth unemployment. Starmer's Labour imply that they can renew public services without spending the money required to achieve that renewal.

Shadow chancellor Rachel Reeves isn't hiding her reluctance to splash the cash. She wants to reassure voters that the Labour Party's moved on from the wild promises of the Corbyn years, not least because of the uncertain state of the public finances.

Starmer has achieved a lot since becoming leader in 2020, remaking the Corbynite Labour Party in his own image and overseeing stunning by-election victories over the Conservatives and the SNP. And he's a lucky general; the governing parties in England and Scotland have self-destructed on his watch.

Despite that, he can't recreate the sense of excitement and buzz that swept Tony Blair to victory. Perhaps memories of Partygate and the Truss debacle will make excitement unnecessary. Johnson brought plenty of buzz, and Truss brought bracing but disastrous radicalism. After so many years of turmoil, Starmer is hoping that boring will come as a relief.

For me, the problem comes with that mismatch between Labour's diagnosis of the dire condition of the country in general – and the public sector in particular – and the lack of anything concrete to fix it. Everyone in politics knows the game: criticise the governing party and imply that only you can save the day without making any promises that can be used against you. This is dishonest politics, but it's so long established as part of the dance of the opposition towards a general election that everyone in the lobby and the commentariat goes along with it. They shouldn't. If you go around saying that the NHS is 'flat on its face', then it's not being honest to pretend you can get it back on its feet with a packet of plasters and a paracetamol. You'll either disappoint the electorate, or have to take action that you didn't mention in the election campaign once in power.

I suspect that one way or another, if Reeves and Starmer triumph at the next election, they'll spend more money on the NHS than they're currently pledging. And when that extra cash arrives, most people won't care that they weren't straight with the electorate. But it will have to be paid for, and honesty about who will foot the bill should be provided before, not after, an election.

As Andrew Neil suggests, *Lying Bastard* started a debate about what we lost when we abandoned the long-form political interview.

Being a debate, not everyone agrees with me. The most common pushback has come from seasoned political journalists. They tend to see how politicians are – and how they behave – as immutable. So when it comes to an argument for change, some (not all) insist that nothing can be done; politicians will always be slippery and risk-averse, and television interviews of the sort that used to enhance our democracy are gone forever. Politicians can't be compelled to do anything that they don't want to do, so, well, nice idea, but let's get real.

Oh, and we already have TV debates at general elections and special editions of *Question Time*. Job done.

Some go further: extended interviews are undesirable. They're boring, they say, and who wants forty minutes of Grant Shapps playing a straight bat and saying nothing? It's easy to get people to agree that it sounds dreadful. What's more, in the social media age, nobody has the time or inclination to watch long, detailed conversations. Forget it.

I can't just dismiss these arguments; they're powerful because they reflect why we are where we are regarding the nature and quality of our political debate. Politicians' reluctance to submit themselves to scrutiny is understandable. Why risk a mistake by doing any more than the bare minimum? It's better to get in and get out fast, and say nothing.

This will stay the same as long as this counsel of despair holds sway. We need to demand better. So dire is the state of our politics and the collapse of trust in our politicians that everyone – political journalists, sympathetic politicians, broadcasters, regulators and citizens – should advocate for a return to proper scrutiny.

Election debates or *Question Time* can sometimes produce moments of revealing spectacle and can change campaigns, but both can be rushed, over-populated and easy for the politicians to navigate. Cast your mind back to 2019, an election that led to Boris Johnson winning a considerable majority. Can you remember anything about the BBC's TV debate? I can't, and I was there. Debate formats favour those who can make the complex simple when the complex isn't simple at all. It's a great skill, but it's a con (remember 'Get Brexit Done').

And then there's what we might call the 'Shapps problem'. Grant Shapps, in his current format – and he's been through umpteen jobs and at least two identities – is the great survivor of the Conservative government. His greatest attribute is that he keeps on going, whatever his personal political setbacks down the years, however deep the political shit the government is in.

Shapps is the minister deployed when someone is required to repeat the government line ad nauseam, no matter how ridiculous or contradictory it might be. He does so in an increasingly weary, almost off-hand and half-asleep mode, but remains just about in the room.

He will argue on behalf of whoever happens to be in charge on whatever issue he's asked to, and from whatever point of view is expedient, even if it contradicts things he's argued for in the past.

So do we really want forty minutes of Shapps, when we could have only seven? I say yes. A well-briefed interviewer, given time to pursue questions properly, would reveal the limitations of his talking points. The BBC's best interviewer, Mishal Husain, did so in a reasonably short but sustained interview about the crisis in Israel and Gaza in October 2023. Her precise, polite and devastatingly logical performance left Shapps resorting to cheap anti-BBC rhetoric. But a longer interview could have achieved even more.

This would be positive. Shapps and the others who deploy a similar style would no longer be so effective in a world where we take political interviews seriously. As for social media, the truth is that longer, more in-depth interviews, while valuable in their own right, are also likely to produce shareable moments of better value than the current, hurried six- or seven-minute format. The content will still be sliced and diced, but the best raw material is delivered by the long-form TV encounter.

Which leaves a final response, or critique, to deal with, and it's the most powerful one. It was put to me most effectively and enjoyably by Richard Kelly, who for many years was head of politics at Manchester Grammar School. A former Tory activist, Richard has a cameo in Chapter 1, and he emailed me after reading *Lying Bastard*. I felt like one of his A level students absorbing his witty and relentless rationale for awarding me a C-minus. I've turned our email discussion into a mini-interview, because I'm all about you having fun.

Kelly (sternly): As its title predicts, the book is inclined to portray interviewers as the good guys: honest and sometimes courageous seekers after truth, confronted by slippery and amoral politicians. But I've always felt this view was unfair, and I waited in vain for a sustained commentary that was friendlier to the perspective of interviewees – and more critical of their interviewers.

Burley (a little crestfallen): I know what you mean about the title; it might make people think that I think they're all lying bastards, which I don't, and I say so. But it's the perfect title. It just works. Sorry. I agree that most politicians are decent people trying to do the right thing, and that some interviewers are shits (no names), but I'm bound to see it primarily from the point of view of the interviewer and the public, not the politician, because that's been my career.

Kelly (undeterred): So, in my view, your excellent book cries out for a sequel or coda – one with a title that goes something like: *Who do these smug fuckers think they are, asking smart-arse questions instead of having a go themselves?*

Burley (pleased Richard liked the book, but still slightly piqued): Well, that's a crap title to start with, but I agree there's a serious point. Political interviews that are designed to catch politicians out for the sake of it or confect a 'gaffe' that will make cheap headlines are part of the problem. I too dislike the 'smug fuckers' with 'smart-arse questions' – as an aside, isn't Richard brilliant at swearing? – who think they're superior to politicians. But there have been numerous attempts by journalists to reset the relationship, and they've all failed because politicians won't risk answering questions truthfully. To be honest, Richard, sorry, *sir*, I'm struggling to give the political class the benefit of the doubt right now. Take what we heard at the Covid Inquiry. The unprofessional conduct, sexism and incompetence of No. 10 was jaw-dropping and disgraceful. And as for the fibbing: it's getting worse.[2]

Worse? Really? Actually, worse than Boris Johnson or Liz Truss (God love her) or Grant bloody Shapps? Well, yes. As we approach the general election in 2024 or early 2025, politicians are getting desperate. It happens that the party behind in the polls and losing its grip on power is the Conservatives, but politicians as a breed can go too far when careers are on the line. In the 2023 Conservative Party conference in Manchester, techniques that would previously have been seen as dishonest and dishonourable were deployed in the conference hall, and defended and amplified outside it. It wasn't pretty.

In July 2023 I found myself at the *Spectator* summer party. It was a sweltering evening, and the garden was rammed with politicians, journalists and advisers. By this point, Sunak's media performances were becoming a problem. They were both robotic and, when challenged, tetchy. If there's one thing the Theresa May years taught us, it's that nobody wants a tetchy robot.

I was curious to know whether Sunak's people were worried about how he was coming across, so I went to find one. This adviser, a likeable and highly intelligent individual, had no idea what I was talking about. As far as Team Rishi was concerned, repeating those tedious pledges was working. It was all going well.

By the autumn, this view no longer held sway. The tide stubbornly refused to turn, and Labour's poll lead remained enormous. It was time for a Rishi Relaunch and a new slogan: 'Long-Term Decisions for a Brighter Future'.

This, the pitch went, was the real Rishi. The message, which he amplified at his party conference, was audacious, even outrageous. He presented himself as the change candidate. This despite being chancellor since 2019 and prime minister for the previous year. And then he went further, using the most important speech of his political life so far to set himself against everyone and everything that had come before him in the previous thirty years. From Major to Cameron and Osborne, May, Johnson and Truss, and, obviously, any Labour leader you might mention, all of them were part of the problem. Rishi could and would do better. You might congratulate him for keeping a straight face, but trying to convince the country that he represented change rather than more of the same was counterintuitive, bold and, on the face of it, bananas.

The case was built on the assertion that he was willing to take tough, long-term decisions that others – including many in his own party – had ducked for years. In September he announced he would delay some aspects of the UK's 'net zero' strategy to cut carbon emissions. His predecessors had nodded through an unrealistic and unnecessary timetable that would clobber ordinary people with unaffordable costs when forced to change their car or replace their boiler. He wouldn't stick to it. Britain would still meet the net zero target carbon by 2050, he said, but there would be less pain for the public.

From there, Sunak made two choices, one rhetorical and familiar, the other more political and unexpected. The rhetorical device was, and you may be ahead of me on this, repetition. Sunak's new interview mantra was that he was tough enough to stand up to those who disagreed with him, accompanied by a challenge that his critics would have to justify why 'they think it's right to impose costs of five, ten, fifteen, twenty thousand pounds on families' when it wasn't necessary to do so. Expect to hear these words again whenever the election comes.

But it's the second choice that Sunak made that was troubling if you're worried about truth in an age of mis/

disinformation. In his speech, and later on social media, Sunak pledged to stop 'taxes on eating meat', 'compulsory car sharing if you drive to work' and a 'government diktat to sort your rubbish into seven different bins'.

Who could blame him? If, like me, you could only afford plant-based burgers because of VAT on meat, have your drive to work in the morning spoiled because you're compelled to car share with Nigel from accounts and his appalling halitosis and have to juggle more than twice as many recycling bins as Liz Truss attended Prime Minister's Questions, then this was music to your ears.

The only trouble was that none of these things were real. There was no meat tax to stop, there were no plans to make car sharing compulsory nor rules requiring seven different types of recycling bin. 'These are all things that have been raised by very credible people,' protested Sunak half-heartedly in subsequent interviews. The truth is he wanted to give the impression that these measures were either already in place or in the pipeline, and that only he could be trusted to stop them.

The cynicism was depressing and amounted to disinformation. He knew these were not policies he could scrap because they were neither in force nor even on their way to being in force. Here Sunak chose to go beyond not answering questions or giving dishonest answers. This was much darker. The pushback that followed, far from being a problem, served the same purpose because it amplified the original lie and elevated it in some people's minds to something either true or worthy of debate.

This approach was cemented a few weeks later when, at Sunak's first conference as Tory leader, it was turbocharged and pointed at Labour. The previously highly rated Claire Coutinho, the secretary of state responsible for net zero, arrived at the conference podium armed with plenty of red meat for the party faithful:

It's no wonder Labour seems so relaxed about taxing
meat. Sir Keir Starmer doesn't eat it. And Ed Miliband is
clearly scarred by his encounter with a bacon sandwich.[3]

Afterwards, Coutinho rocked up to the Sky News conference
studio, basking in the afterglow. If she was expecting a routine
outing, she'd reckoned without Sophy Ridge. Ridge is an excellent interviewer with a unique, discursive style and a warm
on-screen presence that helps break down complex politics into
everyday language. When it came to Coutinho, though, she
decided to channel her inner Jeremy Paxman. She was wonderfully relentless in calling out Coutinho.

The secretary of state's defence was hopeless. Initially, she
implied the comments were merely a 'light moment' and not
something to be taken seriously. But she wasn't prepared to
acknowledge that there was no tax on meat. Instead she blus-
tered on, referring to other Labour policies she regarded as
heavy-handed attempts to meet net zero. 'That's not a meat
tax,' said Ridge. Coutinho ploughed on while Ridge, in a game
of rhetorical whack-a-mole, pushed back: 'It's not a meat tax
though, is it?' she countered before wearily delivering a killer
aside as Coutinho's defence became ever more desperate and
irrelevant: 'Also not a meat tax.'[4]

Before the interview, Coutinho was an obscure figure in the
country but well regarded in her party. After it – and millions
of views on social media – inventing a Labour meat tax and
struggling under tough questioning is what she's best known
for. The risk for ambitious politicians like Coutinho is that they
will be tainted by behaviour like this. Unless today, you're only
tainted if you choose to be (yes, I'm looking at you, Ms Truss).
Perhaps Coutinho will go on defending her speech about a ficti-
tious meat tax for the rest of her career.

If that wasn't bad enough, the transport secretary Mark
Harper plumbed new depths in his address to the Manchester
conference. Harper began by announcing he'd be 'calling time'

on the 'misuse of so-called fifteen-minute cities'. The fifteen-min-ute city is a pretty innocent concept in town planning; it envisages that everyone should be able to live a fifteen-minute walk or bike ride away from the amenities they need – schools, shops, parks, GP surgeries and so on. Some drivers don't like them – after all, they prioritise pedestrians and cycling – but why was Harper 'calling time' on their misuse?

At this point in his speech, Harper should probably have ripped off his suit to reveal the David Icke-style purple tracksuit he wears underneath, complemented by a Matt Le Tissier vintage football shirt that he's too sexy for and a tin foil hat that tops off his conspiracist look. In reality, he offered no visual clues that we were about to go down the rabbit hole, but his words couldn't have been more explicit:

> But what is different, what is sinister, and what we shouldn't tolerate, is the idea that local councils can decide how often you go to the shops, and that they can ration who uses the roads and when, and that they police it all with CCTV.[5]

Given all this, it wouldn't have seemed unreasonable to ask Harper where he stood on the moon landings, Bigfoot and whether 9/11 was an inside job.

As *Wired* magazine put it in an article in February 2023, the idea that fifteen-minute cities are 'sinister' is a crazy fringe-group conspiracy theory:

> [It] has bundled up innocuous ideas in urban development, from traffic calming and air pollution measures to cycle lanes, into a kind of meta-narrative – a meeting point for anti-lockdown activists, anti-vaxxers, QAnon adepts, anti-Semites, climate deniers, and the far right … the 15-minute city concept has become entwined within a much bigger universe of conspiracies based

around the idea of a 'Great Reset' that will see people locked in their homes by climate-obsessed autocracies.[6]

Sounds legit.

It's astonishing that a cabinet minister chose to go deep into Right Said Fred territory. Fifteen-minute cities seek to ensure the provision of essential services within a short distance from people's homes, but the idea that anyone in the UK is having their travel restricted or being told how often they are allowed to go to the shops by local councils is deeply fucking dippy.

I'm not suggesting that politicians have never made false claims in the past. It's not new, of course, and one of the most notorious examples was a Labour, not a Tory, slogan. You could set your clock by the moment in an election campaign when Labour would claim that the Conservatives – despite explicit commitments to retain the NHS free at the point of use – planned to 'privatise' it and urged to vote Labour to 'save it'.

And then, as happens more often than not in British politics, the Tories won. They did not go on to privatise the NHS (although plenty of campaigners take issue with both Labour and Tory extension of private provision used in the NHS). As a result, Labour were able to make the same claim at the following election, apparently with an entirely clear conscience. It's bound to feature in some form or another next time too.

Harper's decision to peddle conspiracy lies would be wrong whenever it took place, but in an era of active disinformation it's irresponsible and shocking to give such corrosive fantasies credibility.

But fear not, a Counter-Disinformation Unit has been set up by the government to, well, counter disinformation. Here's its definition of the word 'disinformation':

The UK government defines disinformation as the deliberate creation and spreading of false and/or manipulated information that is intended to deceive and mislead people, either for the purposes of causing harm, or for *political*, personal or financial gain [my emphasis].[7]

It can only be a matter of time before the Counter-Disinformation Unit opens an investigation into the political parties, their speeches, interviews, manifestos and social media posts. I'm sure Rishi, Keir and the rest will be up for it.

Some Hope.

I emailed Emily Maitlis the other day. I wanted to know if she'd seen Hope anywhere lately. Hope had scarpered again after Harper's wild speech, and I wanted to find her, what with a general election coming soon. As Maitlis had when we'd last discussed all this, she did her best to oblige.

Maitlis stresses the difference between populist Johnson and repetitive Rishi. For Maitlis, the big problem with Boris Johnson was his attitude to the institutions that check the power of politicians: the judiciary, civil servants, parliamentary bodies like the Privileges Committee (aka the 'kangaroo court') and those charged with upholding standards in public life. Sunak, she thinks, respects these guard rails and is not 'hell-bent on trying to circumnavigate them or destroy them'.[8]

This is a low bar, but it's true; Rishi managed to jump over it. Johnson, on the other hand, in what resembled Monty Python's 'Upper-Class Twit of the Year' – look it up on YouTube, kids – repeatedly smashed into, tripped over and destroyed the lowest of ethical hurdles.

But what about lying? Emily raises it as part of the Johnson problem, but it's part of the Sunak problem too. Those comments about compulsory car-sharing and the rest were untrue or, at best, designed to give a false impression.

We saw it again when Sunak sat down with Beth Rigby at the Conservative Party conference in Manchester. The event had been overshadowed by the news, still awaiting official confirmation, that the HS2 rail link between London and, appropriately enough, Manchester was to be axed.

Everyone paying attention knew the decision had been taken and that it would be confirmed the following day in Sunak's speech. Despite this, when Beth asked him whether he'd made a decision, even if he couldn't tell us what it was, he said 'no'. Twice. What's more, he volunteered that he wouldn't be forced into 'premature decisions', as if he continued to weigh the options on HS2.

The following day, to nobody's surprise, he announced his decision, dropping a Rishi video on social media on the subject. The video had been shot at Downing Street before the start of the conference. How could that square with his denial that he'd already made the decision? It couldn't.

It shouldn't have been so difficult. Sunak could have said, 'I've made a decision about HS2, but I'm afraid you'll have to be patient and wait until tomorrow to hear what it is.' Job done. But no, he pretended that all was still to play for.

At his own party conference, Keir Starmer carried his Ming vase around Liverpool, pursuing what Maitlis calls his 'not-fucking-up strategy'. There was some risk-taking: his pledge to build houses, even if that might well upset the view from Middle England's backyard, could easily ignite in the election.

But it was Hamas's barbarous murders of Israeli men, women and children on 7 October and the prospect of the Israeli government response that gave Starmer real trouble. When asked whether it was appropriate for Israel to cut off water and electricity to Gaza, Starmer said, 'I think Israel does have that right.' He claimed he meant the right to defend itself rather than the specific measures he appeared to endorse, but the reaction from his own side was strong enough to give the Ming a wobbly moment. Between now and January 2025 we'll know the fate of Starmer's posh pottery.

As for Rishi Sunak, it was soon time to roll the political dice again. If a week is a long time in politics, then a month is an eternity. By mid-November 2023 the Conservative Party conference in Manchester the previous month was widely regarded as a series of embarrassing missteps by the prime minister. His laughable attempt to present himself as the change candidate and to repudiate the political class – mainly Tories – who'd run Britain for the previous thirty years was dead on arrival, as was the piss-poor dishonesty of the meat tax, the seven recycling bins and the sinister pretence that local government was trying to stop you from leaving your house. None of that guff ignited the imagined passions of the 'Red Wall', and the Tory's poll ratings remained in the toilet.

So Rishi alliteratively reached for a reset, a relaunch, a reboot and, as it turned out, a retread. The big idea – from a man who'd recently written off all of his predecessors live on television – was to bring David Cameron, the first prime minister who'd been a PR man, back into government as foreign secretary.

This move, made possible by the sacking of Suella Braverman, the Trumpian home secretary, seemed to fulfil the promise of the autumn of 2022 by finally bringing the curtain down on Johnson and Truss and dialling down the chaos and populism. Finally, the norms were back!

Or were they? As the dust settled on the reshuffle, attention turned to the Supreme Court, which was about to rule on the legality of the 'Rwanda Plan', the centrepiece of the government's attempt to 'stop the boats' – the small vessels crossing the Channel bringing migrants into Britain.

The Rwanda Plan was designed to deter people from making that (dangerous) journey because, rather than offering those who made it to the UK the prospect of a new life in Britain, it promised to put them on the next flight to Rwanda in East Africa instead.

And once you arrived in President Paul Kagame's one-party state, if you were granted asylum, you'd be invited to make a fresh start there, not in the UK. This prospect, the UK government reckoned, might encourage you to claim asylum wherever you first entered the EU rather than make a perilous and pointless journey across the Channel to British shores.

This was the big idea: remove the allure of the UK to migrants and asylum seekers once and for all by offering a life in Kigali, not Kettering.

Genius.

Before the big idea could be tested, legal challenges held up flights to Kigali International. And then, two days after Lord Cameron of Chipping Norton's sensational return to the cabinet, the highest court in the land, the Supreme Court, ruled the plan unlawful.

Oh shit.

Rwanda's poor human rights record was part of the problem. But the main sticking point was the justices' concern that migrants sent to Rwanda might end up being deported back to their country of origin – or somewhere else – and ultimately find themselves in harm's way. This would breach the European Convention on Human Rights, which prohibits torture and inhuman treatment.

Bloody snowflakes.

Cue outrage. And no one can compete outrage-wise with Lee Anderson, deputy chairman of the Conservative Party. Anderson – not so much a poundshop Donald Trump as one you might pick up at a car-boot sale – had somehow survived the reshuffle. With a mind like a rusty steel trap, Lee was ready to pass his own judgement on the Supreme Court decision. Here, then, is what we'll call the 'Anderson Ruling':

We should just get the planes in the air right now and
send them to Rwanda ... The government need to show
leadership and send them back. *I think we should ignore
the laws* and send them back on the same day.[9]

Ignore. The. Laws.

It's disappointing but not surprising that when asked about
Lee's idea that we should start ignoring laws, Rishi Sunak's
press secretary defended Anderson on the grounds that he had
'strong views' – that's one description of them – and that he
was merely 'representing the views of his constituents'. It was
not a great start on the road back to normal.

But old habits die hard. Sunak and his advisers may eventually
get the hang of their latest strategy, step away from permanent
chaos and embrace boring things like not ignoring laws. Indeed,
a few hours later Alex Chalk, the justice secretary, made clear
that the Conservative government were not, in fact, about to
abolish the judiciary in favour of a common-sense star chamber
of Lee Anderson, Ann Widdecombe and that bloke with the long
hair off *Coast* who tits about on *GB News*. Good process, guys!

After the Supreme Court setback, Sunak had the chance to
lower the temperature, change the subject, perhaps even prepare
the ground for a quiet climb-down. Not this time. He had set
his heart on the Rwanda plan and was determined to press
ahead. A new treaty was drawn up that sought to address
concerns about the system in Rwanda. Then came legislation
that declared Rwanda safe – whatever the Supreme Court said
– and new rules designed to minimise, if not entirely exclude,
the possibility of legal challenges.

The new legislation was drawn up in the Home Office, and
the plan was for Robert Jenrick, the immigration minister, to
help sell the Bill to Parliament and the country. Jenrick was
seen as a Sunak loyalist who'd had to swallow his disappointment when passed over for a cabinet job. So it was calamitous
when Jenrick quit the government because he didn't believe the

legislation would stop the endless legal challenges that had frustrated the Rwanda project so far.

Suddenly Sunak's position had become perilous. The legislation split the party into fragments – there were references to the 'five families' on the Tory right, plus a sizeable 'One Nation' moderate Tory bloc – and when the Bill reached the House of Commons in December, it looked possible that Sunak could go down to a defeat, his authority in such tatters that it would be hard to imagine him continuing as prime minister.

As it was, the government convinced enough MPs on the right to abstain, knowing they'd have the chance to introduce amendments that went further in limiting the scope for legal challenges when the legislation returned to the Commons in early 2024. But there's a big problem: meaningful concessions to the right risk withdrawal of support from the 'One Nation' left. One way or another, it's hard to see how Sunak can keep them all happy.

But you know all this – you have an advantage over me, as I'm writing in mid-December 2023; you'll know how the Rwanda affair ended and whether or not Rishi Sunak survived long enough to lead his party into the next election. Depending on when you read this, you may even know the result. I'll stop, it's making my head hurt.

A general election looms and must arrive by January 2025 at the latest. The democratic moment, when it comes, will be an opportunity for all of us – politicians, journalists and citizens – to do better.

I love general elections. I know most people feel like Brenda from Bristol, whose primal reaction to the news that an election had been called in 2017 – 'You're joking, not another one?' – might be the greatest 'vox pop' in history, but they can become defining moments through which we understand our modern history. One instance was 1979, another was 1997. If Labour maintains its lead in the polls, 2024/25 has the potential to be a third. If they don't, and Sunak holds on, it would be a remarkable survival story.

Let's set aside all our fears and let Hope in. She's not knocking at the window desperate to come back – she's been badly burned before – but it's in her nature. So what could we – politicians, media and the public – do better this time around to keep Hope alive or from permanently pissing off?

I've had a stab but my friend Patsy read this next bit and thought it was patronising, maybe even a little earnest. I know what he means – the bastard – but coming across as a bit preachy is the risk you take when you're arguing for change. Sorry about that. I'll leave it with you, see what you think.

Politicians

Don't lie.

Try to unlearn your media training and be as authentic as you can be. If you find yourself parroting slogans repeatedly and 'pivoting' away from the questions you're asked, consider how your audience will judge you. If you're not in a position to answer fully, then as far as possible explain why rather than changing the subject. People hate that.

Be brave enough to accept invitations from broadcasters to take part in long-form political interviews and debates, which are important. Try to see these conversations as an opportunity to talk about how you want to change the country and promote the ideas that got you into this business in the first place. Be ready to answer the other annoying political questions that will bubble up with good grace but insist on some chunky policy content too.

Oh, and once more with feeling: don't lie. Really.

Media

Be less cynical. Nothing will change unless we give it a chance. Cynicism can infect the tone of interactions with politicians, and that's not a great way to start. And I say that as a cynic myself.

Offer politicians the chance to talk about policy, not just process, in formats that include more extended interviews (fifteen to thirty minutes and beyond). Try to resist the allure of the 'How much is a pint of milk?'-style trick question and care more about content than headlines.

Call out lying and those who don't answer questions, but don't be self-righteous about it.

Don't talk about polls and speculate about post-election deals too much. We'll find out who wins after the vote.

The public

Give politicians a chance! Most of us are sick and tired of how they talk to us and how they avoid difficult questions, but if we've mentally switched off from them before we start, then there's not much point in them doing anything but drumming home their messages.

Engage in the complexity of the choices. Politicians often have an unenviable set of options. Suppose – and it's a huge ask – they come into the election willing to talk frankly about the difficulties. In that case, voters should consider the competing solutions reasonably and realistically rather than wishing a plague upon all their houses. In other words, voters have to put in some work themselves when making an imperfect choice.

Vote. You might as well; you're living with the consequences anyway.

* * *

I feel simultaneously silly and hopeful as I write all this. Silly because, well, why should the lying bastards, or anyone else, listen to *me*? – since I wrote the book, Liz Truss has blocked me on Twitter/X! – and hopeful because without Hope, there's no point in getting out of bed in the morning, let alone writing a book.

The next general election *might* be different from the usual frustrating experience, but it will almost certainly be exactly the same or even worse than what we're used to.

Politicians are not all lying bastards. Most are in it for the right reasons, but they operate in a culture where playing safe and being less than honest is rewarded. And yet, the prize for a politician who connects authentically and for the right reasons could be enormous.

We live in Hope.

Rob Burley, December, 2023

NOTES

INTRODUCTION

1. Neil Thompson, interview with the author.
2. Peter Bull and Kate Mayer, 'How not to answer questions in political interviews', *Political Psychology*, vol. 14, no. 4, December 1993.
3. Peter Bull, lecture to the British Psychological Society, 7 November 2019.
4. Peter Mandelson, 'How I accidentally invented the "boring, snoring" interview', *Financial Times*, 12 September 2014.
5. Andrew Neil, interview with the author.
6. Bull and Mayer, 'How not to answer questions in political interviews'.

1 MARGARET & MARGO

1. *Thatcher: A Very British Revolution*, BBC Two, 2019.
2. Ibid.
3. Richard Kelly, interview with the author.
4. Ibid.
5. *Nationwide*, BBC1, 5 October 1982.
6. ITN interview, 23 February 1958.
7. *That Was the Week That Was*, BBC1, April 1963.
8. Martin Rosenbaum, *From Soapbox to Soundbite: Party Political Campaigning in Britain since 1945*, Palgrave Macmillan, 1997.
9. Sir Robin Day, *Grand Inquisitor: Memoirs*, Weidenfeld & Nicolson, 1989.

10. Ibid.
11. *The Levin Interviews*, BBC2, May 1980.
12. TV-AM, 24 May 1987.

2 BRIAN & MARGARET, PART ONE

1. Brian Walden, quoted in Hugo Young, *One of Us*, Pan Macmillan, 1989.
2. Charles Moore, *Margaret Thatcher: The Authorised Biography; Volume 3: Herself Alone*, Penguin, 2019.
3. Andrew Neil, interview with the author.
4. *The Sunday Times*, 8 May 1988.
5. Ibid.
6. Ibid.
7. Thatcher interview with Kelvin McKenzie for the *Sun*, Margaret Thatcher Foundation Archive, 6 November 1989.
8. Charles Moore, interview with the author.
9. Sir Charles Powell, quoted in *Thatcher: A Very British Revolution*, BBC Two, 2019.
10. Moore, interview with the author.
11. Woodrow Wyatt, *The Journals of Woodrow Wyatt: Volume One*, Pan Macmillan, 1998.
12. Moore, interview with the author.
13. Margaret Thatcher memo, Margaret Thatcher Foundation Archive, 2 October 1989.
14. Nigel Lawson, *The View from No. 11: Memoirs of a Tory Radical*, Bantam Press, 1992.
15. Michael Tracey, *In the Culture of the Eye: Ten Years of Weekend World*, Hutchinson & Co., 1983.
16. Ibid.
17. *Sunday Supplement – Walden Reminisces*, BBC Radio 4, 10 October 2004.
18. Tracey, *In the Culture of the Eye*.
19. *Sunday Supplement – Walden Reminisces*.
20. Moore, interview with the author.
21. Ibid.
22. Brian Walden, *The Walden Interviews*, ed. David Cox, Boxtree Ltd, 1990.
23. David Cox, interview with the author.
24. Walden, *The Walden Interviews*.
25. Moore, interview with the author.

26. Ronald Millar, *A View from the Wings: West End, West Coast, Westminster*, Weidenfeld & Nicolson, 1993.
27. Ibid.
28. Ibid.
29. Andrew Neil, interview with the author.
30. Andrew Marr, interview with the author.

3 BRIAN & MARGARET, PART TWO

1. John Wakefield, interview with the author.
2. Andrew Neil, interview with the author.
3. Bernard Ingham, memo to Margaret Thatcher, Margaret Thatcher Foundation, 22 April 1988.
4. *The Sunday Times*, 8 May 1988.
5. Bernard Ingham, memo to Margaret Thatcher, Margaret Thatcher Foundation, 27 October 1989.
6. 'Is she safe in his hands?' (profile of Brian Walden), *Independent*, 28 October 1989.
7. Ibid.
8. Ibid.
9. Ibid.
10. David Cox, interview with the author.
11. John Wakefield, interview with the author.
12. Ibid.
13. Cox, interview with the author.
14. Ibid.
15. Ibid.
16. Charles Moore, interview with the author.
17. Ibid.
18. *The Walden Interview*, ITV/LWT, 29 October 1989, transcript reproduced in *The Walden Interviews*, ed. David Cox, Boxtree Ltd, 1990.
19. Ibid.
20. Ibid.
21. Ibid.
22. Ibid.
23. Ibid.
24. Ibid.
25. Wakefield, interview with the author.
26. Cox, interview with the author.
27. Ibid.

28. Ibid.
29. *The Walden Interview*, ITV/LWT, 29 October 1989.
30. *The Downing Street Years*, BBC TV, Fine Art Productions, 1993.
31. Wakefield, interview with the author.
32. Woodrow Wyatt, *The Journals of Woodrow Wyatt, Volume Two*, Pan Macmillan, 1999.
33. John Smith, *Hansard*, 31 October 1989.

4 I THINK PADDY ASHDOWN HATES ME

1. *Jonathan Dimbleby*, London Weekend Television, 13 April 1997.
2. *Independent*, 13 April 1997.
3. *Guardian*, October 1996.
4. Barney Jones, interview with the author.
5. Ibid.
6. Ibid.
7. *Kebabbed*, Part 4, BBC Radio 4, 16 April 2000.
8. David Cox, interview with the author.
9. Ibid.
10. Eddie Morgan, interview with the author.
11. Ibid.
12. Jonathan Dimbleby, interview with the author

5 WORDS DON'T MEAN WHAT THEY MEAN

1. Eddie Morgan, interview with the author.
2. *Jonathan Dimbleby*, London Weekend Television, 2 March 1997.
3. 'Euro gaffe wrecks Tory unity', *Independent*, 3 March 1997.
4. Ibid.
5. Morgan, interview with the author.
6. Barney Jones, interview with the author.
7. David Jordan, interview with the author.
8. *On the Record*, BBC One, 16 November 1997.
9. Andrew Rawnsley, *Servants of the People: The Inside Story of New Labour*, Hamish Hamilton, 2000.
10. John Rentoul, *Tony Blair: Prime Minister*, Faber & Faber, 2013.
11. *On the Record*, BBC TV, 16 November 1997.
12. Jordan, interview with the author.
13. Jonathan Dimbleby, interview with the author
14. Ibid.
15. *Jonathan Dimbleby*, Granada London, 13 March 2005.

16. Ibid.
17. Ibid.
18. Memo from Sir David Manning to Tony Blair, 14 March 2002.
19. *Jonathan Dimbleby*, Granada London, 13 March 2005.
20. Ibid.
21. Ibid.
22. Ibid.
23. *The Report of the Iraq Inquiry*, 6 July 2016.
24. *Jonathan Dimbleby*, 'Ask Tony Blair', Granada London, 2 May 2005.
25. *Blair & Brown: The New Labour Revolution*, BBC Two, 2021.

6 SIAN HAS GORDON FOR *BREAKFAST*

1. David Jordan, interview with the author.
2. Barney Jones, interview with the author.
3. Ibid.
4. Andrew Marr, interview with the author.
5. Gordon Brown, *My Life, Our Times*, Bodley Head, 2017.
6. Tony Blair, *A Journey: My Political Life*, Alfred A. Knopf, 2010.
7. Andrew Rawnsley, *Servants of the People: The Inside Story of New Labour*, Hamish Hamilton, 2000.
8. Marr, interview with the author.
9. Ibid.
10. *The Andrew Marr Show*, BBC One, 27 September 2009.
11. Ibid.
12. *Kebabbed*, Part 4, BBC Radio 4, 16 April 2000.
13. Dr Sian Williams, interview with the author.
14. Ibid.
15. Ibid.
16. *Blair & Brown: The New Labour Revolution*, BBC Two, 2021.
17. Marr, interview with the author.

7 IF YOU BUILD IT, THEY WON'T COME

1. *Sunday Politics*, BBC One, 16 June 2013.
2. Ibid.
3. Ibid.
4. Andrew Neil, interview with the author.
5. Ibid.
6. Ibid.

7. Robbie Gibb, interview with the author.
8. Ibid.
9. Neil, interview with the author.
10. Ibid.
11. *Sunday Politics*, BBC One, 16 June 2013.

8 YOU GET FED UP WITH THE BULLSHIT

1. *The Media Show*, Channel 4, Wall to Wall, 29 October 1989.
2. Andrew Neil, interview with the author.
3. Jeremy Paxman, interview with the author.
4. Jeremy Paxman, *A Life in Questions*, William Collins, 2016.
5. John Birt, 'For Good or Ill? The Role of the Modern Media', Independent Newspapers Annual Lecture, Trinity College Dublin, 3 February 1995.
6. Paxman, interview with the author.
7. John Birt, email to the author, 10 August 2022.
8. Paxman, *A Life in Questions*.
9. Ibid.
10. Paxman, interview with the author.
11. Neil, interview with the author.
12. Paddy Ashdown, *The Ashdown Diaries, Volume Two 1997–1999*, Allen Lane, 2001.
13. David Cameron, *For the Record*, William Collins, 2019.
14. Paxman, interview with the author.
15. Jeremy Paxman, James MacTaggart Memorial Lecture, Edinburgh International Television Festival, 24 August 2007.
16. Ibid.
17. *Newsnight*, BBC Two, 8 October 2013.
18. Emily Maitlis, interview with the author.
19. Paxman, interview with the author.
20. Ibid.
21. *Newsnight*, BBC Two, 23 October 2013.
22. Ibid.
23. Ian Katz, 'The death of the political interview', *Financial Times*, 7 September 2014.
24. Russell Brand, *Revolution*, Random House, October 2014.
25. *Newsnight*, BBC Two, 23 October 2014.
26. Paxman, interview with the author.

9 DIFFICULT CHOICES

1. Barney Jones, interview with the author.
2. Andrew Marr, interview with the author.
3. Jones, interview with the author.
4. Ibid.
5. Marr, interview with the author.
6. Ibid.
7. *The Andrew Marr Show*, BBC One, 15 March 2015.
8. *The Andrew Marr Show*, BBC One, 19 April 2015.
9. Gill Thompson, interview with the author.
10. *The Andrew Marr Show*, BBC One, 26 April 2015.
11. David Cameron, Twitter, 4 May 2015.
12. Squeeze, 'From the Cradle to the Grave', *The Andrew Marr Show*, BBC One, 10 January 2016.

10 BREXIT IN FOUR MONTHS OF SUNDAYS AND A TUESDAY

1. *The Andrew Marr Show*, BBC One, 21 February 2016.
2. Ibid.
3. Ibid.
4. *The Andrew Marr Show*, BBC One, 6 March 2016.
5. Ibid.
6. Ibid.
7. *The Andrew Marr Show*, BBC One, 24 April 2016.
8. Ibid.
9. *The Andrew Marr Show*, BBC One, 8 May 2016.
10. *Peston on Sunday*, ITV, 8 May 2016.
11. *The Andrew Marr Show*, BBC One, 22 May 2016.
12. Ibid.
13. Robbie Gibb, interview with the author.
14. *The Andrew Marr Show*, BBC One, 5 June 2016.
15. Ibid.
16. *The Great Debate*, BBC One, 21 June 2016.

11 JEREMY IN THREE PHASES

1. *The Andrew Marr Show*, BBC One, 23 September 2018.
2. Carmel Nolan, interview with the author.
3. *The Andrew Marr Show*, BBC One, 27 September 2015.
4. Seumas Milne, interview with the author.

5. Ibid.
6. Ibid.
7. Ibid.
8. Ibid.
9. *The Andrew Marr Show*, BBC One, 29 November 2015.
10. *The Andrew Marr Show*, BBC One, 17 January 2016.
11. John Prescott, TwitLonger, 17 January 2016, https://www.twitlonger.com/show/n_1so6pca.
12. Milne, interview with the author.
13. Ibid.
14. *The Andrew Marr Show*, BBC One, 10 July 2016.
15. Milne, interview with the author.
16. Ibid.
17. *The Andrew Marr Show*, BBC One, 11 June 2017.
18. Martyn Sloman, interview with the author.
19. *Channel 4 News*, 13 July 2015.
20. *The Andrew Marr Show*, BBC One, 24 September 2017.
21. Gabriel Pogrund and Patrick Maguire, *Left Out: The Inside Story of Labour under Corbyn*, Bodley Head, 2020.
22. Milne, interview with the author.

12 NOTHING HAS CHANGED

1. Andrew Marr, interview with the author.
2. Ibid.
3. Katie Perrior, interview with the author.
4. Ibid.
5. *The Andrew Marr Show*, BBC One, 4 September 2016.
6. Perrior, interview with the author.
7. Ibid.
8. *Sophy Ridge on Sunday*, Sky News, 8 January 2017.
9. Perrior, interview with the author.
10. Ibid.
11. *The Andrew Marr Show*, BBC One, 1 October 2017.
12. Ibid.
13. Ibid.
14. Ibid.
15. Ibid.
16. Ibid.
17. Ibid.
18. Ibid.

13 PARAGRAPH 5C

1. *The Andrew Neil Interview*, BBC One, 12 July 2019.
2. *Politics Live*, BBC Two, 8 March 2019.
3. *Boris Johnson Talks to Kirsty Wark*, BBC Four, 15 February 2005.
4. *The Andrew Marr Show*, BBC One, 23 March 2013.
5. *The Andrew Neil Interview*, BBC One, 12 July 2019.

14 GAFFE MACHINE

1. *The Andrew Neil Interview*, BBC One, 5 December 2019.
2. Ibid.
3. Andrew Neil, interview with the author.
4. Ibid.
5. Ibid.
6. Zion Lights, 'Why I left Extinction Rebellion to campaign for nuclear power', *Daily Telegraph*, 10 September 2020.
7. 'Labour antisemitism: Corbyn not fit for high office, says Chief Rabbi Mirvis', *The Times*, 26 November 2019.
8. Ephraim Mirvis, 'What will become of Jews in Britain if Labour forms the next government?', *The Times*, 26 November 2019.
9. https://www.facebook.com/JeremyCorbynMP/posts/my-statement-following-the-publication-of-the-ehrc-reportantisemitism-is-absolut/10158939532253872/.
10. *The Andrew Neil Interview*, BBC One, 5 December 2019.
11. Neil, interview with the author.
12. Andrew Marr, interview with the author.
13. Ibid.
14. *The Andrew Neil Interview*, BBC One, 5 December 2019.
15. WhatsApp message from Anjula Singh to Seumas Milne, 7 November 2019.
16. WhatsApp message from Anjula Singh to James Schneider, 27 November 2019.
17. Email from Seumas Milne to Fran Unsworth, 4 December 2019.
18. Email from Fran Unsworth to Seumas Milne, 6 December 2019.
19. Milne, interview with the author.
20. *Westminster Insider Podcast*, Politico, 1 October 2021.
21. Ibid.
22. Ibid.
23. Sir Robbie Gibb, interview with the author.
24. Neil, interview with the author.

25. Interview with the author.
26. *The Andrew Marr Show*, BBC One, 20 July 2020.
27. Neil, interview with the author.
28. Ibid.
29. Email from author to Tim Davie, 11 March 2021.

15 AFTER THE CLOWN SHOW

1. *Partygate: The Inside Story*, ITV News, 11 January 2023.
2. Andrew Marr, interview with the author.
3. Ibid.
4. Ibid.
5. Iain Dale, LBC, 12 July 2022.
6. Michael Lake, *Guardian* letters, 12 July 2022.
7. *Sky News*, 18 January 2022.
8. Ibid.
9. Andrew Neil, interview with the author.
10. *Sunday with Laura Kuenssberg*, BBC One, 25 September 2022.
11. *Sky News*, 4 October 2022.
12. Harry Cole and James Heale, *Out of the Blue: The Inside Story of the Unexpected Rise and Rapid Fall of Liz Truss*, HarperCollins, 2022.
13. Emily Maitlis, interview with the author.
14. Ibid.
15. Ibid.
16. *The Beth Rigby Interviews*, Sky News, 24 November 2022.
17. Ibid.
18. Tweet by Jeremy Hunt, 18 April 2016.
19. Marr, interview with the author.
20. Neil, interview with the author.
21. Ibid.
22. Robbie Gibb, interview with the author.

AFTERWORD

1. Entry for 'bleak' at britannica.com.

EPILOGUE

1. *Sky News*, 19 May 2023.
2. Richard Kelly, email to the author, 19 October 2023.

3. Claire Coutinho, speech at Conservative Party conference, 3 October 2023.
4. *Sky News*, 3 October 2023.
5. Mark Harper, speech at Conservative Party conference, 2 October 2023.
6. Peter Guest, *Wired*, 20 February 2023.
7. Fact sheet on the work of the Government's Counter-Disinformation Unit and Rapid Response Unit, 9 June 2023.
8. Emily Maitlis, email to the author, 24 October 2023.
9. Lee Anderson, PA Media, 15 November 2023.

BIBLIOGRAPHY

Archives
BBC
ITV
LBC
Margaret Thatcher Foundation
Sky News

Books and articles
Ashdown, Paddy, *The Ashdown Diaries, Volume Two 1997–1999*, Allen Lane, 2001

Berlinski, Claire, *There Is No Alternative: Why Margaret Thatcher Matters*, Basic Books, 2011

Blair, Tony, *A Journey: My Political Life*, Alfred A. Knopf, 2010

Brand, Russell, *Revolution*, Random House, 2014

Brown, Gordon, *My Life, Our Times*, Bodley Head, 2017

Bull, Peter and Mayer, Kate, 'How not to answer questions in political interviews', *Political Psychology*, vol. 14, no. 4, December 1993

Cameron, David, *For the Record*, William Collins, 2019

Campbell, John, *Margaret Thatcher Volume Two: The Iron Lady*, Vintage, 2007

Cox, David (ed.), *The Walden Interviews* (with foreword by Brian Walden), Boxtree Ltd, 1990

Day, Sir Robin, *The Grand Inquisitor: Memoirs*, Weidenfeld & Nicolson, 1989

Day, Sir Robin, ... *But with Respect*, Weidenfeld & Nicolson, 1993

Gimson, Andrew, *Boris: The Rise of Boris Johnson*, Simon & Schuster, 2006

Lawson, Nigel, *The View from No. 11: Memoirs of a Tory Radical*, Bantam Press, 1992

McBride, Damian, *Power Trip: A Decade of Policy, Plots and Spin*, Biteback Publishing, 2013

Maitlis, Emily, *Airhead: The Imperfect Art of Making News*, Michael Joseph, 2019

Meyer, Christopher, *DC Confidential*, Orion, 2005

Millar, Ronald, *A View from the Wings: West End, West Coast, Westminster*, Weidenfeld & Nicolson, 1993

Moore, Charles, *Margaret Thatcher: The Authorised Biography; Volume 3: Herself Alone*, Penguin, 2019

Nott, John, *Memorable Encounters*, Pen & Sword Politics, 2018

Oliver, Craig, *Unleashing Demons: The Inside Story of Brexit*, Hodder & Stoughton, 2016

Paxman, Jeremy, *A Life in Questions*, William Collins, 2016

Pogrund, Gabriel and Maguire, Patrick, *Left Out: The Inside Story of Labour under Corbyn*, Bodley Head, 2020

Purnell, Sonia, *Just Boris: The Irresistible Rise of a Political Celebrity*, Aurum Press, 2011

Rawnsley, Andrew, *Servants of the People: The Inside Story of New Labour*, Hamish Hamilton, 2000

Rentoul, John, *Tony Blair: Prime Minister*, Faber & Faber, 2013

Rosenbaum, Martin, *From Soapbox to Soundbite: Party Political Campaigning in Britain since 1945*, Palgrave Macmillan, 1997

BIBLIOGRAPHY

Tracey, Michael, *In the Culture of the Eye: Ten Years of Weekend World*, Hutchinson & Co., 1983

Watson, Iain, *Five Million Conversations: How Labour Lost an Election and Rediscovered Its Roots*, Luath Press, 2015

Wyatt, Woodrow, *The Journals of Woodrow Wyatt, Volume One*, Pan Macmillan, 1998

Wyatt, Woodrow, *The Journals of Woodrow Wyatt, Volume Two*, Pan Macmillan, 1999

Young, Hugo, *One of Us*, Macmillan, 1989

ACKNOWLEDGEMENTS

My most important thank you is to Holly, my partner, for her love and patience as I disappeared into the attic for months on end to write this book. She also offered invaluable guidance and editorial help to get it over the line. I want to apologise to Louis for not playing football enough and to Noah for using the attic for something other than games of *FIFA*. Sorry, everyone.

I want to thank all of those who took the time to let me interview them for this book (some more than once): Andrew Marr, Andrew Neil, Jeremy Paxman, Emily Maitlis, Jonathan Dimbleby, Charles Moore, David Cox, John Wakefield, Barney Jones, Dr Sian Williams, Seumas Milne, Katie Perrior, David Jordan, Eddie Morgan, Sir Robbie Gibb, Jo Coburn, Neil Thompson, Gill Thompson, Richard Kelly, Carmel Nolan, Martyn Sloman and Meirion Jones.

Thanks to my agent for this book Martin Redfern, whose enthusiasm for the idea was inspiring, and to Jack Fogg, my agent at Dunn Fogg. I'd also like to thank Hannah Weatherill for all her help. I'd also like to thank my editor Joel Simons at Mudlark/HarperCollins for his belief and support.

I want to thank Jonathan Munro for providing copies of relevant BBC programmes, and Lewis Hare and Robin Bray at ITV for access to their archive.

Thanks to Professor Stephen Fielding for his blog on Margo Leadbetter, Margaret Thatcher and the Tory campaign of 1979, and to Lord Birt for answering my questions via email.

Huge thanks to Anna, Mark and Phil for providing a place, and some space, to write.

Thanks also to Sandy Watson for reading and encouraging, and to Patrick Wynniatt-Husey and Shaun McInerney for laughing at my lame jokes.

Most of all, I'd like to thank my colleagues over the last twenty-seven years. Television is a collaboration. Stars and senior producers often take the credit for successful interviews or programmes, but they shouldn't: it's a collective effort. From the make-up artists to the studio directors, the junior researchers to the graphics team, the camera crews to the cleaners and the floor managers to the picture editors, nothing works unless it all does.

All the political programmes and interviews I've worked on, from ITV and the BBC to LBC and Sky News, only happened because of the effort and talent of the wider team. So I'd like to say thank you to them all. Particular thanks are due to some of those I worked with most closely, many of whom have helped jog my memory for this book:

ITV: Gloria De Piero, Mehdi Hasan, James Macintyre, Alex Gardiner, Rebecca Asher, David Mapstone, Mike Lewis, Ginny Hill, Rachel Clarke, Andy Miller, Jenny Parks, Jonathan Maitland, Richard Conway, Julie Shaw, Colin Stone, Stella Creasy, Jeff Anderson, James Goldston, Roy Greenslade, Jamie Glassman, Fiona Campbell (RIP), Andrew Harrison (RIP).

BBC: Jason Keen, Andrew Alexander, Brian Hollywood, Libby Jukes, Leala Padmanabhan, Brenda Yewdall, Sam McAlister, Gavin Allen, Ian Katz, Rachel Jupp, Neil Breakwell, Lesley Boden, Chris Cook, Sue Lockyer, Hugh Milbourn, John Neal, Hannah Wilkinson, Will Boden, Laura Wilkinson, Joel Massey, Emily Craig, Ed Chivers, Claire Bellis, Kirsty Wark,

ACKNOWLEDGEMENTS

James Bray, Tim Burke, Adam Donald, Paul Duffy, Chris Cook (*Newsnight*), Simon Enright, Lizzi Watson, Jamie Donald, Mark Urban, Adam Livingstone, Steve Smith, Natasha Mardikar, Jon Sopel, Dino Sofos, James Clayton, Tom Lumley, Hannah Macinnes, Martin Rosenbaum, Adam Bullimore, Matt Booker, Stuart Denman, Max Deveson, Elizabeth Glinka, Laura Cooper, Alison Ford (RIP).

LBC: Matt Harris, Ellie Tivey, Jack Maclaren and the technical team at Millbank.

Sky News: Beth Rigby and the team, Cristina Nicolotti-Squires, Jonathan Levy, John Ryley and Sam Coates.

I'd also like to thank the late, great Paul Flynn for being the best boss and giving me a start. RIP.

Parkinson's: Thanks so much to Anna Wilson for the help and support in the scary early days. I'm grateful to Rory Cellan-Jones for his support and for consultation on the Afterword. If you'd like more information on Parkinson's or details of how to donate to charities that help people live with the condition and work to find a cure, please visit parkinsons.org.uk and cureparkinsons.org.uk.

Finally, I'd like to thank my mum. My dad crops up in this book a lot because he did so much to inspire my interest in politics, history and difficult questions. My mum is on the periphery here, which is not like her, but that's just the nature of this particular story. Generally, she was at the centre of every room she was in, holding court and making the weather. She died in February 2017, two years to the day after my dad. I miss them both.